BETRAYAL

Also by Linda Chavez

An Unlikely Conservative
Out of the Barrio

HOW UNION BOSSES SHAKE DOWN THEIR MEMBERS AND CORRUPT AMERICAN POLITICS

BETRAYAL

LINDA CHAVEZ
and Daniel Gray

THREE RIVERS PRESS
NEW YORK

Published in the United States by Three Rivers Press, an imprint of the
Crown Publishing Group, a division of Random House, Inc., New York.
www.crownpublishing.com

Three Rivers Press and the Tugboat design are registered trademarks
of Random House, Inc.

Printed in the United States of America

Library of Congress Cataloging-in-Publication Data is available upon request.

ISBN 1-4000-5260-2

10 9 8 7 6 5 4 3 2 1

First Paperback Edition

For my sons, David, Pablo, and Rudy,
who make me proud.
—L. C.

To Stephen, Chelsea, and Jason,
who make it all worthwhile.
—D. G.

CONTENTS

BETRAYAL

CHAPTER 1

For Sale: The Democratic Party, the American Worker, and the United States Government

Imagine you pick up your newspaper one morning and read that the Republican Party has given control of George W. Bush's reelection campaign to Halliburton, the oil and gas company that has taken on the specter of Darth Vader–like evil to the American Left. It turns out that Halliburton is spending millions of corporate dollars—none of it collected from voluntary contributions—to finance ads and grassroots activity for the Republicans. Halliburton employees also dominate the Bush campaign staff; they are on loan as full-time "volunteers," though they continue to draw their Halliburton salaries. In exchange for the huge amounts of money and other support Halliburton is providing, the president and his staff meet with Halliburton executives to coordinate the message for the reelection campaign. More important, the GOP has granted Big Oil veto power over the Republican platform, refusing to formalize the party's public policy positions and campaign strategies until Halliburton and other oil-company donors have given their approval.

No doubt the nation would erupt in a furor if such an arrangement were revealed—and justifiably so. Armies of reporters would go to work investigating every iota of evidence of the ties between Republicans and their fat-cat patrons in corporate America, with each revelation a front-page story, the lead item on the evening news, and the subject of round-the-clock coverage on the cable news channels. Indignant politicians would call for congressional hearings, a special prosecutor, perhaps even the president's impeachment. Whatever formal steps the government took, the media circus and the outrage over the revelations would ensure that the Bush presidency was over in everything but name. . . .

Amazingly, such a scenario actually played out pretty much as described—except the president running for reelection was not a Republican but a Democrat, and the powerful group pulling the strings in the campaign was not Big Oil but Big Labor.

Even more shocking, the national media and the political establishment barely reacted to the revelation that America's union bosses had systematically bought their way into control of the Democratic Party. There were no calls for congressional hearings, no outrage, no intensive media campaign.

Welcome to the world of modern American politics. Simply put, the leftist labor unions have the Democrats in their pockets. And as a result they wield extraordinary political power at all levels of government—federal, state, and local. Big Labor has corrupted not only the electoral process but also our system of governing. And we're all paying the price.

THE CORRUPT BARGAIN

By now most people simply take it for granted that the labor unions are active in Democratic politics. But unions are no longer labor organizations that dabble in politics; labor bosses have so radically shifted their approach in recent years that unions have become political organizations that deal only incidentally with workplace issues.

Union leaders have never been less effective in their founding purpose: to represent their members to employers. And they have never been more effective in—and dedicated to—their tacit goal of subverting the American political system to their own ends. Few people realize the extent of the unions' political activity or influence. While it has been said that unions are an adjunct of the Democratic Party, now it is more accurate to say that the Democratic Party has become a wholly owned subsidiary of Big Labor.

The American labor movement provides Democratic candidates and the Democratic National Committee with hundreds of millions of dollars in funding every year. In the 2000 election cycle alone, according to one estimate,[1] unions spent $800 million, much of it in critical campaign support that goes unreported in the form of manpower, mailings, advertising, get-out-the-vote drives, phone banks, and much more. And what do the labor bosses get in return? The power to call the shots in Democratic campaigns and on party policy.

This is not mere speculation. A 2001 investigation by the Federal Election Commission (FEC) exposed the quid pro quo arrangement between the unions and the Democrats. According to the FEC, Big Labor has become an *equal partner* with key Democratic organizations like the Democratic National Committee (DNC) in formulating Democratic Party policy and electoral strategies. The Democratic Party has put on its all-important National Coordinated Campaign Steering Committee representatives from the two biggest union players—the American Federation of Labor and the Congress of Industrial Organizations (AFL-CIO), which is made up of more than sixty affiliated unions,[2] and the National Education Association (NEA), the nation's largest union.

The FEC uncovered an internal DNC document from the 1996 campaign that laid out what the Democratic Party called the "Rules of Engagement": "When the DNC and its National partners including . . . the AFL-CIO and the NEA agree on the contents of a plan, each national partner will give their funding commitment to the state." The document further explained that before any campaign plans could be implemented, they had to be "submitted with a signature page" showing the "formal sign off" of the AFL-CIO and the NEA. As the FEC's final report put it, the unions had "authority to approve or disapprove plans, projects, and needs of the DNC and its state parties."[3]

In other words, the Democratic Party gave the deep-pocketed unions unprecedented authority—veto power over its election plans.

Unfortunately, no one paid much attention to the FEC's dramatic revelation. In part this was because both the Democratic Party and the AFL-CIO quickly sued to keep the FEC from releasing the "Rules of Engagement" document and other evidence to the public. Obviously Democrats don't want the details of their unholy alliance with Big Labor known to the American people, but union leaders also need to cover up their infiltration of the Democratic Party. Labor bosses continue to speak in terms of fighting for the rights of working men and women, trying to endow their mission with a noble purpose that elevates unions above other so-called special-interest groups. Thus they obscure the fact that they have essentially abandoned the interests of those working people in order to enhance their own political power.

In the few days before the Democratic Party's and the AFL-CIO's armies of lawyers secured a court order to seal the DNC documents, the details did actually leak to the Associated Press, which gave some indication of the Democrats' corrupt bargain with Big Labor. But the details unearthed in the course of the FEC's 2001 investigation are just a tiny part of a much larger story—a story that until now has not been fully told. And while the FEC investigation focused on the 1996 election, when Democrats Bill Clinton and Al Gore were reelected, the corrupt bargain continues today.

In every subsequent election, Big Labor has thrown its substantial resources behind Democratic candidates and exacted significant concessions for its largesse. In the closely contested 2000 election between George W. Bush and Al Gore, for example, the unions pushed fiercely for the Democratic Party. According to the nonpartisan Center for Responsive Politics, unions gave some $90.1 million to Democrats in the 2000 election cycle.[4] In addition to direct contributions in the form of donations to candidates and soft-money donations, unions also committed $46 million for a grassroots mobilization effort in thirty-five congressional districts in fifteen states,[5] and mobilized thousands of Democratic campaign "volunteers"—many of whom were getting paid by the unions. According to one union, "Political union activists registered 2.3 million new union household voters, made 8 million phone calls to union households, and distributed more than 14 million leaflets at their workplaces."[6] Nor do even these figures reveal the true amount unions spend on politics. In the 2000 election cycle, union PACs alone spent $128.7 million on all their activities.[7] In short, the 2000 presidential election never would have been as close as it was—and we might not have had the long post-election standoff—if it hadn't been for Big Labor's all-out support for Al Gore.

Gore had reason to be beholden to the labor unions even before their help in the general election. Though he had been groomed for years to be the Democratic Party's standard bearer in 2000, he had to fight off a stiff primary challenge from former senator Bill Bradley, and there too Big Labor swept in. The unions were actually divided between Gore and Bradley, but the leader of the AFL-CIO, perhaps recognizing the benefits of being kingmaker, threw his support to Gore, which saved the vice president's faltering campaign. Gore repaid his union patrons immediately, promising the AFL-CIO that he would oppose a series of measures that threatened the hegemony of labor bosses.[8] He would concede even more during the course of the long campaign. (Indeed, at the Democratic National Convention in August, labor delegates represented the largest single interest group, as they made up one-third of the 4,368 total delegates.)[9]

The year 2004 marked another presidential campaign season, and sure enough Big Labor ratcheted up its efforts long before the primaries began. The unions' ultraliberal leadership was undeniably united behind a single goal: removing the Republicans from power. The unions made this quite clear in late 2003, when they committed $8 million to the liberal advocacy group America Coming Together, which was designed to coordinate the campaign efforts of Big Labor and other leftist groups.[10] Interestingly, the driving force behind America Coming Together was, as CNN reported, none other than Hillary Clinton and her leadership committee, HILLPAC, which was set up to funnel contributions directly to Democratic candidates (hard money) and to distribute funds to her handpicked causes (soft money).[11] Although union bosses were rallying with other liberal groups to defeat George W. Bush, they were divided over which Democratic contender to support, just as they had been with Gore and Bradley. Naturally the candidates were tripping over themselves to secure the endorsement of powerful labor unions, for with an endorsement comes money and manpower.

Former Vermont governor Howard Dean gained momentum in late 2003 when he received endorsements from two of the most politically powerful unions in America, the Service Employees International Union (SEIU) and the American Federation of State, County, and Municipal Employees (AFSCME). When AFSCME president Gerald McEntee announced the endorsement, he declared that the union "is going to mobilize the largest and most aggressive grassroots campaign this nation has ever seen."[12] Less than a month later, another official from the government-employee union, Brenda Stokeley, made clear what political positions the union leadership expected in return for its campaign efforts: "The first thing we have to do is remind ourselves that we are fighting for socialism."[13]

Surely Dean recognized how critical Big Labor's support would be to his political fortunes, so perhaps he was pandering to the unions when he veered far to the left on an array of issues, such as taxes and economic policy. Despite his record as a fiscal moderate in Vermont, he resurrected the key campaign promise of 1984's landslide loser, Walter Mondale: higher taxes for Americans, including the middle class.[14] Then, sounding like Brenda Stokeley, he promised more government control of the economy through the "re-regulation" of American business.[15] Moreover, as *Wall Street Journal* political reporter John Fund pointed out, "the need to keep his own union support has prompted Mr. Dean to apologize" for having supported the North American Free Trade Agreement (NAFTA) in 1993; "he is now a rabid anti-free-trader."[16]

The race for the 2004 Democratic nomination provided an object lesson in what political campaign teams are willing to do to earn Big Labor's backing—or to prevent the unions from throwing their support to opposing campaigns. Richard Gephardt of Missouri had spent more than a quarter-century in Congress kowtowing to union chieftains—as John Fund put it, Gephardt "earned his union support with an almost slavish devotion to their agenda"[17]—and perhaps he thought they owed him an endorsement as he sought the 2004 Democratic nomination. He did in fact win the endorsement of some prominent labor organizations, including the Teamsters,[18] but he received a blow when the powerful left-wing unions AFSCME and SEIU endorsed his rival Dean. Certainly a key Gephardt adviser seemed to react as if the Dean endorsements were a terrible setback for her candidate. In early December 2003, Joyce Aboussie, the vice chair of Gephardt's campaign, reportedly threatened to retaliate against the SEIU and AFSCME if they dared to campaign for Howard Dean in Missouri or Iowa. According to SEIU president Andy Stern and AFSCME president Gerald McEntee, Aboussie issued them an "ultimatum," saying that if the unions did not abide by her demands, she would lobby Republicans in the Missouri legislature to repeal the governor's executive order providing state employees with collective-bargaining rights.[19] It is amazing that a high-level representative of "Mr. Labor" Dick Gephardt would apparently be so willing to sacrifice the interests of government employees simply to gain political advantage. So much for the "rights" of workers.

Whatever threats and ultimatums might have been made, the candidates still welcomed the help of armies of union operatives. AFSCME, for example, put 150 union organizers on the ground for the Iowa caucuses to support Howard Dean; according to the union's political director, AFSCME's efforts on behalf of Dean had been "ramped up considerably" from what the union had done for Al Gore in 2000. AFSCME and the SEIU together spent more than $2.6 million on behalf of Dean. Not to be outdone, Richard Gephardt welcomed an army of industrial union volunteers to Iowa. By the time of the caucuses, Gephardt's union backers had 900 organizers in Iowa.[20]

Although these efforts failed to produce the desired results in Iowa—Dean finished third, and Gephardt finished fourth, forcing him to drop out of the race altogether—they were significant in a few respects. First, the unions showed that they remain completely committed to their political activity. They poured millions of dollars and more than a thousand paid operatives into a single state for a single caucus. They are doing much more to try to defeat George W. Bush in the general election. Indeed, Iowa was not much of a setback for union bosses, because they had signaled early and often that they were obsessed with getting rid of Bush but not particularly concerned with *which* Democrat did the job. Second, the desperate maneuverings of the candidates' campaign teams betrayed just how powerful Big Labor's armies of political operatives are in the eyes of the Democrats themselves. Finally, the leftist unions showed that they can still drag candidates to their radical positions by promising millions of dollars and thousands of campaign operatives. After all, Dean veered left, even reversing his position on key issues, to make himself more attractive to the public-sector unions, and Gephardt predicated his whole Iowa campaign on being a friend to Big Labor.

As his presidential campaign gathered steam in 2004, Senator John Kerry began eyeing the unions, whose support he had not gained early in the race. By February of 2004, Kerry had received endorsements from at least ten national unions.[21] The candidate certainly knew that he'd be receiving substantial organizational support from these unions. For instance, Kerry's own press release touting his endorsement from the American Federation of Teachers quoted union president Sandra Feldman as saying, "We will begin immediately to mobilize our members on behalf of Senator Kerry's campaign to achieve policies that will make a positive difference for our nation and all its citizens."[22] When former candidate Dick Gephardt backed Kerry, it ensured that the Massachusetts senator would get even more Big Labor support. Sure enough, the AFL-CIO rushed to endorse the putative nominee.

For the left-wing unions that had initially thrown their support to other candidates, Kerry was hardly a bad option. The senator had pleased Big Labor when he cosponsored a bill in 1993 to make it illegal for companies to hire replacement workers during a strike. He also was far enough to the left to please the ultraliberal union bosses. In fact, the liberal organization Americans for Democratic Action gives Kerry a lifetime vote rating *four points higher* than uber-liberal Ted Kennedy.[23]

Yet the AFL-CIO and other labor organizations had had reservations about Kerry. In his Senate career he had consistently voted for free-trade agreements, including NAFTA and trade pacts with Singapore, Chile, and African nations, and for expanding the president's "fast-track" trade-negotiating authority—votes that were anathema to the unions. But as a presidential candidate he backpedaled, criticizing NAFTA and other trade agreements. On accepting the AFL-CIO's endorsement, he even proclaimed that "I will insist on real worker and real environmental provisions" in future trade agreements. Why the sudden change of heart? Because Kerry knew he had no chance of winning the election without Big Labor. "These are our foot soldiers," a Kerry spokeswoman told the *Baltimore Sun* after the AFL-CIO endorsement. "They will be working very hard to turn out the vote for us." Quite true. The AFL-CIO's backing opened the spigots of campaign volunteers and cash.

On March 10, less than three weeks after the AFL-CIO endorsed Kerry, the labor organization announced its most costly and ambitious campaign effort in its history, a $44 million program to get the Democrat into the White House. And who would pay for this relentlessly partisan program? Why, the union members, of course—whether they liked it or not. (And as we'll see, many union members *don't* like their money going to union political activism.) To generate the $44 million, the labor leaders decided simply to hike up the union dues they force members to pay. And Kerry was happy to let labor bosses dangle their money and manpower in front of him.

Kerry made a splash in the Democratic field by railing against special-interest groups and vowing to throw them out of Washington. At a rallying point in his campaign, he declared, "I have a message for the influence peddlers, for . . . the special interests who now call the White House their home. We're coming, you're going, and don't let the door hit you on the way out."[24] To burnish his image, he even proclaimed that he wasn't taking any money from PACs or lobbyists in his presidential campaign. In fact, his campaign proudly declared that Kerry had "never taken a dime of PAC money" for any of his campaigns, either for the Senate or the presidency.[25]

But the Man of the People act was just that—an act. Senator Zell Miller, Georgia Democrat, summed it up when he said that Kerry "is the Olympic gold medalist when it comes to special-interest money."[26] Charles Lewis, who heads the nonpartisan financial watchdog group the Center for Public Integrity, said, "The idea that Kerry has not helped or benefited from a specific special interest, which he has said, is utterly absurd. Anyone who gets millions of dollars over time, and thousands of dollars from specific donors, knows there's a symbiotic relationship. He needs the donors' money. The donors need favors."[27]

Indeed, Kerry has gotten *major* support from the special interests—including labor unions and union lobbyists. While he trumpeted the fact that his presidential campaign didn't take PAC money, the ambitious candidate found other ways to get his hands on money from unions and other special-interest groups he publicly condemned. The Associated Press reported that Kerry's "boast omits the fact that he was one of the largest recipients of donations from individual lawyers and lobbyists among all senators and that he created a vehicle in 2002 to collect large checks directly from companies, labor unions, and other special interests on the eve of his presidential bid."[28] That is to say, right around the time that Kerry voted for the McCain-Feingold Act, which was supposed to end the influence of soft money in elections, he created a tax-exempt committee, the Citizen Soldier Fund,[29] specifically to bring in bundles of soft money. The fund collected more than $470,000 from unions and other sources before soft money was banned, according to IRS records.[30]

Kerry has also solicited donations from lobbyists, those who represent PACs, and other special interests. By September 30, 2003, the last report available at the time of this writing, Kerry had accepted $227,950 into his presidential campaign directly from lobbyists.[31]

In the past, the senator even put union money directly into his pocket. From 1985 until 1990, when senators were finally banned from being paid for outside speaking engagements, Kerry personally pocketed $120,000 in speaking fees, including from unions such as the NEA.[32]

Although the presidential election is still months away as this is written, the early campaign proceedings allow us to recognize the fundamental truth: The labor unions retain their stranglehold on the Democratic Party. Their dominance extends far beyond presidential campaigns, too. The simple fact is that if you're an important Democratic politician—whether a presidential candidate, a congressman, a state senator, or a local school board member—chances are that you'll have to cater to Big Labor to maintain your political viability.

Perhaps no Democrat better illustrates the need to turn to unions to get elected than Hillary Clinton. In just a few years, the junior senator from New York has become one of the most powerful Democrats in the country, and certainly the party's mightiest fundraiser. But it's easy to forget now that Mrs. Clinton was not a shoo-in for the Senate back when she was first contemplating a run. She had many obstacles to overcome because of her association with various Clinton scandals, because many New Yorkers saw her as a carpetbagger, and because the man who at the time seemed certain to be the Republican nominee, New York mayor Rudolph Giuliani, would be a formidable opponent. Still, she knew where to turn to shore up her candidacy: the unions. In fact, Mrs. Clinton chose to announce her candidacy at the United Federation of Teachers' Manhattan headquarters, where her host was the president of the powerful New York teachers' union.[33] It was a fitting sign of the candidate's dependence on labor, for the unions would ultimately pour $453,000 into Mrs. Clinton's campaign and mobilize an army of volunteers.[34]

And as we'll see in this book, Hillary Clinton has been a grateful beneficiary of Big Labor's support. Though she has tried to keep herself from being publicly tied to union bosses, the reality is that few politicians have been so readily bought by union interests. Like other politicians with national ambitions, Senator Clinton has moved even further to the left in response to the huge amounts of cash and other resources that union bosses have dangled in front of her. In the process, she has flipped her position on a number of issues, and— surprise!—her new stance on an issue usually lines up with what union bosses think.

Even the FEC's investigation in 2001 hasn't stopped the labor unions from trying to buy political influence. Then again, as this book will reveal, union bosses seem to routinely flout the law. Why would we expect a federal investigation to curb Big Labor's political activities? In America today, it is as if the unions operate under an entirely different set of laws, regulations, and privileges from everyone else.

THE WAR CHEST

Union leaders strive to portray themselves as different from other special-interest groups, and in fact it would be a terrible mistake to think of labor unions as just another special-interest group—but not for the reasons Big Labor would have us believe. Unions have a unique power among private organizations: the power to tax. Unlike other politically active groups, unions don't have to collect donations to finance their ad campaigns or get-out-the-vote efforts on behalf of candidates. "Right-to-work" laws enacted by twenty-two states prohibit unions from collecting fees from workers in private jobs covered by union contract as a condition of their employment. These laws often do not cover public employees, however; some thirty-seven states allow unions to collect fees from public employees, including teachers. These fees, often called "agency fees," are supposed to cover the union's cost of collective bargaining and administering the contract. But without better disclosure of how unions spend their revenues—which the AFL-CIO and its constituent unions have fought repeatedly over the years, even filing lawsuits to prevent the Department of Labor from collecting this information—there is no way to know what the true cost of collective bargaining is. So in most states, they can simply force workers to pay union dues as a condition of employment, and these forced dues provide the unions with a massive war chest that gives them overwhelming political power.

In fact, the labor unions collect upwards of *$17 billion* a year,[35] all of it tax-free. This is a staggering sum of money for organizations whose basic function is to negotiate labor contracts. In reality, unions spend just a fraction of their income on collective bargaining and related activities, which means that Big Labor has billions of dollars left over to pay for whatever union officials choose. It is bad enough that many union officials choose to enrich themselves with the money forcibly taken out of workers' paychecks; corruption within the ranks of labor leaders has become endemic, as many union bosses pay themselves lavish salaries and also "invest" member dues in what amount to private slush funds. Even more disturbing is the fact that the labor unions pour so much of these member dues into advancing a political agenda that has almost nothing to do with workers' issues. The unions have so much money at their disposal that they can spend more on politics than do both major political parties combined.[36]

Union militants often claim that Big Labor needs the ability to spend forced dues on politics in order to counter corporate spending, but in fact union contributions dwarf corporate contributions. Of the top thirteen all-time donors to the Democratic Party, *nine* are unions. The top donor, AFSCME, gave $16.5 million between January 1, 1978, and June 30, 2003. That's $6 million more than the largest Republican donor, Philip Morris, contributed during that period. And AFSCME was just one of three unions (the other two being the SEIU and the Communications Workers of America) that gave Democrats as much as or more than the Republicans' top donor contributed.[37] Moreover, corporations—and any other organization that wants to support political causes, including the often-vilified National Rifle Association—are limited to what they can raise via *voluntary* contributions, but the unions' vast reserves of forced dues give labor bosses almost unlimited power.

The unions are also completely dedicated to using their resources so they can be a force in politics, and direct contributions are just a small part of their political support. For example, the NEA now employs an army of some 1,800 political operatives, who are paid out of the forced dues collected from teachers. To put this in perspective, consider that this one union alone has more paid political operatives than the Republican and Democratic National Committees *combined.*[38] Such resources make Big Labor essential to the future of Democrats, and the Democratic Party knows it.

Of course, the unions technically report that they spend *no* money on politics, even though federal tax law requires tax-exempt organizations to report all political expenditures over a hundred dollars in any year.[39] That's right, despite overwhelming evidence that Big Labor annually puts hundreds of millions of dollars toward politics—and many union officials actually boast of their active support for Democrats—the unions report *nothing* to the IRS. How can this be? Because any political contributions would be taxable. By reporting that they spend nothing on politics, the unions keep their funds tax-free. Just as important, they keep from the public and from their own members the details of how the money is being spent. Much evidence indicates that union employees have actually been *fired* just because they didn't want to support the union political program,[40] so it would seem logical that union leaders would do everything possible to cover up the fact that so much of workers' money is going to politics.

Union members have little recourse if they object to how their dues are being spent. This is another reason union leaders who are active in the political arena have a decided advantage over corporate executives, who must keep their political spending in line with stockholders' and customers' interests. The fact is, most union members—no matter their political beliefs—don't want to see their hard-earned money going to fund political activity. According to a survey conducted by the respected polling firm McLaughlin & Associates, fully 80 percent of union members are against having money taken out of their paychecks and spent on politics. Nonunion employees agree; overall, 82 percent of Americans think it unfair to force workers to pay for political activity, as an ABC News/*Washington Post* poll revealed.[41]

Thus, most workers oppose the very idea of having unions spend member dues on politics. But it is even more troubling to consider that labor bosses are spending these dues on a political agenda that most workers would not voluntarily support and that many union members adamantly disagree with. Polls consistently show that 40 percent of union members vote Republican. In the late 1990s, the AFL-CIO's political director actually admitted that of AFL-CIO members who vote, 40 percent vote Republican.[42] Even the NEA, which represents the traditionally liberal teaching profession, reports that a minority of its 2.7 million members are Democrats; 30 percent regard themselves as Republicans, and another 30 percent consider themselves independents.[43] Still, year in and year out, AFL-CIO and NEA leaders, like most other labor bosses, commit virtually 100 percent of their political resources to Democrats.

For all the unions' rhetoric about standing for the rights of working people, taking money from workers' paychecks against their will to pay for a political agenda they oppose is the antithesis of workers' rights.

Why this dramatic difference between the political agenda of labor leaders and the political views of the rank and file? Quite simply, in the interests of self-preservation, Big Labor has given itself over to a radical political agenda. In the process, the unions have abandoned many of the principles on which the American labor movement was founded, not to mention the interests of the workers they are supposed to serve. Their willingness to change course so abruptly has enabled the labor unions to enhance their own political power even while unions themselves have seen their membership plummet and their importance diminish.

Big Labor has put its own power above all else, including its own members' welfare and the public good. Desperate to keep dues money pouring into their coffers, labor leaders push for bigger and bigger government. In fact, the leadership of the American labor movement is now at the far left of the political spectrum—to the point that the single most powerful labor leader in the United States, the president of the AFL-CIO, proudly preaches his socialist worldview.

BIG LABOR, BIG GOVERNMENT

The American labor movement has shifted its emphasis from workers to politics for a simple reason: desperation. After years of seeing their membership rolls grow, unions began losing members—and consequently, losing the all-important member dues. For decades the unions were a major force in the private sector. Union membership among America's private workforce reached as high as 35 percent in the mid-1950s.[44] Certain fields, such as construction, the unions completely dominated; for example, unionized companies had a whopping 87 percent of the construction market in 1947.[45] Private-sector union membership has fallen off dramatically, however. In fact, by 2003 only 8.2 percent of private-sector employees belonged to unions.[46] Even construction workers have largely abandoned the unions: in 2003 only 16 percent of construction workers were union members.[47] And the drop-off shows no signs of ending. In 2003 alone, America's private-sector labor unions lost 369,000 members.[48]

Faced with the exodus of private-sector workers, the unions have had to look for new sources of income: government employees. Unionization among government employees is soaring, even while private-sector workers are fleeing from unions. In 2002, the same year that private-sector unions lost close to half a million members, public-sector unions gained 165,000 members.[49] Back in the 1950s, government employees made up just 5 percent of union members; by 2003 they accounted for 46 percent of all union members. And more and more government workers are being forced into unions, with nearly four in ten government workers now unionized.[50] According to David Denholm of the Public Service Research Foundation, "Within a few years, a majority of union members will work for the government."[51]

Thus, for all the labor bosses' talk of representing "working families," union members aren't as likely to be industrial hardhats as they are to be white-collar government bureaucrats.

As unions move away from representing those who pay taxes (private-sector workers) to those who depend on ever-higher taxes (government workers), it's natural that Big Labor should seek to dominate politics. By putting their own people in charge of the government—management, so to speak—unions effectively control both sides of the bargaining table.

The result is a cycle of corruption in which labor bosses use forced dues to elect politicians—that is, their members' employers—who then give the unions what they want at the bargaining table, and push labor's demonstrably left-wing agenda as well. And the central feature of that agenda is the expansion of government, since the more employees the government hires, the more dues-paying members the unions will have.

The vested interest of government-employee unions is, and always will be, Big Government. Pollster Scott Rasmussen remarks, "Public-sector workers want government to grow first," and the overall health of the economy isn't as relevant to them."[52] As long as the only growth in union membership is among government workers, union bosses will support having more and more government programs, departments, commissions, and regulatory bodies, because more union-dues-paying bureaucrats will be required to staff them. (And of course, no government program will ever become unnecessary or outlive its purpose, which is why the U.S. government still funds a Rural Electrification Project at a time when every corner of America already has electricity.)

A former union insider sums up what has happened to the American labor movement and how it has corrupted the political process. Steve Silberger, who was AFSCME's chief Washington lobbyist in the 1980s, told the *Wall Street Journal* in 2004, "The big story in labor in the last 15 years is that the hard left has taken over the public-sector unions, and no major Democrat will stand up to them. The Democratic Party is becoming a pure party of government—the public interest is being subordinated to a special interest that prospers when government grows."[53]

The shift away from unionization in the private sector is a natural one, as private companies have competed for the best workers by offering good wages and benefits, rendering private-sector unions unnecessary in most cases.

But the shift toward unionization in the public sector is a radical departure for the American labor movement, which long held that government employees shouldn't—indeed, couldn't—be unionized. From the labor movement's founding, union leaders believed that a union's purpose was to organize workers so they could earn their fair share of the employer's profits. But when government is the employer, there are no profits. Money that goes to pay government workers comes from taxes, which means that government unions take money out of the pockets of *all* workers.

Moreover, union leaders recognized that government employees generally have a monopoly on the services they provide (policing, fire fighting, and so on) and should not use that authority to extort from the American public. President Franklin Roosevelt, a strong supporter of unions, summed up the attitude toward government-employee unions when he decried them as "the Hitler methods towards labor."[54] Collective bargaining, said Roosevelt, "cannot be transplanted into public service."[55] Union leaders before and after Roosevelt agreed. As late as 1959, AFL-CIO president George Meany affirmed that "it is impossible to bargain collectively with government."[56]

Unfortunately, this philosophy fell victim to unions' need for new sources of cash—and the need to preserve their own power. The American labor movement did a complete about-face, as many union bosses began to organize public-sector bargaining units.

MOVING BIG LABOR TO THE FAR LEFT

Big Labor's unprincipled reversal on the matter of government-employee unions drove it headlong into politics, and specifically to a pro-Democrat, pro–Big Government platform. But that switch alone was not sufficient to create the extreme-left agenda that marks Big Labor today—an agenda that in many cases has nothing to do with workers' issues.

In fact, it is ludicrous to think that unions use their vast resources solely to promote political issues crucial to working people. Consider just a small sampling of causes and issues that union bosses have put their billions of dollars in compulsory dues behind:

- □ forcing the Boy Scouts to admit homosexuals and atheists
- □ promoting abortion
- □ opposing welfare reform
- □ legalizing marijuana
- □ opposing a balanced budget
- □ advocating statehood for the District of Columbia
- □ encouraging U.S. participation in the United Nations
- □ supporting a freeze on nuclear weapons
- □ urging legislators in Massachusetts to support gay marriage

Whatever one's views on, say, legalizing drugs or forcing the Boy Scouts to accept homosexuals, it's hard to argue that the unions' support for these causes improves union workers' pay, benefits, or working conditions, or even furthers the opportunity to organize more workers. And these are just a few of the many issues behind which Big Labor has rallied, not because of anything to do with the workers it purports to represent but simply because of union leaders' far-left agenda.

Leading the way on this radical agenda is the most powerful labor leader in America, AFL-CIO president John Sweeney. Sweeney became president of the AFL-CIO in 1995—just after the Republicans took control of Congress in the 1994 elections—by trumpeting his own record of political activism. In his thirteen years as head of the SEIU, he had transformed that union into one of the most politically powerful groups in the country. Immediately upon taking control of the AFL-CIO, Sweeney began employing the political tactics he had learned as head of the SEIU. While his predecessors as AFL-CIO president, George Meany and Lane Kirkland, had moved Big Labor far into the political arena, Sweeney made politics almost the single focus of the labor movement.

Sweeney also set about removing all vestiges of moderate and conservative public policy traditionally supported by Big Labor. For decades after the founding of the labor movement, union leaders had eschewed politics because they recognized that their members did not all share the same political beliefs. The father of the American labor movement, Samuel Gompers—who founded the American Federation of Labor (AFL) in the 1880s—pointed out that "there are a number of earnest Republicans in . . . the AF of L, who would not take kindly to the notion if we, who are elected as officers by their votes as well as the votes of others, were to publicly and practically officially use the offices, or the influence which these offices [give], to secure the defeat of their party, and the success of the party to which they are opposed."[57] Even as the unions became politically active in the second half of the twentieth century, they did not wholeheartedly endorse the Left's agenda. For example, until the end of the Lane Kirkland era, the AFL-CIO supported a strong national defense and a foreign policy that opposed worldwide Communism and defended American self-interests. In part this reflected the lingering sense that unions should at least consider their members' interests, for many AFL-CIO workers were employed in the defense industry.

Sweeney, however, has thrown his members' interests to the wind in order to advance his own political beliefs. And he has made no effort to hide his radical agenda. In his run for the presidency of the AFL-CIO, Sweeney sought to mobilize the more active leftist membership by joining the Democratic Socialists of America (DSA), which is, according to its website, "the largest socialist organization in the United States, and the principal U.S. affiliate of the Socialist International." The DSA roundly rejects any "economic order sustained by private profit."[58]

One might think that an organization dedicated to the expansion of socialism and socialist government in America would be at the fringes of American politics, but the DSA—thanks in large part to John Sweeney's unrivaled political clout—has powerful friends at the highest levels of the U.S. government. The Progressive Caucus, the largest Democratic caucus in the House of Representatives and a who's who of leftist politicians, works closely with the DSA, which boasted that these members work with the DSA on a campaign "for economic justice."[59] Among its more than fifty members is the highest-ranking Democrat in the House, Minority Leader Nancy Pelosi. Another notable member is failed presidential candidate Dennis Kucinich, whose campaign rested on a promise to create a Department of Peace, leaving one to wonder why he didn't go all out for meaningless feel-good symbols and promise a Department of Rainbows. The only non-Democrat in this coalition is the founding chairman, Bernie Sanders, the "Independent" congressman from Vermont—a self-proclaimed socialist.

One DSA document, an organizing document geared toward youth, summarizes the organization's strategy of trying to reach out to a broad swath of Americans: "Stress our Democratic Party strategy and electoral work. The Democratic Party is something the public understands, and association with it takes the edge off. Stressing our Democratic Party work will establish some distance from the radical subculture and help integrate you to the milieu of the young liberals."[60]

The Progressive Caucus's ties to the DSA have been extensive. Joseph Farah, a columnist with the conservative website WorldNet-Daily, revealed in a series of exposés that the caucus's own website was hosted by the DSA until 1999, when the website was moved to an official congressional site.[61] When the DSA came under closer scrutiny because of its influence over members of Congress, the group decided to clean up its image. One thing it did was to remove from its website lyrics to several inflammatory songs more suited to the Red Army of the old Soviet Union than to a group with ties to an official caucus in the U.S. Congress. One charming little ditty, sung to the tune of "Frère Jacques," included these lovely sentiments:

> *Are you sleeping? Are you sleeping?*
> *Bourgeoisie, Bourgeoisie*
> *And when the revolution comes*
> *We'll kill you all with knives and guns*
> *Bourgeoisie, Bourgeoisie*

And then there was this fabulous hit, sung to the tune of "When the Red, Red Robin":

> *When the Red Revolution*
> *Brings its solution along, along*
> *There'll be no more lootin'*
> *When we start shootin' that Wall Street throng*

Naturally, the site also featured "The Internationale," the worldwide anthem of communism.

None of this seemed to deter John Sweeney from openly associating himself with the DSA. Featured on the official DSA website is this statement from Sweeney: "I'm proud to be a member of a movement for change that puts the cause of working people at the heart of the matter."[62]

This is the sort of agenda that Big Labor throws its vast resources behind. By using forced dues to buy the cooperation of one of the two major parties, AFL-CIO leader John Sweeney has placed a number of DSA allies in office and controlled the agenda of the Democratic Party. Sweeney has established himself as the Democratic Party's power broker extraordinaire. If nothing else, Democratic candidates have to make the pilgrimage to Sweeney to kiss his ring. Ignoring Sweeney can put Big Labor's massive resources in an opposing candidate's camp and make it almost impossible to win. Thus, in 2003, Democratic presidential hopefuls dutifully courted Sweeney and the AFL-CIO. Dick Gephardt hoped that his almost perfect AFL-CIO voting record would help him win an early endorsement from the labor federation, which requires a two-thirds vote of the group's fifty-four-member executive council, made up of the AFL-CIO's biggest unions. But other candidates trekked to Florida for the AFL's winter meeting as well, including Senator Joe Lieberman, Senator John Edwards, and former Illinois senator Carol Moseley-Braun.[63] In the end, the AFL-CIO decided not to endorse any candidate that early in the campaign, freeing its member unions to go their own way.

DOOM AND GLOOM

At the very least one might hope that the unions would support economic policy that is in the interests of American workers, but here again labor leaders have ignored what is best for workers. In the Sweeney era, the same Marxist notions that characterize the DSA have come to define Big Labor. John Sweeney and other union bosses have tried to portray American capitalism as a nightmare for workers, despite the real-world evidence to the contrary.

Sweeney took control of the AFL-CIO in the boom years of the 1990s, when the United States was in the midst of one of the longest periods of economic expansion in its history—indeed, in the history of the world. Still, he seemed strangely oblivious to the prosperity, apparently because the nation had not conformed to his socialist vision. Adopting the classic Marxist tactic of fostering class resentment, he charged that "corporate America" had declared "war" on American workers. Never mind that this would be a bizarre and self-destructive strategy for any corporation, which depends on these same workers to buy its products and services. In addition, Sweeney loudly proclaimed that the unions were needed more than at any other time in history—a preposterous claim, given the horrid working conditions that had given rise to the labor movement in the first place and that had long since been eradicated.

Readers of Sweeney's 1996 book, *America Needs a Raise*, might actually conclude that America was in the midst of another Great Depression—that is, unless they looked past Sweeney's doom-and-gloom scenario and examined the evidence themselves. Despite Sweeney's dire warnings about how the American working class was suffering, workers were benefiting from the unprecedented boom. By 1996, unemployment had fallen to 5.4 percent from 7.4 percent in 1992.[64] To be sure, some jobs were being eliminated, but in fact new jobs were being created far faster than old jobs were being eliminated. That is always the case in a dynamic economy. Overall, per-capita income—even adjusted for cost-of-living increases—had risen by more than 50 percent in a generation.[65]

And, of course, Sweeney's comments about the economy in subsequent years have been no more on target. In 2003, for example, he said the nation was suffering the "worst job-loss crisis since the Great Depression."[66] But in September 2003, when Sweeney made this statement, unemployment was at 6.1 percent[67]—a far cry from the Great Depression, when 25 percent of Americans were out of work.

So if workers actually prosper in America's modern capitalist economy, why do John Sweeney and other labor leaders proclaim their dystopian vision of America? These ludicrous charges are, in fact, just one example of how union bosses try to maintain their own authority. Needing to convince workers that unions are still relevant, labor leaders must tell American workers that they are in dire trouble, that they are powerless and have no voice. Indeed, John Sweeney portrays workers as having no voice in their lives if they don't join an AFL-CIO–affiliated union.

But the reality is far different: The vast majority of American workers have found the greatest economic opportunities away from the unions. Moreover, corporations have steadily increased the "voice" of workers, *often over the objections of union bosses*, who have a vested interest in limiting the role of workers in negotiating the terms of their own employment.

BIG LABOR: ABOVE THE LAW?

Big Labor's nightmarish vision of America has no root in reality, but the unions have nevertheless had great success in gaining support at all levels of government and in placing like-minded politicians in positions of power. And a key reason union leaders have such extraordinary political influence, of course, is that they control massive amounts of money they take from members' paychecks. This is particularly shocking because, by continuing to play such an active role in the political sphere, union bosses seem to be openly violating the law.

Although the unions derive their political power from the huge amounts of member dues they control, the U.S. Supreme Court has repeatedly and emphatically ruled that unions *cannot* force members to fund union political activity. Perhaps the two most significant decisions were in the 1977 case of *Abood v. Detroit Board of Education* and the 1988 case of *Communications Workers of America v. Beck*. In the former case, the court ruled that government-employee unions could not use compulsory member dues for political purposes unrelated to their core functions of collective bargaining, contract administration, and grievance adjustment,[68] and in the latter, the court applied the same principle to private-sector unions. Writing for the majority in the *Beck* case, Justice William Brennan cited the National Labor Relations Act, which, he pointed out, "authorizes the exaction of only those fees and dues necessary to 'performing the duties of an exclusive representative of the employees in dealing with the employer on labor-management issues.' "[69]

The *Abood* and *Beck* cases also demonstrated just how much unions have departed from their original purpose of representing workers. If collective-bargaining activities are the unions' core function, labor leaders put very little of their ample resources toward those activities. In the *Beck* case the courts found that barely 20 percent of the communications workers' dues was going toward collective bargaining, meaning that the vast majority of member dues was used for illegitimate purposes; the government-employee union in the *Abood* case spent even less on its supposed purpose.[70]

Spending so little on representing workers and instead focusing on politics is not unusual, even today. In fact, Big Labor ignores the Supreme Court's rulings, probably because it knows that any union member who wants to enforce the Supreme Court's decisions must take the union to court. Most workers don't have the financial resources to take on the unions in court, especially because union bosses will spend virtually any sum out of the money they collect from forced dues in order to retain the right to keep exacting dues against the will of workers.

Congress typically acts to codify major judicial decisions such as *Beck* in order to give these decisions the unambiguous force of law, but politicians have been hesitant to take on Big Labor's political might. Without a legislative act to enforce the *Beck* decision, even workers in right-to-work states have no choice regarding the union's political program. If they want to belong to a union, they must allow their dues to be spent for the liberal political agenda, regardless of their own beliefs. And in a forced-unionism state (in which unions have the legal power to force workers to pay dues as a condition of employment), workers can find relief only if they resign their membership—and even then they are forced to pay union "fees."

Aside from the procedural impediments to holding Big Labor to account for its political spending, workers face another major problem when it comes to controlling how their dues money is spent: Most are simply unaware that the unions are violating members' rights by spending money on politics. According to a 1996 poll conducted by Luntz Research, roughly 80 percent were ignorant of the *Beck* decision.[71] Not surprisingly, the AFL-CIO has worked hard to make sure workers remain in the dark, opposing efforts to require that workers be informed of their rights. (For example, unions have lobbied intensively against regulations that would require these rights to be posted in job sites.) But plenty of others are complicit in this attempt to keep workers from knowing their *Beck* rights. The National Labor Relations Board is the government entity charged with enforcing labor law, but it is traditionally staffed with former union employees who are committed to keeping Big Labor's perks. Unfortunately, George W. Bush's administration has not done much to help union members in this regard. If this has been to keep the peace with John Sweeney, the administration's efforts have been wasted, for Big Labor will spend millions of dollars to defeat President Bush in 2004.

Indeed, Democrats are the most willing supporters of Big Labor's agenda, which means that they are the most willing to allow the further victimization of workers. While Democrats give lip service to concepts like "choice," "fairness," and "workers' rights," they sacrifice those ideals for the sake of the hundreds of millions of dollars Big Labor lavishes on them come election time.

Remaining silent on workers' *Beck* rights is just a small part of how Democrats pay Big Labor back. On many issues, Democrats hold the union-boss line. For instance, even though American education is in crisis, Democrats insist on spending more and more money on the same sorts of programs that have done nothing to improve the quality of education in this country, as we'll see in more detail in Chapter 5. In fact, spending on education, adjusted for inflation, has tripled since 1960, but we have witnessed a steady decline in results as demonstrated by the National Assessment of Education Progress, which has been measuring student performance since the 1960s.[72] So why does the Democratic Party take the foolhardy position that all our schools need is more money? Because Democrats have become mouthpieces for the NEA and the smaller American Federation of Teachers (AFT), an AFL-CIO affiliate.

And the payback comes in many other forms as well. Again and again we see how the unions have gained special exemptions because Democrats are willing to accede to union leaders' demands in order to protect their own political power. The unions' funding of Democrats has started a seemingly unending cycle of corruption that has led to devastating real-world consequences for all Americans. Since unions are shielded from measures of accountability and transparency, corrupt labor leaders—some of them closely linked to organized crime families—fleece not only workers but also taxpayers, who must fund public-works projects that are union-run boondoggles. Forced unionism and Big Government—two key pillars of Big Labor's agenda—saddle all of us with higher taxes, poorer services, and much more.

Even more troubling, government-employee unions put the American public directly at risk, using their monopoly power over vital public services like policing and fire fighting to extort concessions from the government.

Unions are so beyond the reach of the law that they can, and often do, resort to violence as a "bargaining" tool that coerces employers into giving them whatever they want. The record of union-orchestrated violence is frightening, but even more disturbing is the fact that the U.S. government lets these terrorist acts go unpunished. In short, the unions have carved out for themselves a form of legalized terrorism.

Union bosses have betrayed the American worker, the founding principles of the labor movement, and the American public in their desperate pursuit of power. That pursuit of power has been remarkably successful, however. Having struck a corrupt bargain with the Democratic Party, they have bought themselves a special set of privileges and are free to act as they please, no matter the consequences for the American people.

It is time to end that corrupt bargain.

CHAPTER 2

Marriage of Convenience: Unions and the Democrats

I f you were looking for an appropriate symbol of the unbreakable bond between Democrats and the labor unions, you would have found it here:

The First Lady of the United States, Hillary Rodham Clinton, was standing before a crowd of reporters and television crews in a New York City office building. It was late November 1999, and everyone assembled for this news conference was expecting Mrs. Clinton to make the announcement that political watchers had been awaiting for months: that she was a candidate for the U.S. Senate. But instead of announcing her intentions directly, she enlisted the aid of a trusted backer, who was now standing beside her in front of the cameras.

The woman by Mrs. Clinton's side was the president of the United Federation of Teachers, Randi Weingarten. Weingarten was also her host that day, as the news conference was being held in the union's Manhattan headquarters. Anyone who watched the announcement on the news that evening could have no doubt about the location, for the teachers' union's white-on-blue banner was prominently displayed behind the two women.[1]

In what the union leader's aides admitted was a scripted exchange, Weingarten fed Mrs. Clinton the opportunity to make her announcement, saying that New York needed a senator "who really cares about education" and then asking her what everyone had come to find out: "So is it yes or no?" Mrs. Clinton still did not answer directly, saying only, "I believe that if we work together, we really can make a difference for the children and families in New York."

In essence the union boss was left to make the announcement for the Democratic candidate. "So the answer is yes," stated Weingarten. As the *New York Times* reported, "If Mrs. Clinton had anything to say beyond that—and it appeared that she might have—it was lost in the tumult of loud cheers and hand-clapping of the union members as they rose to their feet."[2]

To some it might seem odd that Mrs. Clinton would choose to declare her candidacy for the U.S. Senate in this setting. But she did not even have a home in her newly adopted state yet—it would be another month and a half before she moved into her house in Chappaqua, New York. She needed a place to make the announcement, and the headquarters of the teachers' union seemed a natural choice. After all, Mrs. Clinton must have realized how dependent she was on the labor movement. The unions' massive amounts of money and manpower had been the key to her husband's electoral success, and as she embarked on her own political career, the United Federation of Teachers and many other labor organizations—including unions outside of New York—would be critical to her campaign.

Today, of course, Hillary Clinton is in many ways the face of the Democratic Party. To many, she is the best hope for the future of the party, but undeniably she is the Democrats' most reliable fundraiser. So important is Mrs. Clinton to other Democratic candidates that just weeks after taking the oath of office she set up her own political action committee, HILLPAC,[3] which gave $837,000[4] to her fellow Democrats in 2002 and will play a major role in the 2004 election. Indeed, CNN has reported that HILLPAC is the hidden power behind the leftist coalition known as Americans Coming Together, which played a key role in a December 2003 meeting of liberal activists plotting President George W. Bush's political death (one advocate actually publicized the meeting as a "Hate Bush" event).[5]

All this is quite impressive for someone still in her first term of elective office. Clearly, Mrs. Clinton had a national profile long before being sworn in as a United States senator, but it is safe to say that she would not be in such a powerful position today without the undying support of the labor unions. At the time she announced her candidacy in 1999, many observers thought she faced an uphill battle to win the Senate seat. She ended up winning the election handily, however. While it helped that the Republicans' original choice to run against her, New York City mayor Rudolph Giuliani, dropped out of the race for health reasons, the unions were essential to putting her in office. As a senator, she has been careful to keep Big Labor happy.

In a sense, then, Mrs. Clinton's announcement of her Senate candidacy was not the only fitting symbol of the corrupt bargain between the Democratic Party and the labor unions. Hillary Clinton's whole political career provides a fascinating case study of how Big Labor controls the Democrats.

HILLARY CLINTON: PROFILE IN COWARDICE

According to financial documents filed with the Department of Labor, the unions take in some $17 billion each year,[6] much of it from compulsory dues taken from workers' paychecks as a condition of employment. Because so little of this money is spent on collective bargaining or related activities (court cases have revealed unions to be spending as little as 20 percent of member dues on their supposed function),[7] unions can devote substantial funds to politics. Indeed, some experts estimate that unions spend upwards of $800 million a year on politics, which is more than what both major political parties spend combined.[8] A top AFL-CIO official, Richard Bensinger, put the unions' political spending power in perspective in 1995 when he said, "Look at the Christian Coalition. They have $25 million. We have $11 billion."[9]

Bensinger's statement was typical of Big Labor officials, who often boast of their political spending and their influence on American government. Thus it is not surprising that the president of the United Federation of Teachers would be at center stage with Hillary Clinton when she announced her candidacy for the Senate in 1999, or that the union then played an active role in getting her elected. The United Federation of Teachers' support for Mrs. Clinton went far beyond the carefully produced announcement ceremony. The union, through its parent organization's PAC, AFT-COPE, gave Mrs. Clinton the maximum direct contribution allowed by law, $5,000 for her primary campaign and another $5,000 for her general election. The rival National Education Association (NEA) also gave Mrs. Clinton the maximum $10,000 in 2000.[10] But that was only a fraction of the money she raised from the unions. Indeed, the Center for Responsive Politics estimates that she raised some $446,480 from those in the "education" field, making teachers among her principal donors in her bid to become New York's senator.[11] And the United Federation of Teachers and its state affiliate, the 430,000-member New York State United Teachers, also supplied the Clinton campaign with "volunteers" to man phone banks, distribute campaign literature, and work in get-out-the-vote efforts. In all, unions gave some $453,000 in PAC, individual, and soft-money donations.[12]

Mrs. Clinton's union support was not confined to New York either. The president of the Communications Workers of America also endorsed her, for example. At the Working Families Party Convention in San Francisco in 2000, union president Morton Bahr stated that Clinton could be counted on to fight against a national right-to-work act (which would end the forced collection of union dues) and a paycheck-protection act (which would prohibit unions from using members' dues for politics against their will). Interestingly, Bahr admitted that a paycheck-protection bill would "effectively put unions . . . out of the political process,"[13] tacitly acknowledging that union bosses would be hard-pressed to get their members to contribute voluntarily to the unions' extreme political program.

Since taking office, Senator Clinton (or Hillary!, as she referred to herself in her Senate campaign material) has been sure to reward the union bosses who got her elected—and whose continued support will be vital to her quest to fulfill her political ambitions. In fact, she has followed the union line to an embarrassing extent, going so far as to reverse her positions on key issues when her original stance did not correspond with the unions'. And like many other leading Democrats, she has moved further to the left in her pursuit of high office, which undoubtedly pleases the labor movement's radical leadership.

Perhaps most startling is Senator Clinton's about-face on education issues. The group for whom she most loudly professes her support is "the children." She served as chair of the board of the Children's Defense Fund, wrote a book about the "Lessons Children Teach Us,"[14] and said she wanted to be a senator because she (and her union allies) "can really can make a difference for the children." And yet it seems that she has been more than willing to sell out our nation's children at the behest of union leaders.

While her husband was governor of Arkansas, Mrs. Clinton headed up the state's education reform efforts. As head of the Arkansas Education Standards Committee, she advocated and pushed through the state legislature a requirement for teacher competency testing. Arkansas parents had repeatedly said that many teachers were incompetent. Said Mrs. Clinton, "I kept running over and over again into people who said, 'These teachers can't read, they can't spell, they can't do anything.' "[15] As it turns out, the people of Arkansas had good reason to doubt their teachers: some teachers actually *were* incompetent. Mrs. Clinton admitted this when her committee called for teacher testing, saying that her committee "kept coming up against some very legitimate questions about who was in the classroom today."[16]

It can hardly be said that Mrs. Clinton's testing program was stringent, since those who failed had two years to prepare and retake the test. Still, the very notion of these competency tests was anathema to the teachers' unions, which oppose most efforts to hold teachers accountable for basic skill and knowledge requirements.[17] (As we will see in Chapter 5, this is just one example of how the teachers' unions, who are concerned only with keeping government money pouring into the schools and keeping dues-paying teachers on the job, stand in the way of true education reform.) The Arkansas Education Association, the state affiliate of the powerful National Education Association (NEA), went on the attack, lashing out at Mrs. Clinton for advocating teacher testing, picketing her public appearances, and refusing to endorse her husband. But Mrs. Clinton did not back down, and she openly criticized the leadership of the teachers' union.

Even in standing up to the teachers' unions, however, Mrs. Clinton did not do much to advance the cause of education or "the children." Arkansas would remain ranked forty-ninth out of the fifty states in education. According to former Clinton political consultant Dick Morris, that is because Mrs. Clinton handled education reform in Arkansas with all the aplomb and grace that she would later exhibit as she tried to ram nationalized health care down the nation's throat. Morris recounts that the results of Arkansas's teacher competency tests were so bad that the Clintons decided to rig them. In a strategy session with Bill and Hillary, Morris says, Governor Clinton told him that between one-third and one-half of teachers had failed the test. Afraid of the political backlash from releasing this result, the Clintons reportedly ordered Morris to poll Arkansas voters to see what percentage of teachers they expected to fail. Morris's polls showed that 10 percent was an acceptable failure rate to voters, and so, says Morris, that was the figure that was actually released.[18]

Predictably, the teachers' unions were appalled even when those few teachers were dismissed for failing the competency test—many fewer than should have been dismissed, according to Morris. He reports that dismissals created a "firestorm," and this seems to have imparted a valuable political lesson to Hillary Clinton: Don't buck the teachers' unions.

Sure enough, once her ambitions became national, Mrs. Clinton metaphorically kissed the ring of teachers' union bosses and flip-flopped her position. Suddenly, as a U.S. Senate candidate, she became adamantly opposed to teacher testing, publicly stating her opposition to any form of testing for teachers already at work.[19] Those are the teachers who are paying dues to the teachers' unions and give the unions a huge war chest to spend on politics—and specifically on loyal politicians like Hillary Clinton.

The teachers' unions are by no means Senator Clinton's only source of support from labor. Union PACs have been generous contributors, giving her more than $466,000 as of January 2004.[20] And she has proven herself a loyal friend to those unions as well. She has even risked our nation's security to pay back the union leaders who were essential to her election.

After the September 11 terrorist attacks, the House of Representatives passed legislation creating the new Department of Homeland Security just a month after it was introduced,[21] which is light-speed action in the congressional bureaucracy. But when the bill went to the Senate, Senator Clinton repeatedly stalled efforts to create the department in order to get more concessions for government-employee unions. She demanded that union rules trump the president's ability to manage homeland security in times of crisis.

To protest what she claimed was President Bush's plan to "undermine and eliminate the rights of federal workers,"[22] she rallied with one hundred government-union employees, who demanded concessions to the unions.[23] In all, Senator Clinton spent nearly four months stalling Homeland defense, voting for at least four substitute bills that would have granted her union benefactors their every wish but that would have tied the president's hands in a crisis.[24]

Of course, typical of the Clinton brand of doublethink, she now vehemently criticizes President Bush for not reacting quickly enough to secure the country. She has said, "The truth is we are not prepared . . . and our approach to securing our nation is haphazard at best."[25] She has also proclaimed, "We have relied on a myth of homeland security—a myth written in rhetoric, inadequate resources and a new bureaucracy."[26] Never mind the fact that her solution was to create a bureaucracy completely hand-tied and unable to respond to a national emergency because it was completely subject to union-defined rules. She also has remained silent on the issue of the "rights of federal workers" under the Department of Homeland Security, probably because those rights have remained intact even though the final bill did not grant all the concessions the unions and Mrs. Clinton were advocating.

Given how publicly she aligned herself with the unions in announcing her Senate candidacy, how much money and support the unions have provided her, and how she has shifted her position on major issues so as to be more acceptable to union bosses, one might think that Hillary Clinton would not do much to hide her union ties. But as senator she has bent over backwards in her PR efforts to keep herself from being publicly linked to union bosses. For example, the index of her ghostwritten "autobiography," *Living History*,[27] does not mention a single labor leader, despite all the money and manpower the unions gave the Clintons. Not even AFL-CIO leader John Sweeney, who was so valuable to the Clintons, merits a mention.

This is standard for Democratic politicians today. Though the Democratic Party has become a wholly owned subsidiary of Big Labor, Democrats are careful not to telegraph that they have entered into a corrupt bargain with union bosses. The unions, too, work hard to obscure the fact that they have devoted themselves completely to their radical political agenda, as they keep their finances—and thus their political spending—hidden from public view. And for the most part the Democrats and the labor unions have succeeded in obscuring the truth. While many Americans recognize that the labor unions are politically active and are a key Democratic constituency, almost no one understands how much power the unions have and how they have corrupted the system.

Fortunately, the truth sometimes peeks through.

BIG LABOR'S CONTROL OF THE DEMOCRATIC PARTY

The 2001 investigation conducted by the Federal Election Commission (FEC) marked one of those moments when we got a glimpse at the truth. Of course, just as Hillary Clinton carefully distances herself from her union benefactors, the unions and the Democratic Party immediately sued to keep the FEC from making public the records of their quid pro quo arrangement, and a judge agreed to pull the records from public view. But the Associated Press obtained copies in the few days before the judge's ruling, revealing how the Democratic Party has given Big Labor veto power over its election plans and policy decisions.

The Democratic Party's National Coordinated Campaign Steering Committee is responsible for formulating the party's national and statewide campaign strategies and for coordinating political spending on behalf of Democratic candidates. It is not surprising that the committee features representatives from such Democratic groups as the Democratic National Committee (DNC), the Democratic Senatorial Campaign Committee, the Democratic Congressional Campaign Committee, the Democratic Governors' Association, and the Democratic Legislative Campaign Committee. What is shocking is the list of other groups represented on this all-important steering committee. The FEC's investigation revealed that in 1996 the steering committee also included representatives from Big Labor—the NEA and the AFL-CIO. (Reflecting how much the Democrats pander to radical left groups—at least those that are generous donors—the committee even had a representative from EMILY's List, the advocacy group that targets its substantial political contributions to pro-abortion candidates.) Internal DNC documents also showed that the campaign scheme placed AFL-CIO and NEA leaders on the steering committees in each state, meaning that Big Labor controls Democratic election activities throughout the entire country.

Indeed, internal Democratic Party documents memos showed that the DNC and its congressional fundraising arm would contact union officials for approval of their plans—all so the Democrats could turn around and ask for a new infusion of Big Labor money. For instance, Democratic Congressional Campaign Committee official Rob Engel gathered plans for phone banks, direct-mail, and get-out-the-vote programs in sixteen targeted congressional districts and sent them directly to AFL-CIO political official Steve Rogers in September 1996. Engel wrote, "We request the AFL-CIO review these budgets and programs. If you approve them, we ask that you encourage your affiliated unions to contribute to each congressional district coordinated campaign."[28] A few days later, operatives from the congressional campaign were even more blunt, writing in a memo, "Attached is our updated and improved requests for your big bucks."[29]

An internal DNC memo entitled "Rules of Engagement" detailed how the arrangement worked: "When the DNC and its National partners including . . . the AFL-CIO and the NEA agree on the contents of a plan, each national partner will give their funding commitment to the state."[30]

As the Associated Press reported, AFL-CIO general counsel John Hiatt even admitted that the labor federation had veto power over the

Democratic campaign activities it helped finance. "For aspects of campaigns we subsidize, I think we would want veto power," he said matter-of-factly.[31]

Big Labor's role on the national steering committee was just as important as its work on the state committees. According to DNC general counsel Joseph Sandler, this national committee—which had two representatives from the AFL-CIO and one from the NEA—met six to eight times to carry out the coordinated campaigns and discuss financing.[32] The coordinated campaign plan was explicit that state parties must submit election plans to union bosses for approval, requiring that they be "submitted with a signature page which demonstrates the formal sign off of the principal players for each representative of the Steering Committee."[33]

The FEC's final report, marked "sensitive," concluded that as the financial backbone of the Democratic Party, the AFL-CIO and NEA had "authority to approve or disapprove plans, projects and needs of the DNC and its state parties with respect to the coordinated campaign."[34] Even as informed a source as Lawrence Noble, the FEC's chief lawyer, admitted that he was "surprised by the degree of control unions held over Democratic decisions."[35]

But that is what happens when a political party is so beholden to one group's financial contributions and active electoral support. In a sense, the arrangement with Big Labor was merely the fulfillment of a promise that Bill Clinton made back in December 1991, when he was struggling to get his campaign for the Democratic nomination off the ground. Candidate Clinton told an NEA panel, "If I become president, you'll be my partners."[36]

We just didn't realize he meant it literally.

The unions got the Clinton-Gore ticket over the top in 1992; the NEA alone paid 20 percent of its national headquarters staff to work directly for the Clinton campaign.[37] So in 1996 the unions were rewarded—though their rewards were linked directly to how much they had contributed to the reelection effort. In the 1996 elections, the direct contributions that the unions gave—$60.6 million[38]—were just a small part of Big Labor's financial support for Democrats. For example, the AFL-CIO alone spent $35 million on a major advertising campaign to help Democrats win, and that money came from its general treasury, which is funded by the member dues union workers are forced to pay.[39] Labor economist Leo Troy has testified before a House committee that unions spent $315–525 million on the 1996 election.[40]

The 1996 election was in fact a landmark election in that it was the first in the modern era of Big Labor political activism, for it was the first election in which John Sweeney was leading the American labor movement. True enough, the labor unions had been moving ever farther into the political arena before Sweeney took over the AFL-CIO, but Sweeney brought his radical sensibilities and an unwavering commitment to being a political force. Under Sweeney, a dramatic shift was completed: Big Labor became a political movement that concerned itself only incidentally with matters of the workplace. And the 1996 elections provided the first clear evidence that politics had become the true focus of the American labor movement.

Sweeney was still in his first year as president of the AFL-CIO in 1996, but he did not hesitate to signal his commitment to politics or to political spending. In his years heading the Service Employees International Union (SEIU), he had seen the value of using union dues for extensive political action in order to advance his agenda, for he had made that organization one of the most politically powerful government-employee unions in the country. Sweeney's AFL-CIO therefore launched a major political program called "Labor '96—Building to Win, Building to Last." While spending millions on direct contributions to candidates, this program relied far more on paid television ads, direct mail, sending paid political organizers into "battleground" districts, and organizing activists to proselytize union members at work (presumably on the employer's time). For example, the AFL-CIO began training more than three thousand union employees as political activists and organizers stationed throughout the country.[41]

The AFL-CIO first showed how active it could be when, in January 1996, it rallied its forces to elect a Democrat in Oregon's special election to replace embattled senator Bob Packwood, the liberal Republican who had resigned after allegations of sexual harassment. Big Labor openly spent $183,000 on this election, but hidden soft money multiplied this many times over. AFL-CIO documents reveal more than twenty-five union operatives (twelve of them from the AFL-CIO itself) working full-time to elect the Democratic candidate. Steve Rosenthal, the former Clinton administration Labor Department official who became the AFL-CIO's political director under Sweeney, bragged, "We're mailing endorsement pieces to 75,000 union members and persuasion pieces to an estimated 40,000." The AFL-CIO set up phone banks and produced hundreds of thousands of political flyers.[42] Other unions sent out at least 350,000 pieces of blistering attack mail and made 230,000 phone calls to swing voters.[43] All the effort worked: Democrat Ron Wyden became the next senator from Oregon.

Big Labor used these same tactics on the national-campaign level as well, though the efforts were multiplied by a considerable factor. Steve Rosenthal has admitted that the AFL-CIO sent at least 135 union staff members and activists into 120 targeted congressional districts for the sole purpose of "educating" voters—that is, to shill for the Democrats.[44] For instance, in Washington State the AFL-CIO "educated" members at 220 work sites, passing out 75,000 political flyers in the process. Union activists also canvassed neighborhoods, going door-to-door to influence Democratic voters to go to the polls.[45]

Union head Dennis Rivera describes the Labor '96 campaign as an "aggressive program of political action whose twin objectives were to recapture Democratic control of the House of Representatives in the 1996 elections and to conduct a massive member and public issues oriented education program."[46] For politically motivated union heads like Rivera, this campaign was a revelation and a major attraction. Indeed, Rivera had chosen to bring his union, the National Health and Human Services Employees Union, under the AFL-CIO umbrella specifically because he was impressed with John Sweeney's commitment to politics. "The AFL-CIO has placed the rejuvenation of the political role of labor at the center of its activity," Rivera remarked approvingly.[47]

AFL-CIO member unions took up the call for political electioneering, as well. Although Sweeney had moved on from the SEIU, that powerful union remained committed to the Democratic Party. Indeed, reflecting Big Labor's far-left politics, SEIU officials depicted the 1996 elections as a battle of Good (Democrats) versus Evil (Republicans), writing, "We should . . . focus our energy on defeating the evil entirely."[48] The SEIU's Committee on the Future provided the union's mantras: "Member education about the importance of political action needs to be part of all union activities," and "All leadership training needs to have a focus on political action."[49] At the SEIU convention in April 1996, the newly elected successor to Sweeney, Andy Stern, put forth a new goal: He asked "every leader at every level of this union—from the international president to the rank-and-file member—to devote five working days this year to political action."[50] SEIU bosses also declared their goal of putting ten thousand union political organizers in the field, with a minimum of thirty-five activists in each of three hundred targeted congressional districts[51]— and that was for just one union.

Although Big Labor did not succeed in reclaiming Democratic control of the House of Representatives, its Labor '96 program scored big dividends for Democrats across the country. Operating under the radar of most Americans, Labor '96 defeated eighteen Republicans in the House, slashing the GOP majority won in the 1994 campaign. The AFL-CIO's program produced a huge turnout of union voters: In 1992, 19 percent of voters were from union households, but just four years later, 23 percent of voters came from union homes.[52] Had the Labor '96 program turned out just a few more Democratic voters, in fact, it could have swung the House to the Democrats, as House Republican leader Dick Armey acknowledged after the election. "The best-kept secret of the 1996 elections," according to Armey, was that "if just 8,759 voters had switched their votes in ten districts where Republicans won razor-thin margins, Bill Clinton would have a Democratic majority in the House today. That's too close for comfort."[53]

The unions' get-out-the-vote efforts also proved critical to Bill Clinton's electoral fortunes. Just two years earlier, it must be remembered, Clinton had suffered a humiliating defeat as the head of the Democratic Party when Republicans took control of the House of Representatives for the first time in forty years. His reelection was by no means a foregone conclusion heading into 1996, and it would not have been possible without the overwhelming union support he received. According to former AFL-CIO political director Steve

Rosenthal, Bill Clinton and Bob Dole split the nonunion vote evenly, but union voters pulled the lever for Clinton by a staggering 64–28 margin.[54]

To answer why the Democratic Party would hand the keys over to a special-interest group like Big Labor, one need look no further than these statistics: The unions, which take in some $17 billion every year, and own property in the District of Columbia alone valued at more than $300 million[55]—all of it tax-exempt—have a massive war chest that the Democrats need to keep dipping into in order to remain in power. Desperate to keep the union contributions coming, the Democrats apparently are willing to grant Big Labor virtually all of its demands—even formal control over party policy and strategy.

What is perhaps most remarkable about the FEC's 2001 report on the arrangement between the Democrats and the unions is how tame it actually is. According to the Associated Press, Lawrence Noble of the FEC "initially concluded the two sides had illegally coordinated."[56] But the FEC abandoned that finding when, in an unrelated case, a federal judge ruled that such coordinated campaigning was protected under the First Amendment. Noble argued that the FEC should have appealed the ruling and punished the Democrats and Big Labor for illegal coordination, but to no avail. The FEC stopped short of charging the unions and the Democratic Party with illegal actions, though it did document the sordid quid pro quo arrangement.

Noble was right to try to push the case further. The judge who ruled on supposed First Amendment rights didn't address the fact that unions were using compulsory dues money to buy their control of the party, sometimes in shocking ways. The $35 million the AFL-CIO took from the general treasury and spent on behalf of the Democrats was the most visible example of how member dues went to politics, but it was merely one of many examples. For instance, the FEC reported that the AFL-CIO, its affiliated unions, and the NEA were major contributors to the $2.7 million " '96 Project," the stated goal of which was to "hold individual members of Congress accountable" for supporting the Republicans' 1994 Contract with America.[57] According to the FEC, one SEIU local actually took $250,000 from its strike defense fund and put it toward the '96 Project.[58] This sort of sub-rosa raid on a union treasury does nothing but abuse the trust and interests of union members, who are forced to pay tribute to a union in order to keep their job.

THE SHELL GAME

The FEC did a service in revealing how the unions have Democrats in their pockets, but its report was just a small part of a much larger story. The 1996 election might have marked the first major election in which Big Labor gave itself over completely to political activities, but it also marked a point of no return. In every subsequent election, the unions, under the guiding hand of proud socialist John Sweeney, have fully committed themselves to pushing their radical political agenda and to being the Democrats' power broker, whether or not that serves the interests of the working people they represent.

The unions' political efforts in 1996 reveal why it is so misleading to talk about the labor movement's PAC contributions alone. While their direct campaign contributions are considerable, unions hide much of their spending in the sorts of initiatives they employed in the Labor '96 program. Union official Tony Mazzocchi admits, "Every election year, organized labor shells out millions of dollars in direct and indirect contributions to help elect Democrats. We knock on doors, we staff the phone banks, we sponsor get-out-the-vote drives."[59] Another union tactic is to pay "volunteers" to work full-time in political campaigns.

While serving as the AFL-CIO's political director, Steve Rosenthal openly acknowledged that "the [political] parties have become shells to move money."[60] Most union bosses try to conceal this fact in public, but at least internally they sometimes speak openly about using treasury dues money for politics. Years ago, the official publication of the Steelworkers union, *Steelabor,* gave this instructive hint about how to further Big Labor political interests:

> Use local treasury money. It can't go for direct political contributions, but it can do a lot. Mailings supporting or opposing candidates, phone banks, precinct visits, voter registration and

get-out-the-vote drives. Contributions to national, state or local COPEs [Committees on Political Education]. And it can be used to raise voluntary funds for the Steelworkers PAC.[61]

The unions' indirect contributions to Democrats often involve major expenditures. Direct-mail campaigns, phone banks, get-out-the-vote efforts—all these efforts cost money. Paying "volunteers" to work full-time on a campaign represents a staggering political expenditure. In late 2003, the SEIU's New York City local convened a special meeting to plan the union's effort to defeat George W. Bush in the 2004 election. The plan: to give a thousand "volunteers" a one-year leave of absence from their regular jobs so they could campaign for Democrats in battleground states all over the country—with the union paying their regular salaries *and* their travel expenses. The cost: between $35 million and $40 million, according to union sources.[62] In other words, one *local* union planned to spend more than the entire AFL-CIO spent on its vaunted $35 million "air war" media campaign in 1996.

The SEIU local's effort was unusual in that at least a rough estimate of the costs was made public. Most of the time, it is impossible to learn how the unions are spending their money, because they do everything they can to keep their finances hidden from public view. It is clear, though, that unions are spending very little on actual collective bargaining. Remember, in the 1988 Supreme Court case of *Communications Workers of America v. Beck*, the courts discovered that 79 percent of the union's funds were spent on politics and other expenses unrelated to the union's supposed core purpose.[63]

So just how much do the unions spend on politics? To answer that question, one must recognize that the unions' indirect political spending—also known as in-kind contributions—dwarfs their direct funding. In testimony before Congress in 1996, Rutgers economist Leo Troy, who has spent four decades studying organized labor, estimated that the unions' in-kind expenditures "could reasonably be a multiple of 3 to 5 times" the amount they spend through their PACs.[64] Thus, according to Troy's scholarly estimate, Big Labor's political expenses in 1996 alone would be between $315 and $525 million—and this is *in addition to* the $105 million he estimates their PACs spent in direct contributions and other disbursements.

Troy's estimate may even be low—really low. For instance, the Teamsters' PAC reported $2.4 million in direct contributions in the 1992 Democratic campaign. But Gene Giacumbo, a Teamsters International vice president, revealed that Teamsters president Ron Carey "bragged to me that the union gave $56 million" to Bill Clinton that year.[65] That would mean that on just one presidential candidate the Teamsters Union spent *twenty-three times* what it reported in PAC spending for all candidates combined.

Giacumbo revealed more than just how much money union bosses are willing to pour into Democratic coffers. He went on to say that Carey and the rest of the Teamsters leadership gave all that money to Bill Clinton even "after an independent, outside poll the union paid for showed the membership responses preferred [Ross] Perot, then [George H. W.] Bush, with Clinton in third place."[66]

This is no surprise. To labor bosses, the interests and wishes of union members are of no real concern.

"YOU DON'T HAVE A CHOICE"

Polls show that 40 percent of union members historically vote Republican, an even higher percentage in some elections.[67] In 1972, 54 percent of union households voted Republican, sinking George McGovern's presidential hopes in favor of a second term for Richard Nixon.[68] In 1980, union members made up a large portion of Reagan Democrats, with 43 percent of union member households voting for Reagan, and in 1984—even after President Reagan fired the striking air traffic controllers in 1981—union households voted for him in even higher numbers: 45 percent.

In the late 1990s, the AFL-CIO's Steve Rosenthal admitted that a minority of union members actually vote Democratic. Although the unions have poured millions of dollars into their get-out-the-vote efforts and have gotten a number of union voters out to the polls for the Democrats, a sizable percentage of union members still don't vote, according to Rosenthal. He reported that only 60 percent of AFL-CIO members are registered to vote, and of those who are registered, 40 percent don't vote. He also acknowledged that of those AFL-CIO members who do vote, a respectable 40 percent vote Republican.[69]

Moreover, despite the union leadership's far-left agenda, union members often disagree with union bosses on important issues. In 1996, for instance, a poll revealed that 78 percent of union members supported the Republicans' $500 family tax credit, 82 percent backed a balanced-budget amendment, and 87 percent favored the Republicans' welfare reform plan.[70]

So it can hardly be said that union members are dedicated to unswerving Democratic activism. Still, labor bosses aren't interested in what members want. Rosenthal has publicly stated that union members who voted Republican voted "wrong,"[71] which brings to mind Joseph Stalin's insistence that no citizen have political beliefs different from his own. Just prior to the 1996 election, the AFL-CIO commissioned a study by Peter D. Hart Research Associates that showed union members overwhelmingly reject partisanship. An AFL-CIO publication summarized the Hart polling data by stating, "Members want political action to be about them and their needs, not about candidates or political parties. . . . In election campaigns, unions should provide members with information, not voting instructions. . . . Members say they do not want to be told for whom to vote."[72] The AFL-CIO was nevertheless relentless in its support for the Democratic Party in that election.[73]

Even though their leftist agenda does not represent the political beliefs of a great mass of union voters, and labor bosses don't mind confiscating member dues and using them on politics, sometimes their assaults on workers' freedom can be even more grievous. For instance, evidence indicates that in 2001 an SEIU local in New York City actually forced members to work for Democratic mayoral candidate Mark Green during working hours, even if they personally supported another candidate. SEIU members also accused union bosses of requiring workers to use personal leave and vacation days to campaign for Green, and they presented documents to a grand jury to support that claim.[74] One memo copied to the local's vice president, Kevin Doyle, ordered that "all staff should have completed a personal day off or vacation request form" for October 11, 2001, the day Green faced fellow Democrat Fernando Ferrer in a party runoff. And apparently the union was contributing more than manpower: Documents showed that the SEIU local spent more than $731,000 in the 2001 elections. One union reformist, assistant secretary Dominick Bentivegna, told the *Daily News* in 2003, "I believe in a political program, but not one that is going to drain our treasury, and it should be voluntary."[75]

No charges were filed against the union, however. As the *New York Times* reported in July 2003, "Last month, after an 18-month investigation by [New York District Attorney] Mr. Morgenthau, Local 32 BJ agreed to hire a new law firm that would oversee its political campaign activites to help ensure that there were no future violations of election laws. Mr. Morganthau did not bring any charges."[76]

Ordinarily union bosses can do as they please when it comes to politics, because dissenters have no real recourse. As Baltimore steelworker Dave Baker said about the shameful use of his dues, "I'm not happy about it, but I know I can't change it. I don't understand it. You pay your dues because you don't have a choice."[77]

Baker articulated the two great problems with union financing. First, because so many states have forced-unionism laws, many workers have no choice in whether they belong to a union, and they are forced to pay dues to the union as a condition of their employment. Second, union members have no control over how their dues money is spent once it goes into the treasury. If they had a choice, most workers would not want their dues money going to support the unions' political program.

For example, a 1996 poll showed that union members overwhelmingly opposed the AFL-CIO's scheme to spend $35 million in dues on its ads for Democrats. Overall, 62 percent of union members opposed the plan, while just 31 percent supported it. Among newer members, the opposition was even stronger: 77 percent disapproved of the plan and only 19 percent supported it.[78]

The Supreme Court case of *Communications Workers of America v. Beck* arose precisely because union member Harry Beck protested his union's political spending. Beck resigned his membership, so the union then charged him "agency fees"—which were equal to the full dues he had already been paying, even though supposedly he was no longer responsible for subsidizing the union's political spending. By law, the union could charge these agency fees to any nonmember covered by a union contract. When the Supreme Court ruled it illegal for unions to use compulsory member dues for political purposes unrelated to their core functions of collective bargaining, contract administration, and grievance adjustment, the decision in theory prohibited unions from using compulsory dues on politics without the members' consent. The trouble is, this court decision has been notoriously difficult to enforce, at least in part because unions do such a good job of hiding their political spending.

The simple truth is that most union members don't want the unions to take their money and use it to fund political activity. Certainly some members oppose the unions' political program on ideological grounds, but even many staunch Democrats in the unions are against having money taken out of their paychecks and spent on politics. A union charges its members significant fees—hundreds of dollars every year—and if much of this money is being spent on activities unrelated to the union's core functions, union workers quite reasonably would like to see the money in their own pockets instead of in the union's treasure chest.

Because the *Beck* decision has done little to stifle the unions' political activities, other measures have been necessary to protect union members' money. One means of checking union political spending is a paycheck-protection law, which requires unions to secure members' approval before using compulsory dues on political activities. Where such initiatives have been put in place, the vast majority of union members have declined to have their dues spent on politics. For example, after voters in Washington State passed a paycheck-protection initiative in 1992, 85 percent of the state's teachers took advantage of their new freedom and refused to have their dues go toward politics.[79] Needless to say, the union leadership opposes paycheck-protection initiatives and has fought a national paycheck-protection act, because giving workers across the country the same freedom would cripple Big Labor's political program. If even two-thirds of union members declined to support the program (almost 20 percent less than in Washington State), John Sweeney would have trouble getting his calls returned inside the Washington, D.C., Beltway. Unions would have to either scale their political activity way down or take positions closer to the mainstream.

THE RISE OF THE RADICALS

As it is, though, John Sweeney and other labor bosses are major power brokers in Washington. With the massive resources of the American labor movement at their disposal, they have forced their radical political agenda from the fringes of American politics to the highest levels of the U.S. government.

John Sweeney's election as president of the AFL-CIO in 1995 marked a major turning point for the labor movement both because Sweeney immediately moved to make Big Labor a political force unrivaled in this country and because he has unabashedly pushed his leftist, even socialist, agenda. While many have credited Bill Clinton's political success to his centrism, the fact is that the Democratic Party under Clinton gave unions unprecedented power just as Sweeney and his associates were moving the labor movement to the far left.

There can be no mistaking Sweeney's politics. On economics, he spouts Marxist doctrine, proclaiming that the "wildly uneven accumulation of wealth is making the United States the most unequal country in the entire industrialized world" and that the only solution is the redistribution of wealth through more taxes and more government.[80] He regularly condemns corporate America for supposed evils. For example, at the AFL-CIO summit held in January 2003 he declared, dramatically, "What we face . . . is the most central moral challenge of our time: the challenge of helping working men and women come together to improve their lives," and then he identified the source of the problem: "corporate forces that have seized control of our workplaces, our capital markets and our government."[81] Sweeney is also a staunch protectionist who opposes free-trade treaties like the North American Free Trade Agreement (NAFTA) and demands tariffs on goods from a host of nations. He claims, "We have met the enemies, and they are American-based multinational companies."[82] Moreover, he regularly demonizes Republicans, proclaiming, for example, that "there is a conservative conspiracy going on in the Congress, especially the House of Representatives," and that "the sleaziness of the Republicans in the House is the shame of the nation."[83]

It was not as if Sweeney cloaked his leftism as he worked his way up the Big Labor hierarchy. During the 1980s, at the height of Cold War struggles in Central America, he joined a far-left committee of union presidents known as the National Labor Committee in Support of Democracy and Human Rights in El Salvador. In joining this committee, Sweeney, then head of SEIU, came out against anticommunist policies—not of a Republican administration but of the AFL-CIO itself.[84] The labor federation had been firmly anticommunist since the late 1940s, when the AFL purged communists from its ranks. In 1972, for example, AFL-CIO president George Meany refused to back George McGovern because the Democratic nominee pledged to "go to Hanoi" to capitulate to the Communist Vietnamese.[85] At global conventions, the AFL-CIO required its representatives to leave the room when members of procommunist unions entered.[86]

Sweeney, then, was far to the left not only of most Americans but also of the leadership of the labor movement. And as soon as he became president of the AFL-CIO, he set out to rid the labor movement of whatever moderate or conservative policies it had. Almost right away he signaled that he was changing labor's traditionally conservative foreign policy by bringing in Barbara Shailor from the International Association of Machinists to run the AFL-CIO's International Affairs Division. According to labor lawyer Jerome Levinson, Shailor "has gradually weeded out those people who were associated with the old crowd and their Cold War line. They have changed the face of the AFL-CIO."[87]

Sweeney also broke from the labor movement's traditional policies when he pushed the AFL-CIO to support his protectionist tariffs. For decades before Sweeney took over, the AFL-CIO had strongly supported free trade, at least in part because of its anticommunism. AFL-CIO leaders reasoned that as other countries and peoples prospered from international trade, communism would have a more difficult time gaining a foothold. For instance, an AFL-CIO publication from the 1960s declared, "We must also assist the newly developing countries, to whom we are giving economic and technical assistance, to obtain markets for the products of their new industries. . . . Exports can actually mean as much or more to the less developed countries than all the foreign aid they receive."[88] The same thinking held for developed nations: Strong democratic governments would serve as examples to nations under the yoke of Communism. In 1962 the AFL-CIO said, "Japan is a bastion of strength to the free world in the Far East. For both political and economic reasons, therefore, it is important that we keep open our trade lines with Japan."[89] Today, Japan is one of the many nations against which Sweeney's AFL-CIO demands trade tariffs.

But nothing reflects John Sweeney's leftism better than the socialist economic policies he advocates, which also fly in the face of positions that his predecessors took. Where Sweeney calls for taxes to eliminate economic disparities and for state control of the economy, George Meany firmly rejected John Kenneth Galbraith's paean to the redistribution of wealth, *The Affluent Society*, and accepted President Kennedy's assertion that "a rising tide lifts all boats."[90] Sweeney and the AFL-CIO advocate nothing less than European-style democratic socialism, even as many European nations are struggling to reform their systems to avoid national insolvency, stagnant economies, and perpetual double-digit unemployment. Decades of Europe's "pro-worker" policies have wiped out what workers need most: jobs.

Sweeney boldly aligns himself with these policies by being a proud member of the Democratic Socialists of America (DSA), which is dedicated to expanding socialism and socialist government in America. The DSA advances its socialist agenda by working through a coalition of prominent left-wing Democrats in the House of Representatives known as the Progressive Caucus.[91] These Democrats probably employ the euphemism "progressive" to preserve their political viability, and the strategy has worked: The caucus has more than fifty members and includes the highest-ranking Democrat in the House, Minority Leader Nancy Pelosi. Other leading Democrats in the DSA-sponsored Progressive Caucus include John Conyers, Barney Frank, Jesse Jackson, Jr., Sheila Jackson Lee, Dennis Kucinich, Jerry Nadler, Maxine Waters, Henry Waxman, and a host of other representatives whose views are hardly mainstream. Bernie Sanders of Vermont, a founder of the Progressive Caucus, is not even a Democrat; the "Independent" congressman is a proud socialist.[92]

How could Sweeney espouse such radical political views and still ascend to the top of Big Labor's power structure? Perhaps more important, how could he become head of the AFL-CIO—an organization that had only two presidents in forty years—even after openly challenging the leadership's policies? Because as head of the SEIU he had shown himself to be a master political organizer, and by the mid-1990s the labor movement, which was losing more and more members, needed to become more powerful politically in order to protect its tenuous position in American society.

To be sure, Big Labor was active in politics, and specifically Democratic politics, long before John Sweeney took over the AFL-CIO. In fact, George Meany bragged that "we've got the finest political organization in the nation."[93] Originally Meany had agreed with AFL founder Samuel Gompers, who, as Meany said, "took a very practical view that he did not want to run the country" and who thought "our job was to be nonpartisan."[94] But Meany began supporting Democratic candidates in the 1950s, even though he was not a chapter-and-verse leftist. He claimed that Congress had "forced" the unions into the political realm in 1947 by passing the Taft-Hartley Act, which rolled back some of the excessive powers Congress had granted unions during the Great Depression.[95] The Wagner Act of 1935 had given unions the power to force membership as a condition of employment; Taft-Hartley provided that a state could adopt "right-to-work" laws, which would free most workers in that state from having to pay union dues as a condition of employment, although they could still be forced into union-bargained employment contracts.[96]

In other words, Big Labor abandoned nonpartisanship as soon as its own position was threatened. The labor movement's most important ally became the Democratic Party, which could protect Big Labor from further encroachments on its power. (And the Democrats have protected Big Labor: Taft-Hartley, passed nearly six decades ago, represents Congress's last attempt to reform the system of forced unionism it forged in the Depression.) Moreover, as we will see in more detail in Chapter 4, the labor movement shifted its attention to government unions as it began losing private-sector union members, so Big Labor and the Democrats shared another interest: Big Government.

Meany's handpicked successor, Lane Kirkland, who became AFL-CIO president in 1979, moved the labor federation even further into the political arena. He would pay for that decision, however. Having made political results the measure of his own effectiveness, Kirkland was suddenly vulnerable in 1994 when the Republicans, brandishing their Contract with America, seized control of the House of Representatives for the first time in four decades. As the journal *Labor History* reported, "In politics, the critics argued, Kirkland had failed to capitalize on the first period of joint Democratic control of the legislative and executive branches since 1980. The AFL-CIO failed to stop the North American Free Trade Agreement, failed to achieve health care reform, failed to pass legislation banning the permanent replacement of strikers and, ultimately, failed to shift public discourse in a more liberal, pro-union direction."[97] Without the Democrats in control of Congress, Big Labor was in jeopardy of losing its most potent political weapon: the ability to push through its social agenda and maintain its privileged status, exempt from the rules that apply to other organizations.

And therein lay John Sweeney's opportunity. AFSCME president Gerald McEntee, a key Sweeney ally, later summed up the dissatisfaction with Lane Kirkland: "We didn't have a federation that was on the go. It had, institutionally, stood still for any number of years. We had a dwindling of membership without any offsetting activity. We saw our political influence and strength on the wane. We weren't risktakers."[98] Sweeney was, if nothing else, someone who had shown he could wield tremendous political influence, having transformed the SEIU into one of the nation's most politically powerful unions. First Sweeney helped push Kirkland into retirement, and then in 1995, in the first closely fought presidential election in the AFL-CIO's history, he defeated Kirkland's own choice for his successor, secretary-treasurer Thomas Donahue.

John Sweeney, far-left radical, thus became the most powerful labor leader in America, and he swung the labor movement sharply to the left. Other union leaders have joined him on the left fringes. For example, the SEIU's international executive vice president, Eliseo Medina, gave the keynote address at the DSA's 2001 convention.[99] After the September 11 terrorist attacks, Ron Richardson, executive vice president of the Hotel Employees and Restaurant Employees International Union, said a picture should be painted "of a couple of these Republican leaders sitting on the knees of Santa Claus saying 'Thank you for giving us everything we always wanted,' and Santa Claus' face would be that of [Osama] bin Laden."[100]

One of the most vocal supporters of Sweeney's radical agenda is Dennis Rivera, the labor leader who chose to bring his organization into the AFL-CIO because he was so impressed with how Sweeney had "placed the rejuvenation of the political role of labor at the center" of the federation's activity. Rivera is firmly committed to a socialist agenda for the United States—and to using his members' hard-earned dues money to pay for that agenda. He spouts the Marxist creed, stating, "Our goal is to build class consciousness,"[101] and proclaims that the source of all problems in America is "corporate power and the greed that can be personalized in the form of the new high-tech/high-finance robber barons."[102] Rejecting capitalism, he says that "the AFL-CIO needs to put together a comprehensive alternative economic agenda" and that the goals of the labor movement must include "electoral power" and "social upheaval."[103] As to how to accomplish social upheaval, he says, "This means spending a larger percentage of our dues on the political education of our members."[104] Very early in the 2004 campaign, Rivera showed just how willing he is to spend his members' money on his far-left agenda: The union of which he is now president, the SEIU's New York City local, is the union that set aside at least $35 million for its efforts to defeat George W. Bush.

ALL POLITICS, ALL THE TIME

The radical politics of labor leaders like John Sweeney and Dennis Rivera would not be a big problem if Big Labor didn't have such extraordinary political power. Immediately upon his election as president of the AFL-CIO in 1995, Sweeney ramped up the federation's political operation and turned the labor movement into a full-scale political machine. According to Sweeney, his goal was to put together "a seamless garment of activism" and "change the nature of politics itself."[105]

He has been remarkably successful. Under Sweeney, the labor movement has become the single largest political force in America. Big Labor now spends more than both major political parties combined. Remember, in the 2000 election cycle alone, labor PACs spent $128.7 million,[106] including almost $85 million in direct contributions to Democrats[107]—and those expenditures were just a small fraction of what Big Labor gave the Democrats in that election. The unparalleled political influence that the Democrats lent the unions in 1996—veto power over the Democratic Party's policy and campaign decisions—was no coincidence. For the staggering amounts of money that union bosses throw at the Democrats, they have become kingmakers.

As we have seen, in the 1996 campaign Sweeney committed the AFL-CIO to Democratic activism through its significant financial contributions and its electioneering programs, and he rallied other unions to the cause as well. But his commitment to politics was not limited to electoral engineering. One of his first actions as president was to create the AFL-CIO Public Policy Department, which is dedicated to pushing a left-wing policy agenda, and as noted, he also revamped the International Affairs Division. Out were the AFL-CIO's traditional anticommunism and free-trade stances, and in were the radical policy positions of the Democratic Socialists. Within months of winning the presidency, Sweeney began the America Needs a Raise campaign to take down what union leaders called the "unequal distribution of wealth" and to push for far-left policies: a nationalized economy, redistribution of wealth through higher taxes, protectionist tariffs, socialized medicine, and so on.[108]

The political lobbying programs of AFL-CIO member unions exploded under Sweeney, as well. The Steelworkers International Union, for example, put together a Rapid Response Team to pressure Congress to pass the union's pet legislative projects. Under this program, the Steelworkers' headquarters would fax important information on legislative issues to the local unions. (Headquarters provided the locals with their fax machines.) The locals would resend these faxes directly into workplaces—which, incidentally, forced employers to bear some of the cost of the union's lobbying program. The designated Rapid Response Team member in each workplace would then walk out to the shop floor to talk to workers—on company time—and would often carry a cell phone so workers could call their congressman right then, under the watchful eye of the union leader.[109]

Writing in 1996, historian Ronald Radosh observed, "More and more, the one constituency group with money for Democrats is the one they have been counting on since the FDR era: the AFL-CIO." Radosh predicted that in elections to come, "public employee unions and the Hollywood liberal elite will likely be the main backers of the Democratic party—and it will be to these elements that any would-be candidates will have to turn for support."[110]

Radosh was right. The 1996 elections were only the beginning of Big Labor's assault on the electoral process. John Sweeney has become such an important power broker that by the year 2000, *Washington Post* reporter Peter Baker would call Sweeney "perhaps the single most dominant force within the Democratic Party even after decades of [union] decline."[111] Sweeney and the rest of the radical union bosses have taken control of the Democratic Party.

1998: ENDING THE REPUBLICAN REVOLUTION— AND SAVING A DEMOCRATIC PRESIDENT

The labor movement put forth an extraordinary effort on behalf of Bill Clinton and the rest of the Democrats in 1996, and the unions would not stop there. After all, despite having secured Clinton's reelection, Sweeney's AFL-CIO had fallen short of his stated goal of winning back the House of Representatives for Democrats. Looking forward to 1998, Sweeney vowed, "We're going to redouble our efforts."[112]

He did, although the AFL-CIO's approach in 1998 was in some respects different from what it had been in 1996. Whereas 1996 had been marked by the expensive "air war" of paid advertising and large direct contributions, in 1998 the AFL-CIO mainly employed a "ground war." The labor federation still paid a nominal amount for advertising, but it relied more on hidden expenditures. It was a strategic campaign of one-on-one recruitment, phone banks, individual arm-twisting, political endorsements mailed as "member communications," and paid "volunteers" for political campaigns. The plan for the

1998 elections was to come in "under the radar screen," as one Democratic consultant admitted[113]—that is, to spend hundreds of millions on political activity that didn't need to be reported publicly and could be disguised as "legitimate" union expenses such as "member communication," "organizing," and "outreach."

Big Labor's tactic of paying "volunteer" political activists to work for Democratic campaigns was critical in the 1998 elections. According to President Clinton's former secretary of labor, Robert Reich, the AFL-CIO had "about 72,000 [paid] organizers out in the streets" for the last two weeks of the campaign.[114] In other words, the AFL-CIO had a bigger political staff than did the Republican and Democratic National Committees combined.

The unions didn't stint on spending, either. According to the Center for Responsive Politics, unions donated almost $56 million to Democrats during the 1998 election cycle—the most ever spent in a nonpresidential election year up to that point.[115] But that sum includes only actual PAC and soft-money donations and those from individuals who list a union as their employer. It doesn't include the money that unions spent to staff and administer their operations, some $98.2 million in the 1998 election cycle.

These efforts paid off for the unions. The AFL-CIO reported that 76 percent of union members who received union political material voted for Democrats, compared with only 58 percent of members who voted for Democrats if they had not seen the union endorsements.[116] The results were impressive: Democrats actually gained five seats in the House of Representatives, and in the Senate, though they did not pick up any seats, they won major races in two states that would be key to the 2000 presidential election, New York and California. This was a remarkable achievement, considering that the 1998 elections came less than a month after the House had authorized an inquiry into whether President Bill Clinton should be impeached. To many political observers, it had seemed the Democrats would do well if they could simply prevent the Republicans from expanding their majority in Congress.

Perhaps just as important to Big Labor, Speaker of the House Newt Gingrich suddenly resigned. In the previous election, the unions had invested heavily in the '96 Project as revenge against the Republicans' 1994 Contract with America, and now, two years later, the most visible symbol of the Contract and the Republicans' rise to power was gone from office. Big Labor had outlasted the so-called Republican Revolution.

Unions also dedicated major resources to protect their unique power to tax, which gave them so much political clout. Voters in California were presented with a paycheck-protection initiative, which would require unions to get permission from members before spending their dues money on politics. Americans overwhelmingly favored the principle behind this initiative. An October 1997 ABC News/*Washington Post* poll revealed that 82 percent of American workers believed that it was unfair for unions to force workers to pay for political activity with their dues.[117] Another poll found that 80 percent of *union members* opposed the use of their dues for politics without their permission.[118] Nevertheless, union bosses forced 100 percent of members to lobby for the defeat of initiatives that the vast majority of union members supported. Why? Because they were desperate to safeguard their future stream of political money. As National Labor Relations Board chairman William Gould said, California's Proposition 226 would "cripple a major source of funding for the Democratic Party."[119] Big Labor and the Democrats had to preserve that funding at any cost. In California, unions contributed more than $20 million to defeat Proposition 226, with the California Teachers Association alone kicking in at least $3 million. The AFL-CIO set up phone banks to defeat the proposition, and calls were made from as far away as West Virginia, Oklahoma, Florida, Washington, and Nebraska.[120] All this (expensive) political activity worked, as the voters of California rejected Proposition 226.

John Sweeney and the American labor movement achieved another political goal in 1998: They kept President Clinton in office, even in the face of impeachment. Sweeney, in fact, may have been single-handedly responsible for saving the Clinton presidency from ending in a humiliating resignation. In his book on the Clinton impeachment, *Washington Post* reporter Peter Baker recounts that in 1998 Harold Ickes, Clinton's former deputy chief of staff, was meeting with Democratic leaders to develop a delegation to persuade Clinton to resign. According to Baker, Ickes "told people that the only possible way to convince his ex-boss to give up power would be to put together a coalition of interest groups and key senior members from

Congress to go to him as a delegation and tell him there was no way to hold the White House in 2000 unless he resigned."[121] Yet the plan apparently came to an abrupt halt when Ickes presented the idea to Sweeney. Sweeney responded, "Let's wait and see, Harold," and the campaign to engineer a resignation ended then and there, writes Baker.[122]

2000: THE UNIONS TRY TO PUT THEIR MAN IN THE WHITE HOUSE

John Sweeney carried on his congenial relationship with the Clinton administration by deciding early to back Vice President Al Gore for the 2000 Democratic nomination. Gore's only serious Democratic challenger was former New Jersey senator Bill Bradley. Still, the vice president faced a tough fight, because Bradley had locked up some of the more liberal element of the Democratic Party, garnering endorsements from former labor secretary Robert Reich and arch-liberal senator Paul Wellstone of Minnesota.

Gore, meanwhile, had not been able to gain the support of a united labor movement. He had secured the support of some of the more politically active unions, notably AFSCME and the Communications Workers of America, but the Clinton-Gore administration's championing of NAFTA and other free-trade policies made Gore suspect in the eyes of many protectionist unions. Because the unions were divided, the AFL-CIO normally would be expected to stay out of the primary fight and let member unions support whichever candidate they chose. But apparently Sweeney didn't want simply to influence the outcome of the November election; it seems he wanted to play a major role in picking the Democratic Party's standard bearer.

By the time of the AFL-CIO's convention in Los Angeles in October 1999, Gore's campaign was faltering. Though he was Bill Clinton's handpicked successor, Gore was trying to counter public perceptions that he was a weak candidate, and a failure to earn an endorsement from the most crucial element of the Democratic Party could only have hurt him.

Sweeney went to work at the convention, putting unrelenting

pressure on AFL-CIO officials to back Gore. Sweeney's efforts caused some rumbling among his constituents. Teamster president James P. Hoffa opposed the endorsement as a "top-down" dictum to rank-and-file union members. "We disagree not necessarily with [Gore], but with the process," Hoffa complained.[123] Still, Sweeney's backroom dealings paid off: On October 12, 1999, the AFL-CIO endorsed Gore with almost no open discussion. With that endorsement, Gore could suddenly show that he was strong with the Democratic Party's core constituency. (Unions that didn't back Gore—notably the United Auto Workers, the Teamsters, the Steelworkers, and the Mineworkers—stayed neutral rather than backing Bradley.) Sweeney gave Gore momentum when he needed it most. Gore knew how to repay Sweeney. In his speech to the AFL-CIO accepting the endorsement, Gore promised to push Big Labor's complete agenda if elected. He further swore to secure the industrial unions' number-one wish: a ban on replacement workers for strikers. He assuaged the teachers' unions with a vow to adamantly oppose school vouchers. And he made a broad promise to veto all "anti-union" legislation, meaning, presumably, whatever bills Sweeney didn't like.[124]

Sweeney followed up the endorsement by mobilizing the Big Labor machine through the early caucuses and primaries. For the Iowa caucuses, which marked the first votes cast and were therefore crucial for building early momentum, Sweeney spared no expense. The AFL-CIO and AFSCME sent thirty-five paid political operatives to Iowa to oversee the Gore effort. The AFL-CIO sent out four direct-mail letters to potential supporters, including one with a five-minute videotape of Sweeney endorsing Gore. The unions also sent a huge tractor-trailer to Iowa City and parked it outside the Gore headquarters. The trailer served as Big Labor's campaign headquarters and came complete with a "war room," computer systems, and a telephone bank—all of which were critical to bringing out Gore supporters on a cold winter's night for the few hours necessary to vote. AFL-CIO political director Steve Rosenthal bragged that in the last two weeks of the campaign, union operatives made some thirty thousand phone calls on behalf of Gore from that trailer.[125]

The NEA state affiliate, the Iowa State Education Association, also campaigned vigorously to help Gore. The teachers' union sent several letters to member households around the state and regularly endorsed Gore in union publications. The union also ran radio ads urging listeners to "support the party and candidate who has always stood behind our educational agenda."[126]

Gore ended up beating Bradley handily in Iowa, 63 percent to 35 percent. Union voters made up fully one-third of voters.

Gore also benefited from Big Labor efforts in New Hampshire, which held the first Democratic primary. Rosenthal declined to say how many paid operatives the AFL-CIO sent to New Hampshire, but AFSCME admitted to dispatching eleven. Every union household in the state received an average of seven campaign contacts, through direct mail, telephone contact, or personal visit. The AFL-CIO sent another videotape to union households, again with Sweeney's endorsement and pro-union comments by Al Gore. Donny Fowler, the Gore campaign's national field director, even admitted that the AFL-CIO made its phone banks available directly to the Gore campaign; to Fowler, this was merely a sign that the labor federation was "very good partners with Al Gore."[127] In the New Hampshire primary, union households made up 24 percent of the electorate, even though such households represent only about 16 percent of voters in the state,[128] and cast their votes 62 to 37 percent in favor of Gore. Union voters were crucial to the Gore victory in New Hampshire, for his overall margin of victory was much smaller, 53 percent to 47 percent.

In the big prize state of California, the state AFL-CIO organization, the California Labor Federation, sent "Gore for President" videos containing Sweeney's endorsement and Gore's speech to union leaders across the state. In addition, the California federation mailed three separate letters to union households; these letters, designed by the national AFL-CIO, had information on local elections as well as the presidential primary. The California Labor Federation also trained one hundred operatives to conduct "worksite blitzes," where they would pressure workers to vote for Gore. In all, the state federation distributed more than 500,000 pro-Gore flyers.[129]

The AFL-CIO was active even in states not considered to be seriously in play. For example, in Missouri, the AFL-CIO sent at least two mailers to union households.[130] The unions helped Gore lock up the nomination. At the opulent Wilshire Grand Hotel on the night before the 2000 Democratic National Convention in Los Angeles, Al Gore recognized Sweeney's role in handing him the nomination, crowing, "A new chapter began on October 9: The [AFL-CIO] convention catapulted me to victory." He then turned to John Sweeney and gushed, "I love you, buddy."[131] Gore also pledged political payback for the massive resources that union bosses had already spent and had pledged to spend in the upcoming campaign. "I'm running for president to fight for you," he said. "In the Gore-Lieberman administration, we are going to be pro-union."[132]

For his part, Sweeney told his fellow union leaders of his political vision for 2000, saying, "First, we must dominate this convention, then we must dominate this election."[133] If Gore promised that as president he would be a staunch ally of the unions, Sweeney made clear that he expected payback. "We not only want to win," he said, "we want to win big so we can send a signal to every public official we've endorsed that we will hold them to the standards of working-family values that we've established."[134]

Sweeney's influence on the convention itself was almost proportionate to his influence in selecting the nominee. One-third of delegates to the 2000 Democratic convention were union representatives, who represented the largest single special-interest group.[135] The kingmaker himself, John Sweeney, was afforded the opportunity to address the delegates from the convention podium, as were two other union leaders, AFL-CIO secretary-treasurer Richard Trumka and AFSCME president Gerald McEntee. All of this was payback for Big Labor's support of Gore; it was also a radical change from previous years, in which union bosses operated largely behind the scenes.

In the general election, Big Labor was just as committed to Gore's election. Unions sent untold thousands of paid union staffers to work full-time on the Gore campaign. One SEIU local sent forty paid campaign operatives to Pennsylvania and Michigan—and this from a *New York City* local. But union president Dennis Rivera issued a typical rationale: "This resembles the Second World War, when the United States was sending arms to the British so they can fight the Germans."[136]

Direct contributions to political campaigns were only a small part of the resources Big Labor directed toward Gore's campaign, but even these were significant. The Center for Responsive Politics showed that unions gave nearly $85 million in PAC contributions and soft-money donations to Democrats in 2000.[137] Included in this was perhaps the largest check given in post-Watergate politics, a $1 million check from a single local to the Democratic Congressional Campaign Committee; the generous donor was, perhaps not surprisingly, the SEIU's powerful New York City local, run by Dennis Rivera.[138]

The AFL-CIO's battle plan called for a nationwide effort with special concentration in key states: Ohio, Pennsylvania, Michigan, Wisconsin, New Jersey, Missouri, and Florida.

In Pennsylvania, the unions divided the state into five geographic regions, and union operatives met with all the local presidents in the state in order to plug them into the Gore campaign.[139] The SEIU alone paid eighty operatives to work in the political campaign. SEIU president Andy Stern was open about his union's single-party work of SEIU, saying that the goal was to elect Gore as well as Democrats down the ticket. Pennsylvania also figured prominently in Big Labor's efforts to overcome the problems that resulted from his pro–gun control position. Many union members are hunters and gun owners, and Gore's calls for more stringent gun laws were not popular with them. In several key states where the gun issue threatened Gore's chances—Pennsylvania, Michigan, Minnesota, Ohio, Wisconsin, and West Virginia—the AFL-CIO distributed brochures defending the Democratic candidate on the firearm issue.[140] The brochure emphasized that a President Gore would not try to eliminate guns, saying, "Al Gore doesn't want to take away your gun, but George Bush does want to take away your union."

At least in part the AFL-CIO was trying to counter the National Rifle Association's campaign on behalf of George W. Bush, though it should be noted that the NRA funded its campaign with *voluntary* contributions, whereas the unions were using dues money that union workers were forced to pay. (In hindsight, the unions should have sent more of the brochures in West Virginia, a Democratic stronghold that went Republican for the first time in decades, largely because of the gun issue.)

In Florida, Big Labor went beyond union households to continue what has become a staple of Florida Democratic politics: lying to retired seniors about Republican plans for Social Security and Medicare. In this case, the unions mailed letters to retirees claiming that

George W. Bush's plan could wipe out their Social Security benefits but that Al Gore would lower their prescription drug costs.[141]

In Michigan, unions had a real leg up. The United Auto Workers had negotiated with the Big Four automakers for a paid holiday on Election Day, which made it easier for union voters to get to the polls and freed up more activists to work on the union's get-out-the-vote campaign. Michigan's governor, Republican John Engler, called the paid day off "the largest single corporate [political] contribution in American history," saying it "dwarfs the other money in politics."[142] It's easy to wonder if unions actually do any nonpolitical union work in election years, given how many union staffers become paid political "volunteers." The AFL-CIO's newsletter, *Work in Progress,* reported that its staff was leaving to "volunteer" for the campaign's final two weeks. "As a result," the union mouthpiece said, "the next two editions of *WiP* will be abbreviated (one-pagers) and will be available on the Web and via e-mail only. There will be no fax edition for those two weeks."[143]

Those final weeks were busy ones for union operatives. The AFL-CIO organized a "People Powered" bus tour, moving twenty union leaders through twenty-five cities in target states like Pennsylvania, Kentucky, Ohio, Michigan, Washington, West Virginia, and Oregon. The AFL-CIO reports that it sent 60,000 e-mail messages and distributed 3.5 million leaflets as part of its get-out-the-vote efforts. In Texas the labor federation organized a "Truth Squad" to attack George W. Bush's policies. The AFL-CIO's "Working Women Vote" program organized "Ironing Board Brigades" of women supporters for Gore and the Democrats.[144] In black and Latino neighborhoods, union sound trucks roved the streets, blaring out political propaganda.

Late in the campaign, Democratic consultant Tom O'Donnell admitted how important Big Labor's efforts were to his party, saying, "We'd be lost without them." O'Donnell also acknowledged just how much the unions had ramped up their political operation under John Sweeney: "When you look across the political spectrum from right to left, nobody's been as effective as labor and nobody can match them. You didn't say that four or six years ago."[145]

After the election, looking back on the labor movement's frenetic activity, Sweeney crowed, "No other group in America has built a

long-lasting structure that can turn out hundreds of thousands of activists in every township in the U.S."[146]

Sweeney's boast was accurate. In all, Big Labor put together an
estimated 100,000 volunteers for Democrats in the 2000 campaign.
Big Labor assigned more than a thousand paid political coordinators
to train hundreds of thousands of volunteers to do campaign work,
and another five hundred paid coordinators joined the campaign in
the final weeks. The AFL-CIO confirmed that union activists made
8 million phone calls and sent out 14 million pieces of mail; these figures do not even include what state and local unions did on behalf of
Gore.[147]

It is impossible to gauge just how much Big Labor spent on this
ground war, but the program easily cost tens of millions of dollars.
This cost, of course, was in addition to the $128.7 million union PACs
spent in the 2000 election cycle. In short, union members were once
again forced to pay for an all-out political program that might well
have run counter to their wishes and interests.

The total outlay was staggering, but in some respects the investment was worthwhile to union bosses. In 2000, the AFL-CIO registered 2.3 million new union voters to the rolls, which far surpassed
the 1998 total of 500,000 new union voters. Although union members
were 13.5 percent of the population, union households in 2000 made
up a record 26 percent of voters, according to a survey by Peter D.
Hart Research Associates. More astonishingly, union voters supported Gore 61 percent to 33 percent, while the nation as a whole
gave Gore only 48 percent of the vote. Although Gore lost the election
in the Electoral College, he actually won the popular vote—something
he would not have come close to winning without Big Labor's forced-
dues–funded campaign.[148]

Even with the Gore loss, Big Labor was effective for Democrats.
Union political spending was especially influential in Michigan, Pennsylvania, Wisconsin, and Washington. In Michigan, for example, union
voters made up 43 percent of voters (thanks mainly to the holiday
that the United Auto Workers negotiated) and were instrumental in
electing Democrat Debbie Stabenow as senator. Stabenow was just
one of several Democratic senators whom the unions helped elect;
Jon Corzine of New Jersey, Jean Carnahan of Missouri, Bill Nelson of

Florida, and Maria Cantwell of Washington all rode Big Labor to victory. With the 2000 election, the Democrats cut dramatically into the Republicans' Senate majority, picking up five seats for a total of fifty. And in fact they would retake control of the Senate in 2001, when Senator James Jeffords of Vermont defected from the Republican Party. None of that would have been possible without Big Labor.

Nor were the unions' gains only on the federal level. In another example of how labor bosses are continually looking to protect their own power, the unions targeted the Colorado state senate, mainly because it was considering a publicly supported right-to-work bill; the unions were key players in winning Democratic control of the state senate. Additionally, they defeated ballot initiatives in Oregon that would have restricted union political spending and initiatives in Michigan and California that would have allowed school vouchers (see Chapter 5). And Big Labor's efforts on behalf of Al Gore didn't end on Election Day. In the long aftermath of court battles before the election was finally certified in Florida, John Sweeney sent hundreds of union staffers to the state to generate guerrilla theater in protest of the recounts in various counties that kept showing George W. Bush the winner. In rallies at the capitol in Tallahassee and elsewhere in the state, union members demonstrated while Sweeney joined Jesse Jackson and other Democratic luminaries on stage to question the legitimacy of Bush's victory. AFSCME president Gerald McEntee told the crowd, "Our fundamental democracy is under attack in Florida today. . . . The power brokers in Florida and Texas have changed the rules. If they can hijack our votes in Florida, what state is next?[149]

Sweeney also appeared at a demonstration on the steps of the U.S. Supreme Court, as the court considered whether to overturn a Florida Supreme Court ruling that ordered several counties to recount their disputed ballots by hand; he urged protesters to stage vigils around the District of Columbia while the court deliberated.[150] After the court handed down its decision, Sweeney said the justices were "ignoring the fundamental principle of 'one person, one vote' in their decision." In a statement he released, Sweeney declared that the decision "profoundly threatens the faith of citizens in our democracy and our system of justice. That faith will be most sorely tested in minority communities where hundreds of reports of harassment, intimidation, and faulty voting machines now cast a pall over the progress we have made in more than three decades of fighting for voting rights for all Americans."[151]

2004: THE NEXT BIG BATTLE

Although the unions achieved some of their goals in the 2000 election, they of course failed to achieve their main objectives: defeating Bush and giving the Democrats control of Congress. Rest assured, however, that a leadership as radical and as politically motivated as Big Labor's would not abandon its aim of putting its Democratic brethren in power. Once again, the labor bosses under John Sweeney only intensified their efforts. In 2002, according to the Center for Responsive Politics, unions contributed almost $90 million, a new record for a nonpresidential year.

Early in 2003, Big Labor was already signaling that it would go all-out to defeat the Republicans in 2004. AFSCME president Gerald McEntee boasted, "We are better at playing politics than ever before," and he made clear that the unions would be focused on one goal: defeating Bush.[152] At the AFL-CIO convention in March 2003, John Sweeney took to the podium to declare that Bush must go: "They know, we know, you know that the time for change has come," he shouted. "And it's your job, their job, our job to start making it happen."[153]

Big Labor had a dry run in the fall of 2003, when California's Democratic governor, Gray Davis, faced a voter recall. Art Pulaski, head of the California Federation of Labor, admitted spending $5 million to oppose the recall, and the SEIU paid two hundred political operatives to take time off from their jobs and campaign against it. Undoubtedly the unions spent more, but the murky accounting that unions are allowed to practice makes it nearly impossible to determine precisely how much they spent in California. One thing is clear, however: Virtually all of their political support went to opposing the recall or to supporting candidates other than Republican Arnold Schwarzenegger, who ended up winning the election handily. Union leaders were not, of course, rallying against the recall because that is what their members wanted. In fact, exit polls showed that nearly half of union members voted to recall Governor Davis.[154]

For his part, President Bush made some efforts to appease union leaders in hopes of preventing the entire labor movement from focusing its massive resources against him in 2004. Bush should have remembered what he had said when he was marshaling support for military action in Iraq: It is folly to try to appease one's enemies.

Trying to make inroads with the unions—especially the Teamsters and Carpenters unions—President Bush addressed a number of union events, including Labor Day picnics and union training programs.[155] He even invited Teamsters president James Hoffa to sit with First Lady Laura Bush during his 2002 State of the Union address. Hoffa told the *Washington Post* that year, "We have more access to this White House than we did to the Clinton White House." And indeed union officials from the ironworkers', seafarers', bricklayers', and laborers' unions met with Bush White House officials in the early days of his administration on a regular basis, sometimes over lunch in the exclusive White House Mess.[156]

But the cozy relationship didn't last long. That is the problem with appeasement, whether it's governments trying to appease aggressors or Republican administrations trying to woo union bosses: It rarely works. Sure enough, as the 2004 presidential campaign heated up, Big Labor allied itself against the president's reelection. Indeed, the labor movement early on was not *for* any particular candidate as much as it was *against* Bush. The legislative director for the International Association of Machinists and Aerospace Workers, Richard Michalski, set the tone when he declared, "We are at war." John Sweeney yielded to his penchant for hyperbole, saying, "The present administration is probably the worst we've seen, and the most anti-worker and anti-union in every possible way."[157]

AFSCME's Gerald McEntee showed just how good he had gotten at "playing politics" when he announced plans to register 500,000 Latino voters in Arizona, Florida, Nevada, and New Mexico through his union and a new labor PAC, Voices for Working Families. McEntee declared, "Most of our effort will be to get George Bush out of the White House."[158]

Even after sitting at Laura Bush's side during the State of the Union address, Teamsters president James Hoffa said in early 2003 that his union would probably back the Democratic nominee, regardless of who it was, just as it had backed Al Gore in 2000.[159] Later that year the Teamsters endorsed longtime union backer Richard Gephardt of Missouri for the Democratic nomination, but like the rest of the unions, the Teamsters seemed more focused on ousting Bush than on getting a particular candidate elected.[160]

Defeating Bush in 2004 was exactly the motivation behind Dennis Rivera and his SEIU local's $35 million plan to send a thousand paid political operatives to key battleground states across the country—for example, Florida, Michigan, Arizona, Pennsylvania, and Ohio—to work for a full year. The union set up this program well before a Democratic nominee was even chosen, so in no way could the SEIU local have been expressing its enthusiasm for a particular Democratic candidate.[161]

It's interesting to note that because observers pegged New York as a sure state for Democrats in 2004, not one of these thousand agents would work in New York City, where the members who are forced to foot the bill reside.

With each successive election during his tenure as AFL-CIO boss, John Sweeney has promised a larger, more effective political program than the one before. He has been largely successful, thanks to the legally unaccountable use of member dues for politics. As this is written, the 2004 campaign season is just beginning in earnest, so it is too soon to tell whether Big Labor's political efforts—its massive investment in money and manpower—will pay off. But one thing is certain: Union bosses are siphoning this money and manpower from the legitimate purposes for which union members pay dues, and they are doing it without their members' consent. And that is simply undemocratic.

We know something else, too: Several years ago the Democratic Party struck a corrupt bargain with America's labor bosses, and in subsequent years the quid pro quo relationship has only grown stronger. The dirty bond between Democrats and Big Labor is seemingly unbreakable.

CHAPTER 3

An Affair to Remember:
Bill Clinton and the Unions

They might have been just three guys trading golfers' stories in front of a cozy fire that October day in 1994, except that one man stood accused of labor racketeering and the second man had been lawyer to several mob-run unions for more than a decade and now worked as key aide to the third—who just happened to be the president of the United States.

In the Oval Office that day, President Bill Clinton presented his guest with a special gift—a Callaway "Divine Nine" golf club. The visitor, Arthur A. Coia, the debonair head of the 700,000-member Laborers International Union of North America, was touched, and just a few days later, while accompanying the president on a trip to Rhode Island, he would give Clinton a gift of his own, a custom-made driver that, the president would gush, was "gorgeous . . . a work of art."[1]

But as he sat in the Oval Office, Coia was looking for more than just a golf club from the president. Apparently Coia felt his union wasn't getting as large a share of federal contracts as it deserved, even though the Laborers union and Coia himself had been among the president's and the Democratic Party's most generous benefactors.

Look into it, Clinton reportedly instructed the other man present, Harold M. Ickes, Jr., the White House deputy chief of staff. The professorial-looking Ickes was used to fixing labor unions' problems.[2] For years Ickes had been the head of labor practice for the Long Island law firm Meyer, Suozzi and had represented several unions with alleged ties to organized crime, including

- Local 100 of the Hotel Employees and Restaurant Employees International Union, which, according to a civil racketeering suit brought by the U.S. Justice Department under the RICO statute, was under the control of the Colombo and Gambino crime families of New York.[3]

- Teamsters Local 560, which the Justice Department accused, in a 1982 racketeering suit, of using murder and beatings to silence anyone in the union opposed to Genovese crime family mobster and union boss Anthony "Tony Pro" Provenzano.[4]

- The Laborers International Union of North America, Coia's own union, which the Justice Department was investigating for racketeering at the very time of the Oval Office meeting. The investigation had been ongoing for three years, and Justice claimed in its draft civil complaint that Coia had "associated with, and been controlled and influenced by, organized crime figures" and that he "employed actual and threatened force, violence and fear of physical and economic injury to create a climate of intimidation and fear."[5]

The meeting among Clinton, Coia, and Ickes should never have taken place, and certainly not in the Oval Office. Officials from the Justice Department had tried repeatedly to warn the White House about Coia's alleged ties to organized crime before the meeting occurred. They had made desperate phone calls to warn the president's advisers about Coia and the Laborers union, and they had even sent over written warnings.[6] Still, President Clinton held the meeting—

and would maintain a cozy relationship with Coia for years afterward, continuing to take hefty contributions from Coia and his union and in return helping out his patron whenever possible.

Of course, much of what went on in the Oval Office during the Clinton years was seamy and corrupt. But the difference between the Laborers union affair and other Clinton scandals, including the Monica Lewinsky scandal, is that this went way beyond Bill Clinton's personal sleaziness. The Clinton-Coia affair is symptomatic of the institutional corruption that infects the relationship between labor unions and the Democratic Party. Bill Clinton couldn't afford to distance himself from Arthur Coia, no matter how rotten a character the man was. Clinton and the Democratic Party were simply too beholden to the union—and its tainted boss—for the money that put them in power and kept them there.

Unions and the Democratic Party are joined in a symbiotic relationship in which neither could survive without the other. Without men like Coia and unions like the Laborers to fund the party and its candidates, Democrats would have a much tougher time gaining political office. And without Democrats in office, the unions couldn't get their political agenda adopted—an agenda that includes special protection for unions and freedom from the kind of legal scrutiny other organizations must contend with. Still, the case of the Clinton administration's ties to Arthur Coia and his union may go down as one of the most dramatic examples in history of how union bosses can buy influence, access, and even shielding from criminal prosecution by making the "right" political campaign contributions—some of them paid for by union dues over which the union members themselves have little or no control.

THE LABORERS UNION AND THE MOB

Although the Clinton White House would later contend that it was not aware of the Laborers union's apparent links to organized crime, the federal government had identified the union's ties to the mob long before Bill Clinton took office. In 1986, President Reagan's Commission on Organized Crime identified the Laborers International Union of North America as one of the "bad four"—the most corrupt unions in the nation—along with the Teamsters, the Hotel Employees and Restaurant Employees union, and the International Association of Longshoremen. According to congressional testimony by an FBI official, each of these unions' presidents at the time had been "handpicked by La Cosa Nostra."[7] Laborers union president Angelo Fosco (Coia's predecessor) had won reelection despite the fact that he had been under federal indictment for union racketeering; Fosco had won the election through "the use of force and threats of violence against potential competitors," according to the Reagan crime commission.[8]

Violence and intimidation were by no means uncommon in this mob-controlled union of low-skilled workers, who perform undesirable work like removing building rubble from construction sites. As John E. Mulligan and Dean Starkman explained in the liberal, muckraking magazine *Washington Monthly*:

> The mob's grip on the Laborers was particularly ironclad because the union has such broad authority over its workers. If you want work as a Laborer—say, cleaning toxic waste—you don't go to an employer. You go to the union "hiring hall." Local officers there decide who works and who doesn't, so complaining about mob influence gets you blackballed. Real troublemakers might draw beatings or worse. And workers never even see the complicated kickback schemes, real estate frauds, and other misuse of their dues. Such investments are made by union leaders, beholden not to the rank and file but to bosses whose chain of command runs straight to the general president's office and, from there, to the mob.[9]

This was the union leadership through which Arthur A. Coia worked his way up. As reporter Byron York documented in a long investigative piece for *The American Spectator*, Coia's father and grandfather were both Laborers union officials, with his father rising as high as secretary-treasurer, the number-two job in the union hierarchy. Young Arthur got his union card at the tender age of fourteen, went on to college and law school, and began working for the Laborers' local in Providence, Rhode Island.

In 1981, both father and son faced bribery and racketeering charges stemming from a multimillion-dollar insurance scheme that bilked Laborers' members out of insurance premiums for "kickbacks, payoffs, unearned salaries and fees and improper personal expenses," according to their indictment. Also charged in the indictment were reputed Mafia crime figures Santo Trafficante of Tampa, Anthony Accardo of Chicago, and Raymond Patriarca of Providence.[10] But a judge threw out the charges without a trial because the government had unwittingly let the statute of limitations expire before filing the indictments.[11] With that behind them, in 1987 Coia succeeded his father as secretary-treasurer—with the blessings of the Chicago mob, as he later admitted in sworn testimony.[12] Then, in 1993, Coia became president of the union, assuming office just a few weeks after Bill Clinton moved into his. The two became frequent companions. Over the course of the next three years, Coia would have contact with the Clinton White House no fewer than 120 times[13]—an extraordinary amount of access for a man of Coia's dubious background. The Clinton White House invited Coia to state dinners, receptions, the signing of the Israeli-Palestinian peace agreement (Coia didn't attend), fundraisers, even a private dinner; the president became so chummy with the union boss that he had him over to the White House residence to watch the NBA playoffs.[14] But no meeting between the two men was more important than the October 21, 1994, Oval Office visit.

POLITICAL CONTRIBUTIONS BUY ACCESS AND FAVORS

Arthur Coia's amazing access to Bill Clinton was no accident. Before Clinton even took office, the Laborers union was writing checks to help his new friend. Coia lent $100,000 to Clinton's inaugural committee. The day after he met with the president in the Oval Office, Coia wrote a personal check for $50,000 to the Democratic National Committee (DNC).[15] In the next four years, the Laborers union and its political action committee (PAC) contributed $4.8 million to Democratic candidates and the party.[16]

Yet while this was going on, the Justice Department was investigating Coia's and his union's ties to organized crime.

Just prior to the Oval Office meeting, the White House had submitted Coia's name to the FBI for a routine "name check" because it intended to name him to a prestigious presidential commission, the Council on Competitiveness. This kind of background check is the most minimal security clearance the government uses; it is mainly for part-time appointments to the White House's hundreds of commissions. But even with this cursory review, Coia's name set off alarm bells at the FBI. In a memo, investigators wrote, "Coia is a criminal associate of the New England Patriarca organized crime family." The bureau also warned the White House that "within the next several weeks" the Department of Justice "will accuse Coia of being a puppet of the LCN [La Cosa Nostra]." Associate deputy attorney general David Margolis even tried calling the White House several times to warn officials not to get too close to the mob-controlled union boss—to no avail. Although the White House dropped the idea of appointing Coia to the Council on Competitiveness, no one in the White House seemed concerned that the president himself was having Oval Office *tête-à-têtes* with Coia and inviting him to travel at his side to Rhode Island.

Even First Lady Hillary Clinton had raised red flags at the Justice Department. The Laborers union had invited the First Lady to speak at its annual convention in February 1994, which prompted Justice to send one of several written warnings to the White House to maintain distance from the union and its disreputable president.

Despite the Justice Department's repeated warnings, White House counsel Abner Mikva later told a House subcommittee looking into this scandal that he could not recall receiving any warnings. The Associated Press reported that Mikva claimed that no one in his office brought the FBI's report to his attention: " 'There would be no reason for it,' Mikva told reporters during a break in the House hearing on the laborers union. He said it was 'probably a clerk in the office, maybe an intern' who read the FBI report on Coia and didn't pass on the information."[17]

Now, unless the intern's name was Monica Lewinsky and she was otherwise occupied with the president, it defies credulity to claim that a low-level staffer would not bring to the attention of his or her

White House bosses an FBI warning that the president of the United States—or his wife, for that matter—was about to meet with a mobster who was under imminent threat of indictment. To be sure, as a Democratic congressman Mikva had been union-friendly, but he had also served as a judge on the United States Court of Appeals for the District of Columbia, which is generally considered the second-most important court in the nation. It is shocking that a man of Mikva's intelligence and reputation would excuse the Clintons' close association with reputed underworld crime figures. "We don't try to isolate the president and first lady from all human contacts," Mikva told reporters.[18]

Despite Mikva's lame excuse about "human contacts," the Clinton administration's ties to Coia and his corrupt union involved more than just friendly get-togethers. Money changed hands, over and over again. And the money went both ways: Coia and his Laborers union gave money to Democrats, and the administration in turn gave huge grants to the Laborers union.

According to Byron York, Arthur Coia sent $100,000 to the DNC on March 23, 1994, two months *after* the Department of Justice issued its memo warning the White House that Coia was a pretty dangerous character—which, implausibly, no one in any position of authority at the White House claims to have read. On June 20, he sent another $35,000 to the DNC, and on June 24, an additional $10,000. In June, Coia was also the cochair of a DNC fundraiser that raised $3.5 million. In July, the Laborers union sent a check for $100,000 to the DNC.[19] For the entire 1993–94 election cycle, the Laborers union's PAC gave more than $1.4 million to Democratic candidates—and that doesn't even count contributions by the Laborers' state PACs. In the next election cycle, 1995–96, contributions from the Laborers union went up by almost a million dollars, to $2.3 million.[20] Although the Laborers International Union of North America is only a medium-size union, representing relatively modestly paid workers, it became the largest union contributor of so-called soft money to the Democratic Party during the Clinton years and had the fourth-largest PAC among all unions.[21] In a January 1995 memo to the White House, DNC finance chairman Terry McAuliffe identified Coia as one of the Democratic Party's "top 10 supporters."[22]

In addition to the generous outlays to the Democratic Party, Coia gave money to whatever causes he thought might bring him closer to Bill and Hillary. In May 1994, Coia gave $50,000 to the U.S. Botanical Gardens, which raised questions even among his union cronies. Byron York, reporting in *The American Spectator*, noted that the donation "baffled some Laborers." David Caivano, the Laborers official who administered the union's New York State PAC, recalled to York that another union official had to spell out for him why Coia would give so much money to a botanical society. "Because Hillary Clinton is involved and he desperately wants to get next to Hillary Clinton," the other official told Caivano.[23]

It seems Coia and the Laborers union were rewarded for their generosity. Coia, no doubt, liked chumming around with Bill Clinton, but he also had a specific agenda. He must have been gratified when, after their October 1994 Oval Office meeting, the president assigned deputy chief of staff Harold Ickes as point man in facilitating the Laborers union's access to lucrative federal grants. According to a study by the Heritage Foundation, during the first two full fiscal years of the Clinton administration, the Laborers union received nearly $30 million in federal grants.[24] Examined in this context, the union's contributions to the Democratic Party look like an excellent investment, yielding ten dollars in grants for every dollar of political contributions given by the union, according to the Heritage Foundation report. These grants were particularly helpful to the cash-strapped union, which ran an operating budget deficit of nearly $12 million in 1995.[25]

Many of the federal grants went to the union's education and training programs. The Department of Labor and other domestic agencies traditionally give grants to these sorts of programs because apprenticeship programs are in many cases the only way individuals can break into certain jobs. But the Laborers union training programs that Bill Clinton was so anxious to keep funded have traditionally been a major source of criminal activity and corruption. In its draft complaint against Coia and the Laborers union, the Department of Justice alleged that "in or about 1986 to on or about July 31, 1994," union officials, including Coia, sought to "defraud training and education funds of various upstate [New York] locals," using "actual and threatened force" to "induce the locals to surrender control of these funds."[26]

It appears that Clinton was concerned only with ensuring that Coia remained a major donor to the Democratic Party. Of course, the man he assigned to make sure the Laborers union was taken care of, Harold Ickes, was no stranger to mob-run unions, including the Laborers union, having represented them in private practice before heading to the White House. According to published reports, in 1985 Ickes was present at an interview between investigators and the president of the Hotel Employees and Restaurant Employees union's Local 100, Anthony "Chickie" Amodeo, when Amodeo admitted that he had been an associate of Gambino crime family mob boss Paul Castellano for more than forty years.[27] Still, Ickes's law firm professed ignorance of the type of clients they were representing, claiming they were "absolutely not" aware of the ties between their clients and organized crime figures. Similarly, in 2000, when Ickes was running Hillary Clinton's New York Senate race, he attempted to play down his ties to Arthur Coia, telling the *Wall Street Journal*, "As [White House] deputy chief of staff, I handled a lot of matters and Arthur was a person I dealt with. . . . I helped set up, and attended, meetings."[28] What he didn't say was that he was the point man to ensure that the Laborers' cash flowed into Democratic coffers and that government contracts went to the union's affiliates, despite the Justice Department's concerns about the union and its top leadership.

JUSTICE FOR FRIENDS OF BILL

Despite the Justice Department's warnings to the White House that Arthur Coia was trouble—or as the department's draft complaint against him alleged, that he had "associated with, and been controlled and influenced by, organized crime figures"—Coia remained close to the White House and out of jail. As the *Washington Monthly* reported, "On November 4, 1994, Coia was served with a 212-page draft racketeering complaint from the Justice Department's Organized Crime and Racketeering Section." That was just two weeks after his meeting with Bill Clinton and Harold Ickes, and the same day the president sent Coia a handwritten note thanking him for the custom-made golf club.

"But then something strange happened," noted the *Washington Monthly*. Instead of formally indicting Coia, the Justice Department worked out a deal that allowed him to remain a free man and keep his job as well. The Justice Department dropped its 200-plus-page complaint in favor of a one-page agreement, which said that the union "shall be allowed to undertake a period of internal reform, lasting at least ninety (90) days, aimed at further investigating and disciplining individuals within any entity of LIUNA [Laborers International Union of North America] for wrongful association with, or corruption by, members of organized crime." Coia would remain in place to oversee the cleanup of the Laborers union.

"The settlement, when it came, was an enormous victory for Coia," reported the *Washington Monthly*. "Not only did he keep his position atop the union, he also beat back reforms that would have brought real democracy to the Laborers and handed power to the rank and file."[29]

The Justice Department's decision not to move forward with its complaint was shocking, for in all fifteen previous union cases in which Justice had filed racketeering charges, it had taken over the corrupt unions' operations.[30]

Was it just coincidence that Coia escaped that fate, or did his powerful friends at 1600 Pennsylvania Avenue make sure that no one touched their union banker?

Just days before the Justice Department offered the deal, Hillary Clinton traveled to Miami to address the annual Laborers union conference on February 6, 1995. Again, the Justice Department tried to warn the White House that the First Lady's visit might be ill-advised. According to congressional investigators, deputy attorney general Jamie Gorelick discussed the matter with White House counsel Abner Mikva, who, in turn, warned Harold Ickes that Mrs. Clinton should not have any private meetings with Coia.[31]

Although the White House would later assert that no conversations concerning the investigation ever occurred between anyone in the White House and Coia or other Laborers officials, Coia reportedly told others that Bill Clinton did speak to him about the investigation.[32] Byron York of *The American Spectator* interviewed three Laborers union officials who asserted that Coia had told them at a meeting that the White House had promised to take care of the RICO complaint. John Serpico, a Coia rival whom the Justice Department later named as an alleged mob associate, told York that Coia "said he talked to Clinton and Clinton assured him that everything would be OK. Clinton was gonna help him out and take care of this thing." David Caivano remembered that conversation vividly. According to Caivano, Coia turned to Caivano's father, Samuel, who was also at the meeting, and said, "Sam, I talked to Bill Clinton about this. He knows we're not doing anything wrong. Don't worry." York confirmed this version with Samuel Caivano.[33]

Whether or not Hillary or Bill Clinton promised, in so many words, to help bail Arthur Coia out, the Justice Department agreement was clearly a sweetheart deal—and one that produced no genuine union reforms. Coia removed a few lower-level mobsters from the union but kept his own job. He also stayed on Bill Clinton's A-list for invitations. At the end of March, little more than a month after the Justice Department agreement was signed, the president invited the union boss to travel with him aboard Air Force One on a trip to Haiti. Coia couldn't make the trip, but he did write Harold Ickes, thanking him for his "quick and personal involvement in my invitation to join President Clinton in Haiti." In his letter he added that the Laborers' proposal to set up a job-training program in Haiti was at the Agency for International Development and that he hoped to discuss it with the White House in the near future.[34]

The Justice Department deal did not mark the end of the federal government's investigations of Coia and the Laborers union, however. In 1996, a congressional subcommittee investigated the union, though the hearings ended up producing little more than an opportunity for Democrats to demonstrate their fealty to the union bosses. The House subcommittee staff received confidential information that federal prosecutors had actually been thwarted in their efforts to take over the union and rid it of corruption, the *Weekly Standard* reported, but Democrats on the subcommittee blocked subpoenas that would have forced knowledgeable witnesses to testify. Instead they attacked the credibility of witness Ronald M. Fino, who had been business manager of the Laborers union's Buffalo local for fifteen years and a national official for eight—and an undercover FBI informant for the entire time. Over the years, Fino had met with the FBI more than four thousand times to detail the mob's relationship to the Laborers union, but this did not seem to impress the subcommittee's Democrats. Most notable was this mocking query from Democrat Charles Schumer: "Mr. Fino, do you believe space aliens are linked to the mob?"[35]

It is startling that Democrats like Schumer could be so flippant about mob ties to labor unions, since the federal government had been tracking organized crime's involvement in labor unions, and since the Laborers union specifically had been a major focus of investigation for years. Then again, as the *Weekly Standard* pointed out, "It's not hard to grasp why Democratic congressmen wanted to undercut Fino's testimony. The Laborers, under president Arthur A. Coia, had managed to snuggle up embarrassingly closely to the Clinton administration."[36] And defending their party leader might not have been the only reason Democrats seemed willing to look the other way when it came to mobbed-up unions. Most politicians are concerned with their own political survival, and of course many Democrats survive because of Big Labor's hefty contributions.

Consider Charles Schumer. Less than a year after the congressional hearings at which he ridiculed Ronald Fino, Schumer announced that he would run for the Senate in 1998, and Big Labor was quick to back his campaign. In 1997–98, union PACs poured $227,428 into the Schumer campaign; the Laborers' PAC rewarded Schumer for his loyalty by contributing $10,000, the maximum allowed by federal campaign laws. And the unions continue to back Schumer, now the senior senator from New York: by the end of 2003—still nearly a year out from Election Day—union PACs had already given $116,500 to Schumer's reelection effort.[37]

A SLAP ON THE WRIST FOR CLINTON'S FRIEND

The last-minute agreement between the Justice Department and the Laborers union in 1995 saved Arthur Coia's job in the short run, but apparently the man just couldn't keep his hands out of the union cookie jar. Coia lived lavishly, with an opulent home on Rhode Island's Narragansett Bay and another in Florida, plus several Ferraris.[38] And less than five years after signing the surprise agreement with the Justice Department, Coia was signing a different kind of agreement with federal law officials—this time a plea agreement for having defrauded the state of Rhode Island of taxes owed on the purchase of three Ferraris, which ranged in price from $215,000 to $1 million.[39] Coia bought the fancy cars from a Rhode Island Cadillac dealer, Carmine Carcieri, who—not so coincidentally—held the union's $1 million-a-year car-leasing agreement.

Coia stepped down as union president as part of the agreement, but magically he kept his full $250,000-per-year salary—for life. The plea agreement, filed on January 27, 2000, allowed Coia to receive probation on the condition that he "remain retired from LIUNA as General President Emeritus pursuant to the terms of compensation on the date of his retirement and will be barred, whether within or outside LIUNA, from any service as a consultant or adviser . . . to LIUNA or any of its affiliated or subordinate entities. . . . In addition, the U.S. Attorney and the Defendant hereby agree that, as a result of his guilty plea and as a condition of his probation . . . the Defendant will not accept any compensation increases from LIUNA above the level of the current constitutionally mandated salary of the General President."[40] In essence, the government's plea agreement assured that Coia would draw a quarter-million-dollar salary—plus a union pension—for the rest of his life for doing nothing. The agreement also specifically allowed Coia to do work for other unions and labor organizations or to work as a consultant or adviser to employers on union issues.[41] Even when the Rhode Island bar suspended his license to practice law, the punishment didn't last; in February 2003 the bar reinstated Coia after several prominent Democratic politicians and civic leaders wrote letters urging his reinstatement.[42]

The union also conducted an internal investigation into Coia's alleged ties to organized crime, but here too Coia got off easy, perhaps because the investigation was flawed from the start. The sweetheart deal worked out between Bill Clinton's Justice Department and the Laborers union in 1995 appointed former federal prosecutor Robert D.

Luskin as an internal prosecutor of corruption within the union. But Luskin was the very man who had worked out the deal between the Justice Department and the Laborers union. As the *Wall Street Journal* noted in an editorial several months later, "Justice should have seen a glaring conflict of interest at the outset. . . . Was it realistic to expect [Luskin] to turn overnight from Mr. Coia's advocate into Mr. Coia's investigator, while he continued to be paid by the union?"[43] The *Wall Street Journal* also reported that "Mr. Luskin, at the very time he was working out the unprecedented agreement between Justice and Mr. Coia, was allegedly accepting 'hot' money, to the tune of $700,000, from Stephen A. Saccoccia, a Patriarca crime family associate now in prison for money laundering."[44] According to the *Journal*, Luskin received his fees in the form of gold bars and Swiss wire transfers, since his client's assets were frozen under court order at the time. The U.S. Attorney's Office in Rhode Island accused Luskin of "willful blindness" in accepting "surreptitious and anonymous payments," and Luskin eventually forfeited $245,000 of the money from his client's ill-gotten gains.[45]

Luskin did eventually bring charges against Coia, alleging Coia's continued ties to organized crime, but these charges were investigated and adjudicated using the very internal union process set up under the 1995 plea agreement that Luskin negotiated. In the end, Coia got off with a slap on the wrist for his Ferrari deal—a $100,000 fine. Meanwhile, the hearing officer cleared Coia of ties to organized crime, arguing that the witnesses who testified of his extensive dealings with Raymond Patriarca, Jr., son of the New England crime boss who was an associate of Arthur Coia's father when he was a top official with the Laborers union, were not credible.

Although the Justice Department had been careful not to criticize the deal worked out in 1995, the assistant attorney general for the criminal division and the U.S. attorney for the Northern District of Illinois, who conducted the original investigation that led to the draft RICO complaint, issued a statement following the finding from the internal hearing. "We are disappointed with the decision," James K. Robinson and Scott R. Lassar said, adding, "We believe the opinion contains serious factual and legal errors" in clearing Coia of ties to organized crime.[46]

A PATTERN OF CORRUPTION

If the Clinton administration's dealings with Arthur Coia and the Laborers International Union of North America were an isolated incident it would be bad enough, but the corrupting nexus between union money and Democratic political power was especially tight during the Clinton years. As the former governor of a right-to-work state, Clinton would seem to be an unlikely candidate to be taken over by the unions. But Clinton knew how important the unions could be to his campaigns. Unions provide the money and the troops to elect Democrats and keep them in power, and in 1992—before he even took office—he had already begun tapping their resources for his reelection. According to Common Cause, the liberal campaign finance reform group, in the last three months of 1992 the DNC amassed more than $20 million, which was to be put toward Clinton's reelection four years later. Unions accounted for a significant chunk of this money; for example, nearly $400,000 came from a single union, the United Steelworkers Union.[47] Clinton had no intention of being a one-term president. He used the unions' early money to ensure his reelection in 1996, and he built powerful ties to labor leaders like Arthur Coia. In return they rewarded him with soft-money contributions that made his reelection inevitable even before the Republicans had picked their nominee; the unions were a major source of the $35 million in soft money spent to reelect Clinton. And the money didn't just go to Clinton's reelection. Unions spent more than $20 million in an advertising blitz that was part of the effort to win back control of the Congress for the Democrats.[48] In all, unions gave more than $60.6 million in direct contributions to Democrats in 1996.[49]

For all intents and purposes, unions and the Democratic Party operated as one. Yet the media essentially ignored the close ties between unions and the Democrats, focusing much more often on the links between business or conservative religious groups and Republicans. Amazingly, in Bob Woodward's blockbuster book about the 1996 presidential campaign, *The Choice*, the index has *not a single entry* for labor unions, despite the significant—indeed, controlling—role unions played in Clinton's reelection. This 462-page book by one of

the most celebrated investigative reporters in history manages to ignore completely the relationship between Bill Clinton and the unions,
and yet it lists dozens of entries for groups such as the National Rifle
Association, Americans for Tax Reform, the Christian Coalition, and
many other right-of-center groups with ties to Republicans.

Although much of the union money that fed the Democratic political machine in 1996, as in most years, came from union dues—money
spent without the members' consent or, oftentimes, their knowledge—
perhaps the most outrageous misuse of dues money for political
purposes during the Clinton reelection campaign was the money-
laundering operation run by the Teamsters union.[50] This scheme bilked
union members of their hard-earned dues not merely to help elect
Democrats but also to protect the job of one union president. In a clear
display of the crooked partnership between Big Labor and Democrats,
Teamsters officials and paid consultants worked with the DNC and
several Democratic front groups to use those member dues—illegally—
to ensure Teamster president Ron Carey's reelection. Ultimately, this
illegal conspiracy cost American taxpayers at least $41 million.[51]

THE TEAMSTERS' MONEY-LAUNDERING OPERATION

Like the rest of Big Labor in the 1990s, the Teamsters' leadership hi-
jacked the agenda and pushed the union far to the political left. Starting with Dwight Eisenhower in the 1950s and continuing through
Ronald Reagan and George Bush in the 1980s, the Teamsters union
had often endorsed Republicans for president.[52] When Ron Carey,
a former Marine and a registered Republican, was elected president
of the International Brotherhood of Teamsters in 1991, he hardly
seemed like the man who would tie the Teamsters' fortunes to the
Democratic Party. In his 1991 campaign for the union presidency, he
ran on an anticorruption platform, promising to rid the troubled
union of its ties to organized crime and to make the union more democratic. Once installed as president, however, Carey seemed to abandon his concern with reform: dropping his Republican registration,[53]
he quickly brought the Teamsters into the Democratic fold.

The two issues seem to have been linked. Although the union had endorsed Republicans in the 1980s, Republican administrations went after the Teamsters. For example, in 1986, even after Teamsters president Jackie Presser had endorsed President Reagan's reelection in 1984, the federal government indicted him on racketeering and embezzlement charges; Presser died of brain cancer before going to trial.[54] And a Reagan-appointed U.S. attorney in New York named Rudolph Giuliani filed far-reaching racketeering charges against the union in 1987.[55] Charging the Teamsters with having "a devil's pact" with the Mafia, the RICO complaint led to federal supervision of the union in 1989 and the first direct election of a Teamsters president— ironically, the election that produced Ron Carey. Federal supervision meant that the taxpayers footed the bill to supervise Teamsters elections; thanks to union corruption, this would end up costing the taxpayers millions.[56]

Chafing under the federally appointed Review Board that supervised union activities and elections, Carey sought help in 1992 from Harold Ickes, who was then Bill Clinton's New York campaign manager. Not surprisingly, Ickes recognized the opportunity, as Michael Ledeen and Mike Moroney reported in *The American Spectator*:

> Once installed in the White House, Ickes wrote a memo spelling out Carey's great importance to the political ambitions of the Clintons, and urged the president to establish a personal relationship with the Teamsters leader. The alliance promised enormous benefits for both sides. For the Democrats, support from the Teamsters provided the two pillars of political power: money and votes. . . . For the Teamsters, support from the White House could provide, at a minimum, more tolerant treatment from the hated investigators and overseers.[57]

As it turned out, Carey received much more than he had reason to expect from his ties to the Clinton administration.

Bill Clinton wasn't the only one running for reelection in 1996— Ron Carey's term was up that year as well. And with the feds overseeing the election under the terms of settlement of the Giuliani RICO suit, Carey actually had to campaign for the votes of the union's 1.4 million members, an expensive and risky proposition. Carey had become unpopular with the union members who put him in office in

1991. The big problem was that he had squandered the union's treasury, pouring much of it into politics through soft-money donations to the Democrats. In 1991, the union had been worth $157 million, but by 1996 the Teamsters' net worth had fallen to $702,000.[58] In order to make up for the shortfall in funds, Carey proposed to raise Teamsters dues. But when his proposal was put to a vote among the membership, as the union constitution required, Teamsters members rejected it by a 3–1 margin.[59]

Facing stiff competition for the presidency from James P. Hoffa, the son of former Teamsters president Jimmy Hoffa, who disappeared in 1975 and whose body has never been found, the increasingly unpopular Carey needed lots of help to win reelection. So Carey operatives turned to friends at the DNC. Since the Teamsters during Carey's tenure had given Democrats some $8.5 million,[60] it was natural to expect the Democratic Party might return the favor. In his exposé *The Buying of the President 2000*, Center for Public Integrity executive director Charles Lewis notes that from 1991 to 1996, "as the union was careening toward bankruptcy, it was spending more than $18 million on a wide range of political activities and borrowing nearly $16 million to help pay for its activism."[61] Teamster operatives had no trouble finding a receptive audience for their plan. The resulting scheme was typical of the shady Democratic fundraising in the Clinton era; like the Buddhist temple fundraisers and Lippo Group donations that became infamous after the 1996 election, the Teamsters' plan involved unusual donors and sizable contributions that were given in ways meant to conceal their origin.

It is illegal for a union official to spend union dues on his own election campaign, but Carey operatives seem to have figured out a way around the law. They seized on a complicated plot hatched by two consultants who did work for labor unions and other left-leaning groups, Martin Davis and Michael Ansara. According to the findings of a special elections officer appointed by a federal court, Davis and Ansara identified wealthy individuals who would funnel contributions to the Carey reelection campaign in return for Teamsters donations—made in larger amounts—to the individuals' pet advocacy groups or political causes. The Teamsters funneled the money through Democratic front groups, other unions, and the AFL-CIO. Davis even enlisted help from the DNC, as the court-appointed Teamsters election officer reported:

> Mr. Davis told individuals associated with the DNC and the Clinton-Gore '96 Re-election Committee, including Terry McAuliffe, that he wanted to help the DNC by raising more money from the IBT [Teamsters] than the DNC originally anticipated. Mr. Davis asked if the DNC, in exchange, could raise $100,000 for the Carey campaign.[62]

On August 10, 1996, the DNC sent a memo to the Teamsters union requesting donations amounting to nearly $1 million—a hefty sum all at one time, even for the Teamsters. Martin Davis faxed the memo to Teamsters director of government affairs Bill Hamilton, who coordinated the contributions. In a handwritten note on the memo, Davis seemed to recommend that the Teamsters not make the contributions until the DNC delivered on its part of the deal—finding a wealthy contributor for the Carey reelection effort. "I'll let you know when they [the DNC] have fulfilled their commitments," he wrote to Hamilton.[63]

The DNC came up with a donor, a Filipino woman in California who was ready to give. But the Teamsters decided she would not be appropriate, perhaps because federal election law forbids foreigners from donating to U.S. candidates.[64] Nonetheless, Carey personally called Terry McAuliffe, who at that time was the chief fundraiser for the Clinton-Gore reelection committee, to thank him for his efforts. Even though the scheme hadn't panned out, Carey seemed intent on keeping in McAuliffe's good graces.[65]

If the DNC's selected patron did not work out for Carey, the Teamsters were luckier in finding Democratic front groups to funnel money through. The Carey forces spent at least $885,000 in union funds to ensure his reelection, funneling most of the money through three organizations: Citizen Action, Project Vote, and the National Council of Senior Citizens. Citizen Action bills itself as a "campaign finance reform" group, but it apparently saw nothing wrong with accepting Teamsters money, taking a hefty cut—about one-third—for itself, and then forwarding the rest to a direct-mail operation that sent out 1.7 million pieces of Carey campaign literature.[66] Project Vote, a voter registration and get-out-the-vote group aimed at minority and low-income voters, was a pet project of Harold Ickes, who held great sway over the DNC.[67] The National Council of Senior Citizens was an AFL-CIO front group, financed and controlled by Big Labor; it has since been renamed the Alliance for Retired Americans,[68] no doubt in response to the unfavorable publicity surrounding the organization's role in the Carey campaign scam. Other unions contributed to the efforts, too, including the American Federation of State, County, and Municipal Employees (AFSCME), the Service Employees International Union (SEIU), and the AFL-CIO itself.[69]

The scheme worked, at least in the short term. Carey narrowly won reelection over James P. Hoffa. But all the improprieties set off alarms, and eventually some of the figures involved in the plot came under investigation. Perhaps the most notable aspect of those investigations, however, was how many people escaped retribution.

Although U.S. attorney Mary Jo White obtained convictions of Davis, Ansara, and Hamilton, the Clinton appointee did not go after other major figures associated with the scandal, such as Harold Ickes and Terry McAuliffe, who later became chairman of the DNC. She also waited nearly four years before indicting Ron Carey himself. Even when Carey was indicted, it was only on charges related to his claims to investigators that he had not known about the funding scheme. A Manhattan jury ultimately acquitted him.[70] Although Carey was not convicted, several others involved in the scheme were. William Hamilton, who was political director of the Teamsters under Carey, was convicted in 1999 on multiple felony counts in a conspiracy to embezzle $885,000 in Teamsters funds to help reelect Carey. Meanwhile, Jere Nash, Carey's campaign manager, pleaded guilty to siphoning union funds and testified for the government at Hamilton's trial. Michael Ansara, a left-wing operative who ran a Boston-based telemarketing firm, also pleaded guilty, as did Martin Davis, another consultant involved in the scheme, and Charles Blitz, a West Coast fundraiser.[71] Despite his guilty plea in the Teamsters case in 1997, Ansara's firm continued to do business with the DNC until the Democratic convention in 2000.[72]

Clinton's attorney general, Janet Reno, was forced to look into whether Harold Ickes gave false testimony to a Senate committee that was investigating the Teamsters scam, but she declined to appoint a special prosecutor to investigate the charges further. Congressman Peter Hoekstra, who chaired the House panel that held hearings on the Teamsters scandal, criticized Reno's decision. "Our investigation uncovered substantial information indicating that Mr. Ickes may have provided false and misleading testimony to Congress," Hoekstra said. "Ickes told Congress the Clinton administration did nothing to help the Teamsters. But internal Clinton administration documents . . . show a different story."[73] Senator Fred Thompson, who chaired the Senate committee before which Ickes had allegedly perjured himself, also denounced Reno, saying that "the demise of the independent counsel law when it expires . . . may be the most notable 'achievement' of her tenure as attorney general."[74]

Nor did AFL-CIO secretary-treasurer Richard Trumka face charges for his apparent involvement in funding the Carey campaign. Prosecutors accused Trumka of having laundered $150,000 in AFL-CIO funds through Citizen Action to help reelect Carey.[75] A New York grand jury and congressional committees investigating the Teamsters scandals called him to testify, but he exercised his Fifth Amendment right not to incriminate himself.[76] Although AFL-CIO policy, adopted during the George Meany era in response to earlier union corruption scandals, requires officials to step down if they insist on taking the Fifth, Trumka remains the number-two man in the AFL-CIO. In a letter to the AFL-CIO executive council explaining his decision not to remove Trumka, John Sweeney said that the policy, enacted in 1957, "has never been applied by the federation." In defending Trumka, Sweeney claimed that there was "no basis to conclude that there was any unlawful conduct by Secretary-Treasurer Trumka." As Bill Sammon of the *Washington Times* noted, however, "Mr. Sweeney's endorsement of Mr. Trumka directly contradicts the findings of Kenneth Conboy, election appeals master for the Teamsters. On Monday [November 17, 1997], the former federal judge implicated Mr. Trumka in the illegal funding of Teamster President Ron Carey's re-election campaign last year."[77]

The statute of limitations expired without charges being filed against any of the other DNC or union officials who improperly used union dues in an attempt to reelect Ron Carey.

Still, the costs of the scheme were real to the American taxpayer. The federally supervised election in which Carey held on to the union presidency cost taxpayers $24 million, but because of the financing improprieties, the election had to be overturned. Thus the Teamsters had to hold a second round of government-funded voting, which cost another $17.2 million.[78]

Hoffa won the second election, and initially it seemed that he might use the civil antiracketeering statutes to obtain justice for his union members. But in April 2000, when Hoffa filed a civil RICO suit against several union officials and others involved in the crooked election scheme, noticeably missing from the suit were Richard Trumka of the AFL-CIO and Terry McAuliffe of the DNC, despite the evidence that both men were intimately involved in the union dues rip-off. After Hoffa filed the suit, a *Wall Street Journal* editorial noted, "It looks like the fix is in on the Big Labor fraud scandal that threatens top players from the 1996 Clinton-Gore re-election effort, the Democratic National Committee, and the AFL-CIO."[79]

Republicans even made overtures to Hoffa, hoping his bitter experience with union and Democratic Party corruption would persuade him that labor's ties to Democrats often hurt union members. President Bush invited Hoffa to sit with First Lady Laura Bush during the president's first State of the Union address, and the president appeared at several union rallies. But Hoffa ultimately spurned Bush. The final blow came in 2002, when Hoffa endorsed Democrat Bill McBride in the Florida governor's race against Governor Jeb Bush, the president's younger brother. The White House had been hinting to reporters for weeks that the Teamsters would endorse Governor Bush. The Republicans' aggressive courting of the Teamsters and the United Brotherhood of Carpenters and Joiners—whose maverick leader, Doug McCarron, had taken his union out of the AFL-CIO in March 2001—proved even less effective during the tight 2002 Senate and House races. As it turned out, 95 percent of the two supposedly GOP-friendly unions' PAC contributions went to Democrats, while 93 percent of their soft-money donations went to the Democratic Party and its state affiliates.[80]

No matter how much cheating the Democrats engage in, no matter how poorly they serve the legitimate interests of working men and women, Big Labor's love affair with the Democrats grows more passionate by the year. Nothing, it seems, can separate the two groups, joined in this relationship that benefits union bosses and Democratic pols at the expense of union members and the general public. In many cases the damage done is staggering, as we'll see in the next chapter.

CHAPTER 4

Putting the Public at Risk

Prince George's County jail in Lanham, Maryland, houses some of the most dangerous criminals in America: murderers, rapists, and drug dealers from the nation's highest-crime region, right next door to Washington, D.C. It's not the kind of place you'd want to leave unguarded. But that's exactly what happened when members of the local branch of the American Federation of State, County, and Municipal Employees (AFSCME) walked off their jobs. Within half an hour, two hundred of the jail's five hundred prisoners had broken out of their cells, setting fires, destroying jail records, and breaking windows—all while AFSCME guards walked a picket line outside the jail. The county estimated that the inmates caused $50,000 in damage to the facility—and would have caused even more if county sheriffs and state and county police officers hadn't rushed to the jail.[1]

The Prince George's jail guard strike was illegal, as are most strikes by government employees. But while fires burned inside the jail, union guards laughed in the face of the county attorney who served them with emergency court orders to return to their posts, preferring walking the picket line to guarding the community from dangerous inmates. When the president of AFSCME's local affiliate heard that the strikers had been ordered back to work, he told the Associated Press, "I don't know if we'd go back [into the jail] even with a contract. It's a dangerous, life-threatening situation."[2]

Indeed it was life-threatening, but only because the guards had broken the law and abandoned their duty to protect the safety of the community. And the chaos in the jail was by no means the only problem created by the illegal AFSCME strike. The strikers included not only jail guards but also road crews, landfill operators, and office workers. Meanwhile, police protection was lessened countywide as officers had to be diverted to strike areas to prevent violence.

The illegal strike paid off for the union, however: The county, desperate to restore order, ultimately caved in to most of AFSCME's demands.

Alas, this is what happens in the world of modern unionism: The government-employee union puts its own power ahead of everything else—the public good, the community's health and safety, even its own members' welfare. Nearly fifty years ago, Big Labor threw out the idea of primarily looking after its members' interests in favor of expanding its own political power. It was at this time that private-sector union membership began declining, and union leaders suddenly looked to government-employee unions as a means of expansion.

This was a stunning about-face for the unions, which had long opposed government unions and collective bargaining for public employees. In fact, in 1959, just one year before this switch, AFL-CIO president George Meany had declared emphatically, "It is impossible to bargain collectively with government."[3] Meany wasn't alone in believing that unions had no place in the public sector. Even a stalwart pro-unionist like President Franklin D. Roosevelt thought the same thing, referring to government unionism as "the Hitler methods towards labor."[4] Indeed, Roosevelt wrote in a 1937 letter, "All government employees should recognize that collective bargaining, as usually understood, cannot be transplanted into public service. . . . Actions looking toward the paralysis of government by those who have sworn to support it are unthinkable and intolerable."[5]

Roosevelt was right. The government provides many essential services (policing, fire fighting, and much more), and it has a monopoly on those services—they can't be replaced. That is why a public-sector strike is so devastating: It doesn't affect an individual company, but rather it endangers the general public. Of course, that is also why Big Labor has adopted the public-sector strike as one of its main weapons: as the Prince George's County government employees discovered, public-sector unions wield extraordinary power to extort the American people.

EXTORTIONATE TACTICS

In defending the government-union concept, labor bosses often point to laws forbidding public employees from striking. But these laws are routinely ignored, as they certainly were in Prince George's County. Strikes by government workers have only increased with the expansion of government unions. In 1958, the year before Wisconsin became the first state to recognize government unions, there were only 15 strikes against government; in 1980, by which time thirty-seven states had enacted some form of forced government unionism for public employees, there were 536 public-sector strikes.[6] In fact, a study by the Public Service Research Foundation reveals that the frequency of strikes against vital public services *quadruples* after a forced-unionism law takes effect.[7]

The main reason that laws prohibiting government employees from striking are so ineffective is that union bosses routinely negotiate striker amnesty as the first bargaining item during a government-employee strike. Robert Poli, head of the air traffic controllers' union (PATCO) in the early 1980s, recognized this reality when he said, "The only illegal strike is an unsuccessful strike."[8] Of course, when PATCO went on strike in 1981, President Ronald Reagan showed remarkable courage and fired the illegally striking air traffic controllers (with, it should be noted, no loss to air safety), giving Poli the distinction of leading one of the very few unsuccessful government-worker strikes. Reagan proved that public officials don't have to buy "labor peace" with tax dollars, something we would do well to remember.

In the early 1970s, the president of the American Federation of Teachers, Albert Shanker, said, "A strike in the public sector is not economic—it's political. . . . One of the greatest reasons for the effectiveness of the public employees' strike is the fact that it is illegal."[9] He meant that whereas a private-sector strike is designed to harm one company economically, a strike by public employees inflicts political harm by denying essential services to citizens and creating ill will toward the government. During a private-sector strike, consumers can take their business to another company, but citizens have no such recourse during a government strike: the police, for example, have no competition.

The prime weapon of government unions is the threat to eliminate public safety. Police labor bosses have run television ads in local markets implying that violent crime will run rampant if they don't get their way. The union ads flash images of murder victims, with the announcer declaring murder, rape, and robbery on the rise. In the commercials, police telephones are ringing, but no one answers. The voiceover says, "Suppose you called and they didn't come. Think about it."[10]

Such threats are nothing but extortion. Given the success of the AFSCME strike in Prince George's County, it is little wonder that that county's police union has conducted at least two such threatening campaigns. While president of the Prince George's police union, Corporal Darryl Jones boasted of the effectiveness of those extortionate tactics, saying, "We have found that practice to be extremely successful. People are concerned about their safety." Corporal Jones even threatened to put up billboards in the county saying, "Welcome to Prince George's County. Enter at your own risk." County officials caved in to his demands before he did so, however.[11]

Corporal Jones was simply following in the footsteps of Paul Manner, who led the AFSCME strike that sparked chaos in the Prince George's County jail. Significantly, that strike was not even over wages or benefits, issues that had already been resolved over nineteen months of contract negotiations. Instead, Manner was willing to put county residents at risk in order to force the county to expand the union's power. Specifically, AFSCME was demanding

1. a provision to force government workers to pay dues or fees as a condition of employment
2. an extra 126 paid days off to union leaders "to attend conferences" (Is there any other job that requires six months of conferences each year?)
3. a provision that each workplace hire a full-time employee to do nothing but tend to union business as shop steward[12]

The strike had far-reaching effects, even beyond the jailhouse riot and the overburdening of the police force. Three skirmishes occurred at the garbage dump as striking landfill operators forced garbage trucks away. At the county animal shelter, union vandals destroyed records, vandalized vehicles, and set free animals that were being observed for rabies.[13] Even the elderly became pawns in the union's extortion, when AFSCME workers shut down transportation provided to the county's most vulnerable population. "I don't know what I'm going to do if this thing goes on," senior citizen Mary Rattler told the *Washington Post*. "I'm living alone and looking at four walls."[14]

Nor is Prince George's County the only place where government-union leaders have displayed such disregard for the public good. Elsewhere, striking firefighters have walked a picket line while buildings burned and lives were lost,[15] and police strikes have fostered widespread looting and gunfire.

When a government union's threats to the public don't work, direct threats to opposing politicians aren't out of the question. In Manchester, New Hampshire, for example, leaders of the police union staged an apparent armed insurrection in response to rumors that the city was considering a proposal to allow non–police officers to serve as traffic control flagmen. It wasn't an issue that would gain public sympathy in a strike, since most people aren't convinced that it takes a highly trained individual to direct a car around plastic cones. But police officers in Manchester were overwhelmingly paying union dues, so police union bosses sought to preserve their money flow by any means possible.

According to New Hampshire's major newspaper, the *Manchester Union Leader*, the local union head of the Manchester Patrolman's Association, Edward Kelley, led a mob of thirty to fifty uniformed police officers to the homes of the mayor and several aldermen, including that of alderman Ronald Machos. Machos was not at home, but Kelley reportedly said to Machos's wife and son, "You tell him we're going to get him," as he punched his fist into his open palm. According to Mrs. Machos, her six-year-old grandchild burst into tears, crying that they were going to be killed by the police. Mrs. Machos said, "I felt like I had a bunch of thugs coming to my door."[16] And whom was she going to call with these thugs at her door? The police?

Police union boss Kelley was hardly a sterling example of a diligent, hardworking police officer. At the time of this incident, he had already been suspended nine times and received fifteen written reprimands and eleven oral reprimands.[17] It's no wonder that he so staunchly stood by his union: it apparently allowed him to accrue an abysmal service record with no long-lasting consequences. It's almost inconceivable that an employee in the private sector could keep his position while so blatantly ignoring his job requirements.

THE INCREDIBLE SHRINKING LABOR MOVEMENT

The decision to organize the public sector was a fateful one for the labor movement, and it altered not just the face of American labor but the future of American politics as well. In barely forty years, public-employee unions went from being the stepchildren of the labor movement to the head of the labor family. Union membership in the United States peaked in 1956, when 35 percent of workers in the private sector belonged to labor unions.[18] In some fields, union membership was even higher, notably in the building and construction trades—which were the heart of the old American Federation of Labor before it merged with the Congress of Industrial Organizations in 1955, creating the AFL-CIO. In 1947, unionized companies had 87 percent of the construction market.[19] By 2003, however, union members accounted for only 16 percent of construction workers.[20] Overall, the decline in private-sector union membership has been even more dramatic: By 2003 only 8.2 percent of private-sector employees belonged to unions.[21] Between 2002 and 2003 alone, labor unions lost 369,000 members.[22]

In a closed-door session during the 2001 AFL-CIO convention, AFL-CIO president John Sweeney announced to the assembled union presidents, "Not only are the numbers totally unsatisfactory, but if we don't begin to turn this around quickly and almost immediately, the drift in the other direction is going to make it virtually impossible to continue to exist as a viable institution and to have any impact on the issues we care about."[23] This sentiment was echoed by Gerald McEntee, president of the AFSCME and chairman of the AFL-CIO's Committee on Political Education (COPE), who said, "If we go down lower than 10 percent of the American work force—and as I said we've been dropping—we really become, really, no social force in this country, with no power to change national social issues."[24]

Tellingly, Sweeney's and McEntee's biggest concern wasn't the welfare of their members but that Big Labor would lose its ability to have "impact on the issues" and would have "no power to change national social issues."

But while overall union membership has been sliding precipitously downward over the past several decades, public-employee union membership has been steadily on the rise. In fact, while private-sector unions lost 445,000 members from 2001 to 2002, government unions gained 165,000 members.[25] With 37 percent of all public employees now members of unions—and those public employees now accounting for 46 percent of the total union membership—government unions have come to play the dominant role within the AFL-CIO and the American labor movement as a whole.[26]

The days of traditional union organizing are all but gone, despite the AFL-CIO's assertions to the contrary. If it weren't for public employees, the labor movement would be cash-strapped and politically powerless. Public employees keep Big Labor afloat and, in turn, Big Labor uses its deep pockets and political clout to elect federal, state, and local officials committed to expanding the government, which of course will create more government jobs and thus more union members—and more dues. In economist Leo Troy's words, the intent of union political activity is "to redistribute more of the national income from the private to the public economies."[27] We all suffer the consequences of the labor unions' relentless defense of their own power: big government, higher taxes, expanded bureaucracy, and less choice for individual working men and women.

YOU SCRATCH MY BACK, I'LL SCRATCH YOURS

The political clout of public-employee unions extends beyond public-sector jobs, however, as they actually promote union jobs in the private sector as well. While private-sector union membership is in rapid decline, state and local politicians beholden to labor can force even nonunion employers to hire only union workers. A good example of this is the Project Labor Agreement (PLA), a scheme to use government power to give jobs exclusively to unionized workers. PLAs, which have been used in all fifty states and the District of Columbia,[28] require that government construction work go exclusively to companies that are already unionized or that agree to recognize unions as the exclusive bargaining agent for all employees on the job, to use the union hiring hall to obtain workers, to pay prevailing union wages and benefits, and to obey the restrictive work rules and job classifications imposed by craft unions.

The rationale for these agreements is that they ensure "labor peace" by forbidding employee strikes and employer lockouts, ostensibly keeping the construction project on time and on budget while ensuring high-quality workmanship. But the reality is very different. A similar rationale exists in the sweetheart deals on federal work sites governed by the Davis-Bacon Act, which mandates that federal projects pay "prevailing wages" for construction—which is really a back-door way to give preference to union contractors. According to the U.S. Chamber of Commerce, Davis-Bacon inflates spending on federal construction by at least 15 percent and costs taxpayers more than $1 billion a year in extra wages.[29]

By definition, nonunion workers don't go on strike, since their employers would simply replace them. So PLAs are hardly necessary in preventing strikes. One of the reasons unions want PLAs so much is that they pad union coffers. For instance, many PLAs require contractors to pay into union pension funds, which results in a huge windfall for unions. Most union plans require at least five years before vesting fully, and since most contracting projects last less than five years, workers and the contractor who paid into the fund on their behalf simply forfeit this money to the union when the project is completed.

What's more, the promise of "labor peace" doesn't guarantee that a PLA project won't be subject to walkouts. The largest PLA ever awarded—$2.4 billion for rebuilding the San Francisco International Airport—experienced wildcat strikes from union electricians, carpenters, and others, with the resulting delays costing the city $1 million a day. Strangely, union carpenters struck because they were angry with their union, not the contractor. The *San Francisco Chronicle* reported the scene:

> Carrying simple cardboard signs that read "More Money," the jeans-clad members of the Northern California Carpenters Regional Council protesting at the airport yesterday said they wanted $10 more an hour, coffee breaks and every other Friday off. But they are not upset with the contractors, who pay them almost $27 an hour. Instead, they are angry with their own union officials, whom they say sold them out last Saturday by voting on a weak four-year contract.[30]

In essence, PLAs require that all government construction be reserved exclusively for the less than 20 percent of construction workers who are union members while excluding the more than 80 percent of construction workers who choose not to join a union. Forcing contractors to adhere to inefficient union rules and job classifications removes any advantage a nonunionized contractor has in bidding for a job. Even when a contractor is paying "prevailing wages" as Davis-Bacon regulations require, nonunionized companies still have the ability to underbid a unionized company because of their greater efficiency—unless they are made to comply with all union rules.

In other words, the government has given unions an extraordinary power: the ability to circumvent the free market. Quite simply, unionized companies aren't competitive in private construction because higher costs and lower productivity make it impossible to deliver the lowest bid. These free-market forces are precisely why union membership has plummeted in the construction market even while the construction industry has expanded dramatically (2 million new construction jobs were created between 1970 and 2000).[31] It should come as no surprise that those who pay for construction projects out of their own pockets like to contract with those who can do a quality job at a good price. But as PLAs show, the same rules don't apply to government projects.

Government bureaucrats have never been overly concerned with saving the taxpayers money, and why should they be? Their salaries aren't dependent on cost savings—quite the contrary. Instead, government employees—a large portion of whom are union members themselves—worry about keeping unions afloat so that the money stream keeps flowing their way. By keeping nonunionized companies from competing for contracts, government makes sure, at our expense, that unionized construction workers will keep paying union dues when their employers might otherwise go under.

The fact that taxpayers have their hard-earned money confiscated to keep union bosses fat and happy seems to be of no concern to anyone involved. Nor does the government seem to mind that PLAs purposely punish the 84 percent of construction workers who have chosen not to be union members.

Since fewer and fewer private-sector workers are willing to join a union, labor bosses almost universally recognize that the future of Big Labor depends on forcing government workers into unions. At one time, government unionism was the exclusive purview of unions such as AFSCME, the National Education Association (NEA), and the American Federation of Government Employees. Today, however, nearly every union is involved in organizing the public sector to some degree. Government workers today are almost as likely to be organized by the Teamsters or the Service Employees International Union (SEIU) as they are by the traditional government unions.

Liberal politicians are willing to do all they can to further government-forced unionization because they know that forced dues will be used to benefit their campaigns. For instance, one of the first actions that Democrat Bill Richardson took on becoming governor of New Mexico in 2003 was to push through a law forcing the state and all cities, counties, and school boards in New Mexico to recognize unions as collective-bargaining agents, regardless of whether individual workers wanted union representation.[32] Twenty-three states now allow monopoly bargaining by public-employee unions, and although antistrike laws remain on the books in many states, they are rarely enforced against striking government workers, from teachers to firefighters.

This is the dream of Big Labor: an autocratic decree that will force government employees into unions by fiat. Labor leaders have been chasing the dream in one form or another for fifty years. Liberals have proven repeatedly that there is no situation that will keep them from trying to impose unionism on government workers.

TURNING TRAGEDY INTO OPPORTUNISM

The terrorist attack on the World Trade Center on September 11, 2001, killed 343 firefighters, most of whom were members of the International Association of Fire Fighters, an AFL-CIO affiliate.[33] These brave men gave their lives trying to save others and deserve our deepest gratitude; their deaths ought not to have been used as an excuse to force other firefighters into unions against their choice. But that's exactly what the AFL-CIO and some of its Democratic pawns tried to do in the immediate aftermath of the attacks. Senator Ted Kennedy, Big Labor's most reliable ally in Congress, used the tragedy to try to ram through a forced-unionization bill for all firefighters, police, and emergency workers nationwide without even a recorded vote.

Just *two days* after the terrorist attacks, Senator Kennedy pushed the bill (known as the Public Safety Employer-Employee Cooperation Act) out of the Senate Health, Education, Labor, and Pensions Committee, which he chaired at the time, in a closed-door hearing with neither testimony nor recorded vote. A few nights later he tried to sneak the bill through the full Senate by "unanimous consent," a maneuver typically reserved for noncontroversial measures like the designation of National Pickle Week. When that scheme failed, Kennedy tried to attach the measure as an amendment to the must-pass Department of Defense appropriations bill, just as America was gearing up for a war on terrorism. Here Senator Kennedy had a partner—the Democratic leader in the Senate, Tom Daschle of South Dakota, himself a reliable ally of the labor unions. Fortunately for all of us, other senators recognized the amendment for what it was— another power grab by Big Labor—and managed to foil Kennedy and Daschle's plan.[34]

Of course, this wasn't the first time unions tried to hold national security hostage. During the Hitler-Stalin Pact of 1939–41, many communist-run unions in the United States went out on strike,[35] hoping to avert U.S. entry into the war. On the eve of American entry into World War II, United Mine Workers president John L. Lewis took his coal miners out on strike, nearly crippling the nation. Despite making a no-strike pledge for the duration of the war, Lewis repeated this tactic at the height of the war, in 1943, when he led a half-million mine workers on strike. Although the government declared the strike illegal, only 15,000 workers went back to work initially. Big Labor realized that the need for wartime production was so great that its extortionate demands would have to be met. The central demand was to have the Roosevelt administration require miners to pay union dues as a condition of employment.

By holding U.S. industry captive in a time of national crisis, Big Labor achieved its goal of forced union membership. In just two years' time, from 1941 to 1943, the percentage of workers covered by collective-bargaining agreements jumped from 20 percent to more than 60 percent.[36] By the end of the war, union membership had grown to within 2 percentage points of its all-time high.[37] But forced unionism was not totally without costs to the unions themselves. Popular antipathy for unions spread rapidly and helped elect a Republican-controlled Congress in 1946, which, in turn, passed the Taft-Hartley Act in 1947. Still, this law—which United Steelworkers president Philip Murray outrageously called "the first real step toward the development of fascism in the United States"[38]—provided only modest controls on labor unions, and in fact enshrined the concept of the union shop, which forces all workers to pay union dues if they work in a private-sector job covered by a union contract.

Since then, liberals have been on a crusade to force the same rules on state and local government employees by legislative fiat. In 1985, the Supreme Court ruled in *Garcia v. San Antonio Metropolitan*

Transit Authority that Congress could impose labor regulations on state and local governments just as it does on private companies for such matters as minimum wage or maximum hours. Immediately, Congressman William Clay, Democrat of Missouri, introduced a bill that would have mandated forced unionism for all state and local government workers.[39] The measure failed, but it has been continually resurrected in different forms ever since. For example, in 2003 a group of congressmen—both Democrats and liberal Republicans—introduced a bill designed ultimately to corral all state and local government safety employees into a union, whether they wanted "representation" or not. Not only would this coercive action deny hundreds of thousands of government workers the right of freedom of association, it would also have terrifying consequences for the average citizen, as police and fire services would become subject to union strikes. Although the bill failed, chances are the unions' allies in Congress will again fight to consolidate Big Labor's power.

CRIPPLING GOVERNMENT EFFICIENCY

Holding the public hostage to union "labor actions" is only one of the catastrophic effects of government unionism. Sheltering incompetent government employees also has become commonplace as a result of union-enforced policies that have made many government agencies paragons of Third World efficiency. Local union bargaining has stunted government services.

In Philadelphia, for instance, work rules negotiated by AFSCME resulted in a featherbedded system designed solely to load the payrolls with as many union dues–paying workers as possible, all at taxpayer expense. The new rules required an intricate work structure for tasks such as removing sludge from city water pipes. *Forbes* magazine reported that the sludge "was shoveled into trucks, then dumped on the ground and once again shoveled into another truck . . . all this to employ ten persons."[40] Philadelphia workers certainly benefited from the cushy arrangement. Entry-level workers were given fifty-two days off each year—that is, more than ten weeks of paid leave annually. (Later the workers' leave was reduced to forty-three days in a "reform" measure.)

The rise of public-sector unions has also hurt our schools. Though many teachers are dedicated and hardworking, the all-powerful teachers' unions have hamstrung the education system with excessive bureaucracy and bizarre curriculum ideas, as we will see in detail in Chapter 5. The significant rise in teachers' unions and collective bargaining began in 1962, while the decline in SAT scores began in 1963. The government has poured trillions of dollars into education over the past forty years, but the quality of education has actually declined, and teachers' unions must share a good deal of the blame.

GOVERNMENT UNIONISM BETRAYS LABOR'S FOUNDING PLATFORM

Sadly, the rise in government unionism goes against the founding principles of the labor movement in America. Indeed, when George Meany of the AFL-CIO said that it would be impossible to apply collective bargaining to the government, he was following what labor leaders had been arguing for decades. Samuel Gompers, who founded the American Federation of Labor in the 1880s, believed that in a competitive free market, employers would always try to maximize their profits by slashing workers' pay.[41] Thus the unions' role, as Gompers saw it, was to organize workers so they could negotiate with their employers to create a fairer balance between employers' profits and workers' compensation. But this rationale couldn't apply to government, which made no profits. What's more, government wages were relatively high, and benefits and job security were often better in government work than in the private sector.[42] Worst of all, the money that went to pay government workers came from taxes on all workers, which meant that higher wages for unionized government employees would ultimately come from higher taxes on the wages of other union members and unorganized workers. As former union activist Max Green points out in his book *Epitaph for American Labor: How Union Leaders Lost Touch with America*, "What economic gain was to be realized by transferring money from one worker's wallet to another's?"[43]

The labor movement's opposition to public-employee unions melted, however, once it became clear that organizing public employees would be easier than organizing in the private sector, as would winning huge wage and benefit concessions. Private-sector union membership began to decline in large part because many private employers resisted efforts to organize workers, seeing unions as meddlesome troublemakers that made unreasonable demands for higher pay even when profits were low. Government employers, in contrast, weren't spending their own money, so they had far less to lose by caving in to union demands. But even government employers had their limits. As Green notes in his book, "Pay hikes for public employees helped to push spending so high that cities across the country were threatened by fiscal crisis. With their backs up against the wall, city officials started resisting public-employee unions' demands; the public backed the officials."[44]

The public-employee unions soon learned a way around this stumbling block, however. Instead of relying exclusively on the old-fashioned labor strike—which often angered citizens because it deprived them of vital public services, such as trash collection, transportation, or public schooling for their kids—public-employee unions began using political muscle to achieve their objectives. By making elected leaders dependent on union money and manpower to ensure their reelection, the unions ended up controlling the very people with whom they negotiated for higher wages or better benefits. This created an inherently corrupt system, but it has paid off for the unions. For example, unions for sanitation workers, police, firefighters, hospital workers, and many other public employees have contributed money and manpower to elect mayors and city council members, and these officials, in turn, have sat down at the bargaining table to determine how big a raise to give to the unions' members.

Teachers' unions are a good example of how public-employee unions can wield political power. Much of their political activity goes unnoticed, however, because it is focused on the local level. Of special interest to teachers' unions are local school boards: by gaining control of the school administration, they are able to grant themselves unprecedented concessions, including the power to force workers to pay dues as a condition of employment. For instance, when the school board of Long Beach, California, would not order teachers to pay union dues, the local teachers' union targeted the school board for takeover. Using forced dues money from all over the state in these political campaigns, the teachers' union won four out of five school board seats.[45] Not surprisingly, the board promptly gave the union the power to force teachers to pay dues or be fired.[46]

THE SHARP LEFT TURN

The political activism of modern government unions only underscores the American labor movement's radical shift in philosophy. While labor leaders like John Sweeney—a self-identified socialist—are now on the extreme Left politically, the labor movement traditionally reflected its members' more conservative views, at least on social issues. No one better represented labor's conservatism than George Meany, who as president of the AFL-CIO was anathema to the radical Left throughout the turbulent 1960s and 1970s. A gruff, cigar-chomping former plumber from the Bronx, Meany supported the war in Vietnam, refused to endorse 1972 Democratic presidential candidate George McGovern because he viewed McGovern as too liberal, and was derided by TASS, the official Soviet news agency, as "an apologist of the capitalist system, a rabid anti-communist."[47] Upon his death, the *Washington Post* commented that Meany had never led a strike, walked a picket line, or gone to jail for union activities, as had more radical union officials like Eugene V. Debs and Albert Shanker. The *Post* obituary noted that Meany "detested radicals, intellectual phonies, hippies and communists. No matter how acerbic his comments might have been on the business community and its profits, he was devoted to the capitalistic system and free enterprise. He was middle America."[48]

And Meany wasn't alone. The typical union member during the Meany era was a white male who worked at a skilled trade and usually voted for the Democratic candidate for local office or Congress but at least occasionally crossed over to vote for Republican candidates for president. In 1980, for example, some 43 percent of voters from union households voted for Ronald Reagan for president.[49] Thus, under Meany's leadership the AFL-CIO generally favored liberal economic policy, supporting big government spending programs as a way to stimulate the economy, but it was decidedly more conservative on social issues, from racial quotas and feminism to the environment.

Today, however, the AFL-CIO has embraced the entire social agenda of the Left, from feminist "comparable worth" pay schemes to gay rights. The labor federation now has an official lesbian, gay, bisexual, and transgender group, Pride At Work (PAW), which advocates, among other things, laws allowing same-sex marriages, a boycott of the Boy Scouts of America, and abortion on demand.[50] After the Massachusetts Supreme Judicial Court ruled in late 2003 that the state legislature would have to enact a law making gay marriages legal, several Massachusetts unions, representing more than 200,000 union members throughout the state, rallied to support the decision, including the Massachusetts Teachers Association, the SEIU, and several locals.[51] The AFL-CIO's official women's constituency organization, the Coalition of Labor Union Women (CLUW), also puts abortion rights at the top of its agenda, along with "emergency contraception"—otherwise known as the morning-after pill—and "contraceptive equity," which would require states to force insurers to cover contraception among their provided benefits.[52] A devout Catholic interested in traditional union issues—wages, benefits, and so forth—George Meany must be turning over in his grave.

Much, if not all, of the radical cultural shift within the AFL-CIO can be attributed to the growing influence of public-employee unions, which are, for their own survival, dedicated to perpetually expanding the government. Certainly many labor leaders have long since given up the notion that the welfare of their members is their primary concern; union bosses like John Sweeney focus instead on their own political clout, on their "impact on the issues." But it is even more disturbing that Big Labor has also abandoned any concern for the public interest. Union leaders have thrown out the founding principles of unionism and are now willing to use just about any weapon in their desperate attempts to preserve their own power—even if that weapon is aimed directly at American citizens.

Government employees are supposed to serve the American people—indeed, they often provide essential services that we cannot get elsewhere. FDR said it would be "unthinkable and intolerable" for public servants to take advantage of their monopolistic control over certain vital services, but in fact this has become a standard tactic for modern public-employee unions. The leaders of the government unions know full well that they can hold all of us hostage if they deny us essential services. Big Labor, in short, has a dangerous weapon at its disposal: power over our very lives and well-being.

CHAPTER 5

Teachers' Unions: Deep-Pocketed Protectors of Mediocrity

Jaime Escalante was just the kind of teacher most parents dream about for their children. A Bolivian immigrant to the United States, Escalante taught advanced math at Garfield High, one of the worst schools in East Los Angeles—a largely Mexican-American neighborhood better known for its gangs than for academic superstars. Yet he managed to produce top scores among his Mexican-American students. In fact, nearly one-fourth of all Mexican-Americans passing the Advanced Placement calculus exams nationwide at the time were from Mr. Escalante's classes. His success was so dramatic that Escalante became the subject of the inspiring 1988 movie *Stand and Deliver*, starring Edward James Olmos. But his local teachers' union, the United Teachers of Los Angeles, didn't have the same high regard for Escalante.

He apparently angered union members when he reported some teachers for selling real estate from the school lounge and others for calling in sick in order to enjoy longer weekends.[1] They got their revenge. In a 1996 interview in *U.S. News & World Report,* Escalante described how teachers' union militants would come down on him for having "too many" students in his class.[2] Escalante wrote the union president, complaining, "If you looked into what is going on in this school in the name of the union, I think you . . . would be appalled." Eventually, the union harassed Escalante right out of the school, and then sent out a note bragging about it: "We got him out."[3]

This response from the teachers' union is typical. Teachers' unions don't want teachers putting in extra, uncompensated hours and taking on more work. It makes everyone else look bad and makes it more difficult for the union to argue for more teachers and more money. In fact, teachers' unions count on low test scores to justify their demands for more tax dollars; perversely, the unions actually benefit when educational performance slips. Raising student test scores is simply a low priority for the teachers' unions.

The National Education Association (NEA), with its 2.7 million members, is the largest union in America and the most powerful. Founded in 1857 as a professional association "to elevate the character and advance the interests of the profession of teaching and to promote the cause of popular education in the United States,"[4] the group still claims its mission is to improve education. But to understand NEA's true role, it might be better to follow former NEA president Bob Chase's advice: "Watch what we do, not what we say,"[5] Chase told an audience at the National Press Club in 1997, when he was still president of the union. Despite the platitudes the NEA spouts about its commitment to "improving the quality of our schools and the education that America's children receive,"[6] the truth is the NEA cares far more about increasing its political power and promoting a liberal social and economic agenda than it does about quality education. Former NEA president Mary Futrell admitted as much, saying, "Instructional and professional development have been on the back burner for us, compared with political action."[7]

To understand how committed the NEA is to its liberal political agenda, one need look no further than the resolutions passed by the organization's Representative Assembly—the nine thousand NEA members who gather annually to form what the union likes to call "the world's largest democratic deliberative body."[8] These resolutions range far beyond education to cover everything from abortion to world hunger, though the ideological range is decidedly more narrow: from left to farther left. Among its current policies, the NEA supports

- "family planning, including the right to reproductive freedom," even for schoolchildren, given in "community-operated, school-based family planning clinics that will provide intensive counseling by trained personnel"[9]

- "a verifiable freeze on the testing, development, production, upgrading, emplacement, sale, distribution, and deployment of nuclear weapons, materials, and all systems designed to deliver nuclear weapons"[10]

- "strict prescriptive regulations . . . for the manufacture, importation, distribution, sale and resale of handguns and ammunition magazines"[11]

- "statehood for the District of Columbia"[12]

- "the adoption of a single-payer health care plan for all residents of the United States, its territories, and the Commonwealth of Puerto Rico"[13]

- "formal sex education," which the NEA believes should include information about "diversity of sexual orientation" and "homophobia," among other topics"[14]

- "bilingual education programs" to teach non–English speakers almost exclusively in their "native language" until they, magically, become proficient in English[15]

- "U.S. participation in and equitable financing of the United Nations and related bodies"[16]

- "warnings of detrimental health effects of herbal and/or natural performance enhancing weight control dietary supplements"[17]

- "legislation that would prohibit religious organizations that accept federal funds from discriminating in hiring and delivery of services on the basis of . . . sexual orientation, gender identification, or HIV status"[18]

On the other hand, the NEA opposes

- "efforts to legislate English as the official language"[19]

- "tax deductions to businesses for donations of computers to schools unless the computers are designated solely for classroom use, and software and training for users are provided"[20]

- standardized testing in "determining a student's future or as an indicator of school success," or "to make significant decisions about schools, teachers, or children"[21]

- "expenditure of funds on development of nuclear attack 'evacuation' plans"[22]

- "the privatization of public services and public sector jobs customarily provided in the public sector"[23]

- "tuition tax credits for elementary or secondary schools; the use of vouchers or certificates in education; federally mandated parental option or 'choice' in education programs"[24]

- "providing additional compensation to attract and retain education employees in hard-to-recruit positions," or providing "merit pay or any other system of compensation based on an evaluation of an education employee's performance"[25]

- "unreasonable constraints on foreign students and their dependents in the name of national security"[26]

- "governmental intrusion or monitoring of library materials and bookstore records"[27]

Worse, the teachers' unions often use the power of the bully pulpit to promote their far-left political agenda in the classroom. For example, the teaching guides that the NEA distributed nationally on the first anniversary of the September 11, 2001, terrorist attacks actually encouraged teachers to "discuss historical instances of American intolerance"—yes, *American* intolerance. Among the "obvious examples" of such intolerance were the "internment of Japanese Americans after Pearl Harbor and the backlash against Arab Americans during the Gulf War."[28]

The teachers' unions present perhaps the most dramatic example of how Big Labor has given itself over completely to a leftist political agenda. By co-opting the Democratic Party, the powerful teachers' unions have been able to secure practically whatever they want, no matter whether what they want is in the interests of American students.

Like most unions, teachers' unions protect mediocrity and the status quo. They oppose merit as a criterion for reward, proclaim competition to be unfair, believe it more important to foster "self-esteem" than good performance, and take it as a given that government schools must protect children from the wrongheadedness of their parents.

The NEA is totally devoted to escaping any consequence for the failure of the educational system it helped devise, and it opposes any notion of competition or market forces. The American Federation of Teachers (AFT), the NEA's smaller rival, traditionally has been more supportive of education reform and tougher standards for teachers and students, but since 1997, when the AFT's longtime president Albert Shanker—a true education visionary—died, the AFT has become nearly indistinguishable in its policies from the NEA. The unions don't believe that schools or teachers should face any consequences if they do their jobs poorly. Unfortunately, students, their parents, and taxpayers don't get off so easily.

FROM EDUCATION GROUP TO UNION

Since the advent of radical teacher unionism in the schools—which goes back to 1961, the year the United Federation of Teachers won the right to represent New York City's 33,000 teachers in the first major election in the nation in which teachers chose to be represented by a union in barganing with a school board[29]—the quality of education in the United States has fallen dramatically. *U.S. News & World Report* described the consequences in a cover story in 1996: "By embracing old-style industrial-labor tactics, the unionism of traditional auto plants and steel mills, the AFT and the NEA have given teaching the feel of classic blue-collar work, where winning workers big checks for the shortest possible hours has been the aim and the quality of the product is considered to be management's worry."[30]

For its first hundred years of existence, the NEA was not a union but rather an innocuous professional association, controlled by and made up mostly of school administrators. But the 1960s brought a challenge from the smaller, more militant AFT, which pushed the NEA to become more confrontational or risk losing members to its rival. At first, the NEA said that it supported "professional negotiations" on behalf of its teacher-members, but then quickly gave up the façade that such negotiations were any different from collective bargaining. By the 1970s, the NEA had kicked out its administrator-members and adopted policies sanctioning strikes, and the Internal Revenue Service (IRS) had officially designated it as a union.[31]

The rise of this giant union took an enormous toll on educational quality. While the unions claimed that everything they did—from insisting on salary increases to demanding smaller class size—would improve education, in fact most of the changes in education brought about by the unions have either had negligible impact or actually harmed educational achievement for America's students.

LOTS OF MONEY, NO RESULTS

In the past four decades the teachers' unions have been very successful in persuading Americans that schools need more money; that teachers are underpaid and deserve higher salaries and better benefits; that classes must be smaller if children are to learn, which of course means hiring more teachers; and that the surest way to improve the curriculum is to give teachers more say in its development. Yet most of these shibboleths of the teachers' unions are demonstrably untrue.

Clearly, the unions have been very effective at achieving their goals of more money for education—a lot more. In the 1961–62 school year, at the advent of teacher unionism, the U.S. per-pupil expenditure for public elementary and secondary school students was $3,066 (in constant 2002 dollars); that figure has more than tripled since then, to $9,354 in 2002.[32] In the last four years of Bill Clinton's administration alone, annual discretionary spending for the U.S. Department of Education rose more than 50 percent, all the way to $35.6 billion.[33]

The unions have also succeeded in getting school districts to hire more teachers. In 1960, public schools had on average one teacher for every 25.8 students; by 2001 the ratio had dropped to one teacher for every 15.9 pupils.[34] But even those figures do not accurately convey how successful the teachers' unions have been at flooding the school system with new employees (including when student enrollment was actually declining in the 1970s and 1980s).[35] Indeed, teachers are not the only union members to work in the schools; other school personnel include teachers' aides, counselors, school nurses, and support staff—most of them unionized employees. When all school personnel are considered, the student-to-staff ratio has declined even more dramatically. In 1960, the public schools had one employee for every 16.8 students; by 2000, that ratio had fallen to one staffer for every 8.2 pupils.[36]

Not only have the unions been able to get jobs for many more teachers—the number of teachers increased 112 percent between 1960 and 2002—they have also greatly improved teachers' pay. In constant dollars, teachers' salaries grew by almost 50 percent between 1960 and 2002; by 2002 the average teacher was making $44,642 for just nine months of work.[37] Overall, from 1960 to 2002 the amount of money going into public education on a per-pupil basis increased by more than *300 percent*.[38]

So if the teachers' unions were so successful at getting more money for education, reducing class size, hiring more teachers and teachers' aides, and paying school employees more handsomely, surely all this would have brought significant gains in academic achievement, right?

Wrong. The National Assessment of Educational Progress (NAEP) has been charting the educational achievement of U.S. students since 1969, and the results are fairly dismal. According to the NAEP, reading scores have barely increased in the past three decades.[39] In 1971, the average reading score for seventeen-year-olds was 285.2 (on a scale of 0–500, in which a score of 302 indicates proficiency in the subject);[40] by

1999, that number had risen to 287.8—that is, the average score improved .09 percent—an almost infinitesimal change, considering the billions of dollars poured into the public schools. And math scores haven't gone up much faster. In 1978, the average score for seventeen-year-olds was 300.4 (on a 0–500 scale, in which a score of 366 is considered proficient); by 1999, it had gone up only to 308.2.[41]

The billions of dollars poured into education during the Clinton administration didn't necessarily translate into better schooling, certainly not for the most disadvantaged students in the nation. In 2000, the NAEP's reading test for fourth-graders revealed that 63 percent of African-Americans, 58 percent of Hispanics, and 60 percent of children in poverty were basically illiterate.[42] Perhaps even more telling, the gap between average reading scores for white students, on the one hand, and blacks and Latinos on the other actually grew during the 1990s, after having narrowed during the previous decade. Only after President George W. Bush took office did these racial gaps begin to narrow again.

In his excellent book on the teachers' unions, Peter Brimelow shows just what unionization has wrought in the schools. He cites research showing that "in any given year, unionization raised inflation-adjusted per-pupil spending by 12.3 percent compared with nonunion districts and also—intriguingly—that unionization increased dropout rates by some 2.3 percentage points."[43] In other words, the only thing taxpayers have gotten for the extra billions we've poured into education is more unionized employees.

Still, the teachers' unions insist that they are serving America's children. In fact, in 1999 Bob Chase trumpeted what the NEA had achieved when he said, "For Congress, we supported pro–public education stalwarts in the Democratic Party—the folks who have helped Bill Clinton become the best 'education president' in history."[44]

Chase's claim that Bill Clinton was the best education president in history is laughable, as the dismal academic results from 1999 and 2000 reveal.

FAT CATS AND DEEP POCKETS

In school districts that maintain exclusive bargaining agreements with unions—only nine states prohibit collective bargaining in public education[45]—those who work in the public schools must pay union dues (or a portion of them), which fills the coffers of the NEA, the AFT, and their state and local affiliates. In the 2001–2 fiscal year, the NEA's total revenue was $348,717,566[46] and the AFT's was $133,656,427[47]—for a total of nearly half a billion dollars in just one year. It's nearly impossible to know how much money flows into the coffers of state and local affiliates, since federal law does not require many of these affiliates to report expenses, staff salaries, and so forth.[48]

So where does this money go? A good chunk of it goes to pay union officials' fat salaries.

In 2000, the last year for which the IRS has publicly available records, the AFT paid its president, Sandra Feldman, a whopping $354,105. But that wasn't all that this former New York City school-teacher—now the most powerful woman in the labor movement—received from the union. She also got a $74,870 contribution to her employee benefit plan, and an incredibly generous $96,760 expense account—a total package amounting to $525,735, or approximately twelve times the average teacher's salary. And Feldman wasn't the only official in the AFT earning such hefty compensation. The secretary-treasurer of the union earned a total package worth $313,172, and the executive vice president earned $273,554.[49] That's more than $1.1 million for just three employees. The NEA is also very generous to its top employees. During the 2001–2 fiscal year, Bob Chase, then president of the NEA, received total compensation amounting to $348,849. Reg Weaver, the union's vice president (and currently its president) received $387,526, and Dennis Roekel, vice president, received $351,226.[50]

The AFT and the NEA have hundreds of other employees who earn six-figure incomes in addition to their extremely generous benefits. And state affiliates have similar salaries and benefits, as education expert Myron Lieberman has documented. The Indiana state NEA affiliate, for example, gave the directors of its political operation, known as UniServ, sixty days' leave a year and a benefits package that would be the dream of most employees—generous employer pension contributions, deferred compensation, liability insurance, long-term disability coverage, life insurance, and severance pay, plus health, visual, and dental coverage.[51]

These rich salaries and benefits wouldn't be anyone's concern except that they are indirectly paid by taxpayers. These unions can afford to compensate their officials and employees so well only because they have the power to coerce teachers and other education employees to pay union dues or, in the case of the nineteen states that allow them, agency fees. These dues amount to a tax that the unions levy on their members. And even if union leaders succeed in securing more money for teachers' salaries—which they so often do, because they control the school boards and local elected officials with whom they bargain—the union can "tax" that increase by requiring higher dues.

The unions' dues or agency fees, by the way, are taken directly out of teachers' paychecks by most school districts, which don't even charge the unions a fee for being their collection agency.[52]

Meanwhile, many of our children suffer in drug-infested, dangerous, mind-numbing government schools, held prisoner there by politicians who have struck a corrupt bargain with old-time, back-room–dealing, coercive labor bosses.

SEIZING POLITICAL POWER

Teachers' unions are engaged in a cycle of corruption. The unions maintain monopoly power over government schools by controlling the Democratic Party, which protects them at all costs. They are able to control Democrats because of the huge political war chest funded by the forced dues of their members, most of whom would not support the NEA's political machine (or that of the AFT) if they had a free choice. In return for their support, Democrats make sure that the NEA and the AFT never lose the power to force their members to pay dues against their will.

The NEA's Bob Chase summed it up perfectly: In a keynote address to the NEA Representative Assembly in 2000, he said, "Today, too many politicians are on the side of the biggest checkbook."[53] Of course he's right, but it's not as if the NEA is an innocent party in this devil's compact. The NEA has one of the biggest checkbooks in American politics. By July 2003, a full year before the 2004 presidential election, the NEA's PAC—cynically named the NEA Fund for Children and Public Education—had already collected nearly $2 million. In the 2000 election, the NEA's PAC spent almost $5.3 million.[54] Since 1989, the NEA's PAC has spent $22.3 million, and the AFT has spent another $17.8 million.[55] Indeed, of the Democrats' all-time top donors, the AFT ranks number seven while the NEA ranks number thirteen.[56] These figures do not even count the millions that the teachers' unions' state affiliates have raised for their own PACs. Peter Brimelow has estimated that state affiliates spent seven times as much as the NEA itself on political contributions in the 1992 election and that state (and even some local) PACs spent an additional $45 million in the 1999–2000 election cycle.[57]

The teachers' unions' strategy has hardly been secret. As far back as the 1970s, a top NEA official, then–executive director Terry Herndon, bluntly stated the teachers' unions' true priority: "The ultimate goal of the NEA is to tap the legal, political and economic powers of the U.S. Congress. We want leaders and staff with sufficient clout that they may roam the halls of Congress and collect votes to reorder the priorities of the United States of America."[58]

And who are the political leaders that the teachers' unions target? Democrats, of course. Of the more than $40 million that the NEA and AFT have spent since 1989, *98 percent* of contributions have gone to Democratic candidates.[59] Moreover, the teachers' unions have marshaled thousands of troops on behalf of liberal candidates and the Democratic Party.[60] In exchange for this overwhelming political support, of course, the Democratic Party makes sure that the demands of the teachers' unions are met. As we have seen, the contributions from these unions are so vital that they exercise extraordinary influence over the party's platform.

We've heard this quid pro quo described as politics as usual, and indeed it is—for Democrats. But the media—the same media that would almost certainly be in high dudgeon if they discovered that a single company or industry (say, Big Tobacco or Big Oil) had virtual veto power over Republican Party policy—are remarkably nonchalant about the incestuous relationship between the Democratic Party and the teachers' unions. While many different unions are part of the corrupt bargain with the Democrats, the NEA and AFT are particularly important to the Democrats' political fortunes and thus have extraordinary influence.

"It's fair to say the Democrats would be nowhere without them," says Larry J. Sabato, director of the Center for Governmental Studies at the University of Virginia. "In my view, the NEA and AFT are the most effective union players out there because they not only have the money and the muscle, they also have a positive public image from representing teachers that much of labor lacks."[61] Indeed, even though the teachers' unions make no secret of the fact that they are a major political power broker, they escape scrutiny at least in part because they capitalize on the image of their members: the humble, hardworking American teacher.

The NEA's big entry into national politics came in 1976, when the organization endorsed Jimmy Carter, giving him the boost he needed to win the Democratic nomination.[62] Carter repaid the union when he was elected by establishing the Department of Education, leading an NEA official to boast, "We're the only union with our own Cabinet department."[63]

Since then, the NEA has achieved even greater political influence. Before the 1992 election, Bill Clinton told the NEA screening committee, "If I become president, you'll be my partners. I won't forget who brought me to the White House."[64] The organization likes to trumpet its success by displaying in its national headquarters a framed quote from Senator Bob Graham, Democrat of Florida: "No presidential candidate who wants to win in November ignores the National Education Association anymore."[65]

The NEA has gained so much influence not only because of its money but also because of its massive army of professional political operatives, the UniServ division, which coordinates the union's political activity across the country. The NEA employs some 1,800 UniServ directors—meaning that the union's political staff is larger than those of the Democratic and Republican Parties combined.[66] And the NEA's political operatives are dedicated to the same political agenda as any other radical, left-wing group. In 1992, one of every eight delegates at the Democratic National Convention was a member of the NEA, and in the closing weeks of that campaign the union lent about one-fifth of its national headquarters staff to the Clinton-Gore team.[67] The NEA also played a major role in Al Gore's campaign for the presidency in 2000, sending more than 350 delegates to the Democratic National Convention that year.[68] The AFT, meanwhile, sent 152 delegates and alternates to the 2000 convention. Overall, as the AFT proudly pointed out, union members made up a third of all delegates to the 2000 Democratic National Convention and thus represented the largest voting bloc.[69] Make no mistake, though, the nation's largest union—the NEA—still wielded the most power.

KEEPING THE IRS AND TAXPAYERS IN THE DARK

Amazingly, while the teachers' unions pour millions into politics, they report nothing to the IRS on their political spending. Although federal law requires tax-exempt organizations to report all political expenditures over a hundred dollars, the NEA and the AFT have never reported a single dollar spent on political activity—nothing, zero, *nada*. Yet these unions spend millions during each election cycle and openly admit their political activity—indeed, they brag about their political might.

So why don't they report their political spending? It's simple. Any union dollars spent on political activity—other than those that the union's political action committee voluntarily collects, which are reported separately—are taxable, and at the highest rate no less. Which raises a question: Are the NEA and the AFT defrauding American taxpayers out of millions of dollars in taxes they should have paid?

That's exactly what the Landmark Legal Foundation tried to find out. In the summer of 2000, the conservative watchdog group filed complaints with the IRS alleging that the NEA owed millions in back taxes, not to mention penalties and interest.[70] In 2003, Landmark president Mark Levin told the *Washington Times* that the NEA national headquarters spends $47 million and the state affiliates another $43 million a year underwriting the activities of its cadre of 1,800 UniServ political operatives—figures that Landmark forced to be disclosed through its extensive court filings.[71] According to Levin, UniServ represents "the largest army of campaign workers that any organization has." NEA leaders, Levin said, were free to spend on politics if they chose to do so, but "they just have to pay taxes on it."[72] The NEA's first step would be to report its political spending to the IRS, something that other tax-exempt organizations—including some of the NEA's political foes—have certainly felt compelled to do. In 1996, for example, the U.S. Chamber of Commerce reported $14 million in political and lobbying expenses, while the National Association of Manufacturers reported $5.2 million.[73]

The Landmark Legal Foundation wasn't the only group upset about the NEA's apparent tax skulduggery. Two Republican members of Congress, Charlie Norwood of Georgia and John Culberson of Texas, sent letters to the IRS in 2002 asking for an investigation into the NEA's failure to report political activities on its annual return.[74] At this writing it is too soon to know what, if anything, will come of these investigations—which the IRS is forbidden by law from discussing. But similar efforts directed at conservative groups during the Clinton presidency cost those groups dearly.

For example, spurred on by complaints from the Democratic National Committee and the Virginia Democratic Party, the Federal Election Commission (FEC) filed suit against the Christian Coalition in 1996, alleging that the organization had illegally distributed voter guides and political flyers. In 1999, a federal judge dismissed most of the FEC's charges,[75] but with that victory came another setback for the Christian Coalition: the IRS denied it tax-exempt status, saying that the organization was a partisan political operation.[76] The coalition sued the IRS, claiming that the IRS willingly grants tax-exempt status to liberal groups—including the NEA, which directs virtually 100 percent of its political spending to Democrats. Eventually, the Christian Coalition got the IRS to recognize its tax-exempt status, but only after a hard fight.[77]

Even in the face of the evidence of its substantial political spending, the NEA has claimed it is as innocent as the driven snow. Kathleen P. Lyons, the NEA's chief spokeswoman, told the *Washington Times*, "To be sure, NEA uses general treasury funds to pay for political activity in the general sense of the term. But it does not, contrary to [the Landmark Legal Foundation's] assertions, use such funds to pay for the type of political activity expenditures that should be reported to the IRS under that designation."[78] And Robert H. Chanin, the NEA's general counsel, said, "So you tell me how I can possibly separate NEA's collective bargaining efforts from politics—you just can't. It's all politics."[79]

Interestingly, though, Chanin also complained that the NEA had "been singled out because of our political power and effectiveness at all levels, because we have the ability to help implement the type of liberal social and economic agenda that they [the Landmark Legal Foundation] find unacceptable."[80]

Lyons's and Chanin's claims make for an interesting juxtaposition. It seems we are supposed to accept simultaneously that (1) the NEA spends nothing on politics and that (2) it has gained enough "political power and effectiveness at all levels" to implement its "liberal social and economic agenda." It's amazing that a union could have so much political clout without spending a dime on politics.

FOLLOWING THE NEA MONEY TRAIL

In fact, the record indicates that the NEA is far more active politically than Kathleen Lyons would have us believe. According to the NEA's own documents—the documents that became part of the Landmark Legal Foundation's complaint against the union—as much as one-third of the organization's annual budget is spent on politics.[81] And that massive sum doesn't even include money the NEA's PAC gives directly to candidates or political spending the NEA hides in fuzzy categories like "member communication."

Much of this money goes to the NEA's political ground troops, the 1,800 UniServ directors, who are in every congressional district in the country. These 1,800 political organizers and lobbyists give the NEA a political network unmatched by any other organization or union. Working with the NEA's 16,000 local offices, these well-trained political professionals—schooled in such techniques as how to "confront right-wing campaign efforts"[82]—are crucial to Democratic campaign efforts in every precinct in America. Although it's difficult to determine exactly how much UniServ directors are paid, Peter Brimelow estimates that the average salary and benefits of professional staff at the NEA's headquarters in 2002 came to $130,357.[83]

The UniServ directors are specifically responsible for "managing all political activities" within their area.[84] That involves a broad range of duties and activities, but the goal is usually the same: to help Democratic candidates. For example, according to the NEA's own documents, the UniServ operatives raise funds for the NEA's PAC, manage NEA delegates to the Democratic National Convention, and lend support to NEA-endorsed candidates.[85] They also coordinate lobbying efforts, and here, as in so many other spheres, the teachers' unions don't show much concern for the greater good. For instance, in 1992 UniServ and the NEA steered the Fairfax County, Virginia, school system into choosing Prudential as its insurance carrier even though Prudential's coverage cost as much as $2.1 million more than Blue Cross's would have and was, according to some observers, actually inferior to Blue Cross's coverage. Was it just coincidence that Prudential had contributed $300,000 to the NEA's National Foundation for the Improvement of Education?[86]

UniServ also helps the NEA disguise its political spending. As a 2002 study by the Heritage Foundation revealed, PAC expenditures in the states are tiny compared with the dues-funded political spending by the NEA's state chapters. For the twenty-four NEA state chapters that Heritage examined (the only states that responded with information), the average annual UniServ expenditure exceeded $600,000, whereas the average PAC expenditure in these states was only about $18,000.[87]

That's just the tip of the iceberg, though. According to the NEA documents filed with the IRS, the 1996–97 NEA budget allocated $9.6 million to pay a full 10 percent of the union's employees to build a "broad-based" political network.[88] As Mark Levin of the Landmark Legal Foundation revealed in testimony before Congress in 2002, the 1998–99 NEA Interim Financial Statements showed that through

April 30, 1999, the NEA had spent $3,026,212 for "political advocacy support" and had budgeted an additional $2,033,650 for the remaining four months of the fiscal year.[89] And the NEA's 1998–2000 Strategic Plan and Budget provided $386,000 for "organizational partnerships with political parties, campaign committees, and political organizations" and $540,000 to devise a "national political strategy . . . to address issues such as congressional legislative reapportionment and redistricting, campaign finance reform, candidate recruitment, independent expenditures, early voting, and vote by mail programs."

That NEA 1998–2000 budget also revealed that $350,000 went toward "cyberspace advocacy systems." Indeed, the websites of the NEA and its state affiliates are covered with political messages. The Internet is another means by which the union can communicate its positions on issues and candidates to the broader public, though the NEA pretends to be passing on its political endorsements to union members only, calling such advocacy "member communication." The reason for the pretense is simple: Federal law allows unions and other membership organizations to communicate their positions to their own members without considering these expenditures to be contributions to a candidate, which are limited to $5,000 per candidate per election.

Other membership organizations go to great lengths to avoid partisan political advocacy—especially conservative groups that worry they might lose their tax exemption if they aren't scrupulous. For example, the National Rifle Association—liberals' favorite bogeyman—posts the following message on its website: "Unfortunately, election laws severely restrict the information we can make available to nonmembers, so we are unable to post our recommendations to the Web site."[90] The teachers' unions feel no such compunction, however, as a quick tour of their websites confirms. At the top of the NEA home page, the union's Legislative Action Center advises visitors to "urge Congress to vote no on vouchers" (which, as we will see, the teachers' unions have fought feverishly) and to support the Student Testing Fairness Act, which would dilute important reforms that hold schools accountable for actually teaching children.[91] And the AFT's website trumpets union president Sandra Feldman's slamming of "disastrous education cuts"—an amazing feat given the large increases in education spending at virtually all levels of government over the past several decades.[92]

All of this political advocacy is not, despite the NEA's claims about "member communication," meant primarily to encourage union members to become involved politically. The teachers' unions spend millions of dollars on politicking because they are reaching out to the American public, and the ability to do this without censure gives them incredible influence over the political process. They have been doing it for decades. In fact, when one of us worked for the AFT in the late 1970s and early 1980s, the union routinely flouted election laws by printing up hundreds of thousands of campaign brochures and delivering them to candidates and by providing get-out-the-vote telephone banks, which were used to call Democratic voter lists.[93]

In recent years, the teachers' unions have become even more focused on this sort of direct support for the Democratic Party and its candidates, as their well-trained and highly compensated union staff can become intimately involved in political campaigns. The NEA was extremely active in the Democratic Party's effort to reelect Bill Clinton, for example. In 1995–96, two NEA officers—Mary Elizabeth Teasley and John Pacheco—served on the Democrats' National Coordinated Campaign Steering Committee. According to the Democratic National Committee's general counsel, Teasley and Pacheco helped develop "the unified Democratic Party effort," meeting with officials of the Democratic Senatorial Campaign Committee, the Democratic Congressional Campaign Committee, the Democratic Legislative Campaign Committee, the Democratic Governors' Association, the Clinton-Gore campaign, the AFL-CIO, and the pro-abortion political advocacy group EMILY's List. While Teasley and Pacheco were helping organize President Clinton's reelection campaign, the NEA continued to pay their salaries from the general fund. Teasley made $113,264 annually, while Pacheco made $96,375; having the NEA pick up those hefty salaries was certainly a benefit to the Democrats, for funds are precious in any political campaign.[94]

But again, the NEA reports none of this as political spending to the IRS, and thus it does not pay taxes on these expenditures. And NEA officials follow the party line. Teasley, the political director whose six-figure salary was paid from members' dues, told the *Wall Street Journal* in 2001 that "every dime" the NEA had contributed to political campaigns had been given through the NEA's PAC.[95] Direct contributions may have come through the PAC—as federal law requires for federal elections and as state laws mandate for most state and local elections—but tens of millions of dollars more have come out of the general fund each year.

MANNING THE BARRICADES FOR THE UNION POLITICAL REVOLUTION

Perhaps the most important under-the-table political contribution the teachers' unions make is providing the political shock troops for liberal candidates. Since the NEA and the AFT routinely assign staff to work for Democratic candidates at all levels, it's not at all surprising that two high-level NEA officials were actively involved in Bill Clinton's reelection—and remained on the union payroll throughout the campaign. These staffers are allowed to remain on the union payroll—a huge benefit to campaigns, which are inevitably strapped for cash—as long as they communicate only with union-member households. But with no one watching to ensure compliance, the unions' political operatives often ignore these rules, in some cases actually helping run candidates' entire campaigns.

For instance, in 2002, the NEA's Florida affiliate, the Florida Education Association, supplied Democratic gubernatorial candidate Bill McBride with his campaign manager and a spokesman, the two most important positions in any campaign. Not only was the Florida Education Association willing to lend two of its key officials (its director of government relations and its communications director), but it also agreed to continue paying their salaries.[96] And the union's involvement didn't stop there. The *Fort Lauderdale Sun-Sentinel* reported that the Florida Education Association "invested no less than $1.5 million of member dues into a monthlong TV campaign in McBride's behalf" and sent into the campaign "union workers [who] served as 'liaisons' between local teachers and [McBride's] campaign."[97] In addition, the union reportedly staffed a phone bank operation in that campaign.

Surprisingly, the government actually took notice of this overwhelming union involvement. In June 2003, the Florida Elections Commission voted six to three, with four Republicans recusing themselves from the case, that enough evidence existed to show that the union and McBride had violated state laws. The case was referred to an administrative law judge, who, in February 2004, rejected an attempt to have the case thrown out. As of this writing the case was still pending, complicated by charges and countercharges of partisanship among the parties deciding the case.[98]

Unfortunately, campaign activities by teachers' union personnel have become so routine that in most cases the unions can proceed without worrying about government investigation or even about drawing the attention of journalists. Thus, the teachers' unions can be remarkably effective at achieving their political objectives. These unions get particularly exercised about anything that promotes school choice, such as vouchers or tuition tax credits. The reason is that if all parents—not just wealthy ones—could choose which schools their children attended, public school enrollment would drop and some unionized education employees might lose their jobs, which would mean that the unions would lose the all-important dues of these members.

So, for example, in 1993 the California Teachers Association (CTA) mobilized against a statewide initiative for a school voucher program, Proposition 174. First, the CTA tried to prevent the measure from even getting on the ballot a year earlier. The president of one of the two statewide firms that collect signatures from registered voters to qualify ballot initiatives alleges that he was offered $400,000 not to gather signatures. When that failed, the CTA organized a massive phone bank effort to defeat the initiative. In a hundred union locations around the state, union personnel and volunteer teachers made more than one million phone calls to California voters urging a "no" vote. These CTA operatives kept meticulous records on how voters responded to questions about Proposition 174, which allowed the CTA to make follow-up calls to those voters who indicated that they would vote against the voucher initiative. The union even made calls on Election Day to ensure the anti-174 voters made it to the polls. The CTA also targeted absentee voters, who usually cast their votes early. The CTA obtained lists of those voters who requested absentee ballots, sent them anti–Proposition 174 materials, and followed up with phone calls to see how these absentee voters intended to vote.[99] California's voters rejected Proposition 174.

REBELLION IN THE RANKS

As successful as the teachers' union leaders have become at achieving their political objectives, some union members have begun to rebel at the way their "representatives" spend their dues money on partisan political activity. In relentlessly pursuing their far-left agenda, the leaders of the teachers' unions have in many cases ignored the interests of the members they claim to represent. For instance, according to the NEA's own budget, in 2000 the organization spent a remarkable $218 million to defeat school voucher initiatives in Michigan, Arizona, and California.[100] At the very same time, however, an NEA internal poll showed that 61 percent of NEA members believed that it was "not very important" or "not at all important" for the union to take a stand on the school choice issue.[101] (That position on school choice isn't so surprising given the large number of union teachers who send their own children to private and parochial schools. Overall, the percentage of public school teachers who choose private schools for their own children is very close to the national average—12.1 percent versus 13.1 percent.[102] But in urban areas, where poor children would most benefit from voucher programs, a substantial percentage of public school teachers choose to send their children to private schools—for example, Boston, 44.6 percent; Cleveland, 39.7 percent; San Francisco, 36.7 percent; Chicago, 36.3 percent.[103])

That kind of spending without regard for members' interests prompted a small but determined group of NEA members to try to keep the union's political involvement in check. At the 2000 NEA Representative Assembly, the Educators for Life Caucus—a pro-life group that attends each NEA assembly—introduced an amendment that would have allowed NEA members to designate how the political portion of their dues was spent. According to a leader of this caucus, the NEA's ultraliberal political agenda meant that "dues are used for lobbying, amicus briefs and marches on behalf of issues that are morally repugnant to many members."[104] Certainly NEA leaders recognized the truth in that statement, for they knew that only 40 percent of NEA members characterize themselves as Democrats, according to the union's own polling.[105] But no doubt that is why NEA leaders opposed the amendment: If union members could determine how their dues were spent in the political arena, the NEA leadership would lose its financial clout with Democrats.

With NEA leaders opposing the proposed amendment, the measure was defeated in the Representative Assembly by a vote of 6,369 to 2,113. Fortunately for the NEA leadership, the Representative Assembly is made up of delegates who function more or less as employees of the union—their school districts give them paid time off for their union activities and provide them with stipends to attend the Representative Assembly. Thus, while that margin was seemingly decisive, by the standards of the Representative Assembly the protest vote was a strong one, reflecting serious discontent with the NEA leadership. Indeed, the assembly decides 90 percent of motions by simple voice vote; in 1999, in fact, only one vote in several hundred required a roll call.[106] As Peter Brimelow notes, in most cases the members back home cannot even tell how their individual representatives voted on a given measure, or even how state caucuses voted.[107]

The disconnect between the union leadership and rank-and-file members has also been reflected at the state level. In 1998, for example, the CTA's 660-member state council voted unanimously to oppose California's Proposition 226, which would have required unions to get annual written approval from their members before using union dues for political purposes. But as Brimelow reports, internal CTA polls at the time showed that more than 70 percent of union members actually favored the initiative. So the CTA leadership did what the teachers' unions do so effectively: it funded a major initiative to gain support for its position—though in this case it was an "internal campaign," designed to turn its own members around. The CTA spent $500,000 on this campaign, and it worked. Exit polls on Election Day showed that only 30 percent of union members had voted for the ballot initiative.[108]

THE UNIONS WIN BUT THE KIDS LOSE

The teachers' unions continually send the message that all those millions of dollars going almost exclusively to Democratic candidates aren't part of some power grab; it's all for the kids, they say. But the evidence clearly indicates that the teachers' unions and their Democratic allies are not serving the cause of education.

The teachers' unions have a standard response to any questions about the American education system, which, in essence, is this: "We just need to keep doing what we're doing—but spend more money doing it." Quite simply, the teachers' unions have one goal, and it is not to improve education; they are dedicated to maintaining the status quo at any cost—even if it means sacrificing the next generation. They achieve their goal by buying off the Democratic Party.

Once we understand what the unions' true priority is, we realize why someone like Bob Chase could praise Bill Clinton as the "best 'education president' in history": Clinton's contribution was not to educational excellence but to the teachers' unions themselves. A key reason Clinton is so esteemed in the eyes of the teachers' unions is that he funneled so much money into education without challenging the unions' methods or proposals. Moreover, as president he slashed an estimated 40 percent of the budget for the Office of Labor-Management Standards at the Department of Labor—the *only* government entity responsible for auditing the financial reports of labor unions. As a result, union audits decreased from a high of 1,583 in 1984 to a mere 238 in 2001,[109] and the teachers' unions could act with virtual impunity.

As the political power of the teachers' unions grows, they defend their position ever more tenaciously. In 2001, for example, they were able to force President Bush to abandon the most significant reform of his education proposal—a provision to allow vouchers in a handful of school districts that have repeatedly failed to meet standards. The teachers' unions' Democratic allies made it clear that they would rather kill Bush's entire education reform effort than let through even a modest voucher program for children attending the worst schools in America. The unions, once again, proved that their interests were in protecting union dues, not in helping children learn.

Teachers' union leaders were even more fierce in their opposition to school vouchers in Washington, D.C., which has, by almost every objective measure, one of the worst school systems in the country. Although D.C. schools have the highest per-student spending in the country—$13,355 in 2001–02, *70 percent higher* than the national average[110]—their dropout rate is a whopping 42 percent and their average SAT score is more than 220 points below the national average.

Congress first considered a D.C. voucher test program back in 1995, and union leaders fought it from the beginning, arguing that all Congress needed to do to improve the beleagured D.C. school system was to spend *more* money.[111] The unions' lobbying worked, as a reliable ally, Senator Ted Kennedy, led a filibuster to quash the 1995 proposal.

But the D.C. voucher proposals would not go away, meaning that the teachers' unions had to continue to fight. In 1997, a bipartisan group of senators introduced a voucher plan for the District's poorest students.[112] This time the Senate approved the bill, by voice vote late in 1997, but Bill Clinton, ever beholden to teachers' unions, vetoed it in May 1998.[113] Clearly the teachers' unions and their Democratic friends were not interested in what parents wanted. Three days after President Clinton vetoed the voucher plan, the *Washington Post* printed a poll of D.C. residents showing that 56 percent of District residents wanted school choice. Those who stood to benefit most from vouchers—that is, poor parents who could not afford to get their children out of the failing public schools—supported school choice even more strongly. According to the poll, 65 percent of African-Americans with incomes under $50,000 favored the plan.[114]

When the U.S. Supreme Court upheld the use of vouchers in Cleveland, Ohio, in 2002,[115] Congressman Dick Armey, Republican of Texas, and Senator Judd Gregg, Republican of New Hampshire, introduced another D.C. voucher proposal.[116] Again the teachers' union picked up the fight, and their old friend Ted Kennedy helped them out once more. The Massachusetts senator was vocal in his opposition to vouchers, and when the bill was referred to the Senate Committee on Health, Education, Labor, and Pensions, Kennedy, as the committee's ranking Democrat, was able to bog the bill down, effectively killing the measure.

As the next Congress took office in early 2003, President Bush stepped in and proposed a pilot D.C. voucher program. Senator Gregg and Congressman Jeff Flake introduced the legislation again. The measure passed the House by a single vote that summer, but in the Senate it faced yet another Ted Kennedy–led filibuster. Senators were able to get around Kennedy only when they attached the measure to the 2004 omnibus spending bill.

At last, nearly a decade after the first D.C. voucher program was introduced, the District of Columbia would get a test program for school vouchers.

But the teachers' unions and their Democratic partners did not give up even after the vouchers bill passed Congress. Senator Kennedy vowed to defund the program and send the federal money directly to the public schools. "Even after this vote, don't bank on vouchers coming to D.C.," he said.[117]

In addition to opposing school choice with all their might, the teachers' unions also oppose rigorous standards for assessing teachers. The No Child Left Behind Act, which President Bush signed into law in January 2002, requires that all teachers be "highly qualified" by the end of the 2005–06 school year. Being "highly qualified" entails being fully licensed or certified under state law, but in reality, such certification doesn't mean much.[118] In the District of Columbia, for example, teachers can acquire certification by scoring barely above the 20th percentile on the Praxis test, a truly abysmal standard. And, shocking as it is, for most other states that use this particular certification test—twenty-nine in all—the cut-off score for aspiring teachers is in the bottom third of the national range.[119]

Although the NEA claims it supports improving teacher quality, it vigorously fights efforts to ensure that those already in the classroom be tested. "Paper and pencil tests of current teachers are an ineffective means of evaluating current teachers," the NEA warned in an "Urgent Action Needed!" appeal it sent out on April 27, 2001, when Congress was negotiating provisions of the No Child Left Behind bill with the White House.[120] The unions don't just oppose testing teachers, though. They also have little use for standardized testing to gauge how much students are learning. Maybe the teachers' unions are worried that taxpayers who are footing the bill for ever-expanding education budgets will suddenly notice that they are not getting their money's worth. Or maybe the unions fear that federal money for failing local school districts will dry up when schools have to prove that students are actually learning something if they want to receive help from Uncle Sam. Whatever the reason, the 2001 NEA Representative Assembly passed the following resolution: "NEA supports legislation allowing parents to opt their children out of all mandated standardized tests, without penalties for students, parents, teachers, or schools."[121]

FORCING GOOD TEACHERS OUT OF THE CLASSROOM

Teachers' unions have used the forced dues generated by this system to buy an increasing amount of political power, but they have done little to improve life in the classroom for most teachers. Consequently, dedicated rank-and-file teachers across America must deal with bizarre policies and nonsensical administration that the teachers' unions and their friends in government have foisted on the schools. Even more disturbing, teachers' unions often resort to punishing successful teachers in order to protect their own power. Jaime Escalante of East Los Angeles isn't the only teacher to suffer union reprisals. Susan LaVine, a gifted teacher in Illinois, is another. Her last teacher evaluation stated, "I need an entirely new list of superlatives to express adequately my professional and personal opinion of her. She is an outstanding teacher. Her students love her and learn from her." Yet just a few months later, when she questioned the actions of the local NEA boss and refused to pay her dues, the union forced the school board to fire her for "deficient and unsatisfactory performances as a teacher."[122]

Or consider Charleen Sciambi, who taught for thirteen years in the Fremont, California, schools and was, according to the Foreign Language Teachers Association, the best foreign-language teacher in the state. When she objected to paying the union "fees" against her will, though, she was fired. She appealed and won reinstatement, but only on the condition that she pay union dues. Rather than violate her conscience, she resigned. In a letter to her students, she wrote, "My employer is confiscating my wages without my permission. This is the status of a slave. How can I return to you in September and teach you to stand tall as a free man or woman if I cannot?"[123] The local union president responded by calling her "a big hypocrite."[124]

Or what about the group of energetic young teachers in Mount Clemens, Michigan, who volunteered to take extra training in math in order to teach the demanding new curriculum at Martin Luther King Academy? The local teachers' union insisted that the school district would have to compensate the teachers for their time, but the school district didn't have the funds. Even though the young teachers were willing to take the math training without being paid, veteran union teachers objected, arguing that such unpaid training violated the union contract. So the training didn't take place, and both the kids and the teachers lost out.[125]

BEWARE OF NEA-LED EDUCATION "REFORM"

If the teachers' unions are so active in opposing education reforms like school choice and standardized testing, and are so insistent on punishing even successful teachers who challenge the unions' authority, just what sort of educational model do they have in mind? In general, the notion is to stay the course but to ensure that government provides more and more money. Sometimes, however, the teachers' unions propose grand visions of how to reform education—and inevitably the unions themselves are the centerpiece of these plans.

In 1997, for example, Bob Chase told an audience at the National Press Club that he had sought the NEA presidency "to make a difference for children . . . but on a larger scale: By re-creating—*by fundamentally re-creating*—NEA as *the* champion of quality teaching and quality public schools in the United States."[126] Chase promised, "Our new directions are clear: Putting issues of school quality front and center at the bargaining table, collaborating actively with management on an agenda of school reform, involving teachers and other school employees in organizing their schools for excellence."

Chase challenged his audience to "imagine a future where teachers—under their union contract—have responsibility for nearly three-quarters of a school system's budget," where teachers would "use that authority to cut class sizes and boost academic quality." (He did not specify how "academic quality" might be measured.) "Well," Chase bragged, "that future is now. I just described the work of our local union in New Albany, Indiana."

He continued, "Imagine a twenty-first-century school district where the teachers throw out the traditional contract entirely, and replace it with a joint labor-management 'constitution'—an agreement that allows teachers, in effect, to co-manage the school district. Utopian speculation? Hardly. Our affiliate in Glenview, Illinois, has been operating under such an agreement since 1989."

Chase was boasting, but these images ought to strike terror in the hearts of those truly interested in improving education. Such vague, misguided notions of "education reform" are exactly what we get from the union leaders who have so much control over America's schools.

THE REAL GOALS

For all its talk about "education reform," the NEA still seems far more interested in pursuing exotic issues not related to education. The new business items at the 2000 Representative Assembly included distributing gun-control petitions, calling for curtailment of beryllium emissions, denouncing anabolic steroid use, researching working conditions and human rights in overseas apparel manufacturing, and ending the atrocities in Sudan. And the 2001 Representative Assembly concerned itself with opposing the Bush administration's national missile defense system, with making plans to "disseminate information about stem cell research," and—certain that the 2000 presidential election had been "stolen" from Al Gore—with working "with state and local affiliates to ensure proper voting machine programs and practices have been installed and instituted in all fifty states."[127]

Meanwhile, NEA president Bob Chase was apparently convinced that the real threat to schoolchildren comes not from poorly trained teachers or watered-down standards and curriculum but from the Boy Scouts, a private organization that refuses to admit homosexuals (whose right to do so the U.S. Supreme Court has upheld). Chase wrote a letter to the Boy Scouts of America (BSA), stating, "NEA and its affiliates will work to insure that the public schools fully disassociate themselves from BSA and its message of exclusion and intolerance."[128]

Many of the issues the NEA deals with in its policy statements could have come directly from the Democratic Party platform, which is no accident. Ultimately, the NEA's interest is to represent the Democratic Party's view on policy matters, not to represent the interests of its own teacher-members.

Such broad policy statements on everything from beryllium emissions to stem-cell research are not common practice with other professional associations. The American Physical Therapist Association doesn't normally weigh in on bilingual education; nor does the American Chiropractic Association throw its two cents in on standardized testing; nor does the Financial Accounting Standards Board opine on beryllium emissions. Professional associations deal with issues affecting their profession. Labor unions, on the other hand, try to dictate the entire national agenda. The big difference is that professional associations operate with the voluntary contributions of their members, while unions use coerced dues. If an association that funds its operations from voluntary dues goes too far astray of its members' interests and wishes, its leaders get booted or members just quit paying dues and the group folds. But unions don't have to be concerned with pleasing their membership base, because federal and state laws give them the power to keep collecting money no matter what.

The teachers' unions can get away with ignoring their members' real interests—not to mention what's good for education—because their funding source can't be touched. As long as teachers' unions can collect hundreds of millions of dollars from teachers—whether the teachers want to pay or not—and use whatever portion of that money the unions choose to elect candidates and influence legislation at every level of government, genuine education reform has little chance of succeeding.

But in the American labor movement today, the concerns of the broader American public are at best incidental.

CHAPTER 6

Legalized Terrorism

The fire spread so quickly that the revelers had almost no time to react.

On New Year's Eve, 1986, the Dupont Plaza Hotel in San Juan, Puerto Rico, erupted in flames. In just minutes the conflagration moved from the Dupont's ballroom through the atrium and into the twenty-story hotel, making escape impossible for many guests. Ninety-seven people were killed—including eighty-six trapped in the second-floor casino—and 150 others were wounded. It was the second-worst hotel fire in U.S. history.

But this horrible tragedy could not be blamed on faulty wiring or a careless smoker. It was arson—an act of violence carried out by labor union activists.

The three men who later admitted to setting the fire were hotel employees and members of the Teamsters Union Local 901, which was in the midst of an acrimonious contract dispute with the Dupont Plaza management. Just minutes before the fire began, in fact, the Teamsters had voted to strike, and the arsonists started the fire in order to put pressure on the Dupont management, as they later told investigators.[1]

Most shocking was the evidence indicating that the arsonists were just part of a campaign of intimidation and violence. Indeed, in the days leading up to the strike deadline, three other fires had been set at the Dupont Plaza,[2] and hotel manager Brooke Thompson had received at least forty written threats, including one scrawled on the wall saying, "A fire for Thompson . . . Thompson is dead."[3] And when the Teamsters met in the hotel ballroom to vote on whether to strike, witnesses heard one union member say, "[The] hotel wants to screw us. We have to screw them by burning something . . . by set-ting . . . the hotel on fire. . . . I'm going to set a fire." As the final vote was taken, another witness heard a Teamster boldly proclaim, "There's going to be blood here today."[4] Officials of the Teamsters' local might have understood that these were not idle threats: the three men who set the deadly blaze had met with the Teamsters' secretary-treasurer just prior to attending that final meeting in the ballroom.[5]

Sadly, the Dupont Plaza hotel fire was not an isolated incidence of union violence. In fact, labor unions in the United States all too often resort to violence as a bargaining tool, coercing employers into giv-ing them whatever they want. Worse, the U.S. government lets it all happen. The three Dupont Plaza arsonists may have been convicted, but in general unions remain beyond the reach of federal law, even if they orchestrate, encourage, or order this type of violence during labor disputes. Former attorney general Edwin Meese sums up this shocking state of affairs: "A special license [has been] granted to labor unions and their officials to threaten and actually engage in vio-lence to achieve their ends."[6]

In other words, Big Labor is free to terrorize American citizens as long as it is pursuing its supposedly legitimate bargaining goals.

LABOR'S LOOPHOLE

Union violence has become a major problem in the United States. The National Institute for Labor Relations Research documented 2,193 incidents of union violence between 1991 and 2001, including numerous acts of attempted murder.[7] And these figures include only violent acts *reported in the media;* many acts of violence are not reported out of fear of reprisal. Despite the onslaught of union violence, however, law enforcement on all levels has done virtually nothing: out of these thousands of documented terrorist acts, only *ten* people were actually punished—for a shockingly low conviction rate of less than half of one percent. In short, union activists can commit violent acts with impunity.

How does Big Labor get away with this? How can its terrorist acts go unpunished?

The answer is that the government has created a loophole for the unions. The federal government first carved out an exemption for the unions some seventy years ago, with the Anti-Racketeering Act of 1934. The bill was designed to combat organized crime and specifically prohibited the use or threat of violence to force individuals to make payments to an organization against their will. But the American Federation of Labor (AFL), knowing that the unions used these mob tactics, prevailed on its allies in Congress to add this clause: "No court of the United States shall construe or apply any of the provisions of this act in such a manner as to impair, diminish or in any manner affect the rights of bona-fide labor organizations in *lawfully* carrying out the legitimate objects thereof, as such rights are expressed in existing statutes of the United States [emphasis ours]."

Congress had meant to protect only the unions' lawful actions from being prosecuted under the antiracketeering law. But the U.S. Supreme Court in 1942 came to the ludicrous conclusion, in *United States v. Local 807, International Brotherhood of Teamsters,* that if the desired end is lawful, any means to get to that end are protected from federal prosecution. The court found in favor of the Teamsters' Local 807 even though the union had orchestrated a campaign to extort money from nonunion truck drivers entering New York from New Jersey. Teamster members waylaid nonunion drivers and—using guns, beatings, or the threat of beatings—demanded the equivalent of what a Teamster driver would have earned for a day's work. Since the Teamsters' scheme doubled transportation costs, most trucking companies soon signed contracts with Local 807 to stop the coercion. In the world of organized crime, such a scheme would be called a protection racket, but apparently the Supreme Court thought the Teamsters were conducting a legitimate union activity, even if union members happened to be seeking their wages by beating the money out of nonunion drivers.[8]

In response to this outrageous decision, in 1946 Congress passed (over President Truman's veto) the Hobbs Act, an antiracketeering law specifically designed to punish union officials for using violence to extort money from employers. This law is clear:

> Whoever in any way or degree obstructs, delays, or affects commerce or the movement of any article or commodity in commerce, by robbery or extortion or attempts or conspires so to do, or commits or threatens physical violence to any person or property in furtherance of a plan or purpose to do anything in violation of this section shall be fined not more than $10,000 or imprisoned not more than twenty years, or both.[9]

The courts, though, continued in most cases to apply the *Local 807* decision, allowing unions to get away with strike-related violence, including arson and robbery.[10] Then, in the 1973 case of *United States v. Enmons,* the Supreme Court made it nearly impossible to hold union officials accountable for violent acts. The case involved a bitter strike by the International Brotherhood of Electrical Workers (IBEW) against the Gulf States Utility Company, during which, the court reported, union members committed these acts of violence: "firing highpowered rifles at three company transformers, draining the oil from a company transformer, and blowing up a transformer substation owned by the company."[11] The Hobbs Act had been designed specifically to remove the special power of unions to orchestrate such violence. Nevertheless, in *Enmons* a majority of the court said that the IBEW's acts of violence did not violate the Hobbs Act because they took place during a strike and were intended to achieve otherwise "legitimate union objectives"—namely, higher wages.[12] To justify this bizarre conclusion, the court seized on one word in the Hobbs Act's legal definition of extortion: "the obtaining of property . . . by *wrongful* use of actual or threatened force, violence or fear [emphasis ours]."[13] In other words, orchestrated terrorist acts, no matter how dastardly, couldn't be prosecuted under federal law as long as a union was seeking a "legitimate union objective." Again, the union's ends would justify its means.

Enmons was an astounding decision, for it gave labor unions license to threaten Americans or commit acts of violence without fear of federal prosecution. At the time, the Supreme Court rationalized that state and local laws were sufficient to prosecute the type of violent activities at issue in *Enmons,* but we know from more than thirty years of experience that that was not true. In fact, since the decision, at least fifteen states have enacted similar protection for terrorist union bosses so long as they commit their violent acts during the course of a strike.[14]

This is why literally hundreds of acts of union violence every year go unpunished. In 1997, Senate Judiciary Committee chairman Orrin Hatch rightly described the problem when he said that the United States needs to close "a loophole in an existing federal law that, as interpreted—or more accurately misinterpreted—by the Supreme Court in 1973, covers the violent conduct of everyone other than labor unions in this country."[15] As it stands, however, the loophole remains open, leaving all of us vulnerable to union thugs.

TERRORISM AS A BARGAINING TOOL

The unions' special license to commit violence has had deadly consequences. During strikes, unions often destroy company property, as the IBEW did in the *Enmons* case. But many unions have shown themselves willing to target innocent men and women in order to extort compliance during a strike.

Unions have shown themselves especially willing to engage in violence when employers hire replacement workers during a strike—even though an employer has every right to hire substitute workers, as the Supreme Court established in *NLRB v. Mackey Radio* in 1938.[16] As a result, workers who need to provide for their families during a strike are completely unprotected from acts of violent extortion by union terrorists.

This was something William Wonder, a nineteen-year veteran truck driver, learned the hard way. When the Teamsters Union went on strike against Overnite Transportation, a subsidiary of Union Pacific Corporation, in October 1999, Wonder—like nearly all of the company's 13,000 drivers—chose to continue working.[17] That December, as Wonder drove his truck along Interstate 240 near Memphis, a sniper fired several shots through his windshield, hitting the Overnite driver in the stomach. Wonder was able to call for help on his cell phone, which probably saved his life, but he sustained serious injuries nonetheless.[18] Overnite offered a $1 million reward for information leading to the arrest and conviction of the person or persons responsible for Wonder's shooting, but Teamsters president James Hoffa showed no such concern for the driver. Instead he tried to blame Overnite for the sniper attack, saying that the company "bears a heavy responsibility" for the shooting because, after all, the company could "end this strike at a moment's notice."[19] In other words, Overnite was responsible for a sniper shooting because it wouldn't cave in to union demands.

Over the course of the three-year strike against Overnite, Teamsters militants apparently committed dozens of violent acts. In the first year of the strike alone, the company had to spend more than $21 million in extra security and other measures to protect its nonstriking workers—who represented 95 percent of all Overnite's employees—and lost millions more because of disruptions in service and fears of violence.[20] Meanwhile, the Teamsters sought and received $500,000 from the AFL-CIO for their campaign of intimidation.[21] (As Congressman Charlie Norwood, Republican of Georgia, suggested when Hoffa testified before Congress in March 2000, many speculated that the Teamsters took this payment from the AFL-CIO "as some type of quid pro quo for refraining from naming Richard Trumka in any civil action."[22] Indeed, this payment is what prompted a *Wall Street Journal* editorial to say, "It looks like the fix is in on the Big Labor fraud scandal."[23])

In January 2000, fed up with the union's extortionist tactics, Overnite sued the president and executive board of the International Brotherhood of Teamsters for $5.2 million under the federal RICO (Racketeer Influenced Corrupt Organizations) law. Overnite alleged an extensive pattern of violence that included 57 separate acts of attempted murder and 131 acts of extortion.[24] A federal judge rejected the Teamsters' request to dismiss the suit, finding that 55 shootings and assaults aimed at nonstriking drivers were "related to attempted murder."[25] The judge stated, "Firing a gun at a truck driver on the highway may support the conclusion that the person doing the firing acted with an intent to kill. Similarly dropping a cinder block from an overpass while a truck is passing beneath at highway speed or throwing a brick or rock at a truck's windshield when it is traveling at highway speed may be found to constitute attempted murder."[26] The case was ultimately settled out of court, but the details remain sealed.[27] Nor, despite FBI and local police investigations, have charges been filed in the shooting of William Wonder.

Amazingly, when asked about violence during the Overnite strike, James Hoffa told a congressional subcommittee, "I can tell you that it is one of the most peaceful strikes that we have ever had. . . . As you know, we have even had Senator Bill Bradley on our picket line. We have had Vice President Al Gore on our picket line. I have been on our picket lines throughout the country. I have seen no violence."[28] In light of the evidence, Hoffa's defense speaks volumes about his own willingness—and even more disturbing, the willingness of Democratic politicians—to turn a blind eye toward union violence.

Of course, one might expect the president of the Teamsters Union to justify union violence. After all, the Teamsters have one of the bloodiest and dirtiest histories of any union, and the U.S. Department of Justice once described the union as a "wholly owned subsidiary of organized crime."[29] But the Teamsters are hardly the only union that has engaged in violence to extort compliance from employers. One of the most dramatic examples of union-orchestrated violence came during the five-month strike at the New York *Daily News* in 1990. This brutal campaign revealed how strikes are about much more than simply withholding union-member labor, and how just about anyone can be a victim of union violence. When conducting a strike, labor bosses aim to shut down the employer completely by cutting off access to replacement workers, vendors, suppliers, contractors, and customers, and the threat of violence or violence itself has become the unions' most effective weapon.

The *Daily News* employees went on strike not over wage issues but because management tried to introduce some cost-saving reforms into the antiquated system of producing the newspaper. The *Daily News* was a huge money-loser, largely because the paper's ten major unions called the shots. For example, the unions had succeeded in establishing a number of "no-show" jobs—in which individuals (typically union favorites) received wages even though they never actually showed up at work—and work rules that wreaked havoc with productivity. (One rule, for example, insisted that some advertising staffers could only *make* calls *to* clients, while others could only *take* calls *from* clients.)[30] If the *Daily News* didn't do something to stanch the flow of red ink, the paper would probably go out of business—and consequently *every* union member would lose his job. Nevertheless, the unions balked when *Daily News* publisher James Hoge tried to institute reforms to save the newspaper, especially allowing management the right to determine necessary staffing levels.

Simply by walking off the job, however, the employees did not cripple the *Daily News*. In fact, management was well prepared for the strike and was able to make the newspaper operate *more* efficiently once the strike began. The *Daily News* hired permanent replacement workers, and as the *New York Times* reported, "In the days after the strike began on Oct. 25, The *News*'s replacement team performed stunningly, producing a paper without missing a day of publication and getting it loaded onto trucks and on the streets of the city."[31] Replacement workers were, among other things, more diligent about replacing the printer rollers and cleaning the inkwells.[32]

What management was not prepared for was the violence that erupted as soon as the first workers—members of the Newspaper and Mail Deliverers Union of New York and Vicinity (NMDU), who delivered the newspapers to stands all over the city—walked off the job. On the first official night of the strike, hundreds of strikers threw rocks, bottles, and bricks at buses carrying replacement workers. At one *Daily News* plant, strikers chanting "scabs" smashed windows and windshields of buses that had just dropped off replacement workers. In Manhattan, a delivery truck burst into flames; the replacement driver barely escaped without serious injury. In Brooklyn, another driver didn't get off so lucky and ended up in the hospital. Still other strikers in Brooklyn attempted to overturn a bus—with the driver inside—but were thwarted when riot police showed up.[33]

When the *Daily News* put security guards on the trucks, the union began targeting newsstands, even though they weren't directly involved in the labor dispute. The union dispatched thugs to newsstands, which sold 80 percent of all *Daily News* copies. If they found the *Daily News* on sale, they warned the small businessmen about the flammability of their wooden stands. Union emissaries told one dealer that if he continued selling the paper, union militants would "pour gasoline on the newsstand, set the newsstand on fire, and burn him alive," the vendor's lawsuit later alleged. Strikers and union sympathizers grabbed and destroyed copies of the paper whenever it appeared on newsstands. One dealer told how six union terrorists "came and took all the *Daily News* and they made a fire outside. . . . I don't sell the *Daily News* because I have four kids and have to watch myself."[34] In his stunning exposé *Strike: The* Daily News *War and the Future of America*, Richard Vigilante reports that "in just five days, from October 27 to 31, nearly 100 newsdealers told either the *Daily News* or the police that they had been threatened or attacked by strikers, most of them apparently NMDU members."[35] Although union officials claimed that violence was rare, Vigilante notes that sworn testimony of newsdealers, press reports, and interviews with NMDU leaders themselves "suggest a much more systematic campaign."[36]

By the end of the first week of the strike, Vigilante reports, arsonists had completely destroyed eight *Daily News* trucks worth about $35,000 each and damaged sixty others. In addition, two carloads of strikers armed with baseball bats, guns, and other weapons waylaid a truck taking replacement workers to the *Daily News*. Vigilante describes the incident: "One man jumped from the Jeep and fired shots in the air; seven more men, their faces concealed by ski masks, jumped out of the van and started beating on the bus with baseball bats, then hopped back into the van. Both van and Jeep raced away across the bridge into Manhattan before police could arrive."[37]

Union terrorists taped a pipe bomb to the gas tank of a car belonging to a *Daily News* manager; thankfully no one was injured in the explosion. A similar attempt to blow up a bus that transported replacement workers failed when the pipe bomb was discovered before it exploded.[38]

Former *Daily News* columnist Mike McAlary, who went to work for the *New York Post* in the midst of the strike, wrote of one raid in his first *Post* column. Although the piece is strongly prostriker, his report of what took place is nonetheless chilling:

> A scout had walked into the room and whispered, "We're doing a thing in the Bronx tonight." . . . The cars began arriving at the Alexander's [Department Store] Plaza parking lot. . . . I couldn't help the drivers on the picket line. But now I was standing with them. . . . Fairness had just been written into the equation that is the *Daily News* labor war. . . . The drivers stood facing Story Avenue waiting for orders. . . . By 2 a.m., there were 21 cars in the lot. . . . And then the moment for action came. The drivers huddled around the man in the tam-o-shanter. . . . The target, the face under the tam-o-shanter explained, was a *Daily News* drop off point in the Hunts Point Market. . . . "I don't care what you do. But stop the truck. If you want to burn it, go ahead. But if you're going to burn it, remember what the firemen over in Brooklyn told us. Keep the truck doors open. That makes it burn faster." . . . The cars pulled out of the lot at around 2:30 a.m. heading for a confrontation at the Hunts Point Market. . . . The cars rolled into the market in single file. . . .
>
> The strikers parked their cars across the street from a fenced-in truck lot. I saw a couple of guys picking up rocks. In the boredom of waiting for war, they juggled them like oranges. The company's scout car, with two [security guards], rolled onto the street at around 3 a.m. The guards stopped, and seeing the strikers, screeched back up the block in reverse. The driver of the *Daily News* truck, having been warned of the strikers' force, turned around and headed back into the city.[39]

Bombings became common. On October 31, 1990, eleven union terrorists were arrested with homemade bombs. Advertisers in the *Daily News* received death threats. Another advertiser suffered $30,000 worth of vandalism.[40] But instead of provoking outrage from public officials, the union violence had no impact on Democratic support for the strikers. Mayor David Dinkins thwarted one *Daily News* attempt to keep up distribution when he forbade the paper from recruiting salesmen from homeless shelters; management had given copies of the *Daily News* to homeless men and women and allowed them to keep what they earned from sales. The Metropolitan Transit Authority refused to allow the paper to be sold in subway stations.

So what happened to the union leaders who were quite openly operating "war rooms" to plan their course of violent attack in the *Daily News* strike? Not much at all. Unionized police and court officers appeared slow to move against the striking unions for breaking the laws. As Richard Vigilante notes in his book, the New York Police Department chief of detectives, Joseph Borelli, maintained that there was no evidence "that the violence was directed or organized by union leaders," though "he did concede that the NYPD knew some of the attacks were mounted by the same people or the same cars." Borelli repeated his claim that the unions couldn't be linked to the violence when he testified before the New York State Assembly's labor committee, which was chaired by Democrat and union crony Frank Barbaro. He testified, "Each [act of violence] seems to have involved someone getting upset and doing what they did."[41]

But Vigilante was able to learn a great deal about the union's involvement simply by interviewing union members and officials, most of whom spoke on condition that they remain anonymous. He quotes one official telling him that the main operations center for planning attacks was a roofers' union hall in Brooklyn, just a few blocks from the *Daily News* plant:

> Teams were formed and guys had certain tasks to do. . . . They would do all kinds of things to the rag heads, you know the Muslims that sell papers. They would harass them something fierce. . . . If a guy would not stop selling the *News*, guys would visit him and they would say what could happen to him . . . and of course some buildings and stores got burned down completely. A lot of stuff happened. There were a lot of guys that were very good in the field.[42]

Yet the FBI, citing *Enmons*, refused to investigate. The district attorney in New York, Democrat Robert Morgenthau, also declined to undertake any investigation, despite significant damage to *Daily News* property as well as threats against and actual physical assaults on numerous individuals. Two years later, however, indictments were handed down against dozens of NMDU members and officials in a separate, non–strike-related racketeering investigation. Vigilante describes the apparent disconnect: "As one senior official within the district attorney's office told me, the imperative to appear neutral in a labor dispute overwhelmed any interest the office might have had in investigating whether the campaign against the dealers might be directed by the same mob-linked cadres that ran the NMDU's corrupt activities. 'We don't get involved in anything that will give inadvertent support to strikebreaking,' the source told me. But he also said that at the time the office did note 'overlaps' between NMDU members involved in racketeering activities and those involved in violence against replacements and newsstand operators."[43]

As for the police department, Deputy Inspector Dennis Cunningham, in charge of Major Cases for the NYPD, told Vigilante, "We don't investigate union activities. That comes under the category of political matters. It would be like investigating someone for political beliefs. We have to remain neutral."[44] Nor did any of New York's finest investigative reporters at the *Daily News*'s competitors—most of them members of the Newspaper Guild or other unions—think it was worth digging into the police department's failure to investigate union violence. Quite often the newspapers downplayed the violence and took the unions' side in the dispute.[45] The *New York Times* actually ran a headline questioning the *Daily News*'s complaints about the unions' campaign of terror: "Police Rebut *Daily News* on Violence."[46]

In a fitting irony, the strike ended when British billionaire Robert Maxwell bought the *Daily News* and immediately cut one-third of union jobs in order to make the newspaper financially viable. But the union had proven its point: it had brought the venerable newspaper to its knees and restricted, if only temporarily, the right of management to make decisions about staffing needs.[47]

What the *Daily News* strike proved is that union bosses will rationalize violence as a legitimate means to an end—and politicians will let them get away with it. Tellingly, the president of the AFL-CIO did not condemn the *Daily News* strikers and union goons who bashed in heads, set fires, and destroyed property. Quite the contrary. At a union rally held outside the *Daily News* during the strike, then–AFL-CIO president Lane Kirkland echoed Teamsters president James Hoffa talking about the violence committed during the Overnite strike: "The economic violence of stealing people's jobs—that's the root of anything that might be called violence," Kirkland told the cheering crowd.[48]

BLAMING THE VICTIM

According to Big Labor's logic, someone who "steals" a job by continuing to work during a strike is carrying out the only true violence. If we accept Lane Kirkland's twisted reasoning, then we would have to believe that Shucheng Huang was really responsible for all the intimidation she endured when the United Auto Workers (UAW) went on strike against Abex Friction Products, the plant where she worked in Winchester, Virginia. Huang, a Vietnamese immigrant who had come to America to escape tyranny, continued working during the strike in order to feed her four children. Are we to believe it was Huang's fault when someone posted her picture on Abex bulletin boards with the caption "WANTED: DEAD OR ALIVE"?[49] Was Huang to blame when someone put a severed cow's head on the hood of her car and smashed her windows? Was Huang responsible for the photo she received of the severed cow's head on her car, doctored to show her own severed head there instead? No, union militants did all this.

Union militants were also responsible for the intimidation and violence perpetrated during a labor dispute between the United Steelworkers of America and Ohio's AK Steel in 1999. Before AK Steel locked workers out, one union official warned a reporter that AK was "going to get somebody killed by not coming to the [bargaining] table."[50] In a new version of the "devil made me do it" refrain, union leaders were actually claiming that the employer would force them to kill. And they made sure they could follow through on their threats. Soon after bargaining talks broke off between AK Steel and the United Steelworkers, threatening posters appeared on company bulletin boards, inviting union members to "get a gas mask and we will see you at the picket line. Buy your guns and ammo, baseball bats and rocks," according to congressional testimony by David C. Horn, general counsel for AK Steel. Other posters advertised, "Wanted—good reliable small arms, unused explosives (C-4 preferred), names and addresses of all salary employees. Payback time!"[51] Horn testified that in the days that followed, an anonymous voice on the plant walkie-talkie system said that the plant manager should be shot, his wife raped, and his house burned down.

Sure enough, union members resorted to violence almost as soon as they were on the picket line. Union activists committed hundreds of acts of vandalism over the course of the lockout. When AK Steel learned that the union members were planning a violent rally for September 10, 1999, it contacted law enforcement officials but was informed that the law prohibited police from interceding.[52] The rally turned into a mob action, as hundreds of militants, many wearing masks, attacked security guards and replacement workers with rocks and bats. As the mob tried to force its way into the plant, eight of the guards and workers were beaten so badly that they had to be hospitalized. In a later report, a United Steelworkers official proudly proclaimed to a Cincinnati paper, "Yeah, we did send eight scabs and goons to the hospital."[53]

Two weeks later, plant officials discovered one-gallon explosive devices wrapped with nails. Faulty fuses were all that had kept them from exploding when lit. The terrorist threats continued: Picketers threatened guards, saying, "Is it worth it, coming out in a body bag?" A motel that housed replacement workers received a call saying, "You'd better be careful when you go home. We do not like scabs staying at your motel. Do you understand?" and "Scabs, scabs go boom, boom." A restaurant at which replacement workers ate received a bomb threat, as did the plant itself. The bomb-threat call to the plant was traced back to a union terrorist.[54]

A plant employee entered his yard to find a severed pig's head. Another worker opened a letter to find this lovely thought: "Remember, you are only protected 12 hours a day. The only good scab is a dead scab. Get the message?" Union members again threatened guards, saying, "Day is coming boys. We got your names and addresses. We'll get your wife and kid. Them f—ers, too, we'll get them when we get back in."[55]

November 10 brought another bomb threat, and this call was traced back to the union. On November 11, two pipe bombs were tossed into the plant; only one exploded, and fortunately no one was injured.[56]

On December 2, a trucking firm that hauled material for AK Steel received a threatening call warning it to stop doing so. On December 4, someone fired four shots into the trucking office, barely missing the owner and causing a fire.[57] On December 6, 9, and 11, pipe bombs exploded in the mailboxes of workers who did not join the strike. Also on December 11, a bomb placed on a semitrailer truck's fuel tank went off, injuring the woman inside the cab; the owner of the truck had earlier hauled material to AK Steel.[58]

Union goons made numerous other threats, scratching the words "Die Scab" on the cars of nonstriking employees. But the worst incident was narrowly averted when federal authorities arrested a UAW member who reportedly wanted to show his support for the Steelworkers strike by firing homemade rockets into the AK Steel plant.[59] According to the affidavit filed against the UAW member, the man had already distilled propulsion fuel and test-fired his rockets. His goal, it seems, was to put the "scabs" out of work—permanently. Apparently he was not concerned that the rockets probably would have also killed picketing union members; he referred to the possibility of dead United Steelworkers members as "collateral damage."[60]

But it isn't just delusional fanatics who will sacrifice the well-being of workers, including union members. For many union officials the end—increased union power—always justifies the means, whether on strike or at the bargaining table. That's why one of the most common "negotiating tactics" of union bosses is to give up wage and benefit increases in exchange for "union security clauses," which guarantee them the ability to force all workers into paying dues. Again, we see union bosses less interested in the welfare of their members than in their own power.

WORKING WITHOUT UNION PERMISSION: A CAPITAL CRIME

Even while union violence has terrorized American citizens, government officials have continued to resist interfering in what they see as union business. The specious reasoning that the Supreme Court employed in the 1973 *Enmons* decision has been expanded to mind-boggling extremes. For instance, the Amalgamated Council of Greyhound Local Unions called a strike in 1990 and the Greyhound bus line began using replacement drivers, which of course was quite legal. During the strike, snipers shot at the replacement drivers fifty-two times.[61] Greyhound filed a complaint with the National Labor Relations Board (NLRB), the government agency charged with enforcing labor law. The NLRB, which is consistently staffed with union sympathizers, ruled that "although the Union's conduct . . . was substantial and widespread," the sniping did not violate federal labor law because—pay attention, now—it wasn't "aimed directly at employer bargaining representatives."[62] This decision sent the message that as long as you're shooting only at replacement workers, the federal government will look the other way. Just try to avoid shooting the company bargainers, because murdering someone essential to negotiating the contract could be an unfair labor practice.

The *Enmons* decision has also led to a hands-off approach by state and local police. In 1984, for instance, West Virginia state troopers reportedly stood by and watched as striking union miners terrorized those who tried to enter the coal mine. The union miners lined the roads leading to the mine and waylaid coal trucks, pulling the drivers from the cabs and beating them. They also flipped over the cars of nonstriking workers while the drivers were still inside.[63]

West Virginia police also failed to take action during a 1993 United Mine Workers (UMW) strike. Local contractor Eddie York didn't work for the company being struck and didn't belong to the UMW, but a union terrorist apparently felt that York was committing a capital crime by crossing the picket line: York was shot and killed.[64] Four eyewitnesses were willing to testify against union activist Jerry Dale Lowe, but West Virginia authorities, apparently in thrall to Big Labor's political might, declined to press charges against Lowe.[65] Although federal law enforcement sought to right this injustice, it could not bring charges of murder, which is a state crime. Instead the federal government charged Lowe with with "incapacitating" a driver engaged in interstate commerce. Even in pursuing this lesser charge, federal prosecutors were careful not to bring the unions into the matter; U.S. Attorney John Parr said in his opening statement, "This is not a case against the UMW. It is not a case against the unions."[66] Later, however, civil cases were filed naming then–UMW president (and current AFL-CIO secretary-treasurer) Richard Trumka as complicit in York's death. The UMW settled out of court.

Nor were any charges filed against the people who shot Texas boiler worker Bill Hinote, who refused to join the Oil, Chemical, and Atomic Workers International Union in a strike. Hinote was shot five times but survived. While still in the hospital, according to Hinote, the chaplain of the union local wrote to the local newspaper, saying, "Lots of us wished we would have done it [shot Hinote] because of what he did by crossing [the picket line]."[67] It's nice to see what passes for a man of the cloth in Big Labor circles.

If even a chaplain considers crossing the picket line a crime punishable by shooting, it's no surprise that union leaders at the highest levels have taken this position. Charles Minton, who at one time ran for the presidency of the UMW, revealed how then–UMW president Tony Boyle had personally ordered him to kill two nonunion coal operators. Boyle promised to provide for Minton's family and provide legal aid if he was arrested. Minton openly stated that he had dynamited mine installations on order from UMW leaders, but in this case he refused the assignment.[68]

Union leaders can orchestrate substantial campaigns of harassment and intimidation against those who do not obey them, as Teamster member and UPS driver Rod Carter learned. When the Teamsters called their 1997 strike against UPS, Carter, a former football star for the 1987 University of Miami national championship team, felt he had to continue working to support his wife and two daughters. He nearly paid for that decision with his life. Carter received a threatening phone call after stating on the evening news that he did not support the strike. Phone records revealed that the threatening call was placed from the house of the Teamsters Local 769 president Anthony Cannestro, Sr.[69]

The threats were only the beginning, however. According to Carter:

Just after my truck left the UPS warehouse in Hialeah, Florida, my coworker and I stopped at a traffic light. A pickup pulled up next to us, and the guys inside started yelling and cursing. They called us "scabs" and threw a bottle at us, and then one of them yelled, "I'm gonna kill you, you f—ing nigger!" . . .

While we stopped at another red light, six men left their vehicle and surrounded my truck. One of them was brandishing an icepick and trying to puncture my tires.

My unlocked door was pulled open. Then I was jumped by six men, who beat me, kicked me, called me "nigger" repeatedly, and stabbed me five times with an ice pick.[70]

According to police reports, the assailants were six striking Teamsters, and all six were immediately bailed out by the union.[71] Sworn statements taken later revealed that in a meeting of the Teamsters membership, Cannestro and two other union officers had encouraged and sanctioned the use of "ambulatory pickets," in which Teamsters would stalk working drivers to harass and intimidate them. During this meeting, the union promised striking Teamsters that it would provide bail money and lawyers if they were arrested.[72] The Teamsters Union ended up paying damages and settling a suit filed by Carter, who received assistance from the National Right to Work Foundation.

While workers certainly have the right to withhold their labor if they believe wages or conditions to be unfair, that right doesn't extend to preventing those who are willing to work for those wages from accepting work. Yet union bosses consistently rationalize that any form of intimidation is fair play, from yelling racial epithets to murder. The reason they tolerate no dissent during strikes is that they cannot allow a company to operate profitably when a strike is on; even if they have to trample the rights of workers (whether their own members or others), union bosses will protect their own bargaining power. Former UAW secretary-treasurer Emil Mazey said simply, "No one has a right to scab, *despite the law* [emphasis ours]."[73]

POLITICS AS USUAL?

Union leaders also are not shy about using violence for political purposes. During the 1998 election, Teamsters from Local 115 in Philadelphia savagely beat Don Adams and his sister Teri Adams, two protesters demonstrating outside a Clinton fundraiser. At least a dozen Teamsters attacked the Clinton protesters allegedly at the direct order of union leader John Morris; in fact, various news cameras caught Morris himself participating in the attacks.[74]

But district attorney Lynne Abraham apparently didn't want to cross her political ally John Morris and chose to prosecute Don Adams rather than the Teamsters. Because of the news footage, Adams was quickly acquitted, but he was still forced to undergo the emotional and financial strain of defending himself from criminal charges.

A year later, John Morris found himself on the outs with the Teamsters International, and after forty-four years as the local's president he was removed from office. A Teamsters investigation revealed that Morris had routinely shaken down union members and had prepared for a "war" by stockpiling weapons (at union expense), including shotguns, stun guns, and combat fatigues, and purchased a building for use as "a sniper's or sharpshooter's nest."[75] When he passed away in 2002, one obituary described Morris's "44-year reign of industrial terror."[76]

Along with increased violence, the *Enmons* decision has increased organized crime's influence in the labor unions. The 1985 President's Commission on Organized Crime concluded an extensive examination of mob influence in unions by stating that *Enmons* created a "loophole that allows organized crime figures to obtain . . . personal gains through the extortion of employees" and that organized crime used unions to commit "violent acts against a nonunion business competitor . . . in the pursuit of a legitimate, *non-prosecutable* labor objective such as a union organizing effort, when the actual purpose was to eliminate unwanted business competition for the syndicate [emphasis ours]."[77]

During the commission's hearings, witnesses detailed organized crime's control of the Service Employees International Union (SEIU), the Teamsters, the Laborers International Union of North America, and the Associated Building Trades Council. Ken Eto, a mob gambling boss, agreed to testify only after the president of Laborers union Local 1, Vincent Solano, attempted to have him murdered.

Two members of Solano's group fired three bullets into the back of Eto's head, leaving him for dead. Miraculously, he survived, and after this failed hit he became an FBI informant. Eto testified that Mafia capos ran Laborers locals in Chicago.[78] He said that Solano used the Local 1 offices as headquarters for organized crime activities, running a wide-ranging empire of illegal gambling, extortion, and "adult" enterprises.[79]

Interestingly, the President's Commission on Organized Crime heard extensive testimony alleging criminal activity on the part of Laborers union official Arthur Coia, whose father was a convicted felon associated with the Patriarca crime family. Coia was first indicted for embezzlement in 1981 but was not prosecuted because the statute of limitations on his alleged crimes had expired. Despite what this federal commission heard reported about his criminal activities, Coia operated as a union official for many more years, and as we saw in Chapter 3, he held great influence. Once again it seemed the government was not much interested in investigating the labor unions.

Like so much else about the labor unions, federally legitimized union violence is a grave problem, but it's a problem that few in Congress are willing to address. The trouble, of course, is that politicians fear that Big Labor will target them in their next election. Until Congress acts to remove the loophole created by the *Enmons* decision,[80] unions will be free to encourage violence as a "legitimate" method to achieve their aims, and American citizens will be at risk.

CHAPTER 7

Money, Mansions, and Mobsters: Union Corruption

Big Labor's ability to force workers to pay union dues as a condition of employment is a problem not simply because the unions then use those forced dues to fund their left-wing political agenda. Just as troubling, these forced dues produce huge coffers of cash that have proven all too tempting to corrupt union leaders. A number of high-profile cases in recent years demonstrate that corrupt labor bosses betray the very members they claim to represent by lining their own pockets with stolen union funds.

Though union officials traditionally describe themselves as representatives of working men and women, they often operate their unions like fiefdoms over which they exert absolute control. Once elected, local union presidents rarely face tough competition, often keeping their jobs for life or until they move further up the union food chain. And their power is enormous. They can hire and fire at will, filling the union bureaucracy with cronies who will do their bidding. With little oversight or public scrutiny of what they do, they can pay themselves handsomely—with lavish perks to boot—even while their members may be going without pay raises or basic benefits. It's a system that invites corruption and can tempt even honest men and women into a life of skimming off the union treasury. Little wonder, then, that for decades mobsters have been keen on running unions.

CAPITAL CRIMES

One of the most shocking examples of union corruption was exposed in our nation's capital in December 2002, when the FBI raided the homes of several Washington Teachers Union officials and their friends and family. At the center of the case was Barbara Bullock, who had recently been forced to step down as president of the union and give up her position on the Executive Council of the American Federation of Teachers (AFT), the Washington Teachers Union's parent organization. Investigators unearthed a treasure trove of luxury items in the raid: a 288-piece set of Tiffany silverware; a $57,000 silver tea set; dozens of pieces of expensive Herend china and figurines; an assortment of purses from Fendi, Gucci, Louis Vuitton, Bally, and other pricey designers; scores of Bruno Magli and Salvatore Ferragamo shoes; boxes of St. John's knit suits, which usually retail for about $2,000 each; various mink coats and hats; assorted pearl necklaces; Chanel earrings, scarves, and brooches; a $13,000 plasma-screen television; assorted stereo equipment; and a double-barrel shotgun, among other items. Investigators estimated the loot to be worth at least $2 million.[1]

How had Bullock and her associates purchased so many expensive toys? After all, Bullock's generous $106,840 annual Washington Teachers Unon salary[2] couldn't even pay the bill at her Baltimore tailor's shop, where, authorities estimated she spent about $500,000 on stylish outfits over the years. According to tailor Myong Lim, Bullock's last check bounced, leaving the immigrant seamstress holding the bag for $80,000 in unpaid debts and forcing her to lay off workers and take out a loan.[3] Federal prosecutors charged that Bullock, her assistant Gwendolyn M. Hemphill, and several family members and

associates were involved in an elaborate scheme to embezzle an estimated $5 million from the Washington Teachers Union for their pri-
vate gain. The first persons to plead guilty in the case were Bullock's
hairdresser and chauffeur, who pled guilty to money laundering. The
chauffeur, incidentally, recieved $90,000 a year from the Washington
Teachers Union for driving Bullock[4]—nearly twice the average D.C.
teacher's annual salary.[5] Hemphill and the union's former treasurer,
James O. Baxter, were indicted in November 2003, but as of this writing have not been tried.

Bullock pled guilty to mail fraud, embezzlement, and tax evasion
on October 7, 2003, and was sentenced January 30, 2004. No longer the
flamboyant, couture-wearing D.C. power broker, the six-foot-three-
inch Bullock stood under the harsh glare of fluorescent lights in the
U.S. District courtroom awaiting Judge Richard J. Leon's pronounce-
ment.[6] U.S. Attorney Anthony Michael Alexis, Sr., told the judge that
Bullock didn't come from a poor background, but was a "highly educated woman who knew what she was doing." Alexis accused Bullock
of causing the union "to lose its soul" and charged that "children were
hurt and so was society." Bullock's lawyer, Stephen Robert Spivack,
could respond only that one of the contributing factors to Bullock's
crime spree—"not an excuse," he assured the court—was that she
suffered from type 2 bipolar disorder. When Bullock stood to make
her own statement, she explained that she was a "broken and remorse-
ful person." She told the court, "If I could have changed things, I
would. . . . But I would have to say that I didn't know how to stop it."[7]

But Judge Leon would have none of it. "This is a tragedy of self-
destruction, a tragedy of which you were the architect," the judge
said. "You so badly abused a vital institution in this city."[8] He sentenced Bullock to nine years in prison, noting that only her age—
sixty-five—kept him from rejecting the plea agreement altogether
and extending her jail time. He also ordered Bullock to spend three
years at a halfway house after she leaves prison and to perform three
thousand hours of community service "as a down payment toward
the incredible debt you owe this city and its teachers as a result of
your heinous, fraudulent acts." The judge ordered Bullock to pay
$4,662,924 restitution to the union, but acknowledged that she proba-
bly could not come up with the money.[9]

The $4.6 million was stolen from the pockets of the men and

women who teach school in the District of Columbia, money they are forced to pay as a condition of their employment. The Washington Teachers Union collected $643 per year from each of its 5,000 members—in total, more than $3.2 million a year.[10] But apparently even the union's plump treasury wasn't large enough to satisfy these corrupt union officials' appetites. According to the AFT's own internal investigation, the Washington Teachers Union overcharged its 5,000 members to the tune of $800,000—or nearly $160 per person—money that was then used to pay for the lavish lifestyle of Bullock and friends.[11]

The AFT ultimately blew the whistle on the Washington Teachers Union officials, but in fact it had for some time ignored key warning signs, including complaints from D.C. union members. Although the AFT's own constitution requires all its locals to submit audited financial statements every two years, the Washington Teachers Union had not done so since 1995, but still the AFT had not acted. It decided to probe further only when the Washington Teachers Union fell some $700,000 behind in the payments locals are required to make to the national office.[12] In other words, the national organization didn't seem to care that its Washington members were being cheated, but it sat up and took notice when its own trough ran low. Even then, though, the AFT waited six months to take over administration of the Washington Teachers Union, and when it did finally take over the local, it did not remove some officials who had been implicated in the mismanagement and misappropriation of funds. Some Washington Teachers Union members were so disgusted with the AFT's lack of proper oversight that they filed suit in federal court to appoint an independent monitor for the local union. In granting the request, U.S. District Judge Emmet G. Sullivan summarized the frustration of many teachers: "It seems everyone in a responsible position fell asleep at the switch. The only ones who were vigilant were the thieves, who took everything that wasn't nailed down."[13]

It seems that union dues bought more than extravagant luxury goods for a handful of corrupt officials, however. One of those indicted in the scandal, Gwendolyn M. Hemphill, served not only as Barbara Bullock's assistant at the Washington Teachers Union but also as executive director of the Democratic Party in Washington, D.C., and, in 2002, as cochair of Democratic mayor Anthony Williams's reelection committee. It was a setup all too common among union officials and Democratic politicians: Hemphill drew her full salary from the union even while she worked virtually full-time on the mayor's campaign. Hemphill even admitted to using union money to pay for thousands of dollars' worth of T-shirts given as gifts to delegates to the 2000 Democratic National Convention.[14] But as of this writing many other aspects of the Washington Teachers Union's support for the Democrats are under investigation. Investigators from the D.C. Office of Campaign Finance are examining whether union dues paid for parties for Williams and his staff. They are also investigating whether the mayor illegally accepted in-kind contributions from the Washington Teachers Union for his campaign without declaring them. In addition, investigators are looking into the Washington Teachers Union's use of its telephone banks—call centers set up at union headquarters to try to mobilize voters on Anthony Williams's behalf in the 1998 and 2002 elections.[15] As of this writing, no action has been taken. Although unions are allowed to call their members' homes to urge support of union-endorsed candidates, they often—illegally—make calls to general Democratic voter lists, something one of us regularly witnessed at the AFT headquarters while working for that teachers' union in the 1970s.

The evidence indicates that the Washington Teachers Union had plenty of influence in the District's Democratic administration, which is not surprising given the union's active role in getting Mayor Williams elected. According to a former official at the D.C. Office of Boards and Commissions, Hemphill routinely submitted names of people she wanted appointed to government boards, and the mayor obliged. Union president Barbara Bullock also lobbied the mayor's office to award a $300,000 contract to a firm run by a brother of the union's treasurer, James O. Baxter, now facing his own trial. And Baxter himself benefited. Between September 1997 and October 2000, Baxter earned $130,000 from his union treasurer post while he also worked full-time as director of the D.C. Office of Labor Relations and Collective Bargaining, earning another $96,000 per year.[16] It's hard to know which was worse, forcing D.C. teachers to pay a six-figure salary to a union official who worked full-time somewhere else or having taxpayers foot the bill for an employee who was really a union hack. Whichever, Washington Teachers Union officials apparently convinced Mayor Williams to ignore the impropriety of having someone concurrently on the union payroll while ostensibly managing the city's labor relations office. The *Washington Post* reported, "Baxter's dual roles were a concern for the Williams administration during the mayor's first year in office, according to several officials who said efforts to remove him were repeatedly stymied by the lobbying of then-union president Barbara A. Bullock and her assistant, Gwendolyn M. Hemphill."[17]

Washington Teachers Union officials' influence in the mayor's office was both extensive and routine, according to the *Washington Post:*

> Mark A. Jones, the mayor's former deputy chief of staff, said he witnessed several examples of Bullock and Hemphill exerting influence over personnel situations. Jones said the mayor told him to hire Hemphill's husband, Lawrence Hemphill, as director of the D.C. Office of the Public Advocate. On another occasion, the mayor mentioned Bullock and Hemphill as he told Jones to stop an employee from being fired, Jones said.[18]

Like many other Democratic officeholders, Mayor Williams no doubt felt he owed his job to the unions—and he wouldn't be wrong in that assumption.

Nor were local elected officials the only ones the Washington Teachers Union tried to influence. Bullock also contributed $9,000 to the Democratic National Committee and $2,000 to Hillary Clinton's 2000 New York Senate race—paid for with her union American Express card.[19] In January 2003, the *Washington Post* reported, vaguely, that "those funds have since been returned to the AFT,"[20] but one could conclude that Mrs. Clinton and the Democratic Party did not want to be tied publicly to a corrupt union. In any event, returning Bullock's contribution would not have been a hardship for Mrs. Clinton, who of course was flush with cash from her many other union supporters.

MIAMI VICE

Except for his full head of white hair, which is worn slicked back, pompadour-style, Pat Tornillo is a dead ringer for Uncle Junior, the Mafia elder statesman on HBO's popular series *The Sopranos*. And the similarity turns out to be more than skin-deep. Tornillo served as president of the AFT's Miami affiliate, United Teachers of Dade (UTD), from 1962 until 2003, when an FBI investigation into his alleged misuse of union money forced him to take a "leave of absence." Like the Washington Teachers Union's Barbara Bullock, Tornillo served as a vice president of the AFT, sitting on the organization's powerful Executive Council for more than twenty-two years, from 1981 to 2003. And like Bullock, Tornillo used his union's treasury to satisfy all his hedonistic desires—which ran less to Bullock's taste in Herend china and Tiffany tea sets and more to python-print pajamas and "sexual instruction" videos.

Tornillo's troubles began when the FBI raided the UTD offices on April 29, 2003. The raid came after a whistleblower reported that UTD officials were making extravagant purchases on the union dime.[21] As in the Washington Teachers Union scandal, UTD leaders seemingly decided that the forced dues of teachers were their own private honey pot, which they could dip into whenever the urge hit them.

Pat Tornillo's tenure at the UTD helm illustrates how the union system breeds corruption. Tornillo actually started off as a union reformer. In 1962, he ran for president of the Dade Classroom Teachers Association, the UTD's predecessor, promising to integrate the then all-white union with its black counterpart. He won the election, and the union became the first integrated teachers' local in the Deep South.[22] In 1968 he led the first—and only—statewide teachers' strike, forcing the courts to recognize public employees' collective-bargaining rights.[23] In 1974, he rammed through the state legislature a collective-bargaining bill for Florida public employees. In 2003, after the UTD scandal broke, a former general counsel for a statewide Florida teachers' union told the *Orlando Sentinel*, "It was through the force of Pat

Tornillo's personality . . . that public employees were able to coalesce and the collective-bargaining bill was passed. It was remarkable to watch."[24] But not as remarkable as the transformation that erstwhile reformer Pat Tornillo underwent.

The old saying that "power corrupts and absolute power corrupts absolutely" certainly seems to apply in the Tornillo scandal. The UTD was the largest labor union in the South, representing some 28,000 teachers and support staff in the nation's fourth-largest school district.[25] Then, in 2000, Tornillo achieved his longtime goal of merging the state's two rival teachers' unions into a single organization, the Florida Education Association. At least when two unions had vied for the same members, elected leaders had had to worry that their competitors might expose excesses if they paid themselves too well or dipped into the union treasury for personal luxuries. But that natural check on union leaders was removed once Tornillo co-opted the competition and merged the rivals into a single, all-powerful union.

Although Miami teachers, on average, earned only $39,275 a year in 2002,[26] Pat Tornillo earned $243,000 a year, including $42,700 for "union expenses."[27] And Tornillo wasn't alone in pulling in the big bucks; at least a dozen UTD staffers drew six-figure salaries in 2002–3,[28] and the union's total annual payroll amounted to more than $4 million.[29] Despite those handsome salaries, Tornillo and a handful of other union officials apparently thought they deserved even more. According to investigators, these officials set up a private, off-the-books slush fund—the "transition reserve fund"—that would pay them handsomely when they left the union for whatever reason, even if they lost a union election (a highly unlikely event). Under the scheme, Tornillo was due to receive at least $663,000 in supplemental cash payouts when he left, and former UTD president Murray Sisselman was due some $406,000[30]—all of which would have come from union dues that had been siphoned off into the account over many years.

The private slush fund swelled to $2.2 million,[31] but the money was never paid out—not because union officials suddenly developed guilty consciences about their secret retirement scheme but because Tornillo decided to raid the fund to cover up other problems he had helped create at the union. Tornillo's tiny stature belied a huge ego, inflated by the political power he wielded. He was already in his late seventies, and having built the UTD from the ground up, he wanted to leave behind something concrete that would mark his tenure. So he embarked on a costly venture to build a new union headquarters, which would be the envy of other public-employee unions and stand as a monument to his memory. The lavish, seven-story headquarters on posh Biscayne Boulevard in Miami, which opened in 2001, carries a mortgage of some $13 million but may have cost as much as $22 million to complete, according to some union insiders.[32] Cost overruns on the project drove Tornillo to empty out the private slush fund to pay for the building, which helped contribute to his eventual downfall.

With the fund depleted, Sisselman, who was seriously ill from cancer, feared that his heirs would not receive the nearly half million dollars from the fund that he wanted to leave them. In an extensive investigative report, *Miami Herald* reporters Joe Mozingo and Manny Garcia described what happened next:

> Murray Sisselman, 73 and dying of cancer, walked into the Rascal House deli near his home on Feb. 25 to meet with James Angleton Jr., the chief financial officer of the United Teachers of Dade. Sisselman, who served as UTD president for 27 years, wanted to come clean in his final days. He directed Angleton to a file cabinet packed with records showing that longtime union chief Pat Tornillo and his wife were apparently reimbursed for at least $155,000 in personal expenses in less than three years.[33]

The *Miami Herald* reported that Tornillo had submitted the following items to the union for reimbursement: $10,200 for a short stay in St. Bart's, which included airfare, hotels, meals, jewelry, and French perfume and cosmetics; $8,671.98 for a five-night stay at the Pierre Hotel in New York; $4,158 for clothing at Silvio Bresciani couture in New York; and $1,400 for a visit to the Silverado Resort in Napa Valley, California.[34] But this was just the tip of the iceberg.

During its exhaustive reporting on the case, the *Miami Herald* obtained twenty-one months of credit card records, which demonstrated a pattern of abuse by Tornillo and his wife that defies the imagination. Reporters Mozingo and Garcia offered a striking example of the corruption:

On the morning of Nov. 19, 2002, United Teachers of Dade President Pat Tornillo excoriated school leaders over low teacher salaries and demanded "a hunt for spare dollars that could go toward raises." But Tornillo himself wasn't so frugal. That night, he spent teachers union dues to stay in a $2,000-a-night suite at the Mandarin Oriental hotel at Brickell Key. Tornillo slept eight nights at the opulent hotel and charged it to a UTD credit card. Total cost: $20,138.53.[35]

Amazingly, the Mandarin Oriental was located just three hundred *yards* from Tornillo's condominium, paid for—you guessed it—by the good teachers of Dade County.[36]

Teachers also paid $49,715 for Tornillo and his wife to take a three-week excursion to California, Australia, and New Zealand in September 2000. The cost of the trip, the *Miami Herald* pointed out, was equivalent to the total annual salary of a Miami teacher with fifteen years' experience and a master's degree.[37] "In terms of the union, it cost the annual dues of 59 teachers," the *Herald* reported.[38] The next year, 2001, teachers paid for the Tornillos to tour Switzerland, India, Thailand, and Cambodia for two weeks, at a cost of at least $27,000.[39] Everywhere they went, the Tornillos traveled first-class, stayed in luxury hotels, and bought expensive gifts for themselves— all at union expense.

Five-star hotels and first-class travel were not all that the union paid for. The union also subsidized Tornillo's day-to-day living. In addition to paying the rent on Tornillo's apartment, the union owned the home in which he and his wife lived.[40] The UTD also paid his phone, electric, and cable bills, his home insurance, and his housekeeper, who earned $22,510 annually and received $1,800 a year for expenses.[41] Tornillo even used the union credit card to try to spice up his sex life, ordering python-print pajamas and a matching robe for himself and paying for several sessions at the Sinclair Intimacy Institute so that he and his wife could share "Better Relationships, Better Sex."[42] And this was all on top of Tornillo's $43,000 expense account, for which he didn't even need to submit receipts. How did Tornillo get away with such profligacy? According to union insider David Albaum, the UTD's former in-house financial consultant, the union paid Tornillo's expenses without question. The *Miami Herald* reported:

Albaum acknowledged that he approved many of the checks. He never confronted Tornillo and never told the executive board during its monthly meetings. His explanation: "Tornillo demeaned people. He'd tell them, 'Get outta here.' " Albaum said the board never questioned Tornillo either. In one financial report prepared for the board, Tornillo's spending is listed under a line item, "Community Affairs and Organizational Relations."[43]

Both Albaum and UTD chief financial officer James Angleton, Jr., were cooperating witnesses for the FBI in the investigation into corruption in the union.[44]

But even if the union was ignoring Tornillo's abuse of the union treasury, Tornillo's extravagant lifestyle and the cost overruns on the union's fancy new headquarters were crippling the UTD. The union was so broke that it had to take out loans to pay for normal expenses, and in the spring of 2003 the UTD reportedly even "borrowed" money from its own members—without their permission, unfortunately. Shortly after the FBI raided UTD headquarters in May 2003, the Public Employee Services Company (PESCO), a Tallahassee insurance company that provided supplemental insurance to UTD members, announced that the union was $300,000 in arrears in paying its members' premiums. The standard procedure was for the school district to deduct the premiums directly from union members' paychecks and turn the money over to the UTD, which was supposed to pay the premiums to PESCO. According to union insider Albaum, however, the cash-strapped union instead deposited the $300,000 from the school district directly into union accounts so it could pay staffers and its bills. As Albaum explained, "They were robbing Peter to pay Paul."[45]

In August 2003, federal prosecutors reached a plea agreement with Tornillo. The union boss pled guilty to one count of mail fraud and one count of tax evasion, admitting that he had siphoned funds from the union to pay for his luxurious lifestyle. In return, prosecutors sought only twenty-four to thirty months of prison time in a minimum-security facility.[46] At the press conference announcing the plea bargain, U.S. Attorney Marco Jimenez said that all agencies involved with the investigation, including the Miami-Dade police and the FBI, had agreed to the terms.

But the agreement quickly came under fire. Miami-Dade police director Carlos Alvarez denied that he had signed off on the plea bargain, telling reporters, "We were not in agreement."[47] Those most angry with federal prosecutors' kid-glove treatment of Tornillo were Miami-Dade teachers. More than eight hundred teachers wrote U.S. District Judge Adalberto Jordan asking him to reject the controversial deal, saying they wanted prosecutors to force Tornillo to testify about alleged backroom deals with politicians, lobbyists, and contractors. Prosecutors defended the plea agreement by saying that the seventy-eight-year-old Tornillo, who was in poor health, might not have lived through the long trial process. Even if he were convicted, they said, he could have died during the appeals process, and the conviction could have been tossed out, meaning that Tornillo's heirs would not be required to pay restitution to the union.[48]

On November 23, 2003, Judge Jordan sentenced Tornillo, who came into court attached to a portable oxygen tank, to twenty-seven months in prison, three months longer than prosecutors had recommended during the hearing. The judge also ordered the former union boss to repay the UTD $800,000, including $150,000 to help defray the legal and accounting bills his activities had cost the union. In addition, Tornillo had to pay $160,000 in federal back taxes, as well as an estimated $200,000 in interest and penalties.[49]

In an amazing display of chutzpah, Tornillo's attorney argued that the $1.02 million that prosecutors claimed Tornillo had misused represented just 1.2 percent of the $83.7 million in union dues collected during the ten-year period Tornillo was pilfering funds. In other words, the lawyer said, the money Tornillo stole represented less than $7.50 per member per year. But this ignored the main reason teachers were so angry with the plea deal: They believed that Tornillo had stolen much more money than that. In fact, the union filed a civil suit in November 2003 to reclaim the rest of the $3.5 million that an audit showed Tornillo and the late Murray Sisselman had misappropriated.[50] As of this writing, state officials are continuing their own probe into Tornillo's misdeeds; although the plea agreement protects Tornillo from further federal prosecution, he could still face charges from the state.[51]

But as federal prosecutors pointed out, part of the difficulty in prosecuting Tornillo was that the union provided him with such extravagant perks that it was sometimes difficult to determine what was criminal conduct and what was a by-product of business-as-usual. The judge agreed, noting that Tornillo was allowed to run the union as his "personal fiefdom"—a frequent state of affairs among labor bosses. "It's inconceivable to me that this went on for this amount of time without someone figuring out that something was not quite kosher," Judge Jordan commented.[52]

Tornillo's stealing was only part of the UTD's serious misuse of members' money. Ever since Tornillo had succeeded in merging the two state organizations into one statewide union, Florida's local teachers' unions had paid dues to the AFT, the National Education Association (NEA), and both the AFT's and NEA's state organizations. And in one of the earliest signs of the UTD's financial problems, by 2002 the union owed millions of dollars in delinquent dues to the Florida Education Association and the NEA, jeopardizing its members' right to vote at the NEA's 2002 national convention.

The fact is that most unions are immune from public scrutiny, their finances hidden even from members' view. Consequently, even though full UTD members paid $840 a year or more for the privilege of union membership, they had no access to information about the local's finances and knew nothing about the UTD's problems with the state and national organizations, according to the *Miami Herald*. " 'We wanted to know exactly what the financial situation was, and they said they were not at liberty to speak,' said Paula Mark, an English teacher and [union] steward at Hialeah Senior High School. 'We basically got no information. . . . It shocks me that this would not all be revealed . . . I believe there is an effort to keep information very close to the vest under the fear that if any negative things are said that it will weaken the union in terms of collective bargaining.' "[53]

Not that Tornillo had anything to worry about in terms of being reelected, year after year. As the *Miami Herald* reported in May 2003, "Despite the trappings of a democracy—a constitution, election schedules, rules for campaigns—not a single ballot has been cast at the United Teachers of Dade in more than 20 years. Pat Tornillo held the title of president, but in reality he was king."[54] The UTD elected its officers every three years, but the elections took place with a single slate of candidates sponsored by the Unity Caucus, the union's version of a political party, which controls power within the AFT and most of its locals. Since the 1970s, the Unity Caucus has rarely been beaten in local or national elections. Damaris Daugherty of the Teachers Rights Advocacy Coalition, a Miami lawyer who has tried for years to challenge the UTD, summed up Tornillo's role to the *Orlando Sentinel:* "He's a despot. He believes he owns the organization the same way Castro believes he owns Cuba. We've been screaming it for years: The union is taking our money to fund their lavish lifestyles. Everybody is getting rich on the backs of teachers."[55]

The Teachers Rights Advocacy Coalition and members of the UTD may have been "screaming" for years about corruption within the UTD, but the claims went uninvestigated for so long because of the enormous power the union wielded. The teachers' union, like many other public-employee unions, operated in the public sphere, supposedly under the oversight of publicly elected officials. Teachers who felt the union was misusing dues should have been able to take their complaints to elected officials—school board members, the city council, perhaps even the mayor—who had jurisdiction over school budgets and with whom the union negotiated teacher contracts. But the problem is, in Miami-Dade County, as in most unionized school districts, the union owned these elected officials, who wouldn't have been in office in the first place if it hadn't been for the union's support in their elections. The *Miami Herald* described the cozy relationship this way: "The union has become a formidable force in Miami-Dade County, where its roster of school board candidates with rare exception wins at the polls."[56] Union-supported candidates for school board had consistently won the majority of seats over a decade or more. "Such ballot box power has given the union dominion over the $4 billion school district," noted another *Miami Herald* article. "The UTD, negotiating with politicians it helped elect, now commands the highest average teacher salaries in Florida."[57]

And as we have seen, winning elections turns into big bucks for a union and its cronies. In the case of the UTD, Tornillo reportedly turned his political influence directly into cash. According to the *Miami Herald:*

Tornillo demanded that the [school] board give a nine-figure contract to HIP Healthcare in 1996 and again in 2001 against a consultant's advice. The company's lobbyist, and Tornillo confidant, Ric Sasser, pocketed at least $4 million on the deal. The union also ensured, as part of its contract, that only one supplemental insurance broker could come to schools and sell products to the county's largest workforce: the Public Employee Services Company.[58]

That's the same PESCO whose premiums the UTD did not pay in 2003, thus jeopardizing members' coverage. But not to worry, PESCO had very close ties to the union—it had been founded by a Tornillo friend, Mike Sheridan, and it rented space on the ground floor of the UTD's new offices. The *Miami Herald* reported that the union owned 19,000 shares of PESCO, and Tornillo sat on the board of directors of another Sheridan-owned company, the Fringe Benefits Management Co., which the school board had employed since the mid-1980s to administer supplemental insurance plans.[59]

The UTD's political clout extended far beyond the local school district, however. The evidence of Pat Tornillo's active role in Florida's Democratic politics provides yet another example of how unions have become the main political force within the Democratic Party—how in the past thirty years the Democratic Party has essentially become the U.S. Labor Party. By pouring funds into Democratic coffers, the unions have gained tremendous power within the party, not only over platforms and other Democratic policy but even in picking the party's nominees. Indeed, in Florida in 2002, it seems that Tornillo essentially handpicked the Democratic gubernatorial candidate to run against incumbent governor Jeb Bush.

As with so much of what went on behind the scenes at the UTD, the teachers' union's involvement in the 2002 Florida governor's race had about it the stench of corruption, so much so that in the summer of 2003 the Florida Elections Commission voted to move forward with an investigation of potential election-law violations, which has yet to be resolved as of this writing.[60] In January 2002, Tornillo was instrumental in persuading the state teachers' union, the Florida Education Association (of which the UTD is an affiliate), to endorse a political unknown, attorney Bill McBride, over former U.S. attorney general Janet Reno for the Democratic gubernatorial nomination. Then Tornillo and his union helped engineer an early endorsement for McBride at the state AFL-CIO convention—a coup for McBride, given that the organization represented a half million current or retired union members. (As the *Tallahassee Democrat* reported at the time, "It was clearly the schoolteachers driving the early endorsement.")[61] Tornillo explained to the Associated Press his reasoning for supporting McBride: "Beating Jeb Bush is the No. 1 priority. Reno carries too much baggage."[62] And of course the candidate was delighted to have the teachers' unions' backing. "The endorsement is particularly important to my campaign because it gives you an army of volunteers," McBride gushed. "They do the hard work, phone-banking and going door-to-door, fund raising. This gives me the kind of boost I need for name identity and momentum."[63] There's nothing wrong with unions' endorsing and working to elect a candidate who they think will better serve their members' needs, but the evidence indicates that a great deal was wrong with the way the teachers' union went about trying to elect Democrat Bill McBride.

After defeating Janet Reno in the primary, McBride acknowledged how vital the Tornillo-engineered endorsement from the Florida Education Association had been. "They were real warriors and real soldiers," McBride told the *Fort Lauderdale Sun-Sentinel*. "Even when we were back at 5 percent in the polls, they were out on the street corners. They were out working."[64] But the Florida Education Association's help went far beyond standing on street corners. According to the *Sun-Sentinel*, "The labor group invested no less than $1.5 million of member dues into a monthlong TV campaign on McBride's behalf. The ads boosted his standing and helped him creep past Janet Reno in the campaign's final weeks. The group also loaned staff members and other organizers to the McBride campaign. Union workers served as 'liaisons' between local teachers and the Tampa lawyer's campaign. And at every union staff meeting for months, brochures and other information about McBride were circulated."[65] In fact, the Florida Education Association virtually ran the McBride campaign, with the union's own political director, Kathy Kelly, becoming campaign manager right after the primary.

Florida election law allows individuals to donate only $500 to a political candidate, but as in most states, organizations can spend an unlimited amount on so-called issues ads, as long as they don't actually advocate a vote for a particular candidate. Evidence indicates, however, that the Florida Education Association donated a total of $1.88 million—most of it paid for by union dues—to a union subsidiary, the Quality Public Education Corporation (QPEC), which, starting early in the 2002 gubernatorial campaign, ran television ads introducing McBride to Florida voters.[66] The ads bought instant name recognition for McBride and also established his image as a pro-education candidate. In all, QPEC spent more than $2 million on the McBride ad campaign, and his numbers soared in public opinion polls within weeks.[67]

None of this was necessarily illegal under Florida law, but allegedly the union's dummy corporation hired McBride's own campaign consultants—Doak, Carrier, O'Donnell & Associates—to produce and place the ads. It is illegal under Florida election law for ostensibly independent groups to use unregulated soft-money donations in a coordinated effort with a candidate's campaign in order to influence the general voting public, because doing so circumvents limits on campaign contributions. The Florida Education Association had run into problems with the Florida Elections Commission over similar campaign expenditures three times previously, and though it always managed to avoid prosecution, the commission did warn in one ruling that "future violations will be dealt with harshly."[68] Consequently, QPEC, the McBride campaign, and the Florida Education Association as of this writing face the possibility of millions of dollars in fines if the state elections commission finds that they have violated the law. McBride himself potentially faces more than $5 million in fines and QPEC more than $3 million,[69] and teachers themselves would end up paying for the latter through their dues.

During the campaign, Pat Tornillo revealed that he would exploit nearly any advantage available to him in order to increase his own political power. He wasn't even above trying to manipulate school-children into carrying the union's political message home to their parents. In an e-mail to UTD members, Tornillo asked teachers to send notes home to their students' parents asking them to support the Democratic candidate and three union-backed amendments on the ballot. According to the *Tallahassee Democrat*, the Tornillo e-mail suggested that the following note be sent home: "As your child's teacher, I am asking you to vote on Nov. 5. Miami-Dade County's teachers support Bill McBride, Amendments 8, 9 and 11" (these measures would provide free pre-kindergarten for all four-year-olds in the state, reduce class size, and dismantle Governor Bush's proposal to create a single state Board of Education to oversee all public education in the state). "We feel the future of public education has never been at greater risk," Tornillo encouraged teachers to tell parents; McBride, he said, "will significantly improve public education in Florida."[70]

On the campaign trail, Governor Bush blasted the Florida Education Association, complaining of "the incredible power this union has—they organized [McBride's] campaign, they funded his campaign, they do this sort of thing and it's just wrong." Although Bush won reelection handily, so, too, did the union-backed ballot measures, saddling the state with billions of dollars in new debt.[71] But apparently such concerns are immaterial to the unions. After all, that's for the taxpayers to worry about. As long as union officials preserve their own power (and certain corrupt officials are left alone to line their pockets with money from union members), Big Labor doesn't have to worry about anything else—like, say, the public interest.

LEADER OF THE PACK

Barbara Bullock and Pat Tornillo reflect two of the most dangerous strains of union corruption: leading a lavish lifestyle at the expense of union members and using union funds to buy political influence. Perhaps Bullock, Tornillo, and other corrupt union leaders are merely taking their cue from the top. After all, as we have seen, AFL-CIO president John Sweeney is the embodiment of Big Labor's desire for political influence and has pushed the labor movement even further into the political arena. Yet Sweeney's career also reveals how easily labor bosses can take advantage of their position in the union hierarchy for personal gain. Before becoming president of the AFL-CIO, Sweeney worked his way up the power structure of the Service Employees International Union (SEIU), and during his time at the SEIU, the near-bottomless source of forced member dues was apparently a grave temptation to him.

Before becoming the SEIU's president in 1981, Sweeney served as head of the union's local New York City affiliate. Though he moved on from the New York union, he did not stop receiving a salary from the local; in fact, he continued to take money from the local until *1994*, a full thirteen years after he had left. Sweeney gave up the second salary only when he was campaigning for the presidency of the AFL-CIO in 1995 and the double-dipping was exposed. The Associated Press at the time reported that Sweeney had profited handsomely from the arrangement, as the local union had paid him at least $449,642 between 1982 and 1994.[72] All of this was in addition to the substantial salary the union's Washington headquarters paid him— $210,952 in 1994 alone. Thus, for a period of thirteen years the local paid Sweeney an average of about $35,000 annually for a job he did not hold (though the New York City union deemed him an "executive adviser"). In some years he took as much as $80,000 from his former local. In 1994 he showed remarkable restraint in taking only $10,059 from the local, and then he cut the funds off entirely as he approached the 1995 AFL-CIO election. A spokesman for Sweeney said that the payments had halted because Sweeney "decided both the amount of time he was spending with the local and the amount of money he was receiving was inappropriate."

"Inappropriate"? That's putting it mildly, especially considering that this double-dipping was forcibly taken from hardworking union members as a condition of employment. Even a representative for the pro-union group Association for Union Democracy was forced to concede, "In most of these double salaries, the second job is fictitious."[73]

Equally appalling, Sweeney made sure that his successor as president of the New York City local, Gus Bevona, got paid by the international union as well as by the local. Bevona was a dictatorial boss who ruled the local for eighteen years, and while Sweeney was president of the SEIU, Bevona received more than $70,000 a year from the international union. This generous contribution from the international helped make Bevona the nation's highest-paid union boss at one point; overall he made nearly $500,000 from various union sources. He also had a Manhattan penthouse worth $6 million—and paid for by forced member dues.[74] Bevona stepped down in 1999 after union members sued him for improper use of more than $2.4 million in funds. Still, when he was forced out, he left with a $1.5 million golden parachute.[75]

Fortunately for Sweeney, these cases of apparent double-dipping did not prevent him from seizing control of the AFL-CIO. His damage control helped. For instance, when asked about having drawn a salary from the local for so many years after he had moved on to the international union leadership, Sweeney said, "I work for that salary, I work very closely with the officers of that local and I'm heavily involved in the activities of that local."[76]

Sweeney did actually have a seat on the executive board of the local, and it's good to know that he takes responsibility for the local's actions, which included using union dues to hire private detectives to tail union dissidents. In fact, that is what ultimately led to Sweeney crony Gus Bevona's resignation as head of the local. In 1991, Bevona had hired private detectives to tail union dissident Carlos Guzman after Guzman criticized Bevona's salary and alleged that the union was selling jobs for bribes. Guzman sued the union boss for spying on him and was awarded $100,000. But Bevona went all out in defending himself in the case, paying his lawyers $1.65 million from union funds and spending another $600,000 on a hardcover, 142-page "history" of the local that touted his own accomplishments and criticized Guzman and another union dissident. In 1997 the two dissidents sued the union leader to recover the $2.4 million in misspent union funds. When two court rulings went against Bevona, he made a deal: He stepped down as union president, and in return the dissidents dropped their suit; the local was placed under federal supervison.[77]

WISE GUYS AND HARDHATS AT MoMA

Just as many labor leaders have figured out how to profit at the expense of union members, mobsters long ago recognized the potential to skim millions from the unions.

The Museum of Modern Art in New York City, known to most New Yorkers as MoMA, might be the last place you'd expect to find organized crime figures hanging out with union bosses. But that's exactly where FBI agents eavesdropped on wise guys and hardhats scheming to bilk builders and taxpayers out of millions of dollars on both private and public construction sites throughout New York City. By planting listening devices in a construction trailer on the job site of MoMA's $858 million renovation,[78] investigators were able to gather enough evidence to indict forty-two members of the Genovese and Colombo La Cosa Nostra crime families and leaders of Locals 14 and 15 of the International Union of Operating Engineers. "What the F.B.I. heard was nothing modern or artful," said James B. Comey, the U.S. attorney in Manhattan. "Instead, what they heard was something as old as the criminal justice system, and that was an effort to strong-arm."[79] According to state attorney general Eliot Spitzer, every construction and demolition job in the city was affected. Spitzer said the two Operating Engineers locals—which provide operators for cranes, loaders, elevators, and other heavy machinery—"had been held captive for decades by a greedy joint venture between the Genovese and Colombo crime families."[80]

The scheme was typical of mob-run unions: force contractors to pay for workers who never show up—and if the company resists, shut down the job site and crack a few heads. In the case of Locals 14 and 15, no-show union workers were on the payroll of construction and renovation jobs at MoMA, the New York Mets' and Yankees' minor-league stadiums, city schools, waterfront condominiums, shopping plazas, and even a new federal courthouse in Brooklyn.[81] According to the indictment, the Colombo crime family made $2 million in union wages and benefits for work that was never done, while the Genovese organization made $1.6 million.[82] Union officials also benefited, apparently: a predawn raid on one union official's home in February 2003 netted a half million dollars in cash in tightly packed bricks of hundred-dollar bills.[83] In addition to the no-show workers' scheme, the mobbed-up locals also sold union memberships for $10,000 apiece.[84] "The financial impact here touches all of us in the form of higher construction costs," U.S. attorney Roslynn R. Mauskopf told the *New York Times.* "In the case of public works projects, taxpayers foot the bill."[85]

As of this writing, a total of nine defendants have pled guilty to charges stemming from the indictments, including Ernest M. Muscarella, who was sentenced to five years in prison and three years of supervised release when he gets out,[86] and Nicholas Lupari, who was given five months' imprisonment, two years' supervised release, and five months' home detention, and ordered to pay $73,985.60 in restitution.[87] The remaining thirty-three persons indicted of more than 130 felony counts still face hearings.

For decades, organized crime has been heavily involved in running labor unions. According to the FBI, in the early 1980s Gambino family boss Paul Castellano reportedly said, "Our job is to run the unions."[88] Indeed, one-third of the fifty-eight mobsters arrested at the infamous Apalachin conference of organized crime bosses in upstate New York in 1957—which changed the way law enforcement fights organized crime—listed their employment as "labor" or "labor-management relations."[89] The FBI's own website notes that over the years La Cosa Nostra has systematically infiltrated and controlled the International Brotherhood of Teamsters, the Hotel Employees and Restaurant Employees International Union, the Independent Laborers Association, and the Laborers International Union of North America, among others. The Teamsters, especially, have been closely identified with organized crime, and in fact four of the past eight Teamsters Union presidents have been indicted on criminal charges.[90]

Because of organized crime families' active role in labor unions, the Department of Labor has an Office of Labor Racketeering and Fraud Investigations. In just the months from October 1, 2002, to March 31, 2003, the Labor Department's investigations resulted in 337 indictments, 191 convictions, and more than $55.6 million in monetary recoveries.[91] And these figures do not include the results of the FBI's New York construction union investigations.

Unfortunately, corruption is endemic to the union structure itself, which has few checks and balances to keep dishonest individuals in line. Transparency—requiring unions to make public all information about their finances, management, and activities—would at least allow union members and the general public to know what goes on in these multimillion-dollar organizations. President John F. Kennedy led the effort to require labor unions to report their financial activities more than forty years ago, but the rules regulating disclosure (specifically, certain provisions of the Landrum-Griffin Act) are so weak and outdated that most unions can simply hide information from their members and the public. Members of most unions have no way of knowing the true salaries and benefits their elected officials and top staff earn. Disclosure forms don't even reveal how much of the union's dues go to such activities as organizing new members or servicing existing contracts—or how much goes to political activity. In fact, the NEA, the biggest and most politically powerful union in the nation, claims to the IRS that it spends nothing on politics, which, as we have seen, is preposterous.

Big Labor has fought tenaciously to preserve its murky accounting—aided, of course, by its Democratic allies. In 2002, President George W. Bush's secretary of labor, Elaine Chao, proposed updating the Department of Labor forms used to report union income and expenses, and the unions cried foul. AFL-CIO president John Sweeney was all for better disclosure for businesses, arguing that "transparency, accountability and full and accurate disclosure should be the central goals of financial regulation."[92] But when it came time to report how unions spend their members' money, unions suddenly found that such regulations were punitive and burdensome. So they turned to their friends in Congress, the very people whom they helped elect, in many cases by misusing union dues.

At the time Chao proposed the disclosure-form changes, Senator Tom Harkin, Democrat of Iowa, chaired the Labor Appropriations Subcommittee, which funds the operations of the Labor Department. One of Big Labor's most stalwart supporters—unions donated more than $372,000 in his 2002 reelection[93]—Senator Harkin put the following language into the Appropriations Committee's report on the Labor Department's fiscal year 2003 funding bill: "The Committee directs the Secretary of Labor not to revise, amend, or change in any way, whether by rulemaking or otherwise, the reporting requirements imposed on labor organizations under the Labor Management Reporting and Disclosure Act. Further, the Committee expects the Secretary to provide the Committee her rationale for any reporting requirement changes being considered by the administration."[94]

Democratic opposition to the tightened disclosure rules was so strong that Chao could not move forward with her reforms until after the Republicans took back control of the Senate in the 2002 elections. But in 2003, the union-backed Democrats in Congress continued the fight to prevent transparency in union accounting, even after shocking reports of union corruption had come to light, including the Washington Teachers Union and United Teachers of Dade scandals. In June 2003, for example, at a Senate hearing prompted by the Washington and Miami scandals, Senator Hillary Clinton did not call for greater oversight of unions but rather took the opportunity to complain about the Department of Labor's proposed disclosure requirements. "It does strike me that with the enforcement of all our labor laws, the administration has been less than enthusiastic," Clinton declared. "This is the only labor law the administration is willing to enforce." Senator Ted Kennedy, always willing to stand shoulder-to-shoulder with his union patrons, chimed in that the new regulations were "the same old anti-union bias."[95] What neither senator mentioned was that the Labor Department's new rules might prevent exactly the kind of corruption that robs union members, like the teachers in Washington and Miami, of their hard-earned wages.

When even those protests from the unions' loyal Democratic allies failed to bury the new disclosure requirements, Big Labor had to act on its own. In December 2003, just a month before Secretary Chao's new disclosure rules were to take effect, the AFL-CIO sued the Bush administration to block the regulations. Then at the last minute the unions were given at least a temporary reprieve: On New Year's Eve a federal judge ruled that the new regulations could not take effect for another year, stating that unions needed more time to comply with the rules.[96]

The judge's ruling was a setback for union workers and for labor reform. The fact is, however, that even if more stringent disclosure requirements were in place, the Labor Department could barely afford to monitor unions—which do need monitoring. From 2001 to 2003, the Labor Department found financial mismanagement or embezzlement in forty of the AFL-CIO's sixty-six affiliates.[97] The Labor Department averages eleven new convictions a month.[98] And it does this with a skeleton crew. For example, the Office of Labor-Management Standards, which oversees union finances, had only 260 auditors in 2001 but was able to win 101 criminal convictions for union fraud and embezzlement.[99] By contrast, the Occupational Safety and Health Administration (OSHA), which oversees employers' workplace abuses, had 1,052 inspectors that year but obtained only 4 criminal convictions. One of the main reasons that the Office of Labor Management Standards is in such peril, despite the corruption it continually exposes, is that the Clinton administration—so dependent on the unions' political support, as noted in Chapter 3—cut back severely on pursuing union fraud and abuse. During the Clinton years, staffing authorization for the Office of Labor-Management Standards decreased 40 percent, from 431 employees to 260, and audits went down by 70 percent, from 800 to 238.[100] It seems that the extraordinary support the unions gave to Bill Clinton's presidential campaigns paid off. When Republicans finally won back control of both houses of Congress in 2002, the Bush administration was able to increase funding for the Office of Labor Management Standards, authorizing the agency to increase its staff.[101]

Because so many politicians are desperate to curry favor with the powerful labor unions, the public knows little about the extent of union corruption and abuse. It's not just the government that obscures union abuse, however. Most newspapers bury stories about embezzlement and fraud among labor unions or don't even report them in the first place. Even a story as big as the New York Operating Engineers' racketeering bust, which involved two of the most notorious organized crime families in the nation, was buried on page three of the *New York Times*'s Metro section. (The *Miami Herald*'s excellent coverage on the United Teachers of Dade scandal is a notable exception.)

The silence about such corruption is startling, because *all of us,* not just union members, pay for union corruption. As the FBI notes on its website on labor racketeering, "FBI investigations over the years have clearly demonstrated that labor racketeering costs the American public millions of dollars each year through increased labor costs that are eventually passed on to consumers."[102] Until we demand the same level of transparency and accountability of unions that we do from American businesses, the cost of union corruption will keep rising.

CHAPTER 8

Choking the Golden Goose: How Big Labor Harms the American Economy

W e don't want to kill the golden goose. We just want to choke it by the neck until it gives us every last egg." That's how union leader Rick Dubinsky summed up his negotiating philosophy. And like other powerful labor bosses, Dubinsky proved himself quite adept at choking the golden goose. As president of the Airline Pilots Association (ALPA), he squeezed every last egg out of United Airlines in "bargaining" for a new labor contract—to the point that the once mighty United had to declare bankruptcy in December 2002.[1]

The United case not only demonstrated the unions' extraordinary power to squeeze employers for sky-high wages, lavish benefits, and bizarre work requirements—even when businesses are crumbling—it also revealed labor leaders' utter lack of concern for the devastating economic consequences of their extortionate demands. In large part because of the overwhelming costs that the unions forced on the airline, United hemorrhaged money, losing $3.2 billion in 2002 alone—

almost $9 million per day.[2] And United was not alone. US Airways also filed for bankruptcy that year,[3] and in 2001 American Airlines bought TWA out of bankruptcy court—even though American itself had teetered on the brink of Chapter 11, averting disaster only when union leaders made last-minute concessions.[4] To be sure, September 11 hurt the airlines (as at least partial compensation, they received a massive taxpayer bailout), but much more damaging were the unreasonable demands of unions unwilling to compromise with management, demands that had been going on for years. In fact, long before September 11, labor disputes had permanently grounded such airline stalwarts as Eastern, Braniff, and Pan Am. Significantly, the only airlines today that earn a profit are those that have been able to streamline their labor costs—such as Southwest, JetBlue, and Frontier.

The economic damage that union leaders inflict goes far beyond the airline industry, however. Intransigent labor leaders have all but obliterated the once-thriving steel and coal-mining industries, for example, and onerous union work rules and wage and benefit demands have forced many employers—indeed, whole industries—to move production overseas or close up shop altogether. Union leaders claim to represent working men and women, but by forcing companies out of business and driving industries overseas they have actually caused millions of union members to lose their jobs.

Other economic consequences are less noticed but no less devastating. Even when union leaders' demands do not drive companies out of business, they drastically increase the ordinary costs of doing business, and companies must pass these higher costs on to consumers. In other words, each and every one of us has to pay to support the unions. Moreover, Big Labor has been remarkably successful at pushing government officials to mandate that public employees belong to unions—thirty-seven states now have forced-unionism laws—and this only takes money out of the pockets of Americans, including union members. The taxpayers have to bear the burden of the expensive contracts negotiated by public-employee unions, which is why taxes are higher in forced-unionism states than in states that allow workers to choose whether or not to join a union (free-choice, or right-to-work, states). Amazingly, for all the unions' rhetoric about improving the lot of workers, forced unionism also lowers real wages, increases the cost of living, limits job opportunities, and in general weakens the economy. Then, of course, there is the extraordinary drain on the American economy that comes with the far-left economic policies that labor leaders like John Sweeney of the AFL-CIO push relentlessly. Big Labor's unrivaled political power—which is derived from its huge war chests of forced member dues—allows it to install Democrats in power at all levels and in all branches of government, and therefore labor bosses can push for higher taxes and bigger government. The extent of the damage Big Labor inflicts on the American economy is simply staggering.

CREATING CHAOS

The most effective way for unions to achieve their often outrageous demands is to bring an employer to its knees. That is why unions often resort to labor strikes, and why many strikers have organized campaigns of violence and destruction. But unions can do incredible economic damage without going on strike, as the employees of United Airlines demonstrated in their campaign to extort new labor contracts from the airline.

United's troubles began in earnest in 2000 as United's pilots, mechanics, and flight attendant unions staged a work slowdown that the unions accurately dubbed CHAOS, for Create Havoc Around Our System. Pilots actually flew their planes more slowly in order to create flight delays, while hundreds of union employees called in sick, leading to canceled flights and angry passengers. Mechanics and flight attendants took two or three times longer to perform their regular duties, slowing service and delaying takeoffs. According to an exhaustive *New York Times Magazine* article by Roger Lowenstein, pilots taxied on runways at 3 knots instead of 15, flew too low so as to burn additional fuel, and opened landing gear prematurely to increase wear and tear on the aircraft, thus driving up operating costs.[5]

Lowenstein reported that pilots delayed flights, often to the point of forcing cancellation, by insisting on the repair of trivial items such as coffeemakers or reading lights before taking off.[6] One pilot announced that because of "low clouds" he wanted to recheck his instruments. He kept the passengers on the tarmac for three hours while he supposedly recalibrated the aircraft to deal with clouds. Another pilot walked off a packed 747 flight, stranding it, because of "nerves."[7]

The overall passenger reaction was predictably harsh. Ryan Murphy, council representative of the Association of Flight Attendants, boasted that he routinely hid in the cockpit after landing in order to avoid the backlash from passengers to the poor service.[8] United canceled 23,000 flights. Its on-time performance, once the best in the business, dropped to 40 percent. The airline lost $700 million during the slowdown.[9]

In order to get employees back to work, United executives capitulated to union demands, giving pilots the best pay in the industry, with an immediate raise of 22 to 28 percent and a 4.5 percent raise promised annually after that. The machinists eventually received similar industry-topping concessions, with entry pay jumping 43 percent and top pay leaping 38 percent.[10] These raises put United pilots in the top 5 percent of all wage earners in America, with senior pilots making more than $300,000 per year in 2002 for an average of fifty hours of work per *month*. Senior mechanics earned $70,000, while comparably experienced flight attendants made about $50,000.[11] Concessions to the unions set up a situation at United in which labor costs absorbed 50 percent of all revenues in 2002 (as opposed to 25 percent at financially solvent JetBlue).[12]

Meanwhile, union work rules at United forced the airline to hire many more employees than the company needed or could afford. At other, more profitable airlines, workers routinely carry out functions as needed. Pilots and flight attendants might pick up trash between flights, while gate agents might help with baggage loading.[13] But the concept of multitasking was prohibited under union rules at United— each separate task required a separate employee. And the unions made sure that United did not try to shave costs by using low-paid employees; for example, they insisted that high-cost mechanics guide in jets, whereas competing airlines often used lower-paid ramp agents for that task.

The unions were also successful at featherbedding—that is, at requiring that extra, unneeded employees be hired. For instance, United was required to have three pilots in the cockpit, as opposed to the two pilots used at other airlines.[14] At the same time, union contracts prohibited United from outsourcing to companies that could perform some functions more cheaply, as other businesses typically do.

Union-negotiated vacation plans at United also necessitated even more employees to cover the time off that union members now "earned." Senior flight attendants received as much as ten weeks of paid vacation under the union contract, while pilots seemed to have a endless supply of paid days off. Union rules required that pilots be released, with pay, from any flights that overlapped a scheduled vacation day. One pilot boasted to the *Wall Street Journal* that as a supposedly full-time employee who averaged fewer than forty hours of work per month, he was able to use these rules to squeeze twenty-five paid days off from just five actual vacation days.[15]

The unions were able to force all of these concessions in an industry that even in the best of circumstances is a low-profit enterprise. During the most profitable period in the airline industry's history, the economic boom from 1995 to 1999, airlines on average made only 3.5 cents in profit for every dollar of sales. (For the entire decade, the profit margin was even slimmer: only one cent for every dollar of revenue.)[16] Not surprisingly, United couldn't sustain even these small profits following the concessions it made to the unions in 2000. The airline began to bleed money at this point. By the end of 2002 (the temporary decline in airline traffic after the September 11 attacks hastened the airline's economic decline), United had lost all the money it had made in the previous five years.[17] With passengers deserting the airlines in droves and planes virtually empty, United began to plead with pilots to stay home, even though union rules required the airline to pay them 80 percent of their salary in such situations. The reason the airline was willing to pay pilots for not showing up was that, as Lowenstein reported, otherwise the pilots could earn *full* pay simply by showing up, even if they remained inactive.[18]

Thus intransigent union leaders forced United to lose staggering amounts of money and ultimately to declare bankruptcy, as the unions disregarded the long-term consequences of their demands. This is all too common, for unions rarely consider how their excessive demands will affect the economic health of the employers on whom union members depend for their livelihoods. Many union leaders are interested primarily in protecting their own privileges, but perhaps even more important, the socialist mindset of most unions today demonizes employers and the idea of profit seeking. Yet Big Labor often gets so caught up in treating employers as the enemy that it cuts off its nose to spite its face, for without profits, companies can't grow and create new jobs. At United Airlines, years of caving in to union demands drove labor costs higher than the market would bear, and it was only a matter of time before United was on the brink of financial ruin. The unions' bargaining victories proved to be illusory, however, as United's financial problems became so severe that union members eventually had to agree to pay and benefit cuts and massive layoffs (tens of thousands of workers lost their jobs).

Perhaps the most puzzling aspect of the unions' role in bringing down United was that the airline's workers actually owned a majority of the company at the time. In the early 1990s, as part of another effort to deal with skyrocketing costs and precarious profits, United had agreed to sell its pilots, machinists, and nonunion employees 55 percent of the company's stock in exchange for employee "givebacks" in wages and benefits. United became the largest "employee-owned" company in the United States, and leading labor figures such as Clinton labor secretary Robert Reich touted the United model as the wave of the future for America's airlines.

But as Roger Lowenstein noted in his *New York Times Magazine* article a decade later, the optimism didn't last long. "Yes, you could turn employees into owners," Lowenstein wrote, "but could you get them to act that way? Could you get them to place the same value on their stock as on their weekly paycheck?"[19] Certainly not with the socialist mentality that dominates so much of the labor movement today. Even though the unions gained three seats on the company's board of directors, they never behaved like true owners of the company, interested in turning a profit and increasing shareholder value. Instead, the unions behaved like camels with their noses in the airline's tent, ready to pull down the entire structure in order to satisfy their own appetites. The ALPA's Dubinsky noted ominously, "You can't eat stock," so the unions, after initially agreeing to wage and benefit givebacks, started demanding increases. With union reps on the board and a new, union-friendly CEO in charge, wages rose 43 percent throughout the 1990s, even though airfares rose only 6 percent during that time. Lowenstein reported, "It may be unkind to say the company lived in fear of upsetting its employees, but everyone, especially at United, knew what the unions were capable of doing."[20] At the time of the union buyout at United, the airline's stock was selling for more than $22 a share; by November 2003, the stock had fallen to barely $1 a share.

The unions representing United employees should have recognized that treating the employer as an enemy will only hurt union members in the long term. But even after the unions became a part of management, they had trouble sustaining their commitment to keep the company on sound financial footing. It's as if union leaders believed that the company could magically produce the cash to pay for their demands, regardless of what the accountants showed the bottom line to be. Unfortunately for the workers, however, reality—and basic economics—determined that the unions had put the airline in an unsustainable position.

FORCED UNIONISM: RECIPE FOR ECONOMIC DISASTER

Inflicting financial harm on employers—who ultimately must be able to pay wages—is just the tip of the iceberg when it comes to the economic harm unions inflict on workers, union members or not. Those who live in heavily unionized states and cities ultimately pay more taxes, experience a higher cost of living, and earn less in adjusted dollars than workers living in free-choice, or right-to-work, states.

But you will never hear that from the unions, who try to convince potential members that without unions, workers would be little better than serfs. Unions are expert propagandists. Take the Bakery, Confectionery, Tobacco Workers, and Grain Millers union (BCTGM). Its website proudly proclaims:

The difference between being represented by the BCTGM and not having a union job is the difference between a living wage and a sub par wage; between health benefits and none; between a secure retirement and an uncertain pension; between a safe workplace and a hazardous one; between a voice on the job and powerlessness.[21]

These statements are typical of union organizing rhetoric. But no matter how many times these falsehoods are repeated, they don't become true. Quite obviously the 92 percent of private-sector workers who aren't unionized aren't all living in abject poverty and despair.

In fact, objective standards comparing forced-unionism states with free-choice states show that workers in free-choice states (where a much lower percentage of workers are union members) are much better off economically in every measurable way. For instance, contrary to BCTGM's claim that union membership is essential to having health insurance—that it is the difference "between health benefits and none"—the statistics reveal that workers in free-choice states do indeed secure health insurance without benefit of the unions. In fact, from 1987 to 2001, the number of people covered by health insurance increased by 17.1 percent in free-choice states but only by 6.1 percent in forced-unionism states.[22]

And that is just one measure of how free-choice, or right-to-work, states are much better off economically than forced-unionism states, despite union organizing claims such as BCTGM's. Table 1 reveals how, across a range of economic measures, free-choice states outperform forced-unionism states.

Contrary to union propaganda, which argues that forced unionism improves the lives of all working men and women, the facts demonstrate that forced unionism does considerable economic damage. Numerous studies have documented the damage that unions do. For example, one study released by the Allegheny Institute of Public Policy confirms that the states with the lowest levels of unionization led highly unionized states in income growth, job growth, and reducing poverty.[23] In fact, in most cases the higher the unionization rates, the slower the income and job growth. Another study by Ohio University economists Lowell Gallaway and Richard Vedder reveals that

TABLE 1

Forced-Unionism States vs. Free-Choice, Right-to-Work States: A Comparison of Objective Economic Factors

ECONOMIC FACTOR	FORCED-UNIONISM STATES	FREE-CHOICE STATES
Percentage growth in nonfarm private-sector employees (1992–2002):	16.8%	29.1%
Percentage growth in construction employment (1992–2002):	45.7%	57.9%
Average after-tax weekly pay adjusted for cost of living (2000):	$468	$484
Share of households who own their own homes (2001):	67%	70%
Percentage growth in manufacturing establishments (1987–2000):	–6.1%	1.4%
Mean two-earner household income in metro areas, adjusted for cost of living (1999):	$63,236	$64,425
Percentage growth in patents annually granted (1992–2000):	64%	80%
Percentage growth in real personal income (1992–2002):	25.8%	37.3%
Aggregate poverty rate, adjusted for cost of living (2000):	12.9%	10.8%
New privately owned single-family housing units started per 1,000 residents (2000):	3.4%	6.0%
Percentage growth in real value added by manufacture per production worker (1990–2000):	14.1%	21.4%
Percentage growth in private employees with employer-provided pension benefits (1988–1999):	32%	58%

Source: "Right to Work States Benefit from Faster Growth, Higher Real Purchasing Power," National Institute for Labor Relations Research, August 2003.

unions have cost America trillions of dollars in lost productivity, led to higher unemployment, and wiped out entire industries.[24]

The statistics also expose the absurdity of Big Labor's frequent claim that a state's right-to-work law is really a "right-to-work-for-less law," for they reveal that union workers in states allowing forcible unionism earn less (when adjusted for cost of living) than nonunion workers in free-choice states. Additionally, workers in those forced-unionism states lose more of their income to taxes and suffer with poorer public services than those in free-choice states.

Interestingly, a major AFL-CIO union has actually provided the strongest evidence for the case that union members on average have less purchasing power than workers in free-choice states. Because of the need to evaluate the worth of salaries in areas with widely varying living costs, the American Federation of Teachers (AFT) commissioned its Research and Information Services Department to determine the comparable worth of wages across the country.[25] The AFT's Interstate Cost of Living Index, updated in 2003, showed that the cost of living in free-choice states is almost 9 percent lower than the national average. In fact, every right-to-work state, without exception, enjoys a lower cost of living than the nation as a whole. Meanwhile, forced-unionism states' cost of living is more than 3 percent higher than the national average.

The differences are even more eye-opening when you look at individual cities. The ACCRA cost-of-living index, compiled at George Mason University, uses a scale that puts 100 as the average for all participating places.[26] If a particular city's cost of living is 10 percent higher than average, its index number will be 110; if a city's cost of living is 10 percent lower than average, its index number will be 90. The cost to live in forced-unionism cities is extraordinary:

ACCRA COST-OF-LIVING INDEX

FORCED-UNIONISM CITIES	FREE-CHOICE CITIES
Boston, 135.5	Tampa, 90.5
Los Angeles, 137.8	Houston, 90.8
San Francisco, 182.3	Phoenix, 95.1
New York (Manhattan), 216.2	Atlanta, 98.1

As unions promote welfare-state government policies in areas where they are strongest, the resulting higher taxes and cost of living make it much more difficult for the typical family to get by. The CNN/*Money* magazine website provides a calculator comparing buying power in different cities.[27] It shows that someone making $30,000 in right-to-work Phoenix would need to make $41,083 to have the same purchasing power in forced-unionism Los Angeles. Likewise, someone making $20,000 in right-to-work Tampa would have to earn $45,072 in forced-unionism New York City.

The AFT scale shows a dramatic difference between the average cost of living in forced-unionism states and free-choice states—12 percentage points—but that AFT scale doesn't even take into account differences in tax rates, a significant omission given that forced-unionism states tend to have higher taxes. Higher taxes, higher costs, and fewer job opportunities leave workers in highly unionized states much worse off. As George Mason economist James Bennett points out, "In states without Right-to-Work laws, high taxes and the high cost of living erode the purchasing power of income so much that families in states with Right-to-Work laws are, on average, better off."[28]

VOTING WITH THEIR FEET

Big Labor has been successful in persuading politicians to adopt its high-tax, big-government, job-destroying policies in forced-unionism states, but it hasn't been able to persuade employers or the population to remain in those states. In a study by the Federal Reserve Bank of Minneapolis using data from the Census Bureau, Thomas Holmes demonstrates that "on average, manufacturing employment increases by one-third when one steps over the border" from a forced-unionism state to a right-to-work state. [29] In fact, the study shows that where forced-unionism and free-choice states share a border, the manufacturers are disproportionately located within twenty-five miles of the border on the right-to-work side, proving that it's not just the weather that leads to employers to abandon states in the highly unionized Northeast for the right-to-work Sunbelt.

The corporate relocation industry, which specializes in helping businesses find the best place to move, confirms these findings. The vice president of one such relocation firm, the Fantus Company, writes:

> Approximately 50 percent of our clients indicate . . . that they do not want to consider locations unless they are in right-to-work

states. . . . As a result, states that are not right-to-work states, and the communities in them, are eliminated from the initial phase of the site selection process, no matter how strong their other advantages for a facility might be.[30]

Similarly, a study by the University of Tennessee showed that the right-to-work law in a state is even more important than "tax concessions" or "government support for site acquisition."[31]

Employers aren't the only ones who flee from forced-unionism states. The leftist political policies typically adopted in these states, with the resulting higher taxes and lower employment, have contributed to a mass exodus of the population from these states. Most notable was the exodus from California in the late 1990s. From 1995 to 2000—a period when Democrats controlled the legislative and executive branches of the state government—an amazing 2.2 million citizens fled the state and its forced unionism. Even with an influx of immigrants during this time, California had a negative migration figure for the first time in its history: the state had a net loss of 750,000 people.[32]

While individuals are probably not making conscious decisions to move based on a state's labor law, the right-to-work status of a state has a domino effect on other policies. Politically strong unions push for big-government programs, because government workers are where unions are growing. This naturally leads to higher taxes. Big Labor's active campaigning for Democrats and lobbying for anti-employer legislation fosters more regulation, higher prices, lower real income growth, and lower employment. Faced with this dismal situation, people will naturally make a beeline for the door.

According to the U.S. Census Bureau, the forced-unionism states had a net migration loss of more than 2.3 million from 1995 to 2000. Meanwhile, free-choice states—with the resulting lower tax and cost burden and higher employment and income growth—had a net gain of more than 2.3 million during the same time period.[33]

WHEN IN DOUBT, RAISE TAXES

Is it possible that this is all coincidence and unions aren't really interested in raising taxes on the rest of us? A look at what happened in California when unions began calling the shots ought to dispel any doubts. Bucking a national trend that has seen union membership decline nationally, unionization in California has gone up dramatically in recent years. In 2002, the University of California's Institute for Labor and Employment reported that from 1997 to 2002 union membership in the Golden State had increased by half a million, to nearly 2.6 million members.[34]

Unions, especially the state's powerful public-employee unions, managed to reelect the widely unpopular Governor Gray Davis in 2002 and maintain Democratic control of both houses of the state legislature since 1996. According to the *Los Angeles Times*, unions provided logistical support and get-out-the-vote efforts critical to Davis's reelection,[35] not to mention the money and troops to run his campaign. The main hurdle to reelection that Davis faced was a budget crisis that threatened the state's fiscal health (and ultimately led to Davis's recall one year after his reelection). Though California revenue in 2002 was almost 20 percent higher than just four years earlier, spending had increased even more in that time, resulting in a $35 billion budget shortfall.[36] The spending increases were largely the result of pressure from Big Labor. For instance, even while it was widely acknowledged that the state was on the verge of financial ruin, Big Labor lobbied for—and got—a transportation budget that was $207 million more than even Governor Davis had wanted, for a total of $938 million.[37] Davis, under pressure from unions, also signed the first-ever paid parental and medical leave law in the nation, granting six weeks of paid leave at a huge potential cost to employers. Another law Davis signed required employers, including small businesses, to pay for health-care coverage for their workers by 2006, which was estimated to cost California employers an additional $5.7 billion.[38]

Meanwhile, the California Federation of Teachers (CFT) posted an eye-opening fiscal proposal on its website. In "Closing the Gap: What CFT Members Can Do About the Budget Crisis," the CFT displayed Big Labor's typical expand-government-at-all-costs logic. The union declared that the way to deal with California's financial woes was to enact or raise six different taxes and push for new legislation that would make it even easier to raise taxes in the future.[39] Naturally, the concept of cutting spending never entered the discussion.

Of course, the CFT claimed that these tax hikes were needed to "save public education" but didn't tie the increases to any improvement in student performance. The CFT apparently felt that the key to improving education quality in California was to oppose the Bush administration's policy in Iraq, or at least that is the impression the union's website gave. The site featured prominent photos of union leaders protesting the war and statements about how union convention delegates proudly "unconvened" to join war protests (one might think teachers could use a *real* word). It also thoughtfully reprinted a diatribe about the war on terrorism from liberal icon Senator Ted Kennedy.[40]

Big Labor's actions in California were not unique. In nearly any forced-unionism state—where compulsory dues turn union bosses into political kingpins—the unions push for higher taxes. In New York, another forced-unionism state, with its own extreme financial problems, government-union leaders have lobbied for higher taxes while talking about the need for shared sacrifice. What they mean is that taxpayers should sacrifice to pay more taxes so government growth can continue unabated, even though New York State already has the second highest per-capita taxation level in the country, a level more than twice the national average.[41]

In 2003, for example, union leaders in New York asked the state for higher income taxes, business taxes, property taxes, and sales taxes. In New York City a local chapter of the Communications Workers of America spent $300,000 on television ads attacking Republicans for talking about spending cuts instead of—you guessed it—raising taxes on "the rich." District Council 37, the scandal-plagued municipal union, spent another $500,000 on television ads to demand higher taxes. Big Labor's unique logic was on display in these ads, which stated, "Middle-class New Yorkers are paying higher fares and property taxes because of the budget crisis." So, of course, the solution proposed for these "higher fares and property taxes" was to raise different taxes. The Sanitation Workers, similarly, spent $70,000 on a media buy (including three full-page newspaper ads) demanding higher taxes as opposed to cuts in spending.[42]

These government unions refused even to consider cutting any government jobs despite the fact that New York had 160,000 more government employees than the national per capita average and despite the fact that those government workers earned 22 percent more than government employees in other states.[43] Nearly 300,000 taxpayers in New York had lost their jobs in the recession, but still the government-union leaders would not reduce their demands. Like the head of the United Airlines pilots' union, New York's labor bosses just wanted to choke out every last concession, no matter what the cost to taxpayers.

BIG LABOR DRIVES LOCAL GOVERNMENTS TO BANKRUPTCY

Big Labor's refusal to consider government spending cuts can have the same result as labor bosses' unyielding demands on employers in the private sector: bankruptcy.

Scores of cities have declared Chapter 9 bankruptcy, perhaps most notably Bridgeport, Connecticut. In 1991, the city declared bankruptcy because labor bosses refused to budge on union contracts. City officials could not cut even $12 million from a $308 million budget because of the demands of union contracts, which accounted for 60 percent of the city's expenses.[44] City officials explained that bankruptcy was the only way Bridgeport could renegotiate "onerous and economically burdensome" union contracts.[45]

In the early 1990s, Philadelphia faced a similar crisis because of fat government union contracts that left the city unable to cut costs. The city had raised taxes nineteen times in the 1980s, and it now had the third-highest tax burden in the nation. (A family of four earning $25,000 paid 13 percent of its income to the city.)[46] The middle class fled Philadelphia en masse, with 350,000 inhabitants deserting the city for the suburbs. This left Philadelphia with 1.6 million citizens, more than half of whom were classified as low-income.[47]

With a smaller tax base, Philadelphia continued to raise taxes in a fruitless effort to maintain the same revenue (and showing the typical government bureaucracy's shocking ignorance of the law of supply and demand). By the summer of 1990, Philadelphia could no longer find buyers for city bonds and was in danger of defaulting on both pension and vendor payments. Its credit rating dropped to B (highly speculative), and bond values fell to 86 cents on the dollar.[48]

Through all this, entry-level city employees were getting fifty-two paid days off each year—or one vacation day per week—and receiving unprecedented benefits. City workers were also receiving annual raises of 5 to 8 percent per year, far in excess of the rise in cost of living.[49] Was it only coincidence that Earl Stout, president of District Council 33, one of the city's most influential municipal-employee locals, went to jail for mail fraud, embezzlement, and racketeering activities in 1992?

While city residents were enduring higher taxes and declining public services, public-employee unions were busy ensuring that they had enough "work" to keep their members busy. As noted in Chapter 4, the featherbedding projects that cost the city dearly included a purposefully inefficient scheme to remove sludge from the city's water pipes that employed ten workers.[50] Another union-imposed work rule required the Philadelphia Museum of Art to maintain a full staff on duty at all times, even on days the museum was closed.[51]

Mayor Ed Rendell, faced with financial collapse, made the case to union officials: Either they could make concessions on wages and productivity or they would have to accept layoffs. Union leaders refused both choices and called a strike.

Eventually, union officials made grudging concessions—heralded as historic—that allowed Philadelphia to creep back from the precipice of financial ruin, but only after Rendell took his case to the public. Labor bosses agreed to let the mayor cut $374 million from the budget over four years, even though the budget needed $1.2 billion slashed. They also agreed to the city's cruel demand to reduce their paid time off from fifty-two days per year to a measly forty-three—still a full two months of the working year. They even gave the city "permission" to use volunteers for some tasks, provided that union bosses were notified in advance.[52]

Driving an employer—even the government—to the brink of ruin has been a long-standing modus operandi with Big Labor, as also seen in New York City's struggles. Today, of course, labor bosses refuse to make concessions even though New York faces major budget shortfalls, but even more famously New York City was on the brink of bankruptcy in the mid-1970s.

It's still perhaps the most famous tabloid headline in American history: "Ford to City: Drop Dead." In 1975, faced with bankruptcy, New York City turned to President Gerald Ford for a federal taxpayer bailout, but Ford rejected the request (at least initially). Amazingly, America's largest city was close to defaulting on its debts, and the reason was that Big Labor contracts had given union bosses control of the city, padded payrolls, and made cost cutting impossible.

New York's problems began in 1967, when Mayor John Lindsay signed Executive Order No. 52, giving union leaders such management duties as "workload and manning" and essentially turning over day-to-day operation of the city to Big Labor. By the late 1970s, the situation was so bad that the mayor complained that governing the city was near impossible because all but two thousand of the city's managers were union members accountable to union bosses. Taxes went up nearly every year and spending grew exponentially.[53]

New York City recruited an army of municipal employees, fielding 320,000 government workers, or one for every 24 citizens (as opposed to one for every 73 in Chicago).[54] The cost was staggering, with $8 billion of the city's $12 billion budget being spent on pensions and salaries.[55] Mayor Abe Beame kept the city afloat with complex financial gimmickry, such as issuing notes based on future state and federal funding, using actuarial tables from 1914 to project city expenses, and charging the final paycheck of the year to the next fiscal year.[56]

As deficits grew, union bosses refused to talk about cutbacks and stated a preference for city bankruptcy on the grounds that then everyone would be equally miserable. Said police union leader Kenneth McFeely, "Then nobody gets paid . . . the unions, welfare, the bankers. We'll all be in the same boat together."[57]

At one point in 1975, it looked as if powerful unions would come to the rescue of New York's Mayor Beame. The city's most powerful unions, including AFSCME's District Council 37 and the Teamsters, pledged union pension funds to keep the city from defaulting on bank loans. It also seemed that New York's teachers' union, the United Federation of Teachers, would help cover the city's shortfall. The union's president, Albert Shanker—who was also president of the national union, the AFT—promised the mayor $150 million from the United Federation of Teachers' pension fund, but then he threatened to back out of the deal. Shanker wanted to use his significant leverage to secure preferential treatment for the union in any future austerity program. This was the win-at-all-costs approach to negotiating that Woody Allen had parodied in his 1973 film *Sleeper,* in which's Allen's character awakes from a two-hundred-year sleep and learns that a horrible war has occurred: it all started when "a man named Albert Shanker got hold of the Bomb," he is told. Sure enough, with New York facing financial ruin, Shanker knew he had a powerful weapon. Only under intense pressure from New York Governor Hugh Carey did Shanker give the order to honor United Federation of Teachers' commitment, and even then it was just forty-five minutes before the funding deadline. "Woody Allen said if I had a nuclear weapon in my hand I would use it," Shanker told *Newsweek.* "Here I had it and I didn't use it."[58]

Still, New York City's finances were a disaster, mainly because of the long-standing policy of running up the city's debt in order to avoid cutting costs. The city could no longer find buyers for its bonds. Finally the state of New York stepped in, giving literally billions of dollars to the city to keep it afloat, thus burdening the citizens of the entire state with the cost of New York City's forced-unionism empire. And despite the famous tabloid headline, in December 1975 President Ford did approve a federal bailout of New York City, authorizing $2.3 billion in annual loans through 1978. Thus, every American taxpayer was forced to subsidize Big Labor's massive government-union program in New York City.

Whether in private industry or in government, Big Labor has a long history of "choking the golden goose." The assumption that the employer has a secret cache of unlimited currency leads hostile union negotiators to demand higher wages and benefits, unproductive union work rules, and featherbedding practices that would cripple even a financially thriving enterprise. When faced with any downturn in revenue, employers don't have the power to tighten their belts, because union bosses won't allow it. It's little wonder that these practices have driven companies out of business and cities into bankruptcy.

Again and again, Big Labor shows itself willing to damage the well-being of everyone else—including union members—in order to protect its own privileges. Union bosses often seem oblivious to the job losses that will occur when they push employers into bankruptcy. And they seem even more callous about the effect their demands have on taxpayers—again, including their own members.

UNION PENSION FUNDS: THE NEWEST WEAPON IN LABOR'S ARSENAL

Big Labor's influence extends beyond state capitals and local governments to a sector of the American economy most people rarely associate with labor unions—Wall Street. AFL-CIO chief John Sweeney may not have much respect for the stock market, once referring to "the vultures on Wall Street,"[59] but that hasn't stopped labor unions from becoming some of the biggest investors in the nation through union-controlled pension funds. Public-employee union pension funds alone invest $2 trillion of their aggregate $3 trillion in holdings in the stock market, making them among the most powerful players on the Street.[60] In all, workers' pension funds amount to $6 trillion—the biggest single source of investment in the stock market.[61] To understand just how powerful a weapon union-controlled pension funds have become—and their even greater potential to exert influence over the U.S. stock market and the economy down the line—it's important to understand how employee pension funds usually work and how labor union funds sometimes operate outside the normal rules.

Unions in both the public and private sector negotiate for employer contributions to union-controlled pension funds. Union members themselves usually exert little or no control over these funds, which pension fund managers oversee on the members' behalf. Federal law requires fund managers to act solely for the benefit of plan members,[62] following what is usually referred to as the "prudent man rule," which stipulates that the manager will act "with the care, skill, prudence, and diligence under the circumstances then prevailing that a prudent man acting in a like capacity and familiar with such matters would use in the conduct of an enterprise of a like character and with like aims."[63]

The idea is that fund managers invest funds to ensure a good return to fund members, not to promote social-engineering projects or the political or organizational goals of labor unions. Or more accurately, that *was* the idea before President Clinton's secretary of labor, Robert Reich, loosened fiduciary standards to allow fund managers to promote social causes.[64] Reich's move was largely a payoff to the Clinton administration's union benefactors. With their ability to use pension funds as tools to pursue their social agenda, union leaders now can use their power as major shareholders to push causes that have little relationship to a corporation's economic performance but instead are pet issues, such as lowering executive compensation or campaigning for more unionization.

According to a November 2003 report in *Business Week*, union pension funds now wield their clout to pressure corporations and state and local governments to settle strikes, maintain health benefits, block privatization, and grant union recognition, among other things. For example, the Service Employees International Union (SEIU) has been very successful in using its pension funds to help the union organize building janitors around the country, especially in California. The union successfully lobbied its public-employee locals—many of which invest their pension funds in real estate, purchasing controlling shares in large commercial buildings—to adopt "responsible contractor" policies. *Business Week* reported that the California Public Employees' Retirement System (CalPERS) and the Ohio Public Employees Retirement System forced the management companies that operated pension fund–controlled buildings to hire union companies to clean their buildings.[65] The practice has certainly helped the

SEIU, which was involved in a nasty janitors' strike in 2000 that alienated many building owners. But it also hurt investors, for it made the investments less profitable by adding to labor costs.

It's bad enough that these activities may end up costing retired union members by limiting them to investing in stocks that may deliver poor returns, but the practice ends up harming other investors as well, especially when unions succeed in forcing companies to make bad economic or governance decisions. Most investors—individuals and pension fund managers—care primarily about the return they receive on their investment. They don't buy a company's stock because they think the company treats its workers "fairly" or is a "good" corporate citizen. Indeed, such standards are highly subjective and have little relationship with—or may even hurt—the company's profitability and stock price. So a private fund manager normally wouldn't attempt to use the fund to engage in social engineering, because doing so would drain time and resources that the manager could use instead to increase the fund's performance—which of course determines how well the fund manager is paid.

But what if fund managers' compensation is no longer tied to the funds' performance? This is what happens when a union controls the pension fund. Suddenly fund managers are free to use their union-controlled shares to put pressure on corporations to accede to unions' demands.[66] And the interests of the unions are not necessarily those of union members, much less of other investors.

Shareholder resolutions are one way that the unions can leverage their control of pension funds to lobby for their political agenda. Any shareholder who has held a certain minimal number of shares for at least one year can inform the corporation in advance that the shareholder will present a proposal at a shareholders' meeting, and Securities and Exchange Commission (SEC) rules require the corporation to put the proposal to a vote by all shareholders.[67] The unions have embraced this power. In fact, the number of shareholder resolutions brought by unions and union-controlled pension funds has more than doubled recently, from 105 in 2001 to over 200 in 2003,[68] making union pension funds among the most activist investor groups.[69]

The unions have wielded shareholder resolutions in their ongoing campaign to restrict executive pay, which is a key component of Big

Labor's leftist agenda. This campaign has been directed from the very top: John Sweeney himself has urged unions to use their status as shareholders to fix the "gap between the pay of a handful of top executives and everyone else in American society."[70] This goal might make good propaganda fodder but has little or nothing to do with return on investment for the pension plan's stockholders. Nevertheless, the unions have obeyed. In 1997, for example, the Teamsters successfully placed a shareholder resolution on General Electric's proxy statements that would have put a limit on the base salary of General Electric's executives.[71] Fearing that such a limit would cripple its ability to attract and retain top management personnel, General Electric urged shareholders to reject the proposal. The resolution garnered only 9 percent of the vote, but this was enough to allow the Teamsters to claim that more and more investors were advocating limits on executive pay.[72] Since then, the unions have only increased their efforts, and in fact union and public-employee pension funds have won more than two dozen campaigns to limit executive pay or benefits in recent years.[73] Although these efforts might strike a populist chord, they also send a signal to corporate leaders that they had better play ball with the union or they will jeopardize their own pay and tenure.

Unions have also found a way to work around ordinary regulations to maximize their influence over corporations. For example, to escape the SEC requirement that a certain number of shares be held for one year before a shareholder can force a resolution onto a company proxy statement,[74] union leaders often send representatives to annual meetings to propose floor resolutions. As Teamsters Union corporate affairs coordinator Bartlett Naylor explained, "It frees us up to make longer arguments."[75] Unions use floor resolutions to promote another of their objectives, unionization of the target corporation. In 1996, the Teamsters were engaged in a bitter struggle with Union Pacific over unionization, and perhaps not coincidentally, the union used a shareholders' meeting to attack the Union Pacific corporate leadership. First, on the day of the shareholders' meeting, the Teamsters ran full-page newspaper ads attacking the executives' pay.[76] Union representatives then appeared at the shareholder meeting and proposed a resolution that would have forced out CEO Drew

Lewis. A Union Pacific spokesman noted, "They didn't appear at any annual meetings before the organizing drive started."[77] The success of this effort prompted the Teamsters to boast, "Looks like Lewis is losing control of his non-union baby."[78]

In 1997, the United Food and Commercial Workers (UFCW), in its fight to unionize workers at Albertson's grocery company, took the tactic one step further, attacking Albertson's directors on other boards where they served.[79] The UFCW held up the reelection of the entire board of directors of an unrelated company, Pier 1 Imports, because one of Pier 1's directors was also a director at Albertson's.[80] The Albertson's directors' great offense, it seems, was that they refused to recognize UFCW as the bargaining representative of its employees without an official National Labor Relations Board election. In other words, the union punished the directors because they refused to cave in to the union's demands but instead insisted that the UFCW follow the law. The UFCW had no interest in Albertson's governance policies before it began its organizing drive, and in fact, the union owned only forty-three shares of Albertson's stock when the campaign against the company started.[81]

As legal scholar Marleen O'Connor noted in a laudatory study of union pension power, "For the most part, the use of [union] shareholder activism in corporate campaigns is limited to companies that are having some type of labor dispute."[82] For example, the Union of Needletrades, Industrial, and Textile Employees (UNITE) and the Teamsters Union succeeding in preventing Kmart from spinning off a subsidiary and pressured management into removing its CEO, but its real motive may have been to get Kmart to accept a union shop in North Carolina. O'Connor reported that union pension power was particularly effective in forcing Wheeling-Pittsburgh Steel Corporation to settle a strike with the Steelworkers Union in 1997: "The union persuaded the major shareholder of Wheeling-Pitt's parent, Dewey Square Investors Corp., to encourage the management of Wheeling-Pitt to settle the strike. The union was able to exert influence because Dewey Square's parent, United Asset Management Corp., manages $10 billion in union pension money."[83]

Unions are becoming increasingly sophisticated in using their pension fund clout to pressure companies to do their bidding. The

AFL-CIO has an Office of Investments, whose director has warned that unions would move to unseat key board members of companies that fail to adopt executive-compensation limits favored by Big Labor.[84] The AFL-CIO also funds the Center for Working Capital, which runs courses to teach unions how to use their investments to promote Big Labor's social agenda, among other things. Moreover, according to O'Connor the AFL-CIO has taken two steps under its Capital Stewardship Program to turn private, multiemployer pension funds into a voting bloc. First, the organization has developed guidelines on proxy voting for union pension trustees; these assert that fiduciaries should not seek to maximize short-term gains that conflict "with the long-term economic best interests of the participants and beneficiaries"—in other words, the best interests of the unions.[85] The real purpose of this measure is to encourage unions to use their pension funds to oppose profit-enhancing measures such as streamlining the workforce, reducing labor costs, and outsourcing jobs—even if doing so would bring far higher returns on pension investments. Second, the AFL-CIO conducts surveys to monitor whether the fiduciaries who manage union pension funds are following the guidelines. With literally billions of dollars at stake, this strategy has the potential to transform equity investing in the United States and to harm not only the union members who are investors in the funds but also the American economy as a whole.

Worse, union pension funds are one of the chief sources of union corruption and racketeering. As of 2002, 44 percent of the Justice Department's 357 pending racketeering investigations involved union pension and welfare funds.[86] No case better illustrates the hypocrisy of union bosses when it comes to protecting their members' pension investments than the sordid case of the Union Labor Life Insurance Corporation, known as Ullico, a privately held insurance company whose stockholders are primarily union pension funds and union officials.

In 1997, Ullico invested $7.6 million in Global Crossing, a company with strong ties to Democratic National Committee chairman Terry McAuliffe, whose own $100,000 investment in Global Crossing reaped him an $18 million profit.[87] Ullico's union pension investors didn't fare nearly as well as McAuliffe, however. Global Crossing declared bankruptcy in 2002—with Ullico still holding 60 percent of the stock it had originally purchased.[88] The value of Ullico's fund plunged as a result. But while pensioners were left holding the bag, many on Ullico's board made out like bandits. Because Ullico is a privately held company, its board can behave in ways that leaders of a public corporation never could. As the *Wall Street Journal* explained it, the insiders on the board "bought Ullico shares at a guaranteed low price and quickly sold them back to the company at a guaranteed higher price, even as Ullico's underlying value plummeted." The board members, the *Journal* wrote, "authorized both the share price and their own buyback—which wasn't available to most of Ullico's big pension fund shareholders. Some 20 directors and officers raked in about $13.7 million in connection with the changing share price."[89]

Among the biggest winners was Ullico chairman and chief executive officer Robert Georgine, who made $837,760 in pre-tax profits on the deal. This was on top of the $1 million he was already earning in his post as Ullico chairman and the $264,000 he made as the head of the AFL-CIO's Building and Construction Trades Department.[90] Georgine was forced to resign as chairman in the spring of 2003.

Another board member, Jake West, collected the same profit as Georgine. West was president emeritus of the International Association of Iron Workers, and he was also a trustee of the ironworkers' pension fund. A lawsuit filed in 2003 charged West with failing in his trustee duties to protect the ironworkers' pensions. That is, he apparently let the ironworkers' pension plan remain invested in Ullico even though he knew that the stock would plummet based on its Global Crossings holdings.[91] Of course, by 2003, West had already pled guilty to a separate charge of embezzling pension money and member dues. In October 2003, he was sentenced to three years in prison and fined $125,000.[92]

That same month, a congressional committee issued a report based on hearings it had held on the Ullico scandal. On issuing the report, the chairman of the House Education and the Workforce Committee, Republican John Boehner of Ohio, said, "Millions of workers deserve to know whether Ullico directors violated the law and made millions at the expense of rank-and-file union members they represent." As of this writing, investigations into the legality of the Ullico board members' actions are still ongoing at the Labor and Justice Departments, the Securities and Exchange Commission, a federal grand jury, and the state of Maryland's insurance commission.[93] But one thing is certain: As the *Wall Street Journal* wrote, "The compulsory dues-paying rank and file deserve to know that the offenders will be held accountable every bit as much as Enron executives."[94]

AFL-CIO secretary-treasurer Richard Trumka has noted, "There is no more important strategy for the Labor Movement than harnessing our pension funds and developing capital strategies so we can stop our money from cutting our own throats."[95] But with Big Labor's socialist, redistributionist agenda, its commitment to featherbedding and undermining productivity, its corrupt practices, and its love of Big Government and high taxes, these union pension funds could end up being used to cut the throat of American free-market capitalism.

That would be no surprise, for union leaders have shown over and over again that they will hinder true economic growth as long as they can protect their own power and, even better, feather their own nests.

CHAPTER 9

Ending the Cycle of Corruption

Americans now live under a system of legal apartheid. While most of us abide by a common set of laws, the labor unions enjoy special privileges and operate under an entirely different set of laws and regulations.

Many Americans bemoan the influence of special interests in Washington, D.C., but somehow the extraordinary power of America's labor bosses has escaped notice. The fact is, the unions have a stranglehold on the Democratic Party and now can operate essentially as they wish. The Democrats know they can't win elections without Big Labor's money and troops, so they are willing to grant union bosses concession after concession.

As we have seen, the Democratic Party has actually given the unions veto power over its policy decisions and campaign strategies. Again, to put this arrangement in perspective, simply imagine the uproar if the Federal Election Commission revealed that the Republican Party had given that same sort of control to a corporate interest like

Halliburton. (In truth, a corporate entity could never offer up the sort of support that labor unions do. Corporations are limited by what they can raise via *voluntary* contributions, whereas the unions have the unique power to take money out of workers' pockets to finance their political activism and whatever else they want.)

As shocking as the Democrats' arrangement with the unions was—or should have been—that was just the beginning of the sellout. The labor unions currently take in some $17 billion in tax-free income a year, but the exodus of private-sector workers from the unions— remember, in 2002 alone the private-sector unions lost 445,000 members—jeopardizes the future stream of member dues. With workers fleeing from the unions, labor leaders desperate to maintain their power focus their attention on government—that is, Big Government. The bigger government gets, the more dues-paying union employees will be hired. That is why America's union bosses throw all their weight behind the Democratic Party—to push their Big Government agenda. For their part, the Democrats kowtow to Big Labor because they are so dependent on the unions' political machine.

In other words, the unions pour hundreds of millions of dollars into Democratic coffers every year as a means to keep *billions* of dollars rushing into their own treasuries. The Democrats also want billions of dollars in member dues to continue streaming into Big Labor's treasuries, because as long as that revenue comes in, the unions will keep raining money on Democratic candidates and organizations. The cycle of corruption is seemingly endless.

The corrupt bond between Democrats and the unions only grows stronger. With every election, union bosses ratchet up their efforts on behalf of Democrats; as *Wall Street Journal* political reporter John Fund noted in early 2004: "Some unions now routinely deplete their entire treasury in election years."[1] AFL-CIO president John Sweeney, a self-proclaimed socialist, has pushed the unions to the far left and has also made politics practically the singular focus of the American labor movement. Today, unions spend a tiny fraction of their members' hard-earned money negotiating and servicing contracts, even though these activities are their raison d'être.

The Democrats, meanwhile, have become ever more faithful to the union bosses' radical political agenda. Not only do they move to the left to please their union patrons, they also stand in the way of much-needed reforms that would threaten Big Labor's special privileges. Since the unions are failing to attract workers in the free market, union bosses depend on their Democratic allies to preserve forced unionism. If workers won't join and pay dues of their own volition, the unions and their allies in government will *coerce* workers into contributing to the treasury as a condition of employment. Someone working a job covered by a union contract suddenly loses his First Amendment right to associate with whomever he chooses, for freedom to choose only one alternative is no freedom at all. The sole purpose of forced-unionism laws is to extend the power and privilege of labor unions.

For the Democrats, being in Big Labor's pocket also means helping the unions hide their operations from their members' view and the public's. Even though court decisions have guaranteed the right of union members to get back that portion of their money not used specifically for collective bargaining, contract administration, and employee grievance adjustment, the process of retrieving money is cumbersome and most workers are unaware of their rights in the first place. Worse, the lack of transparency and accountability allows labor unions to hide from their members and from the IRS how they are spending their money. As long as the government lets them guard the secrets of how they allocate their money, union bosses will continue to shake down their members and focus their efforts on securing as much political power as possible.

To understand how important the unions have become to the Democratic Party, one can look at the leading Democrats and see that they are beholden to the unions. Consider just a few examples from the rogues' gallery of Democratic politicians who have bent to the will of union bosses:

- *Hillary Clinton:* Now the most powerful member of the husband-and-wife political team, Mrs. Clinton has gotten as far as she has because of the unions. After all, this was the Democrat who chose to announce her Senate candidacy in the headquarters of New York City's powerful teachers' union, with the union leader standing proudly by her side. And the unions backed her to the hilt in her 2000 Senate campaign, contributing $453,000, plus hundreds of volunteers to man phone banks, distribute campaign literature, and get out the vote. As a senator she has been loyal to her union patrons, opposing more stringent financial-disclosure regulations for unions, stalling the creation of the Department of Homeland Security for months by pushing for unreasonable concessions to government-employee unions, even flip-flopping her position on the issue of competency testing for teachers. But even as First Lady she cozied up to union bosses, including the leader of the Laborers International Union, who according to the Justice Department had "associated with, and been controlled and influenced by, organized crime figures."

■ *Bill Clinton:* President Clinton was far chummier with the leader of the Laborers union than even his wife. Laborers leader Arthur Coia gave the Democrats hefty contributions throughout the Clinton presidency, and in exchange, Bill Clinton's administration gave the Laborers a massive chunk of federal grants, while also letting Coia himself off the hook on racketeering charges. This relationship, of course, was merely the most dramatic example of how Bill Clinton let union bosses buy influence. Remember, it was for Clinton's 1996 reelection campaign that the Democratic National Committee gave Big Labor actual veto power over the Democrats' policy platform and campaign strategies.

■ *Al Gore:* In his 2000 presidential campaign, Gore was so grateful to John Sweeney and the AFL-CIO for their overwhelming efforts on his behalf that he made clear that Big Labor's wish was his command. He told Sweeney publicly, "I love you, buddy," pledged that as president he would be "pro-union," and made clear his devotion to union bosses by denouncing just about any law or regulation that Big Labor opposed. He had reason to be grateful since unions produced a huge turnout on his behalf in the 2000 election, with tens of thousands of union activists leading get-out-the-vote drives in key states such as Pennsylvania and Michigan— which ended up helping Gore win the popular vote.[2] During the post-election recounts and court battles, unions trucked in hundreds of "volunteers" to stand guard[3] as officials in Democratic counties recounted ballots, while other union members and AFL-CIO honchos, including John Sweeney, demonstrated alongside Jesse Jackson outside the state legislature.

- *John Kerry:* As soon as Kerry became the presumptive 2004 Democratic nominee, after winning the Wisconsin primary and twelve out of fourteen other primary elections and caucuses through early February, the AFL-CIO quickly jumped aboard his bandwagon, endorsing him on February 19, 2004. Although the AFL-CIO had been split before the first primary votes were cast—with the big public-employee unions endorsing Howard Dean and many of the more traditional industrial unions supporting Dick Gephardt, Sweeney was anxious to show labor's clout, and Kerry's liberal voting record made him a natural ally. Kerry has voted with labor 90 percent of the time over his Senate career.[4] And while he claims to have rejected PAC contributions, including those of labor unions, he was happy to accept almost half a million dollars from corporations and unions in 2002 for his "Citizen Soldier Fund," through a loophole in the soft-money ban passed in the McCain-Feingold campaign finance reform bill. Given labor's record in the last several presidential elections, John Kerry can expect tens of millions of dollars—hundreds of millions, according to some experts—in direct and indirect contributions to his presidential campaign.

- *Howard Dean:* The former Vermont governor became one of the leading Democratic contenders in 2004 (indeed, the early front-runner), and he owed a lot of his success to the endorsements he received from the powerful government-employee unions AFSCME and SEIU. One AFSCME official declared, "The first thing we have to do is remind ourselves that we are fighting for socialism," and Dean certainly adopted the union leaders' radical leftist platform. He opposed the war in Iraq, called for higher taxes, even on the middle class, and promised more government control of the economy.

- *Richard Gephardt:* Though Gephardt fizzled out as a presidential candidate, it wasn't because of lack of union effort. The former

House Democratic leader's slavish adherence to the Big Labor agenda earned him the early backing of an array of industrial unions, who put some nine hundred union operatives on the ground for him for the Iowa caucuses. Moreover, a top Gephardt campaign aide allegedly threatened the heads of AFSCME and SEIU in an attempt to prevent them from campaigning for Dean. To that Gephardt official, it seems, the unions' power to influence elections was quite clear.

- *Ted Kennedy:* One of the last old-style liberals in the Senate is, of course, one of the unions' fiercest defenders. In his 2000 Senate race, Kennedy received $352,750,[5] even though he faced barely any real opposition for re-election. Along with Hillary Clinton, he adamantly opposed the Labor Department's calls for more stringent financial-disclosure requirements for the unions. In addition, just *days* after September 11, 2001, he tried to sneak through a bill that would have forced firefighters, police officers, and emergency workers to be unionized—a nice sop to Big Labor. When that attempt failed, another leading Democrat, Senate Minority Leader Tom Daschle, swooped in to try to push through the union power grab.

- *Charles Schumer:* Even before he became the senior senator from New York, Charles Schumer was eager to support the future junior senator, Mrs. Clinton, and her husband—not to mention his union backers. Rather than taking seriously the evidence of corruption and mob influence in Arthur Coia's Laborers union, Schumer dismissed an FBI informant's credible claims by saying, "Do you believe space aliens are linked to the mob?" Big Labor—including Coia's Laborers union—rewarded Schumer by giving him hundreds of thousands of dollars for his next campaign.

- *Nancy Pelosi:* The leftist congresswoman Nancy Pelosi became the highest-ranking Democrat in the House of Representatives when she was elected House minority leader in 2002. Pelosi belongs to the Progressive Caucus, the left-wing group with close ties to the Democratic Socialists of America, of which the

AFL-CIO's John Sweeney is a proud member. Sweeney's political power has helped the left-wing Progressive Caucus become a political force. And Pelosi has fought to make sure the unions keep up their support for their liberal brethren. On March 8, 2004, the Capitol Hill newspaper *Roll Call* reported that she held a special meeting with Sweeney and other labor leaders to make sure the unions didn't throw any support to moderate Republicans in the election. Pelosi, apparently, wanted to be Speaker, and she didn't want the unions doing anything to prevent the Democrats from taking the House.

With so many Democrats in the grip of Big Labor, it is no surprise that the unions have been able to protect their special legal privileges. But the corrupt bargain between the Democratic Party and union bosses has devastating consequences. Many American workers are forced to pay dues to unions they don't want to belong to and see their money going to pay for a radical political agenda they oppose. Some workers have been fired simply for asking about how their dues money was being spent; others, like teacher Jaime Escalante, have been forced out of jobs because union militants were upset with their efforts to make employees more productive and accountable. Many Americans have actually lost their jobs because unions have blocked employers' efforts to increase productivity, modernize, and remain competitive. By insisting on unsustainable wages and benefits and outdated business practices, unions have caused companies to fold and have forced entire industries overseas.

Union bosses have so much power over—and so little regard for—their members that they can operate essentially as they please. Their power applies to far more than how they decide to spend members' money. So dictatorial is union rule that in 1998, after the members of Seattle Iron Workers Local 86 voted down the contract negotiated by union bargainers—not once, but twice—the international union imposed a trusteeship on the Seattle local and signed the contract on behalf of the membership. The union charged at least one protesting member with "inciting dissension."[6]

The special powers and privileges given to Big Labor have yielded a corrupt and rotten system. Shielded from measures of accountability and transparency, corrupt labor leaders have fleeced union members, living lavishly by skimming from union treasuries. Mobsters also recognize the potential to skim millions from the unions, which is why organized crime has infiltrated so many labor unions.

All of this is troubling, but it is also important to remember that workers under union contracts are not the only ones who pay. We *all* pay. To begin, when Big Labor succeeds in expanding government, the American taxpayer has to foot the bill for growing budgets. Furthermore, as government-employee unions grow stronger, more and more public-works projects become union-run boondoggles, and taxpayers are responsible for those costs as well. The problem gets worse when mobbed-up unions are in charge and the mobsters use the taxpayers' money for their own purposes. As we have seen, too, states where forced unionism prevails have higher taxes and a higher cost of living on average.

Among the most powerful unions are the teachers' unions, and these organizations routinely oppose real educational reform. Thanks to the unions' fierce resistance to meaningful change, the taxpayers have had to pour more and more money into an education system that produces poor results. While even some of the most incompetent teachers have been able to keep their jobs permanently, generations of American schoolchildren have suffered at the hands of a bureaucratic system controlled by the teachers' unions.

Perhaps the most frightening aspect of the unions' ability to operate as if they are above the law is that they can put Americans at physical risk. America's government-employee unions put their own power ahead of all else, including public safety. Although laws in most states prohibit government employees from striking, these laws are often ignored as powerful unions negotiate striker amnesty into strike settlements. And strikes give government unions extraordinary leverage, for government employees have a monopoly on the services they provide, many of which the public cannot do without, whether it is policing, fire fighting, emergency services, or public transit. We are all at the mercy of the powerful unions.

Then, of course, there is the matter of legalized union terrorism— the loophole that gives striking unions license to commit acts of violence as long as they are pursuing supposedly legitimate bargaining objectives. When unions are granted an exemption to terrorize American citizens, something is terribly wrong.

FIGHTING BACK

Big Labor has become a dinosaur in the U.S. economy: a big beast with a huge appetite, powerful enough to cause trouble for whomever it opposes. But like the dinosaur before it, Big Labor could face extinction unless it adapts to changing conditions.

Federal labor law is largely a product of 1930s, Depression-era America.[7] The premise behind labor laws created during this era was a now-discredited Marxist theory—that management and labor are natural and eternal enemies, and that since all the advantages are stacked in management's favor, balance can be achieved only by permitting unions to control the supply of labor. It's arguable whether these laws were needed in the 1930s, but they are certainly unnecessary today—and, furthermore, they are actually detrimental to America's place in the world economy.

The American economy has changed dramatically over the years. For example, in 1950 more than one-third of American jobs were in manufacturing, but by 2000 this figure had plummeted to 14 percent.[8] The days of big manufacturing businesses signing union contracts covering thousands of workers are largely a thing of the past. Today, most Americans work for small businesses or in the service industry. Meanwhile, the American economy has become more integrated into the world economy, with exports growing from 3.8 percent of gross domestic product in 1950 to almost 10 percent today, while imports have jumped from 3.2 percent to almost 14 percent.[9] This competition from foreign workers makes it important for employers to maintain a flexible workforce or face extinction.

Unions, however, are anything but flexible; they seek to protect the status quo. This is a main reason why so many workers, when given a choice, have left the unions. Most employees understand the changing nature of the American economy and now seek the type of working conditions that unions often vehemently oppose. For instance, national polls reveal that 65 percent of Americans want more flexible work schedules, while 58 percent would choose paid time off rather than overtime wages—a concept that is anathema to union leadership.

The trouble is, Americans cannot simply wait around for unions to become extinct. For five decades the labor movement has watched workers run away from the unions, but America's union bosses have been remarkably successful at preserving and even enhancing their power. Labor bosses will not accept their fate; they are desperate to keep member dues coming in, even if it means having the government force workers to hand over their money. That is why their political activity has become their main (or only) focus.

The only way to eliminate Big Labor's abuses is to wipe out the system of legal apartheid that Congress has adopted and the courts and government bureaucrats have furthered. As long as Big Labor is given exemptions to laws that apply to everyone else and privileges that no others enjoy, working men and women, the American taxpayer, and the American public will be at the mercy of these organizations.

The following reform proposals would help eliminate the privileges granted to Big Labor. Passing these laws won't be easy as long as so many members of Congress owe their jobs to Big Labor. But the measures might be the only way to restore the rights of American workers, to protect the American people—and to end the corrupt bargain between the unions and the Democratic Party.

1. Give workers true freedom of choice—and remove the special privileges of labor leaders

Federal law now dictates that if barely more than half of employees (50 percent plus one) vote to be represented by a union, then that union is the exclusive representative of every employee, whether or not a particular employee voted for the union.[10] In fact, it may be that *no* current employee voted for the union—the election could have taken place fifty years earlier, before some employees now on the job were even born. But that union-representation election binds every employee of the company virtually in perpetuity; to call for a new representation election, the employer first must go through a cumbersome procedure to decertify the union. The rules for decertification are heavily weighted in favor of the unions and require dissatisfied employees to expose themselves in ways that almost guarantee union retaliation.[11]

Of course, all workers should be free to join unions or choose other representation, but they shouldn't be forced into accepting representation because others voted for it. Even in right-to-work states, workers can be forced into a binding employment contract against their will. This amounts to unconscionable coercion in a democratic society predicated on freedom of association. In fact, the founder of the American labor movement, Samuel Gompers, himself recognized the problems with compulsory unionism. Gompers told the 1924 AFL convention that "no lasting gain has ever come from compulsion." He went on to note, "The workers of America adhere to voluntary institutions in preference to compulsory systems which are held to be not only impractical, but a menace to their rights, their welfare and their liberty." Gompers also told followers, "There may be here and there a worker who for certain reasons . . . does not join a union of labor. It is his legal right and no one can or dare question his exercise of that legal right."[12]

Removing forcible exclusive representation is important not just because it would establish true voluntary unionism and would be faithful to the founding spirit of the American labor movement. Significantly, it would eliminate many of the concerns about union political spending. If unions represented only those persons who voluntarily chose to join, and no one else was forced to accept the terms of the union contract or pay fees to the union, then what the union did with its money would be its own business.

An excellent legislative model is New Zealand's 1991 Employment Contracts Act, which has revitalized New Zealand's economy. According to Charles Baird, economics professor at California State University and founding director of the Smith Center for Private Enterprise Studies, passing the law was politically difficult, since 85 percent of the population initially opposed it. By 1999, though, 73 percent of employees said they were "satisfied" or "very satisfied" with their working conditions and terms of employment.[13] In just five years after the Employment Contracts Act went into effect, New Zealand's unemployment plunged from 11 percent to 6 percent.[14]

Quite simply, the Employment Contracts Act allows for complete freedom of choice in representation. An individual can represent himself and negotiate his own terms of employment, or he can choose to have a union collectively bargain for him. In fact, he may have a choice among several unions, since the law does not prohibit multiple unions from representing the same class of workers at a single workplace. The competition forces unions to be more responsive to their members, while other individuals are free to act on their own behalf, as they see fit.

So why does U.S. law expressly forbid individuals from choosing their own representatives? What can be so bad about letting workers choose for themselves?

Union leaders oppose the concept because it would force them to be responsive to members. Since Big Labor can force people to join and pay dues regardless of union actions or service, it's no wonder that unions have come to ignore the best interests of the people they ostensibly represent in favor of the best interests of union leaders themselves. Big Labor knows that if choice becomes the operative force, their membership will plunge even faster than it already has, along with their cash flow. Forced representation is simply a matter of preserving labor bosses' perks and power.

2. Stop Big Labor from spending members' dues on politics without their permission

Without a doubt the true source of the unions' overwhelming political power is their war chests filled with member dues. Even if the monopoly power of exclusive representation were not eliminated, Big Labor would suffer if it lost its power to force workers to pay for its private political agenda. After all, most unions spend a little of their budgets on true union representation and funnel lots of money to political activities.

Union members—as well as nonmember agency-fee payers—are not, contrary to John Sweeney's apparent belief, uniform, lockstep socialists. Surveys repeatedly show that some 40 percent of union members vote Republican. But even Democratic union members are having their freedom abused. Given a choice of keeping their hard-earned money or giving it to the union for a political program, most union members would opt not to have their wages confiscated.

Legislation to prevent a worker's wages from being confiscated for political purposes would essentially enforce the U.S. Supreme Court's 1977 decision in *Abood v. Detroit Board of Education* and its 1988 decision in *Communications Workers of America v. Beck,* which held that unions could not force members to pay for anything other than collective bargaining, contract administration, and grievance adjustment. Just as *Brown v. Board of Education,* which outlawed segregation in public schools, didn't lead to instant desegregation, the *Beck* and *Abood* decisions haven't yet cut into the unions' improper political spending.

The first President Bush issued an executive order requiring federal contractors to inform workers of their *Beck* rights.[15] But one of the first things President Clinton did when he took office was to rescind the order, as his labor secretary, Robert Reich, called it a "burden without a benefit."[16] Later, the pro-union National Labor Relations Board, the administrative agency that is charged with hearing labor complaints, ruled that unions should self-audit to determine for themselves what expenses were related to collective bargaining; the board required no outside verification.[17] The National Labor Relations Board also ruled that the requirement that members be notified of their rights could be satisfied just by putting a small notice annually in a union publication.

We can see just how effective this has been. A 1996 poll by Luntz Research revealed that 78 percent of union members were not aware that they had the right to obtain a refund of the portion of their union fees that go toward political and other non–contract-related expenses.[18]

When members are aware of their rights, they are sometimes punished for daring to raise the issue. For instance, when AFSCME member Robert Murray asserted his constitutional right not to pay for the union's leftist political program, the union "deducted" the political expenses and then *raised* his fees from $28.96 a month to $29.79.[19] That's right, empowered by the ability to self-audit its expenses, AFSCME claimed that contract bargaining expenses were a dollar more per month than those same expenses plus political costs. Perhaps the union bosses were determined to punish Murray and serve up an object lesson for other dissenters.

Some who complain are the subject of unrelenting union intimidation. Airline mechanic Kerry Gipe testified in congressional hearings:

> The union began an almost immediate smear campaign against us . . . portraying us as scabs, and freeloaders. . . . We had our names posted repeatedly on both union property and company property accusing us of being scabs. We were thrown out of our local union hall, and threatened with physical violence. . . . We were accosted at work, we were accosted on the street. We were harassed, intimidated, and threatened. We were told that our names were being circulated among all union officials in order to prevent us from ever being hired into any other union shop at any other location.[20]

Typical paycheck-protection legislation doesn't go far enough. Several states have tried to protect workers' rights—five since 1992—but these bills generally put the onus on the employee rather than the union, for under these bills the worker has to ask for his money back. Unions should be required to get annual written permission up front for political use of a worker's dues money.

Furthermore, even in right-to-work states, workers need the ability to belong to a union if they choose without paying for the union's political agenda. Under *Beck,* a person who asserts his right not to pay for political activity must resign his union membership and must pay agency fees (the amount of the dues less the political portion). The problem is that even if he is no longer a union member, he is still forced into collectively bargained contracts—and his only opportunity to vote on these contracts comes with membership. A worker shouldn't have to pay for a political program he opposes in order to be able to vote on a contract that will bind him.

3. Repeal laws that allow unions to fleece the government

The Davis-Bacon Act, which mandates that the federal government pay "prevailing wages"—a euphemism for inflated union rates—for construction projects, is one of the many ways in which the government gives unfair preferences to unions. Perhaps more shocking, however, is that the legislation itself is deeply rooted in racism.

Congress passed the law in 1931 to keep nonunion workers from competing for federal construction jobs, and since nonwhites were commonly barred from union membership, the legislation helped protect the jobs of whites in the fiercely competitive Depression job market. One of the supporters of the bill, Congressman Miles Clayton Allgood, Democrat of Alabama, made no bones about his motivation for supporting Davis-Bacon. In a speech on the floor of the House of Representatives, he complained openly of "cheap colored labor" that "is in competition with white labor throughout the country."[21] AFL president William Green, whose organization actively supported the bill, testified before the Senate Committee on Manufacturers that Davis-Bacon was needed because "colored labor is being brought in to demoralize wage rates."[22]

While those supporting Davis-Bacon today may not be racist, the law still has a racially discriminatory effect. First, Davis-Bacon imposes arcane work rules that hurt many unskilled workers, who are still disproportionately from the racial groups that Davis-Bacon was originally meant to exclude. One rule requires that a worker who performs a variety of jobs must be paid at the highest applicable skilled journeyman rate, which means that a general laborer who hammers a nail must be classified as a carpenter and paid as much as three times the company's regular rate.[23] Many companies simply cannot afford to pay unskilled workers the government-determined prevailing wage, and so these laborers have difficulty finding work on government jobs. And because training workers can be done only through costly, highly regulated apprenticeship programs (often run by unions and paid for by tax dollars), these unskilled laborers face a major barrier to entering the job market.

Evidence shows that repealing Davis-Bacon would create hundreds of thousands of new jobs. For instance, Ohio University economist Richard Vedder showed that when Michigan suspended its prevailing-wage law from 1994 to 1997 (because the law violated federal pension regulations), it created eleven thousand new jobs.[24]

Davis-Bacon also has the effect of discriminating against minority contractors. Most minority-owned firms are small companies, and small construction firms cannot afford to operate under Davis-Bacon's rigid job classifications. What's more, the extensive paperwork necessary just to bid on a federal contract—never mind actually fulfill it—requires a staff of lawyers and accountants, an expense well beyond the means of most small businessmen. Indeed, repealing Davis-Bacon would do far more to increase minority contracting than extending the racial bidding preferences and minority set-asides currently mandated by federal and state laws.

Besides opening up the labor market to more unskilled workers and minority contractors, repealing Davis-Bacon would have enormous benefit to working, taxpaying Americans. American taxpayers shelled out billions of dollars in inflated construction costs because of Davis-Bacon. It's bad enough that so-called prevailing wages are significantly higher than market wages, but evidence indicates that the U.S. Department of Labor has sometimes relied on faulty data in determining what constitutes the prevailing wage in certain areas. The Oklahoma Department of Labor, for example, found that the data on which the U.S. Labor Department based its wage determinations for the state were actually fraudulent, jacking up wages way beyond prevailing rates.[25] Davis-Bacon requirements inflate federal construction costs by as much as 50 percent. In fact, the Congressional Budget Office has reported that repealing Davis-Bacon would save the American taxpayer almost $3 billion in just four years.[26]

But Davis-Bacon isn't the only statute on the books that forces companies that want to do business with the government to pay union wages and benefits or, in some cases, even to give unions the power to hire employees for the job. The Service Contract Act, also known as the McNamara-O'Hara Service Contract Act, also requires companies who provide service workers to the government—for example, janitors in government buildings or food service workers—to pay prevailing rates. Like Davis-Bacon, this law makes it more difficult for the government to contract with nonunion companies, including minority-owned contractors and subcontractors. The General Accounting Office (GAO) has recommended repeal of this law because its enforcement by the Department of Labor historically has been arbitrary and capricious. Citing the Department of Labor's "inability to administer the act efficiently and effectively," the GAO said that "it is impractical, in our opinion, to make 'prevailing wage' determinations under the act in a consistently equitable manner."[27]

True reform would also call for revoking all Project Labor Agreements entered into by federal, state, and local governments. These agreements—often mandated by laws or regulations at the federal, state, and local level—force government agencies to contract exclusively with union shops or force nonunion employers to recognize the union as the exclusive bargaining representative of all its employees. Although the ostensible purpose of these agreements is to guarantee "labor peace" on the job, PLA projects are frequently beset with strikes and other "job actions." The agreements also penalize nonunion firms unfairly and increase costs.[28]

4. Give workers the flexibility that unions won't give them

One reason that unions have been allowed to remain inflexible is that labor laws have not changed with an evolving economy and society. The Fair Labor Standards Act, another Depression-era law, establishes work rules for most nonmanagerial workers, including standards for minimum wages and overtime pay. Passed originally in 1938 and amended several times since, the Fair Labor Standards Act is best known for establishing the standard forty-hour workweek. Since its passage, however, the American economy and workforce have changed so dramatically that the act has become a burdensome anachronism for many employees.

When the Fair Labor Standards Act was passed in 1938, few women were in the workplace and the American economy was dominated by manufacturing. By 2000, women made up 47 percent of the workforce,[29] and jobs had shifted to service- and technology-dominated fields. By 1999, 71 percent of married couples with children had both parents working,[30] and families with two working parents have a new need for flexibility in work schedules. For instance, the Fair Labor Standards Act mandates that someone who works forty-two hours one week gets the extra financial reward of two hours' overtime pay. But a working mother may prefer the option of working thirty-eight hours (with pay for forty) the next week so she can attend her child's recital; such an arrangement is commonly called flex-time or comp-time. Union officials adamantly and consistently oppose changes in the law that would give workers this type of choice, despite the fact that the federal government granted its employees this freedom as far back as 1978.[31]

The Fair Labor Standards Act also restricts hourly employees from being paid bonuses or being otherwise compensated outside the hourly wage structure. The rigid hour-and-wage law forces workers into the union's outdated hourly-wage-plus-overtime model in an age when even some relatively low-skilled workers have become wealthy through other compensation means, such as stock options.

5. Allow workers to choose options outside of unions

Although private-sector workers have been fleeing the unions for decades, that exodus is not the only sign that workers are rejecting the union model. Polls indicate that a mere 20 percent of workers would choose a union to address workplace concerns. In fact, most workers—63 percent—would prefer cooperative employer-employee committees to deal with such issues.[32] But the National Labor Relations Act (which also had its roots in the 1930s) does not give workers their preferred option, as it forbids companies from "assisting" any labor organization, including employer-employee involvement programs. The purpose of this clause was to outlaw any discussion of employment issues that takes place outside union-sponsored collective bargaining, a provision that effectively limits any alternatives to unions. But the National Labor Relations Board and the courts have extended this prohibition to nonunion workplaces as well.

Most significantly, in 1994 the Seventh Circuit Court of Appeals upheld the National Labor Relations Board's decision that Electromation, Inc.'s employer-employee involvement program was an illegal labor organization, as the Teamsters union had charged after it lost a union certification election.[33] The court ordered Electromation to disband five "action committees" for addressing these forbidden topics: absenteeism/infractions, no-smoking policy, communications, pay progression, and attendance bonuses. Having stripped the employees of any other voice, the Teamsters narrowly won a second union certification election at Electromation. Thereafter, companies all over America—including Polaroid, which had run such committees for forty years—disbanded their employer-employee involvement programs rather than face potential protracted litigation with unions, thereby depriving their employees a voice in the management of their company.

Of course, most employees would welcome the chance to influence their company's absentee policy, but union leaders have made sure that no worker can have that opportunity unless a union is involved. In fact, the distinctions laid down by the *Electromation* decision are nonsensical at best. For instance, workers may discuss an attendance policy, but they may not discuss absenteeism. The arbitrary nature of the ruling prompted Howard Knicely, executive vice president of TRW Inc., to testify before the Senate, "It is virtually impossible for an employer and its employees to know what they can and cannot do under current law." Even Clinton-appointed Labor Secretary Robert Reich's Commission on the Future of Worker-Management Relations recommended "removing the legal uncertainties" in this unfathomable decision.[34]

The law, as interpreted, means that the only recourse for private-sector employees who want their voice heard is to join a union. They have no alternative.

Thus, Big Labor has ensured that workers have no say about working conditions unless it's through a union. It's extraordinary that the unions, who represent a mere 8.2 percent of America's private-sector workforce, have been able to set the terms for nearly 92 percent of this country's private-sector employees. Until the National Labor Relations Act is amended to allow employees and employers to establish company policies cooperatively, the unions will retain that power over nonunion employees.

6. Prevent union-paid organizers from sowing dissent in the workplace simply to push workers to unionize

The National Labor Relations Act prohibits employers from discriminating against workers solely on the basis of their membership in a union.[35] But the U.S. Supreme Court has interpreted the law to protect paid union organizers, legitimating the union practice of "salting" the workplace.[36] A salt is a paid union activist who seeks a job with a nonunion company for the sole purpose of sowing dissent and eventually organizing that company for his true employer, the union. If a salt is unable to gain enough employee support to unionize, he'll harass the employer by filing an endless stream of unfair labor practice charges, health and safety violation complaints, and worker compensation claims until the employer gives in and just recognizes the union as the employees' bargaining agent.

The Supreme Court ruled that a business could neither fire nor refuse to hire a salt—even if the salt knocks at the company door and announces he's a union organizer, and even if he is a $100,000-a-year union official who hasn't worn a tool belt in twenty years, as long as he meets the basic job qualifications.

This is akin to hearing a knock at your front door and answering it to find a man accompanied by a police officer, who informs you that his cohort is a burglar and you are required by law to let him into your home and allow him free rein with your possessions. If you try to stop the burglar from entering or attempt to eject him before he's destroyed your home, you'll be arrested. Oh, and by the way, you should pay the burglar for his time while he ransacks your house.

Basic fairness mandates removing the protected employment status of salts, but that can be accomplished only by changing federal law, which would effectively overturn the Supreme Court case that extended protection to these union officials, *NLRB v. Town and Country Electric*.

7. Open up the unions' books

The Landrum-Griffin Act, passed in 1959, was designed to prevent union corruption, but it has largely failed to do so and badly needs revising. One of the purposes of the act was to protect union members' right to know how their union dues are being spent, but the unions' finances remain murky.

Currently, the annual reports the unions file with the Department of Labor do not contain enough information to assess union expenditures.[37] Although Secretary of Labor Elaine Chao has made some important changes that improve the reporting mechanism, these reforms don't go far enough. For example, even under the new rules, which don't require unions to use the new reporting forms until March 2005 at the earliest, unions don't have to report on individual expenditures under $5,000, and they can lump expenses used for political purposes and lobbying in one category.

The most important reform that could be enacted would be to mandate yearly, independent audits of union finances, using the Generally Accepted Accounting Practices required of corporations. And just as legislation passed in the wake of the Enron and Worldcom scandals now requires CEOs to attest to the accuracy of information contained in their companies' financial disclosure forms, so, too, should we pass a law requiring union presidents to be held personally accountable for the accuracy of financial information in the forms they file with the Department of Labor. In addition to LM-2 forms, which the DoL now makes available on the Internet, independent audits should be publicly available, as well, so that union members and the general public can know how unions are spending the dues they collect.

Requiring audits by independent accountants would go a long way toward revealing corruption. Perhaps if such procedures had been in place when Barbara Bullock ran the Washington Teachers Union, she and her associates would not have been able to embezzle more than $4.6 million (see Chapter 7). No one suspected that millions in members' dues were being siphoned off until Bullock suddenly raised teacher dues $144 in order to meet the Washington Teachers Union's per capita payment to the national union. Although some dissident union members had tried to get the American Federation of Teachers (AFT) to audit the local union's finances, the AFT had ignored the request for years, until its own dues were at risk. Barbara Bullock might still be embezzling teachers' dues today if she hadn't made the mistake of getting behind in her payments to the AFT.

8. Take away Big Labor's license to commit violent acts

Surely the most basic right of every employer and employee is the right to be free from violence in the workplace. Yet every year, hundred of acts of violence occur during the course of union disputes. According to one study by the National Institute for Labor Relations Research, the media have reported more than 10,000 incidents of union violence, with more than 200 persons killed, since 1975. Despite this record of union-related—and even more often, union-inspired—violence, no federal law currently forbids this activity. As detailed in Chapter 6, the Supreme Court ruled in *U.S. v. Enmons* that the Hobbs Act—an antiracketeering law prohibiting orchestrated violence as a method of extortion—didn't apply to unions as long as they were trying to achieve "legitimate union objectives." The acts of violence in the *Enmons* case were hardly minor: Striking members of the International Brotherhood of Electrical Workers fired high-powered rifles at three electrical transformers owned by the Gulf States Utilities Company and blew up yet another transformer, for example.

The power to orchestrate violence to achieve "union bargaining objectives" has resulted in millions of dollars in property damage and countless assaults and even deaths. The prime targets for union militants are workers who choose to work during a strike. Of course workers should have the right to withhold their labor if they feel their wages or working conditions are not adequate, but they do not have the right to stop others from working who may be satisfied with those wages and conditions. (The courts have upheld a company's right to hire replacement workers during a strike.) Threats, physical intimidation, bombings, arson, assaults, shootings, and other acts of orchestrated violence should not be ignored by law enforcement merely because the thugs involved are working for "legitimate union objectives."

Congress must close the legal loophole created by the *Enmons* decision. The Freedom from Union Violence Act (a version was introduced in April 2003 by Congressman Joe Wilson, Republican of South Carolina) would amend the Hobbs Act and bring down penalties on union officials and members who engage in violent acts in order to further the aims of an otherwise legitimate strike. Such union violence would be punishable by a fine of up to $100,000 and/or imprisonment for up to twenty years.[38] It would be a critical step in calling the unions to account for actions that threaten innocent Americans.

None of these measures will be easy to push through, particularly because, as we have seen, so many politicians jump at the first sign of trouble for union bosses. Frankly, too, even those politicians who have not become tools of union bosses are not likely to take on the unions, simply because most fear what can happen when Big Labor turns its political machine against them. Investing so heavily in politics certainly has its rewards for Big Labor: If union bosses can reward their Democratic allies, they can also severely punish anyone who dares challenge the Big Labor agenda.

But the cycle of corruption must be stopped, and it is possible to reform the system if enough Americans demand it. Union bosses have been successful to date largely because most Americans are oblivious to the corruption, influence-peddling, and power-brokering that goes on in labor unions today. But simply examining the record of abuses reveals how we are all suffering at the hands of union bosses and the political establishment they keep in power.

All of us foot the bill for this corrupt system. Now it's up to us to do something about it.

Big Labor's Big Loss in 2004

Big Labor lost big time in 2004. And needless to say, so did the Democrats.

For years labor leaders have committed themselves to their corrupt bargain with the Democratic Party. And in the 2004 campaign they redoubled their efforts. Big Labor's investment in the election was simply staggering, and union hacks boasted about their electoral clout at virtually every turn. One day before the election, the Service Employees International Union (SEIU), now the largest union in the AFL-CIO, issued a press release hyping its "Role in Bringing Home a Victory for America's Working Families"—meaning a victory for John Kerry and the Democrats.

Of course, on November 2 President George W. Bush was reelected and Republicans gained four more Senate and four additional House seats. The election should have been a wake-up call to organized labor, but instead it has simply spurred on the efforts of those union leaders who believe electing Democrats is the labor movement's number one priority.

The SEIU alone spent $65 million to try to defeat President Bush and Republicans in Congress. According to the union's own pronouncements, this amounted to "the largest investment by a single organization in the history of American politics."[1] Yet that massive investment represented just part of the union's political expenditures. In its press release, SEIU bragged that it also contributed $26 million to America Coming Together (ACT), a so-called 527 organization that could collect and spend unlimited amounts to try to defeat the president. That donation made the union the single largest contributor to ACT, exceeding even the contributions of billionaires George Soros and Peter Lewis, chairman and CEO of Progressive Corporation, the nation's fourth largest auto insurance company, and a top donor to left-wing causes. The union also gave $1 million to the Democratic National Committee and "made large donations to groups that share our goals, like Rock the Vote and the New Democratic Network."[2]

The union bragged that it "recruited more than 2,750 members and staff willing to take a leave from their jobs to do full-time political work with organizations like ACT, allowing the union to reach beyond the labor movement for the first time to conduct real voter contact with a wider universe of workers."[3] But those "volunteers," whom the SEIU dubbed "Heroes," were often "on the clock," paid for by SEIU members—some of whom may not have wanted their union dues spent to fund anti-Bush activities. The union's press release acknowledges $35 million for "SEIU Hero Program Cost," an amazing figure for what was supposed to be volunteer time donated by individuals. But part of the reason the program was so expensive was that, as the union's press release acknowledged, "roughly 40 percent of SEIU's full time activists, or 'Heroes' don't live in the battlegrounds, so they packed their bags—nearly 1,000 of them as early as April and July—and temporarily moved to 16 key states." And these numbers didn't include the "weekend warriors"—50,000 strong—involved in SEIU's get-out-the-vote strategy.

In all, SEIU credits its political organization with registering nearly 4.5 million new voters, including 355,403 in battleground states, and with mailing 4 million pieces of campaign literature, making 19 million phone calls, and knocking on 10 million doors across the country.[4] In addition, the Evergreen Freedom Foundation estimated that the union spent $3 million on federal independent expenditures for TV and radio ads, including $1.4 million for three TV and six radio spots in Wisconsin on health care, and a half million dollars for Spanish language TV ads in Florida two weeks before the election.[5]

And all that was just one union's activity.

Of course the AFL-CIO also kicked in its own hefty contribution, spending $44 million, supposedly to mobilize "union households," a euphemism for any Democrats it could muster. The American Federation of State, County, and Municipal Employees (AFSCME) spent another $48 million. The Laborers Union (LIUNA) spent $8 million. The American Federation of Teachers (AFT) gave $1 million to the Media Fund and another $250,000 to ACT.

None of these contributions included money given directly to political candidates. In all, union political action committees (PACs) contributed more than $52 million in the 2004 cycle. Of that, 86 percent went to Democrats. That's an overwhelming amount when you consider that some 43 percent of union households voted for Republican George W. Bush in 2004, according to analyses of exit poll data, but amazingly, 86 percent was less than unions have given to Democrats in previous years.[6] After years of giving virtually all their money to Democrats, in 2004 labor leaders did make some concession to the political reality that Republicans control the White House and both houses of Congress. But the handful of Republicans who did receive some of labor's largess were union-friendly legislators, like Senator Arlen Specter, Pennsylvania Republican, whom unions helped against a more conservative Republican primary opponent, former congressman Pat Toomey.

And once again, unions proved adept at using campaign finance laws to their advantage. Unions were in the forefront of advocating limits on political spending—for everyone but themselves. Half of the top ten 527 committees—which can accept unlimited donations to promote political issues and thus can basically skirt other federal campaign contribution limits—were funded exclusively or in major part by labor unions.[7] The SEIU gave more than $48 million to 527s for the 2004 election, while AFSCME gave more than $30 million, the AFL-CIO gave $11 million, and the Laborers gave almost $4 million.[8] Most if not all of this money came directly out of the unions' treasuries, collected from union dues, without members having a direct say in how this money would be spent. As ever, Big Labor's leaders simply ignored the wishes of the many union members who supported Republicans.

All that money and manpower going to Democrats produced a much larger turnout of union voters and a much closer election as a result. In 2004 union households comprised 27 percent of the total vote,[9] a much larger share than would be expected from the overall proportion of union members in the population—which dropped to 12.5 percent of all workers in 2004, according to the latest Department of Labor figures.[10]

Those figures betray the desperation of Big Labor's approach. As unions continue to lose members, labor leaders devote themselves more and more to their political agenda in a fevered attempt to retain influence. In 2004 their Democratic gamble failed again. And it also triggered some discontent in surprising circles.

Even though the SEIU played the partisan political game with great gusto in 2004, SEIU president Andy Stern was having some second thoughts about his union's relationship to the Democratic Party—and ultimately whether a politicized and partisan labor movement was in the best interests of union members. At the time of the Democratic convention in July, Stern had a candid interview with *Washington Post* veteran political reporters David Broder and Thomas Edsall.[11] Stern worried aloud that his own efforts to revitalize union organizing might not survive the election of a Democratic president, who, Stern predicted, would co-opt union leaders into the partisan establishment, siphoning off money and manpower from union efforts. It wasn't the first time Stern criticized union leadership either. At his own union's annual meeting a month earlier, Stern said, "Our employers have changed, our industries have changed, and the world has certainly changed, but the labor movement's structure and culture have sadly stayed the same." Stern's criticisms rankled some other union leaders, including AFL-CIO president John Sweeney, who told Broder that Stern's harsh comments were "not justified."[12]

The rift between Stern and Sweeney now threatens to dismantle the AFL-CIO. At the labor federation's March 2005 meeting in Las Vegas, Sweeney temporarily defeated a measure proposed by Stern and his allies—including the Teamsters and the Laborers and accounting for about 40 percent of the AFL-CIO's entire membership—that would have forced the AFL-CIO to rebate as much as half the per capita payments the federation collects from individuals so long as the unions used those funds to organize more members. Instead, Sweeney proposed an increase in money individual unions would be forced to contribute to the AFL-CIO's political efforts, amounting to half of all the payments unions make to the federation.[13] Talk about pouring good money after bad. No wonder Stern is talking about taking his 1.8 million members out of the AFL-CIO. And he's not alone. Bruce Raynor, president of the newly merged UNITE Here, a conglomeration of needle-trade unions and hotel and restaurant workers, says his group may pull out as well. "I think disaffiliation is a real threat," *Washington Post* columnist Harold Meyerson quoted Raynor saying soon after the AFL-CIO shot down reform proposals at the March meeting.[14] The Carpenters union has already disaffiliated from the AFL-CIO, and if the Teamsters, Service Employees, Laborers, and UNITE Here depart as well, it will leave the AFL-CIO a mere shadow of its former self.

For John Sweeney and other Big Labor leaders, that would be a disastrous turn of events, since it would mean an end to their political cachet. A turn away from the political arena could prove nearly as damaging to the Democrats, who rely so much on the unions' bushels of money in order to compete in national elections.

Andy Stern would like to revitalize the labor movement by following UNITE Here's model, folding several smaller unions into fewer, more powerful unions. Ideally, he'd like to see the AFL-CIO's current fifty-eight unions merge into about twenty bigger units organized along labor sectors and with the clout to bargain nationally with big employers.[15]

The problem with all these reform strategies is that they don't address the real problem that causes unions' waning power and influence. Unions have stopped speaking for the average working man or woman by allying themselves with the most left-wing elements in American politics. They've become corrupt, concentrating power in the hands of a few "leaders" who have lost touch with the aspirations and values of working people. These union bosses take their members' hard-earned money and squander it, with little to show for their outrageous profligacy. No wonder fewer and fewer Americans choose to join labor unions. Now fewer than 8 percent of private-sector workers are unionized, and union membership is even down slightly among government workers, from 37.2 percent in 2003 to 36.4 percent in 2004.[16] That downward spiral, which has been steady for some fifty years now, will continue until unions quit ignoring the wishes of their own members, and no amount of political hyperbole will stop it.

NOTES

CHAPTER 1 For Sale: The Democratic Party, the American Worker, and the United States Government

1. Stefan Gleason, "Laboring for a Solution," *Washington Times,* February 20, 2001, A17. Rutgers economist Leo Troy testified on March 21, 1996, before the Committee on House Oversight, U.S. House of Representatives, that unions spent at least $500 million on politics in the 1996 election cycle, basing that information on money raised by the unions for politics and an estimate of the amount of unreported spending for staff, campaign literature, and other political activity.
2. See the AFL-CIO's website: www.aflcio.org/aboutaflcio/.
3. Larry Margasak and John Solomon, "Democrats, Unions Work Side by Side," Associated Press, July 19, 2001.
4. www.opensecrets.org. Labor: Long-Term Contribution Trends from 1990 to 2004 are available at www.opensecrets.org/industries/indus.asp?ind=P& Format=Print.
5. Ruth Marcus, "Hidden Assets: Flood of Secret Money Erodes Election Limits," *Washington Post,* May 15, 2001, A1.
6. "Labor's Role Was Crucial in November Elections," *On Campus,* American Federation of Teachers, December 2000/January 2001.
7. Federal Election Commission, PAC Financial Activity, 1999–2000, www.fec.gov/press/053101pacfund/tables/pacsum00.htm.
8. In his speech at the 1999 AFL-CIO convention accepting the organization's endorsement, Gore promised to outlaw the replacement of striking workers (thus giving Big Labor the extortionate power to literally shut a business down permanently if demands aren't met); oppose school vouchers (because competition for public schools would lessen the power of America's largest union, the NEA); put provisions for "workers' rights" in future trade agreements (meaning requirements for forcibly unionizing workers); and veto any "anti-union" legislation (meaning that Gore would oppose anything the labor bosses told him to).
9. Jonathan D. Salant, "Unions Gear Up for Fall Election," Associated Press, August 15, 2000.
10. John Mercurio, "Democrats in Hillarywood," CNN.com, December 2, 2003.
11. Ibid.
12. "AFSCME Endorses Howard Dean for President," press release, *AFSCME News,* November 12, 2003 (see www.afscme.org/publications/political/pr031112.htm.)
13. Melanie Hunter, "AFSCME Official Endorses Socialism After Union Backed Dean," CNSNews.com, December 19, 2003.

14. Dean made a number of eye-opening proclamations about the need to raise taxes. For example, he reportedly told an AARP forum in Iowa, "I tell you what we need in America. What we don't need are middle-class tax cuts." (See Mark Halperin et al., "The Note," ABCNews.com, October 16, 2003.) Dean also declared, "What I want to know is what in the world so many Democrats are doing supporting tax cuts," and he stated, "We must repeal the entire package of [tax] cuts—both those signed today and those passed in 2001." (See Jonathan Chait, "Howard Dean and the Tempting of the Democrats," *New Republic,* July 28, 2003, and Thomas Beaumont, "Dean Touts Wiping Out Tax Cuts," *Des Moines Register,* May 31, 2003.)

15. Jim VandeHei, "Dean Calls for New Controls on Business: Democrats Seeks 'Re-Regulation,' " *Washington Post,* November 19, 2003, A9.

16. John Fund, "Meany vs. Deanie: Big Labor and Big Government Are Increasingly One and the Same," *Wall Street Journal,* January 19, 2004.

17. Fund, "Meany vs. Deanie."

18. Paul Farhi, "Dean Works to Be Labor's Man: Candidate Trails Gephardt in Union Endorsements," *Washington Post,* November 23, 2003, A5.

19. Dan Balz, "Union Leaders Want Gephardt Aide Fired," *Washington Post,* December 4, 2003.

20. Fund, "Meany vs. Deanie"; Dan Balz, "Democrats Flood Iowa with Ground Troops," *Washington Post,* January 11, 2004.

21. See John Kerry's campaign website: www.johnkerry.com/endorsements/organizations.html (accessed February 10, 2004).

22. "Kerry Wins Support of the American Federation of Teachers," press release, February 4, 2003, www.johnkerry.com/pressroom/releases/pr_2004_0204a.html.

23. While Kennedy rates only an 88 lifetime average, Kerry has a lifetime average of 92. See www.adaction.org (accessed February 10, 2004).

24. *CNN Live,* January 28, 2004.

25. John Kerry for President, "John Kerry Ranks 92nd out of the 100 Senators in Contributions from Special Interest PACS and Lobbyists," press release, February 3, 2004.

26. *Hannity & Colmes,* Fox News, February 3, 2004.

27. John Solomon, "Kerry Blocked Law, Drew Cash," Associated Press, February 4, 2004.

28. John Solomon, "Kerry, Edwards Boasts About Special Interest Money Don't Tell Whole Story," Associated Press, February 2, 2004.

29. IRS form 8871 organizing Citizen Soldier Fund.

30. Solomon, "Kerry, Edwards Boasts About Special Interest Money Don't Tell Whole Story."

31. See www.opensecrets.org.

32. John Solomon, "Kerry Pocketed Speaking Fees," Associated Press, February 9, 2004.

33. Jay Nordlinger, "Super Dem: Hillary Clinton Blazes Ahead," *National Review,* December 20, 1999.

34. Center for Responsive Politics, www.opensecrets.org. These figures include PAC donations and contributions from individuals who list a union as their employer.

35. In 2002, the last year for which complete records are available, the Department of Labor reports that those unions that are required to file disclosure forms with the Department under the Landrum-Griffin Act (only large unions with at least some private-sector employee members) had receipts of $16.88 billion.

36. Sharon Theimer, "RNC Fundraising Edge Over DNC Felt," Associated Press, January 6, 2004.

37. Charles Lane, *The Buying of the President 2004* (New York: Avon Books, 2004), 124–125.

38. Theimer, "RNC Fundraising Edge Over DNC Felt."

39. A union must disclose how much of its general operating funds has been devoted to politics on line 81 of IRS Form 990; if political expenditures in a given year exceed $100, the union must file an extra disclosure form with the IRS—Form 1120 POL.

40. For example, the United Farm Workers union allegedly forced the dismissal of strawberry pickers who refused to pay for the labor organization's political program; leaders of United Food and Commercial Workers reportedly ordered a Rite Aid cashier to be fired because she didn't want her money funding the union's political work; and two US Air mechanics who refused to pay for the union's political program lost their jobs allegedly at the demands of Machinist union officials. See Fred Alvarez, "UFW Is Accused in Firing of Pickers," *Los Angeles Times*, December 18, 2003, B1; and "Worker Rights Advocate Blasts AFL-CIO for Hypocrisy," *U.S. Newswire National Desk, Labor Reporter*, October 12, 1999.

41. Mark A. De Bernardo, "Last Gasp for Unions' Political Clout," *Legal Times*, May 18, 1998.

42. Steve Rosenthal, "The AFL-CIO Political Program," in Jo-Ann Mort, ed., *Not Your Father's Labor Movement: Inside the AFL-CIO* (London: Verso, 1998), 101.

43. Myron Lieberman, *The Teacher Unions* (New York: Free Press, 1997), 36.

44. Max Green, *Epitaph for American Labor: How Union Leaders Lost Touch with America* (Washington, DC: AEI Press, 1996), 5.

45. Barry T. Hirsch and David A. Macpherson, "Union Membership and Coverage Database from the Current Population Survey 1973–2002," U.S. Historical Tables, Private Construction Workers 1983–2002.

46. U.S. Department of Labor, Bureau of Labor Statistics, *Union Members in 2003* (USDL 04-53).

47. Ibid.

48. Ibid.

49. Ibid.

50. "Union Members in 2003," Department of Labor, USDL-04-53.

51. Fund, "Meany vs. Deanie."

52. Ibid.

53. Ibid.

54. Paul Sultan, *Right to Work Laws: A Study in Conflict* (Los Angeles: UCLA Institute of Industrial Relations, 1958, 46.

55. Lee Anderson, "All Should Be Free to Choose," *Chattanooga Times Free Press*, June 1, 1999, B7.

56. Green, *Epitaph for American Labor*, 162.

57. Amity Shlaes, "Labor's Return," *Commentary*, October 1996, 49.
58. See www.dsausa.org/about/index.html.
59. Greg Pierce, "Inside Politics," *Washington Times*, November 13, 1998.
60. www.dsausa.org/about/newlit.html.
61. See Joseph Farah, "Congress' Red Army Caucus," "Congress' Red Army Caucus part 2," and "Pelosi Leader of 'Progressive Caucus,' " all of which are available on the WorldNetDaily website: www.worldnetdaily.com.
62. See www.dsausa.org.
63. Tom Ramstack, "AFL-CIO Focusing on 2004 Elections," *Washington Times*, February 26, 2004.
64. *Statistical Abstract of the United States* (Washington, D.C.: GPO, 1997), 397.
65. In 1975, per capita disposable income (in constant 1992 dollars) was $13,404; in 1998 it was $19,790. Source: *Statistical Abstract of the United States* (Washington, D.C.: GPO, 1999), 464.
66. Barry Flynn, "More Jobs Disappear; Despite the Grim Statistics, Other Areas of the Economy Seem to Be Solid," *Orlando Sentinel*, September 6, 2003.
67. www.bls.gov/eag/eag.us.htm.
68. *Abood v. Detroit Board of Education*, U.S. Supreme Court, 431 U.S. 209 (1977).
69. *Communications Workers of America v. Beck*, U.S. Supreme Court, 487 U.S. 735 (1988).
70. Edith Hakola and Rex Reed, "Labor Day: Labor Plays Politics with Its Members' Dues," *Washington Post*, September 1, 1996; Leo Troy, Professor of Economics, Rutgers University, Statement before the Senate Committee on Rules and Administration, April 12, 2000.
71. "GOP Firm Issues Poll on Use of Union Dues," Congress Daily, *National Journal*, May 2, 1996.
72. National Center for Education Statistics, *Digest of Education Statistics, 2002* (Washington, DC: GPO, 2002), Table 166.

CHAPTER 2 Marriage of Convenience: Unions and the Democrats

1. Adam Nagourney, "Moving to Ease Doubts, First Lady Says She Will Enter Senate Race," *New York Times*, November 24, 1999, A1.
2. Ibid.
3. "Clintons Return $28,000 in Gifts," *Pittsburgh Post-Gazette*, February 8, 2001, A6.
4. Center for Responsive Politics, www.opensecrets.com.
5. John Mercurio, "Democrats in Hillarywood," CNN.com, December 2, 2003.
6. The U.S. Department of Labor, Employment Standards Administration, Office of Labor Management Standards, 2002 e.LORS data.
7. Edith Hakola and Rex Reed, "Labor Day: Labor Plays Politics with Its Members' Dues," *Washington Post*, September 1, 1996; Leo Troy, Professor of Economics, Rutgers University, Statement before the Senate Committee on Rules and Administration, April 12, 2000.
8. Stefan Gleason, "Lobbying for a Solution," *Washington Times*, February 20, 2001, A17.

9. Peter T. Kilborn, "Prospective Labor Leaders Set to Turn to Confrontation," *New York Times*, October 25, 1995, A1.

10. Since the UFT is an affiliate of the American Federation of Teachers, donations from both organizations cannot exceed the $5,000 limit on PAC contributions per election. See: Federal Election Commission, www.fec.gov.

11. See www.opensecrets.org. 2000 race: New York Senate by industry.

12. Ibid.

13. Morton Bahr, "Introduction of Hillary Rodham Clinton," Working Families Party Convention, March 26, 2000, available on the Communications Workers of America website (www.cwa-union.org).

14. Hillary Rodham Clinton, *It Takes a Village: And Other Lessons Children Teach Us* (New York: Simon & Schuster, 1996).

15. David Lauter, "Clinton: Healer or Waffler?" *Los Angeles Times*, January 14, 1992.

16. *Arkansas Democrat-Gazette*, July 13, 1985.

17. Although the United Federation of Teachers' parent organization, the American Federation of Teachers, is slightly better than its bigger rival, the National Education Association, on the question of testing for teacher competency, neither group is exactly pushing to rid the field of incompetent teachers. United Federation of Teachers president Randi Weingarten got high praise for her suggestion in January 2004 that the New York City school system streamline its process for dismissing incompetent teachers. But her idea of speeding up the process would still allow teachers in danger of being fired to remain on the payroll 180 days after they were deemed unfit and would require additional "peer counseling" for "troubled teachers." In most instances, union contracts make it very difficult to discharge teachers, and the process often takes many months or years. See David Herszenhorn, "Failing Teachers Face a Faster Ax," *New York Times*, January 15, 2004, A1; and Nat Hentoff, "Questions for Hillary," *Village Voice*, October 31, 2000.

18. Dick Morris, "How Hillary Sold Out School Reform," *New York Post*, March 21, 2000.

19. New York Senate debate, NBC, October 28, 2000.

20. Center for Responsive Politics, www.opensecrets.org.

21. H.R. 5005, Roll Call Vote #367: Passed 295–132: R 207–10; D 88–120; I 0–2, July 26, 2002.

22. Douglas Turner, "Quinn Takes On a Key Role," *Buffalo News*, August 11, 2002.

23. Jeff Johnson, "Democrats Rally to Protect Unions at New Security Dept.," CNSNews.com, September 5, 2002.

24. S.A. 4471 to H.R. 5005, Roll Call Vote #218: Cloture Motion Rejected 50–49, with Clinton Voting Yes: R 0–48; D 49–1; I 1–0, September 19, 2002; S.A. 4471 to H.R. 5005, Roll Call Vote #225: Cloture Motion Rejected 49–49, with Clinton Voting Yes: R 1–47; D 47–2; I 1–0, September 25, 2002; S.A. 4471 to H.R. 5005, Roll Call Vote #226: Cloture Motion Rejected 50–49, with Clinton Voting Yes: R 1–48; D 48–1; I 1–0, September 26, 2002; S.A. 4471 to H.R. 5005, Roll Call Vote #241: Motion to Table Agreed to 50–47, with Clinton Voting No: R 48–0; D 1–46; I 1–1, November 13, 2002.

25. "Hillary Faults Bush on Security," New York *Newsday*, January 25, 2003.
26. Ibid.
27. There is some discrepancy as to how to categorize Hillary's book. She labels it in her author's note as a "personal memoir," while the publishers label it on the cover as a "biography," which, considering the number of authors involved, could be a more honest description.
28. "Hillary Faults Bush on Security."
29. Ibid.
30. Larry Margasak and John Solomon, "Democrats, Unions Work Side-by-Side," Associated Press, July 19, 2001.
31. Ibid.
32. Ibid.
33. Ibid.
34. Ibid.
35. Ibid.
36. Carol Innerst, "Democrats Make Bid for Teacher Support," *Washington Times*, December 13, 1991.
37. *How Compulsory Unionism Corrupts Politics* (Springfield, Va.: National Right to Work Committee), 6.
38. Center for Responsive Government, www.opensecrets.org. Labor: Long-term Contribution Trends.
39. *How Compulsory Unionism Corrupts Politics*.
40. Leo Troy, Statement Before the House Oversight Committee, March 21, 1996.
41. Amity Shlaes, "Labor's Return," *Commentary*, October 1996, 49.
42. Marshall Wittmann and Charles P. Griffin, "Compulsory Union Dues Pay for Politics," Heritage Foundation, February 1, 1996, www.heritage.org/Press/Commentary/ED020196.cfm (visited December 5, 2003).
43. Grover G. Norquist, "Labor's Last Stand: Facing Falling Numbers and Growing Apathy, Big Labor Plays Big Spender to Stay in Power," *American Spectator*, August 1996, 60.
44. Steve Rosenthal, "The AFL-CIO Political Program," in Jo-Ann Mort, ed., *Not Your Father's Labor Movement: Inside the AFL-CIO* (London: Verso, 1998), 101.
45. Ibid., 106.
46. Dennis Rivera, "Labor's Role in the Political Arena," in Gregory Mantsios, ed., *A New Labor Movement for the New Century*.
47. Ibid., 233.
48. Patricia Lippold and Bob Kirkman, "Blocking Bridges: Class-Based Politics and the Labor Movement," in Gregory Mantsios, ed., *A New Labor Movement for the New Century*, 228.
49. "A New Voice for SEIU Members," final report of the SEIU Committee on the Future, adopted at the SEIU Convention, April 1996.
50. Lippold and Kirkman, "Blocking Bridges," 225.
51. Ibid.
52. Rosenthal, "The AFL-CIO Political Program," 107.
53. Quoted in ibid., 107.

54. Robert Dreyfuss, "Rousing the Democratic Base," *American Prospect,* vol. 11, Nov. 6, 2000.

55. Charles Lewis, *The Buying of the President 2004* (New York: Avon Books, 2004), 30.

56. Margasak and Solomon, "Democrats, Unions Work Side-by-Side."

57. Larry Margasak, "Unions Don't Cite Political Funds," Associated Press, August 6, 2001.

58. Dreyfuss, "Rousing the Democratic Base."

59. Tony Mazzocchi, "Building a Party of Our Own," in Gregory Mantsios, ed., *A New Labor Movement for the New Century* (New York: Monthly Review Press, 1998), 245.

60. Dreyfuss, "Rousing the Democratic Base."

61. "How the 'Union-Free Environmentalist' Is Targeting Your Job, Its Security and Hard-Won Benefits in 1980," *Steelabor,* United Steelworkers of America, July 1979, 9. Since the Supreme Court's *Abood* decision in 1977, which had the potential of forcing unions to refund general-fund political spending to members (later confirmed for private-sector unions by the *Beck* decision of 1988), labor leaders have become increasingly cautious about advocating in their official publications ways to expand their political spending by using the general treasury, funded with member dues.

62. Juan Gonzalez, "Union to Be Out Beating the Bushies," New York *Daily News,* October 23, 2003, 8.

63. Hakola and Reed, "Labor Day"; Leo Troy, Professor of Economics, Rutgers University, Statement before the Senate Committee on Rules and Administration, April 12, 2000.

64. Leo Troy, Professor of Economics, Rutgers University, Testimony Before House Oversight Committee, March 21, 1996.

65. F. C. Duke Zeller, *Devil's Pact: Inside the World of the Teamsters Union* (Birch Lane Press, 1996), 346.

66. Ibid.

67. Merrill Harston, "Union Leaders Satisfied with Mondale Effort," Associated Press, Nov. 11, 1984.

68. Ronald Radosh, *Divided They Fell: The Demise of the Democratic Party 1964–1996* (New York: Free Press, 1996), 180.

69. Rosenthal, "The AFL-CIO Political Program."

70. Frank Luntz and Tony Zagotta, "Union Members Furious About Attacks on GOP," *Insight on the News,* vol. 12, July 22, 1996.

71. Susan Crabtree, "Big Labor Is Spending Big Bucks on Elections," *Insight on the News,* vol. 12, November 4, 1996, 11.

72. "Ten Rules for Talking to Union Members About Politics," available on the website of the International Association of Fire Fighters, www.iaff.org/politics/us/pdfs/AFLCIORules.pdf.

73. Susan Crabtree, p. 103.

74. David Saltonstall, "Campaign Role Limits for Union," New York *Daily News,* June 8, 2003, 13; Steven Greenhouse, "Building Workers' Union Is Set to Limit Politicking," *New York Times,* June 9, 2003.

75. Saltonstall, "Campaign Role Limits for Union."
76. Steven Greenhouse, "Worker Says Union Fired Her for Testifying on '01 Primary," *New York Times,* July 24, 2003, B9.
77. Brooks Jackson, "Republicans Fume Over Labor's Political Spending," CNN All Politics, April 18, 1996, www.cnn.com/ALLPOLITICS/1996/news/9604/18/union.dues/index.shtml (visited December 5, 2003).
78. Luntz and Zagotta, "Union Members Furious About Attacks on GOP."
79. Michael McMenamin, "Labor Lost," *Reason,* November 2000. Not surprisingly, the Washington Education Association found ways around the law. According to *Insight on the News,* the union changed the name of its "Political Education" program to the "Community Outreach" program. Then, instead of "contributing" funds, it "loaned" money to political organizations and then forgave the debt. *Insight on the News* reported that the union employed this policy "to avoid the law." The magazine also quoted sworn testimony from a Washington Education Association lobbyist who said, "It was an internal ploy to raise more WEA-PAC money." When challenged on its spending, the union responded by suing the teachers who helped bring the wrongdoing to light. The judge presiding over the case pointed out that the teachers were simply exercising their First Amendment rights of speech and association. The lawsuits were ultimately dropped. See Hickey, "Unions Pony Up for Their Party"; "WEA Drops Vindictive Lawsuit Against Teacher Support Group," *PR Newswire,* April 26, 1999; "Critics, Teacher Union Agree to Settlement," *Spokane Spokesman-Review,* April 28, 1999, B4; Evergreen Freedom Foundation, press release, "WEA Drops Lawsuit Against Teachers Who First Sparked Investigation of Union's Illegal Political Activities," April 29, 1999 (www.effwa.org/press_releases/1999_04_28.php).
80. John Sweeney with David Kusnet, *America Needs a Raise: Fighting for Economic Security and Social Justice* (Boston: Houghton Mifflin, 1996).
81. "Union Organizers Swap Strategies for Strength at Organizing Summit," AFL-CIO statement, www.aflcio.org/aboutaflcio/ns01132003a.cfm (visited December 5, 2003).
82. Sweeney with Kusnet, *America Needs a Raise.*
83. Jennifer G. Hickey, "Battles Heat Up on Capitol Hill," *Insight on the News,* December 31, 2001.
84. Simon Rodberg, "The CIO without the CIA," *American Prospect,* vol. 12, July 2, 2001.
85. Amity Shlaes, "Labor's Return."
86. Rodberg, "The CIO Without the CIA."
87. Ibid.
88. "Get America Back to Work," AFL-CIO, 1962. Quoted in Max Green, *Epitaph for American Labor* (Washington, D.C.: American Enterprise Institute, 1996), 90.
89. Ibid.
90. Amity Shlaes, "Labor's Return."
91. "What Is Democratic Socialism?" dsausa.org/pdf/widemsoc.pdf (visited December 5, 2003).

92. See bernie.house.gov/pc/members.asp (visited December 5, 2003). In the 108th Congress (2003–4), the members of the Progressive Caucus were Dennis Kucinich, cochair; Barbara Lee, cochair; Lynn Woolsey, vice chair; Peter DeFazio, officer; Jesse Jackson, Jr., officer; Major Owens, officer; Bernie Sanders, officer; Hilda Solis, officer; Neil Abercrombie; Tammy Baldwin; Xavier Becerra; Corrine Brown; Sherrod Brown; Michael Capuano; Julia Carson; William "Lacy" Clay; John Conyers; Danny Davis; Rosa DeLauro; Lane Evans; Eni Faleomavaega; Sam Farr; Chaka Fattah; Bob Filner; Barney Frank; Raul Grijalva; Luis Gutierrez; Maurice Hinchey; Sheila Jackson Lee; Stephanie Tubbs Jones; Marcy Kaptur; Tom Lantos; John Lewis; Jim McDermott; James P. McGovern; George Miller; Jerry Nadler; Eleanor Holmes Norton; John Olver; Ed Pastor; Donald Payne; Nancy Pelosi; Bobby Rush; Jan Schakowsky; Jose Serrano; Pete Stark; Bennie Thompson; John Tierney; Tom Udall; Nydia Velazquez; Maxine Waters; Diane Watson; Mel Watt; and Henry Waxman.

93. Ralph De Toledano, *Let Our Cities Burn* (New York: Arlington House Publishers, 1975), 28.

94. Archie Robinson, *George Meany and His Times* (New York: Simon & Schuster, 1981), 91.

95. Ibid., 154.

96. Labor-Management Relations Act (Taft-Hartley), 29 U.S.C. Sec. 141 et seq. Other major provisions of the Taft-Hartley Act included:
   □ Outlawing the "closed shop," in which workers were forced to join a union before being employed in unionized companies, in effect allowing union bosses to pick employees. The "union shop" is still allowed, however, in which employees are forced to join or pay fees after accepting employment in non–right-to-work states.
   □ Making management employees such as supervisors ineligible for unionization.
   □ Giving management the right to speak during union certification elections, rather than allowing union officials to campaign without opposition.
   □ Requiring that disputed election items have a hearing before a union certification election.
   □ Outlawing "secondary boycotts," in which unions coerce neutral employers to pressure the employer with which the union has a dispute.
   □ Allowing the president of the United States, when he believes a strike will threaten the nation's health or safety, to appoint a board of inquiry. If warranted, the president can then ask a federal judge for an injunction against the strike that will allow eighty days of further negotiation.

97. Taylor E. Dark, "Debating Decline: The 1995 Race for the AFL-CIO Presidency," *Labor History,* August 1, 1999, vol. 40, no. 3, 323.

98. Harry Bernstein, "Gerald McEntee: Bringing Labor into the National Political Debate," *Los Angeles Times,* March 2, 1997.

99. See dsausa.org/convention2k1/eliseo.html (visited December 5, 2003).

100. Hickey, "Battles Heat Up on Capitol Hill," 10.

101. Rivera, "Labor's Role in the Political Arena," 238.

102. Ibid., 241.

103. Ibid.

104. Ibid.

105. Sweeney with Kusnet, *America Needs a Raise*.

106. Federal Election Commission, PAC Financial Activity, 1999–2000, www.fec. gov/press/053101pacfund/tables/pacsum00.htm.

107. Center for Responsive Government, www.opensecrets.org. Labor: Long-Term Contribution Trends.

108. Lippold and Kirkman, "Blocking Bridges," 222.

109. Rosenthal, "The AFL-CIO Political Program," 109.

110. Ronald Radosh, *Divided They Fell: The Demise of the Democratic Party, 1964–1996* (New York: Free Press, 1996), 235.

111. Peter Baker, *The Breach: Inside the Impeachment and Trial of William Jefferson Clinton* (New York: Scribner, 2000).

112. Juan Gonzalez, "Interview with John Sweeney," in Mort, ed., *Not Your Father's Labor Movement*, 225.

113. Laura M. Litvan and Daniel J. Murphy, "How the Democrats Pulled It Off," *Investor's Business Daily*, November 6, 1998, A1.

114. *Hardball with Chris Matthews*, MSNBC, Nov. 4, 1998.

115. www.opensecrets.org. Labor: Long-Term Contribution Trends.

116. Jonathan D. Salant, "Unions Gear Up for Fall Election," Associated Press, August 15, 2000.

117. Karlyn Bowman, "Labor Union Dues: Whose Money Is It?" *Roll Call*, October 30, 1997.

118. Mark A. De Bernardo, "Last Gasp for Unions' Political Clout," *Legal Times*, May 18, 1998.

119. Jennifer G. Hickey, "Unions Pony Up for Their Party," *Insight on the News*, June 22, 1998.

120. Hickey, "Unions Pony Up for Their Party."

121. Baker, *The Breach*.

122. Ibid.

123. Timothy Burn, "Teamsters Oppose AFL-CIO on Gore; Hoffa Resists Rush on Endorsement," *Washington Times*, October 19, 1999, A1.

124. Remarks of Al Gore, 23rd Constitutional Convention of the AFL-CIO, October 13, 1999.

125. Arthur Sanders and David Redlawsk, "Money and the Iowa Caucuses," in David B. Magleby, ed., *Getting Inside the Outside Campaign* (Salt Lake City: Center for the Study of Elections and Democracy, Brigham Young University).

126. Sanders and Redlawsk, "Money and the Iowa Caucuses."

127. Linda L. Fowler, Constantine J. Spiliotes, and Lynn Vavreck, "The Role of Issue Advocacy Groups in the New Hampshire Primary," in Magleby, ed., *Getting Inside the Outside Campaign*.

128. Figures extrapolated from census data on union members, voter registration data, and average household size, *Statistical Abstract of the United States* (Washington, D.C., 2001), 412.

129. Diana Dwyre, Bruce Cain, Ray La Raja, Joe Doherty, and Sam Kernell,

"Outside Money in the 2000 Presidential Primary," in Magleby, ed., *Getting Inside the Outside Campaign.*

130. David Magleby, "Issue Advocacy in the 2000 Presidential Primaries," in Magleby, ed., *Getting Inside the Outside Campaign.*

131. Joel Connelly, "Labor Basks in Democratic Spotlight," *Seattle Post-Intelligencer,* August 14, 2000, A12.

132. Dave Boyer, "Labor Puts Its Brand on Gore," *Washington Times,* August 14, 2000, A13.

133. Connelly, "Labor Basks in Democratic Spotlight."

134. Boyer, "Labor Puts Its Brand on Gore."

135. Salant, "Unions Gear Up for Fall Election."

136. Steven Greenhouse, "Labor Tailors Its Vote-for-Gore Message, State by State," *New York Times,* November 2, 2000.

137. Lewis, op. cit.

138. Jim Drinkard, "Union Chief Hand Delivers $1M Check to Democrats," *USA Today,* June 8, 2000, A1.

139. Dreyfuss, "Rousing the Democratic Base."

140. Greenhouse, "Labor Tailors Its Vote-for-Gore Message, State by State"; Ronald Brownstein, "NRA, Unions Fight for Blue-Collar Voters," *Los Angeles Times,* October 22, 2000.

141. Greenhouse, "Labor Tailors Its Vote-for-Gore Message, State by State."

142. Jim Suhr, "Unions Step Up Efforts for Democrats," Associated Press, October 27, 2000.

143. *Work in Progress,* AFL-CIO, October 22, 2000.

144. "In the 'Cliffhanger' Presidential Election, Massive Mobilization and High Turnout by Union Members Made the Difference in Key States," AFL-CIO news release, November 8, 2000.

145. E. J. Dionne, "To Unions, It's Do or Die," *Washington Post,* September 22, 2000, A25.

146. "In the 'Cliffhanger' Presidential Election."

147. Kathy Barks Hoffman, "Labor, Black Votes Made Difference for Democrats," Associated Press, December 2, 2000.

148. "In the 'Cliffhanger' Presidential Election."

149. Pat Kelly, "Demonstrators from Across Florida Rally Before Capitol," *Bradenton Herald,* December 7, 2000.

150. Andrea Billups and Arlo Wagner, "Outside, Protestors Wave Signs of the Times," *Washington Times,* December 12, 2000.

151. John Bowman and Jay Hancock, "Blacks, Others Question Legitimacy of Bush Presidency," *Baltimore Sun,* December 14, 2000.

152. Mark Murray, "On the Ropes," *National Journal,* March 8, 2003.

153. Ibid.

154. Joseph Perkins, "Holding Labor Unions Accountable," *San Diego Union-Tribune,* October 17, 2003.

155. "Bush Building Up for '04, One Carpenter's Union at a Time," Hotline, *National Journal,* September 3, 2002.

156. Mike Allen, "Bush Courts Unions to Split Off Unions," *Washington Post,* March 31, 2002, A5.

157. Murray, "On the Ropes."
158. "Labor Targets Voters in Battleground States," Gannett News Service, October 7, 2003.
159. Robert Novak, "Teamsters vs. Bush," Townhall.com, March 1, 2003.
160. Paul Farhi, "Dean Works to Be Labor's Man: Candidate Traills Gephardt in Union Endorsements," *Washington Post*, November 23, 2003, A5.
161. Gonzalez, "Union to Be Out Beating the Bushies."

CHAPTER 3 An Affair to Remember: Bill Clinton and the Unions

1. Byron York, "Mob Rules: Bill and Arthur's Beautiful Friendship," *American Spectator*, April 1997.
2. "Coia's Connections, " *Wall Street Journal*, October 24, 1997.
3. A 1992 settlement placed the local under federal trusteeship. See Robert L. Bartley, "New York: Another Rotten Choice," *Wall Street Journal*, October 28, 2002, A19.
4. Local 560 was placed under federal trusteeship on June 23, 1986. See Chairman Peter Hoekstra, Opening Statement, "Lessons Learned from the Teamsters Local 560 Trusteeship," Hearing Before the Subcommittee on Education and the Workforce, U.S. House of Representatives, June 30, 1999.
5. Micah Morrison, "Who Is Harold Ickes?" *Wall Street Journal*, October 26, 2000.
6. Eugene Methvin, "A Corrupt Union and the Mob," *Weekly Standard*, August 31, 1998.
7. York, "Mob Rules."
8. Ibid.
9. John E. Mulligan and Dean Starkman, "An F.O.B. and the Mob: Laborers' International Union of North America Pres. Arthur A. Coia," *Washington Monthly*, May 1996.
10. Joe Pichirallo, "Laborers Union Official Indicted in Kickbacks," *Washington Post*, September 25, 1981.
11. York, "Mob Rules."
12. Methvin, "A Corrupt Union and the Mob."
13. Ibid.
14. Ibid.
15. Ibid.
16. Ibid.
17. Marcy Gordon, "First Lady's Aides Told of Government Action Against Union, Memo Shows," Associated Press, July 25, 1996.
18. Ibid.
19. Ibid.
20. Ibid.
21. Kenneth R. Weinstein, "LIUNA, Organized Crime, and the Clinton Administration," Heritage Foundation, October 20, 1996.
22. "White House Allies," *Wall Street Journal*, November 11, 1997.
23. York, "Mob Rules."
24. Weinstein, "LIUNA, Organized Crime, and the Clinton Administration."

25. Ibid.
26. *United States District Court Northern District of Illinois Eastern Division v. Laborers' International Union of North America*, AFL-CIO, draft available at www.ipsn.org/laborers/international/draftRICOcomplaint.htm.
27. Morrison, "Who Is Harold Ickes?"
28. Ibid.
29. Mulligan and Starkman, "An F.O.B. and the Mob."
30. Jodie T. Allen, "The Clintons and the Mob," *Slate*, August 3, 1996.
31. York, "Mob Rules."
32. Jennifer G. Hickey, "Union Payoffs," *Insight on the News*, September 29, 1997.
33. York, "Mob Rules."
34. Ibid.
35. Methvin, "A Corrupt Union and the Mob."
36. Ibid.
37. These figures were compiled from campaign finance reports the Schumer campaign filed with the Federal Election Commission (FEC). To find out more about union contributions to political campaigns, consult the website of the Center for Responsive Politics (www.opensecrets.org), a nonpartisan, nonprofit research group that tracks money in politics. The FEC offers the most comprehensive resource for information on political contributions; see its main website (www.fec.gov) or the site that enables visitors to conduct detailed searches on candidates and contributors (herndon1.sdrdc.com).
38. Methvin, "A Corrupt Union and the Mob."
39. Mike Stanton et al., "Coia Agrees to Plead Guilty to Tax Fraud," *Providence Journal*, January 28, 2000.
40. U.S. Department of Justice, United States Attorney, District of Massachusetts, Re: Arthur A. Coia, January 27, 2000.
41. Ibid.
42. Tracy Breton, "Coia Regains Law License," *Providence Journal-Bulletin*, February 20, 2003.
43. "A Corrupt Union Escapes Justice," *Wall Street Journal*, July 27, 1998.
44. Ibid.
45. Ibid.
46. Steven Greenhouse, "Laborers' Union President Is Cleared of Links to Mob," *New York Times*, March 10, 1999.
47. Michael Wines, "Study Finds Money Flowed to Clinton Late in '92," *New York Times*, March 4, 1993.
48. Fred Wertheimer, "Campaign Finance Abuses," *Orlando Sentinel*, November 10, 1996.
49. Center for Responsive Politics, www.opensecrets.org, Labor: Long-Term Contribution Trends.
50. Kenneth C. Crowe, "GOP Attacks Quindel Over Teamsters Race," *Newsday*, October 16, 1997.
51. Bill Sammon and Jerry Seper, "Carey Done as Teamsters Chief; Ruling Says He Laundered Money," *Washington Times*, November 18, 1997, A1.
52. Stephen Dinan, "Republicans Woo Teamsters President," *Washington Times*, August 1, 2000.

53. Kevin Galvin, "Former UPS Driver Claims Second Win to Head Teamsters," Associated Press, December 14, 1996.

54. "Past Teamsters' Presidents and Their Legal Woes," Associated Press, November 18, 1997.

55. Kenneth B. Noble, "Giuliani Will Head U.S. Drive to Take Over Teamsters," *New York Times*, September 16, 1987, B5.

56. Kenneth C. Crowe, "GOP Attacks Quindel Over Teamsters Race."

57. Michael Ledeen and Mike Moroney, "The White House Joins the Teamsters," *American Spectator*, November 1998.

58. "The Teamsters Issue," *Wall Street Journal*, May 6, 1998.

59. Ledeen and Moroney, "The White House Joins the Teamsters."

60. This figure represents donations from Teamster PACs, soft-money contributions from the Teamsters, and contributions from individuals who listed the Teamsters as their employer. See Center for Responsive Politics, www.opensecrets.org/industries/contrib.asp?Ind=P&Cycle=1996.

61. Charles Lewis, *The Buying of the President 2000* (New York: Avon Books, 2000), 34–35.

62. "Decision of Teamsters Election Officer Kenneth Conboy to Disqualify Int'l Brotherhood of Teamsters President Ron Carey," U.S. District Court, Southern District of New York, November 17, 1997.

63. Ken Fireman, "DNC Paid Firms Tied to Teamsters Scheme," *Newsweek*, September 19, 1997.

64. Ledeen and Moroney, "The White House Joins the Teamsters."

65. "Decision of Teamsters Election Officer Kenneth Conboy to Disqualify Int'l Brotherhood of Teamsters President Ron Carey."

66. Ibid.

67. Ledeen and Moroney, "The White House Joins the Teamsters."

68. "New Retiree Alliance Launched," *American Teacher*, April 2001.

69. "Match Made in Democratic Heaven," *Washington Times*, April 2, 2001.

70. Associated Press, "Former Teamsters Chief Acquitted," *Washington Post*, October 13, 2001.

71. Frank Swoboda, "Calif. Fund-Raiser Pleads Guilty in Teamsters Election Case," *Washington Post*, August 18, 1998, C3.

72. Chris Mondics, "Democrats Sever Ties to Telemarketing Firm: Employees Involved in Teamsters Scandal," *Washington Post*, August 17, 2000.

73. Jerry Seper, "Reno Says No to Independent Counsel for Ickes," *Washington Times*, January 30, 1999.

74. Ibid.

75. "Who Is Richard Trumka?" *Wall Street Journal*, May 11, 2000.

76. Jerry Seper, "Teamster Scandal's Scope Widens," *Washington Times*, November 29, 1999.

77. Bill Sammon, "AFL-CIO Leader Won't Oust Deputy Who Invoked Fifth," *Washington Times*, November 22, 1997, A3.

78. Kenneth C. Crowe, "GOP Attacks Quindel Over Teamsters Race."

79. "Who Is Richard Trumka?"

80. Stefan Gleason, "Confrontation Not Concession," *Washington Times*, November 14, 2002.

CHAPTER 4 Putting the Public at Risk

1. Margaret Shapiro, "1500 Employees of P.G. County to Strike Today," *Washington Post*, August 12, 1980.

2. Tom Stuckey, "Inmates Take Over Jail After Guards Strike," Associated Press, August 12, 1980.

3. Max Green, *Epitaph for American Labor: How Union Leaders Lost Touch with America* (Washington, DC: AEI Press, 1996), 162.

4. Paul Sultan, *Right to Work Laws: A Study in Conflict* (Los Angeles: UCLA Institute of Industrial Relations, 1958), 46.

5. Lee Anderson, "All Should Be Free to Choose," *Chattanooga Times Free Press*, June 1, 1999, B7.

6. David Y. Denholm, "Beyond Public Sector Unionism," Public Service Research Foundation, www.psrf.org.

7. Ibid.

8. Austin Wilson, "Air Traffic Controllers Threaten June 22 Strike," Associated Press, May 23, 1981.

9. Albert Shanker, "Exploring Alternatives to the Strike," *Monthly Labor Review*, September 1973, 33.

10. Patrick Boyle, "Scare Ads Effective as Police Fight Cuts," *Washington Times*, March 26, 1992.

11. Ibid.

12. Shapiro, "1500 Employees of P.G. County to Strike Today."

13. Margaret Shapiro, "P.G. Workers Strike Sparks Jail Riot," *Washington Post*, August 13, 1980.

14. Neil Henry and Jefferson Morley, "County, Union to Meet U.S. Mediator: Strike Delays Some P.G. Services, Cuts Off Others," *Washington Post*, August 14, 1980, C1.

15. Many of these strikes took place in the 1970s, at the very time the unions were fighting for the legal right to strike. See, for example, "Dayton Homes, Apartments Burn as City's Firemen Continue Strike," *Washington Post*, August 10, 1977, A6.

16. John Toole and Dale Vincent, "Machos Wants Kelley Fired," *Manchester Union Leader*, March 28, 1994.

17. "Union Head Slammed: Kelley Suspended," *New Hampshire Sunday News*, October 9, 1994.

18. Green, *Epitaph for American Labor*, 5.

19. Barry T. Hirsch and David A. Macpherson, "Union Membership and Coverage Database from the Current Population Survey 1973–2002," U.S. Historical Tables, Private Construction Workers 1983–2002.

20. "Union Members in 2003," Department of Labor, USDL-04-53, 2004.

21. Ibid.

22. Ibid.

23. Steven Greenhouse, "Labor Leader Sounds Do-or-Die Warning," *New York Times*, February 15, 2001, A10.

24. David Y. Denholm, "Unions Turn to Public Sector as Membership Declines," *Labor Watch*, April 2003, 4.

25. "Union Members in 2002," U.S. Department of Labor, Bureau of Labor Statistics.
26. "Union Members in 2003," op.cit.
27. Leo Troy, *The New Unionism in the New Society: Public Sector Unions in the Redistributive State* (Fairfax, Va.: George Mason University Press, 1994), 24.
28. "Project Labor Agreements: The Extent of Their Use and Related Information," General Accounting Office, May 1998, 6.
29. See www.uschamber.com/government/issues/labor/davisbacon.htm.
30. Lisa Fernandez, "Carpenters at Airport Protest Against Union Leadership," *San Francisco Chronicle*, May 21, 1999, A18.
31. Herbert R. Northrup, "Government-Mandated Labor Agreements in Construction: A Force to Obtain Union Monopoly on Government-Financed Projects," study prepared for the 79th Meeting, Transportation Research Board, Washington, DC, January 11, 2000.
32. Deborah Baker, "Governor Signs Collective Bargaining Bill," Associated Press, March 7, 2003.
33. See www.aflcio.org/aboutunions/sept11/victims.cfm.
34. John Tate, "Forcing Unions In," *National Review Online*, March 20, 2002.
35. Green, *Epitaph for American Labor*, 150.
36. David Kendrick, "Compulsory Unionism During World War II," National Institute for Labor Law Research, June 11, 2001.
37. Green, *Epitaph for American Labor*, 150.
38. Ibid., 151.
39. Charles W. Baird, "Congress and Public Safety Unionism," Smith Center for Private Enterprise Studies, www.sbe.csuhayward.edu.
40. Robert Lenzner with Lisa Coleman, "The Philadelphia Story," *Forbes*, November 9, 1992.
41. Of course, Gompers underestimated the full role that competition plays in a free-market system, forcing employers to pay higher wages for the best workers or see them leave for competitors who will.
42. Ibid.
43. Green, *Epitaph for American Labor*, 162–63.
44. Ibid., 164.
45. David Hadane, "L.B. Teachers Get 'A' in Politics as Supporters Get School Board Seats," *Los Angeles Times*, June 9, 1988.
46. "Long Beach: Vote Approves Dues for Non-Union Teachers," *Los Angeles Times*, January 19, 1989, 2.
47. J. Y. Smith, "Leaders in Many Fields Join in Mourning George Meany," *Washington Post*, January 12, 1980, B9.
48. J. Y. Smith and Kenneth Crawford, "George Meany, 85, Giant of U.S. Labor Movement," *Washington Post*, January 11, 1980, B5.
49. Merrill Harston, "Union Leaders Satisfied with Mondale Effort," Associated Press, Nov. 11, 1984.
50. See www.prideatwork.org/issues.html.
51. Raphael Lewis, "Unions Lend Voice, Might Back Gay Marriage," *Boston Globe*, January 27, 2004, A1.
52. See www.cluw.org/legaction.html.

CHAPTER 5 Teachers' Unions: Deep-Pocketed Protectors of Mediocrity

1. Peter Brimelow, *The Worm in the Apple: How the Teacher Unions Are Destroying American Education* (New York: HarperCollins, 2003), 44.
2. Toch et al., "Why Teachers Don't Teach," *U.S. News & World Report*, February 26, 1996.
3. Brimelow, *The Worm in the Apple*, 44.
4. See www.nea.org/aboutnea.html.
5. Bob Chase, "The New NEA: Reinventing Teacher Unions for a New Era," Address to the National Press Club, February 5, 1997.
6. See www.nea.org/schoolquality/.
7. Mary Hartwell Futrell, *Los Angeles Times* interview, summer 1982.
8. See www.nea.org/ra/.
9. *NEA Resolutions, Legislative Program, and New Business 2001–2002* (Washington, DC: National Education Association), 367.
10. Ibid., 364.
11. Ibid., 370.
12. Ibid., 363.
13. Ibid., 362.
14. Ibid., 300.
15. Ibid., 292–93.
16. Ibid., 409.
17. National Education Association 2003 Representative Assembly, www.nea.org/annualmeeting/raaction/amendments.html.
18. Ibid.
19. *NEA Resolutions, Legislative Program, and New Business 2001–2002*, 375.
20. Ibid., 402.
21. Ibid., 403.
22. Ibid., 408.
23. Ibid., 409.
24. Ibid., 398.
25. Ibid., 340–41.
26. National Education Association 2003 Representative Assembly, www.nea.org/annualmeeting/raaction/amendments.html.
27. Ibid.
28. Abraham Cooper and Harold Brackman, "Terrorism: The Reality Factor in Educating Children About Sept. 11," *Los Angeles Times*, September 1, 2002.
29. Myron Lieberman, *The Teacher Unions: How the NEA and AFT Sabotage Reform and Hold Students, Parents, Teachers, and Taxpayers Hostage to Bureaucracy* (New York: Free Press, 1997), 13–15.
30. Toch et al., "Why Teachers Don't Teach."
31. Charlene Haar, Myron Lieberman, and Leo Troy, *The NEA and AFT: Teacher Unions in Power and Politics* (Rockport, Mass.: Pro Active Books), 12.
32. National Center for Education Statistics, "Digest of Education Statistics, 2002," Table 166 (Washington, D.C.: GPO, 2002).

33. Department of Education, "Summary of the 2001 Budget," February 2000, available at www.ed.gov/offices/OUS/Budget01/BudgetSumm/summary.html.

34. National Center for Education Statistics, "Digest of Education Statistics, 2002," Table 65, "Public and Private Elementary and Secondary Teachers, Enrollment, and Pupil/Teacher Ratios: Fall 1955 to Fall 2001."

35. National Center for Education Statistics, "Digest of Education Statistics, 2002," Chapter 2.

36. Ibid., Table 80.

37. Ibid., Table 77.

38. Ibid., Tables 77, 166, and 65.

39. National Assessment of Educational Progress, "1999 Long-Term Trending Reading and Mathematics Tables for Age 17 Student Data."

40. National Assessment of Educational Progress, "The Nation's Report Card, 2002 Assessment Results, Map of Selected Items on the Reading Scale, Grade 12."

41. National Assessment of Educational Progress, "Map of Selected Items on the Mathematics Scale, Grade 12."

42. "NEA Violated Federal, State Tax Laws," *Washington Times*, August 13, 2001.

43. Brimelow, *The Worm in the Apple*, 37.

44. Bob Chase, Keynote Remarks to the 1999 NEA Representative Assembly, July 3, 1999.

45. Lieberman, *The Teacher Unions*, 48.

46. Form LM-2, p. 5, filed by the NEA with the U.S. Department of Labor, December 18, 2002.

47. Form LM-2, p. 4, filed by the AFT with the U.S. Department of Labor, September 26, 2002.

48. Federal law requires only unions that represent at least some private-sector employees to file the appropriate form (the LM-2) with the U.S. Department of Labor.

49. IRS Form 990, 2000, for the American Federation of Teachers.

50. Form LM-2, p. 9, filed by the NEA with the U.S. Department of Labor, December 18, 2002.

51. Lieberman, *The Teacher Unions*, 130–31.

52. Brimelow, *The Worm in the Apple*, 80.

53. Bob Chase, Speech to the NEA Representative Assembly, 2000.

54. See FEC 2000 general election reported as amended at herndon1.sdrdc.com/cgi-bin/fecgifpdf/.

55. "IRS and the NEA," *Washington Times*, April 11, 2002, A22.

56. Charles Lewis, *The Buying of the President 2004* (New York: Avon Books, 2004), 124–25.

57. Brimelow, *The Worm in the Apple*, 110.

58. Quoted in testimony by Bob Williams, president, Evergreen Freedom Foundation, Subcommittee on Workforce Protections, U.S. House of Representatives, June 20, 2002.

59. Brimelow, *The Worm in the Apple*, 110.

60. George Archibald, "NEA Challenged on Political Outlays," *Washington Times*, April 7, 2003, A1.

61. Jeff Archer, "Unions Pull Out Stops for Elections," *Education Week*, November 1, 2000.

62. Casey J. Lartigue, Jr., "Dems of Cheney's School," *New York Post*, August 22, 2000.

63. "The Nation's New School Mistress," *Newsweek*, Nov. 12, 1979.

64. Myron Lieberman, 79. See also William F. Buckley, Jr., "National Education(?) Association," *Dallas Morning News*, June 25, 1993.

65. Glenn Burkins and Glenn R. Simpson, "Political Lesson: As Democrats Meet, The Teachers' Unions Will Show Their Clout," *Wall Street Journal*, August 23, 1996, A1.

66. Brimelow, *The Worm in the Apple*, 59.

67. Committee on House Oversight, U.S. House of Representatives, "Influencing Political Activity of Labor Unions," Hearing, March 21, 1996 (unpublished transcript), statement of Reed Larson, president, National Right to Work Committee. See: adnetsolfp2.adnetsol.com/ssl_claremont/campfin/reedlarson.cfm.

68. See www.nea.org/he/advo00/advo0010/aline.html.

69. "Inside AFT, Week of August 21, 2000," www.aft.org/publications/inside_aft/previous/2000/082100.html.

70. Larry Margasak and John Solomon, "NEA's Political Activities Detailed," Associated Press, June 22, 2000.

71. Archibald, "NEA Challenged on Political Outlays."

72. Ibid.

73. "Labor Unions Not Reporting Political Expenses," Associated Press, August 7, 2001.

74. "Lawmakers Request IRS Investigation into NEA's Political Expenditures," *Bulletin's Frontrunner*, July 10, 2002.

75. Richard L. Berke, "Ruling Bolsters Christian Group," *New York Times*, August 2, 1999, A1.

76. Michael Isikoff, "Taxing Times for Robertson," *Newsweek*, June 21, 1999.

77. Marc Davis, "Christian Coalition Claims Victory Over the IRS," *Virginian-Pilot*, July 26, 2000, B2.

78. Archibald, "NEA Challenged on Political Outlays."

79. Archer, "Unions Pull Out Stops for Elections."

80. "NEA: Lawbreaker," *Washington Times*, April 24, 2002.

81. Archibald, "NEA Challenged on Political Outlays."

82. "NEA Counters Attacks," *NEA NOW*, December 12, 1988.

83. Brimelow, *The Worm in the Apple*, 118.

84. "NEA's Paper Chase," *Wall Street Journal*, April 22, 2002.

85. Archibald, "NEA Challenged on Political Outlays."

86. Peter Baker, "Fairfax Contract Called Proper but Pricey," *Washington Post*, June 3, 1992; Peter Baker, "Contracting Process Draws Heat," *Washington Post*, May 21, 1992.

87. "A Hard Look at Soft Money," *Washington Times*, March 20, 2002.

88. Archibald, "NEA Challenged on Political Outlays."

89. Congressional Testimony of Mark Levin before the Subcommittee on Workforce Protections, House Education and Workforce Committee, June 20, 2002.

90. National Rifle Association Institute for Legislative Action. See www.nraila.org/VoterInfo.asp. (Site visited September 25, 2003.)

91. See www.nea.org. (Site visited September 25, 2003.)

92. See www.aft.org. (Site visited September 25, 2003.)

93. See Linda Chavez's account of her role in delivering campaign endorsement brochures to the Ted Kennedy for President campaign during the 1980 presidential primaries in *An Unlikely Conservative: The Transformation of an Ex-Liberal* (New York: Basic Books, 2002), 133.

94. Archibald, "NEA Challenged on Political Outlays."

95. William McGurn, "Teacher's Pets," *Wall Street Journal,* August 2, 2001.

96. Bob Mahlburn and John Kennedy, "Vote Totals Not Expected to Close Gap: Presumed Winner Bill McBride Plans to Announce Running Mate Soon," *Orlando Sentinel,* September 17, 2002, A9; Wes Allison and Adam C. Smith, "McBride Embraces Union's Help," *St. Petersburg Times,* September 12, 2002, 1B.

97. Mark Hollis, "Teachers View Themselves as Winners of the Primary: 'No One Can Take Us for Granted Again,' " *Fort Lauderdale Sun-Sentinel,* September 15, 2002, 21A, quoted in "Where the NEA Pulls Strings," *Washington Times,* November 14, 2003, A22.

98. Lloyd Dunkelberger and Gary Fineout, "Conflict Further Ties Up McBride Election Case," *The Ledger* (Lakeland, Fla.), February 1, 2004, A27.

99. Haar, Lieberman, and Troy, *The NEA and AFT,* 75–77.

100. "Report of the Program and Budget Committee," 2000 NEA Strategic Plan and Budget, FY 1998–2000 (modified 1999–2000), presented to the Representative Assembly July 1999.

101. Mike Antonucci, "Summer School," Education Intelligence Agency, July 2, 2001, www.eiaonline.com.

102. Denis P. Doyle, "Where Connoisseurs Send Their Children to School: An Analysis of 1990 Census Data to Determine Where School Teachers Send Their Children to School," The Center for Education Reform, May 1995.

103. Ibid., Tables 37 and 38.

104. "Pro-Life Caucus Seeks Change in NEA," *Education Reporter,* no. 175 (August 2000).

105. Myron Lieberman, *The Teachers Unions* (New York: Free Press, 1997) 34.

106. Brimelow, *The Worm in the Apple,* 64.

107. Ibid.

108. Ibid., 60–61.

109. D. Cameron Findlay, Deputy Secretary, U.S. Department of Labor, testimony before the Subcommittee on Employer-Employee Relations, Subcommittee on Workforce Protections, Committee on Education and the Workforce, U.S. House of Representatives, April 10, 2002.

110. "Rankings and Estimates Update," National Education Association Research Department, Fall 2003.

111. Albert Shanker, "A Battle in D.C.," *AFT Where We Stand,* January 21, 1996, www.aft.org/stand/previous/1996/012196.html.

112. The senators who introduced the District of Columbia Student Opportunity Scholarship Act of 1997 were Republicans Dan Coats of Indiana, Sam

Brownback of Kansas, and Judd Gregg of New Hampshire and Democrats Joseph Lieberman of Connecticut and Mary Landrieu of Louisiana.

113. The District of Columbia Student Opportunity Scholarship Act of 1997 was vetoed on May 20, 1998.

114. Sari Horwitz, "Poll Finds Backing for D.C. School Vouchers: Blacks Support Idea More Than Whites," *Washington Post,* May 23, 1998.

115. *Zelman v. Simmons-Harris* (00-1751), 234 F.3d 945, decided June 27, 2002.

116. H.R. 5033/S. 2866.

117. Spencer S. Hsu and Justin Blum, "D.C. School Vouchers Win Final Approval," *Washington Post,* January 23, 2004.

118. See "Teacher and Paraprofessional Quality," home.nea.org/www/htmlmail. cfm?type=printer.

119. Peter Schrag, "Getting Better Teachers and Other Herculean Tasks," *Sacramento Bee,* June 19, 2002.

120. See Federal Legislative Update Archives, April 27, 2001, available at www.nea.org/lac/arch0401.html.

121. NEA Resolution B-57 (1978, 2001). NEA Resolutions 2001–2002, p. 305.

122. Sally Reed, *NEA: Propaganda Front of the Radical Left* (National Council for Better Education, 1984), 65.

123. Samuel Blumenfeld, *NEA: Trojan Horse in American Education* (Paradigm Company, 1985), 205–6.

124. Ibid.

125. Thomas Toch et al., "Why Teachers Don't Teach."

126. Chase, "The New NEA."

127. See Mike Antonucci, "The National Everything Association," A Report of the Education Intelligence Agency, August 2001, members.aol.com/ educationintel/everything.pdf.

128. *Connections,* National Education Association Gay and Lesbian Caucus, vol. xiii, no. 2 (December 2000).

CHAPTER 6 Legalized Terrorism

1. "Judge Imposes 99-Year Terms in San Juan Fire," *New York Times,* June 23, 1987, A1.

2. Ibid.

3. Helen J. Simon, "Judge Rules That Arson, Murder Trial May Proceed," Associated Press, April 1, 1987.

4. Helen J. Simon, "Witnesses Say Defendant Threatened Fire," Associated Press, February 4, 1987.

5. Manuel Suarez, "3 Admit Setting Hotel Fire That Killed 97 in San Juan," *New York Times,* April 25, 1987, A-8.

6. Testimony of Edwin Meese III, U.S. Senate Judiciary Committee, September 3, 1997.

7. National Institute for Labor Relations Research, interview with Cathy Jones, July 22, 2003.

8. *United States v. Local 807,* 315 U.S. 521.

9. 18 U.S.C. § 1951(a).

10. Charles W. Baird, "Labor Relations Law," *Cato Handbook for the 108th Congress*, 2003.
11. *United States v. Enmons*, 410 U.S. 396.
12. Ibid.
13. 18 U.S.C. § 1951(b)(2).
14. Deroy Murdock, "Closing the Union Violence Loophole," Scripps Howard News Service, June 5, 2003.
15. Statement by Senator Orrin Hatch, Chairman, U.S. Senate Judiciary Committee, September 3, 1997.
16. *NLRB v. Mackey Radio*, 304 U.S. 333 (1938).
17. By 2001, only 400 of the 13,000 drivers remained on strike, which was not settled for another year. John D. Schults, "A Long, Strange Trip," *Traffic World*, October 2001.
18. "Striker Shot in Memphis," Associated Press, December 2, 1999.
19. Chip Jones, "Overnite Says Threat Rising to Drivers," *Richmond Times-Dispatch*, December 23, 1999.
20. Richard Thompson, "Overnite's 4th Quarter Loss Linked to Teamster Violence," *Commercial Appeal*, January 21, 2000.
21. Alice Ann Love, "AFL-CIO to Aid Teamsters Strike," Associated Press, February 9, 2000.
22. "The International Brotherhood of Teamsters One Year After the Election of James P. Hoffa," Subcommittee on Oversight and Investigations, Committee on Education and the Workforce, U.S. House of Representatives, March 28, 2000.
23. "Who Is Richard Trumka?" *Wall Street Journal*, May 11, 2000.
24. Amy Green, "Overnite Sues Teamsters for $5.2M," Associated Press. January 24, 2000.
25. Reed Larson, "Up with the Right-to-Work Bill: Teamsters' Mob Is Corrupt and Tyrannical," *Washington Times*, January 4, 2002.
26. "Court Permits Hoffa Teamsters RICO Trial to Proceed," Overnite Transportation media release, March 12, 2001.
27. July 19, 2002. *Overnite Transportation Comany v. International Brotherhood of Teamsters et al.*, U.S. District Court for the Western District of Tennessee.
28. Subcommittee on Oversight and Investigations, Committee on Education and the Workforce.
29. Frank Swoboda, "Former Teamsters Head Indicted," *Washington Post*, January 26, 2001.
30. Richard Vigilante, *Strike: The Daily News War and the Future of American Labor* (New York: Simon & Schuster, 1994), 154.
31. Alex Jones, "How the Strike at the News Took on a Life of Its Own," *New York Times*, March 17, 1991.
32. Leslie Wines, "Daily News First Run Cut by Labor-Management Sniping," United Press International, March 22, 1991.
33. Vigilante, *Strike*, 199–200.
34. Ibid., 220.
35. Ibid., 221.
36. Ibid.

37. Ibid., 218.

38. David Gonzalez with James C. McKinley, Jr., "Violence and the News Strike: Anger, Blame and Distrust," *New York Times*, March 2, 1991, A-1.

39. Mike McAlary, "Behind the Lines as News' Union Drivers Go to War," *New York Post*, November 12, 1990, 2.

40. David Gonzalez with James C. McKinley, Jr., "Violence and the News Strike: Anger, Blame and Distrust."

41. Vigilante, *Strike*, 247.

42. Ibid., 225.

43. Ibid., 250.

44. Ibid., 249.

45. David Kendrick, "Violence: Organized Labor's Unique Privilege," National Institute for Labor Relations Research, 1996.

46. Ibid.

47. Alan Finder, "Daily News Strike Ends, and Maxwell Marches In to Take the Reins," *New York Times*, March 21, 1991.

48. Bruce Lambert, "Labor Leaders Rally to Support News Strike," *New York Times*, November 15, 1990.

49. "Severed Cow's Head Dumped on Car in Strike-Related Violence," PR Newswire, July 15, 1996.

50. Testimony of David C. Horn, Employer-Employee Relations Subcommittee of Education and the Workforce Committee, U.S. House of Representatives, September 26, 2002.

51. Ibid.

52. Ibid.

53. Ibid.

54. Ibid.

55. Ibid.

56. Ibid.

57. Ibid.

58. Ibid.

59. Paul Singer, "Man Charged with Plotting to Bomb Steel Mill in Sympathy with Locked-Out Union Workers," Associated Press, March 30, 2002.

60. Testimony of David C. Horn, September 26, 2002.

61. James Bovard, "Union Goons' Best Friend," *Wall Street Journal*, June 2, 1994.

62. Ibid.

63. David Kendrick, "Freedom from Union Violence," Cato Policy Analysis No. 316, September 9, 1998.

64. Testimony of Reed Larson, U.S. Senate Judiciary Committee, September 3, 1997.

65. Statement by Senator Orrin Hatch, Chairman, U.S. Senate Judiciary Committee, September 3, 1997.

66. Maryclaire Dale, "Testimony Upsets Coal Contractor's Widow," *Charleston* (West Virginia) *Gazette*, June 16, 1994.

67. Bill Hinote, "Victim of Union Violence Recounts Story," *Unreported News*, Foundation for Economic Education, January 25, 1997.

68. Thomas O'Hanlon, "Anarchy Threatens the Kingdom of Coal," *Fortune*, January 1971.

69. Janelle A. Weber, "UPS Worker Stabbed in Miami Settles Lawsuit Against Teamsters," Associated Press, April 12, 2001.

70. Testimony of Rod Carter, U.S. Senate Judiciary Committee, September 3, 1997.

71. Joan Fleisher Tamen, "Teamsters Plan to Ask Broward Judge to Move Assault Case to Miami-Dade," *Fort Lauderdale Sun-Sentinel*, January 26, 2000, 1-D; Janelle A. Weber, "UPS Worker Stabbed in Miami Settles Lawsuit Against Teamsters," Associated Press, April 12, 2001.

72. "UPS Employee Files Civil Conspiracy Lawsuit After Stabbing by Teamsters Union Assailants," U.S. Newswire, September 1, 1999.

73. Hearings of the Select Committee on Improper Activities in the Labor or Management Field, U.S. Senate, 85th Congress, 2nd Session, 8,980.

74. "Three Additional Teamsters to Be Charged in Assault of Clinton Protestors," Business Wire, August 27, 1999.

75. Meki Cox, "Teamsters Leader Removed," Associated Press, November 15, 1999.

76. Harold Jackson, "Obituary: John Morris: Discredited US Union Boss," *Guardian* (London), May 8, 2002, 18.

77. President's Commission on Organized Crime, Record of Hearing VI, April 22–24, 1985, Chicago, Illinois, Organized Crime and Labor Management Racketeering in the United States, Supt. of Docs. No. 85-603235.

78. President's Commission on Organized Crime, 19–42.

79. Ibid.

80. In April 2003 Congressman Joe Wilson, Republican of South Carolina, introduced a bill to eliminate this loophole. The Freedom from Union Violence Act was referred to the House Subcommittee on Crime, Terrorism, and Homeland Security in May, but the bill had not moved out of the subcommittee as of the close of the 2003 session of Congress. The threat of Big Labor's political machine makes it unlikely such a bill would receive widespread support in Congress.

CHAPTER 7 Money, Mansions, and Mobsters: Union Corruption

1. "Teachers Union Scandal: An Inside Look," *Washington Post*, January 16, 2003, T4.

2. Brian DeBose, "Mayor Suspends Aide Tied to Probe: Grand Jury Looks at Teachers Union," *Washington Times*, January 9, 2003, B1.

3. Justin Blum, "D.C. Union Chief a Conspicuous Consumer," *Washington Post*, December 21, 2002, A1.

4. Allan Lengel and Neely Tucker, "Ex-Chauffeur Aids Union Probe, Sources Say," *Washington Post*, February 6, 2003, B1.

5. F. Howard Nelson and Rachel Drown, "Survey and Analysis of Teacher Salary Trends 2002," American Federation of Teachers, 2003, p. 7.

6. Nathan Paul Mehrens, who provided research assistance with this book, attended the Bullock sentencing on January 30, 2004, and provided many of these details.

7. Carol D. Leonnig, "Ex-Teachers Union Chief Gets 9 Years," *Washington Post*, January 31, 2004, A1.

8. Ibid.

9. Mehrens.

10. Valerie Strauss, "Forgery of D.C. Union Check Unreported, Audit Finds," *Washington Post,* January 18, 2003, B5.

11. Brian DeBose, "Williams: No Ties to Teachers Union," *Washington Times,* January 16, 2003, B1.

12. Ibid.

13. "The AFT's Malfeasance," *Washington Times,* May 4, 2003, B2.

14. Craig Timberg and Avram Goldstein, "Appointees Say Williams Aide Urged Donations," *Washington Post,* February 16, 2003, A1.

15. Justin Blum and Yolanda Woodlee, "Union Chief Lobbied for Aide's Brother, Suit Says," *Washington Post,* January 15, 2003, B5.

16. "Teachers Union Scandals," *Washington Times,* June 19, 2003, A22.

17. Yolanda Woodlee, "Union's Treasurer Violated D.C. Code," *Washington Post,* January 26, 2003, C1.

18. Ibid.

19. Justin Blum, "Audit Says Union Lost $5 Million to Theft: Teachers Group Sues Eight from D.C. Local," *Washington Post,* January 17, 2003, A1.

20. Ibid.

21. "Education Scandal Spreads," *Florida Times-Union,* June 8, 2003, G2.

22. Maya Bell, "Probe Casts Shadow on Educator's Legacy," *Orlando Sentinel,* May 1, 2003, A1.

23. Ibid.

24. Ibid.

25. Charles Savage, "Longtime Union Leader's Empire Facing Challenges from Dissenting Teachers, Others," *Miami Herald,* October 6, 2002, L1.

26. American Federation of Teachers, "Survey and Analysis of Teacher Salary Trends 2002" (Washington, D.C.: AFT, 2003), 7.

27. "Union Leader Gives Up Salary," *Orlando Sentinel,* May 20, 2003, B5.

28. Manny Garcia and Joe Mozingo, "UTD Leaders Had Secret Pension Fund," *Miami Herald,* May 25, 2003, B1.

29. Joe Mozingo and Larry Lebowitz, "Teachers' Union Raided in Miami-Dade," *Miami Herald,* April 30, 2003.

30. Ibid.

31. Ibid.

32. Matthew I. Pinzur, "We're Taking Back Our Union," *Miami Herald,* June 7, 2003, B1.

33. Joe Mozingo and Manny Garcia, "Union Paid Private Bills for Tornillo," *Miami Herald,* May 11, 2003, A1.

34. Ibid.

35. Manny Garcia and Joe Mozingo, "Union Paid for Chief's Opulent Lifestyle," *Miami Herald,* May 18, 2003, A1.

36. "Report: Union Head Was Reimbursed $350,000 for Private Expenses," Associated Press, May 19, 2003.

37. Garcia and Mozingo, "Union Paid for Chief's Opulent Lifestyle."

38. Ibid.

39. Ibid.

40. Matthew I. Pinzur, "Teachers Union Is in Debt over Dues," *Miami Herald*, May 8, 2003, B1.

41. Joe Mozingo and Manny Garcia, "Tornillo's Maid Was Paid by His Union," *Miami Herald*, May 25, 2003, B1.

42. "Teachers Union Scandals."

43. Garcia and Mozingo, "Union Paid for Chief's Opulent Lifestyle."

44. "Report: Union Head Was Reimbursed for $350,000 for Private Expenses."

45. Matthew I. Pinzur, "Teachers Union Fails to Pay Its $300,000 Insurance Bill," *Miami Herald*, May 22, 2003, A1.

46. Larry Lebowitz, "Tornillo Sentenced to 27 Months in Prison for Misusing Teachers Funds," *Miami Herald*, November 24, 2003.

47. Jim Defede, "U.S. Prosecutor, Dade Police Chief Trade More Shots," *Miami Herald*, January 15, 2004, B1.

48. Larry Lebowitz, "Tornillo Gets 27 Months," *Miami Herald*, November 25, 2003.

49. Ibid.

50. Ibid.

51. Joe Mozingo, "Tornillo Facing New Scrutiny," *Miami Herald*, October 24, 2003, B1.

52. Lebowitz, "Tornillo Gets 27 Months."

53. Pinzur, "Teachers Union Is in Debt over Dues."

54. Pinzur, "Disgruntled Teachers Map Strategy for Next Election," *Miami Herald*, May 21, 2003, B1.

55. Bell, "Probe Casts Shadow on Educator's Legacy."

56. Joe Mozingo and Larry Lebowitz, "Teachers' Union Raided in Miami-Dade."

57. Savage, "Longtime Union Leader's Empire Facing Challenges from Dissenting Teachers, Others."

58. Ibid.

59. Ibid.

60. Peter Wallsten and Lesley Clark, "TV Ad Blitz for McBride Under Scrutiny," *Miami Herald*, June 7, 2003, B1.

61. Bill Cotterell, "Beating Bush Is the Priority," *Tallahassee Democrat*, March 25, 2002, A1.

62. "FL: McBride Beats Out Reno for Union Endorsement," *Bulletin's Front-runner*, March 25, 2002.

63. Cotterell, "Beating Bush Is the Priority."

64. Mark Hollis, "Teachers View Themselves as Winners of the Primary," *Fort Lauderdale Sun-Sentinel*, September 15, 2002, p. 21A.

65. Ibid.

66. "Elections Regulators Will Proceed with McBride Investigation," Associated Press, June 7, 2003.

67. See "Florida: McBride Makes Gains in Yet Another Mason-Dixon Poll," *The Hotline*, September 26, 2002; Mark Silva and Bob Mahlburg, "Teachers Union Paid for McBride Ad," *Orlando Sentinel*, September 28, 2002, B5.

68. Wallsten and Clark, "TV Ad Blitz for McBride Under Scrutiny."

69. Gary Fineout, "McBride May Face Fines in Election Violations," *Lakeland Ledger*, June 7, 2003, A1.

70. Bill Cotterell, "Florida Governor Blasts Teachers Union Efforts for McBride," *Tallahassee Democrat*, November 2, 2002.

71. Bill Hirschman, "State Class Size Limits, Pre-k for All Given the Nod," *Fort Lauderdale Sun-Sentinel*, November 6, 2002, p. 1A.

72. Kevin Galvin, "Candidate Receives Salary from Former Local," Associated Press, August 24, 1995.

73. Ibid.

74. Derek Rose, "Union Prez Challenged, Ax Follows," New York *Daily News*, April 11, 2002.

75. William Murphy, "Sweeney's Salary: Janitors Gave AFL-CIO Boss Hundreds of Thousands," New York *Daily News*, February 4, 1999.

76. Jeffrey Goldberg, "State of the Union," *Daily Telegraph* (Sydney, Australia), July 27, 1996.

77. Ivan G. Osorio, "The Service Employees International Union: Part 2: Conflicts Over Control, Corruption, and Politics," Labor Watch, Capital Research Center, July 2002.

78. Julie Salamon, "Collaborating on the Future at the Modern," *New York Times*, December 26, 2003, E45.

79. Benjamin Weiser, "42 Are Indicted in Investigation of Mob Control in Construction," *New York Times*, February 27, 2003, B3.

80. Ibid.

81. Michele McPhee, "Building Biz Bust Nets Mob, Unions," New York *Daily News*, February 27, 2003, 10.

82. John Lehmann, Al Guart, and Andy Geller, "Mob Families $3 Million Grab: No Show Jobs at Major Projects," *New York Post*, February 27, 2003, 20.

83. Ibid.

84. Ibid.

85. Weiser, "42 Are Indicted in Investigation of Mob Control in Construction."

86. *USA v. Muscarella, et al.*, U.S. District Court Southern District of New York, Criminal Docket for Case # 1:03-cr-00229-NRB-ALL.

87. *USA v. Cacace, et al.*, U.S. District Court for the Eastern District of New York, Criminal Docket for Case # 1:03-r-00191-SJ-ALL.

88. See www.fbi.gov/hq/cid/orgcrime/lcn/laborrack.htm (visited August 3, 2003).

89. See www.fbi.gov/hq/cid/orgcrime/lcn/laborrack.htm (visited August 3, 2003).

90. See www.fbi.gov/hq/cid/orgcrime/lcn/laborrack.htm (visited August 3, 2003).

91. "Semiannual Report to the Congress Highlights," Office of Inspector General, U.S. Department of Labor, October 1, 2002–March 31,2003, vol. 49.

92. Statement, June 6, 2000. Quoted in Edwin Meese III, "Disclosure Benefits Business and Labor," *Washington Times*, January 28, 2003, A19.

93. See www.opensecrets.org/races/blio.asp?ID=IAS2&cycle=2002&special=N.

94. Senate Report 107–216, Departments of Labor, Health and Human Services, and Education and Related Agencies Appropriations Bill, 2003.

95. Joe Mozingo, "UTD Case Prompts Federal Debate," *Miami Herald*, June 20, 2003, 1.

96. "Judge Delays Rules on Union Member Dues," Associated Press, January 2, 2004.

97. "Protecting Workers Through Union Transparency Reform," U.S. Department of Labor, March 24, 2003, 2.
98. "Sandbagging Secretary Chao," *Wall Street Journal*, March 3, 2003.
99. "Protecting Workers Through Union Transparency Reform," 13.
100. Sam Dealey, "Unions, Busted: But There Is Much More 'Busting' to Do," *National Review*, December 23, 2002.
101. Larry Yud, Deputy Director, Office of Labor-Management Standards, Employment Standards Administration, U.S. Department of Labor, Testimony Before the Senate Health, Environment, Labor, and Pensions Committee, June 19, 2003.
102. See www.fbi.gov/hq/cid/orgcrime/lcn/laborrack.htm (visited August 3, 2003).

CHAPTER 8 Choking the Golden Goose: How Big Labor Harms the American Economy

1. "Summer of Hell Exacts Heavy Toll," *Chicago Tribune*, July 15, 2003, 1.
2. John Schmeltzer and Thomas A. Corfman, "UAL Expects $3.2 Billion Loss in 2002," Chicago Tribune Online Edition, December 31, 2002.
3. "US Air Files for Bankruptcy," CNN/*Money*, August 12, 2002. (money.cnn.com/2002/08/11/news/companies/usair/).
4. "AMR Takes TWA Aboard," CNN/*Money*, January 10, 2001 (money.cnn.com/2001/01/10/deals/amr_twa/).
5. Roger Lowenstein, "Into Thin Air," *New York Times Magazine*, February 17, 2002, 40.
6. Ibid.
7. Ibid.
8. Edward Wong, "United Air's Family Is Anything But," *New York Times*, October 6, 2002, sec. 3, p. 1.
9. Ibid.
10. Ibid.
11. Ibid.
12. Susan Carey and Scott McCartney, "United Urges Its Union to Concede on Issues," *Wall Street Journal*, March 2, 2003.
13. David Grossman, "United Airlines Goes Fishing for a Solution," *USA Today*, August 14, 2003.
14. Lowenstein, "Into Thin Air," 40.
15. Carey and McCartney, "United Urges Its Union to Concede on Issues."
16. Lowenstein, "Into Thin Air," 40.
17. Ibid.
18. Ibid.
19. Ibid.
20. Ibid.
21. www.bctgm.org/organizing/Organize-intro.htm, October 15, 2003.
22. U.S. Census Bureau, Health Insurance Coverage Status and Type of Coverage by State, All People, 1987 to 2001, Table HI-4, www.census.gov.

23. Paul F. Stifflemeyer, Jr., "Unionism and Economic Performance: Pennsylvania and Peer States," Allegheny Institute of Public Policy, Report #0302, May 2003.

24. Richard K. Vedder and Lowell E. Gallaway, "Do Unions Help the Economy," *Journal of Labor Research,* Winter 2002 (vol. 23, no. 1).

25. F. Howard Nelson, "An Interstate Cost of Living Index," American Federation of Teachers Research and Information Services Department, February 1989. A subsequent version of this paper was published in *Educational Evaluation and Policy Analysis,* Spring 1991, vol. 13, no. 1, 103–11.

26. Daniel Henninger, "Blue State Pols Are Emptying Their Own State," *Wall Street Journal,* August 29, 2003.

27. cgi.money.cnn.com/tools/costofliving/costofliving.html.

28. Bennett, "A Higher Standard of Living in Right to Work States."

29. Thomas J. Holmes, "The Effects of State Policies on the Location of Industry: Evidence from State Borders," Federal Reserve Bank of Minneapolis Research Department Staff Report 205, December 1995, 3.

30. Phillip D. Phillips, letter to Michael Dolton, Greater Twin Falls (Idaho) Chamber of Commerce, June 27, 1986.

31. David A. Hake, Donald R. Ploch, and William F. Fox, "Business Location Determinants in Tennessee," Center for Business and Economic Research, College of Business Administration, University of Tennessee, October 1985.

32. Henninger, "Blue State Pols Are Emptying Their Own State."

33. Marc J. Perry, U.S. Census Bureau, "State-to-State Migration Flows: 1995–2000," CENSR-8 (2003).

34. Nancy Cleeland, "Unions Gain Ground in Golden State," *Los Angeles Times,* August 31, 2003, part 3, p. 1.

35. Gregg Jones, "Davis, Simon Make Final Bids," *Los Angeles Times,* November 4, 2002, 1.

36. Gary S. Becker, "The States Should Find Their Own Way Out of This Hole," Business Week Online, May 26, 2003.

37. David M. Drucker, "Unions Influence Davis Budget," *Inland Valley Daily Bulletin,* June 1, 2003.

38. Milt Freudenheim, "Many California Employers Face Health Care Mandate," *New York Times,* September 17, 2003, A-14.

39. See www.cft.org/councils/ec/news/budget_crisis.html.

40. See www.cft.org/home_news/cftanti-war.html.

41. "Budget Watch '03," Public Policy Institute of New York State, November 19, 2002, updated January 3, 2003.

42. Steven Greenhouse, "Unions Take On City Hall and the Rich in Ad Campaign," *New York Times,* April 25, 2003.

43. David Shaffer, "Public-Employee Unions Think 'Sacrifice' Is a One-Way Street," Policy Points, Public Policy Institute of New York State, April 2003.

44. Leo Troy, *The New Unionism in the New Society: Public Sector Unions in the Redistributive State* (Fairfax, Va.: George Mason University Press, 1994), 76.

45. George Judson, "Anguished Plea from Bridgeport for Fiscal Relief," *New York Times,* June 8, 1991, 1.

46. Robert Lenzner with Lisa Coleman, "The Philadelphia Story," *Forbes*, November 9, 1992.
47. Ibid.
48. Ibid.
49. Ibid.
50. Ibid.
51. *Morning Edition*, NPR, August 18, 1992.
52. Lenzner with Coleman, "The Philadelphia Story."
53. Ken Auletta, *The Streets Were Paved with Gold: The Decline of New York, an American Tragedy* (New York: Random House, 1979).
54. David M. Alpern with Phyllis Malamud and Barbara L. Davidson, "New York's Last Gasp?" *Newsweek*, August 4, 1975, 18.
55. Ibid.
56. Ibid.
57. Ibid.
58. Michael Ruby with Phyllis Malamud, Holly Camp, Eric Gelman, and Rich Thomas, "New York's Near D Day," *Newsweek*, October 27, 1975, 16.
59. Heather Pauly and Francine Knowles, "AFL-CIO Chief Opposes Plan," *Chicago Sun-Times*, May 4, 1998, 45.
60. *Social Security Bulletin*, vol. 63, no. 2 (2000).
61. See Center for Working Capital website: www.centerforworkingcapital.org/who/index.html.
62. See the Employee Retirement Income Security Act, 29 U.S.C. § 1104.
63. 29 U.S.C. § 1104(A)(1)(a), et seq.
64. Interpretive Bulletin 94-1, 59 *Federal Register* 32,606 (June 23, 1994).
65. Aaron Bernstein and Amy Borrus, "Labor Sharpens Its Pension Sword," *Business Week*, November 24, 2003.
66. Charles M. Nathan, "Lip Service," *The Deal*, September 29, 2003.
67. 17 C.F.R. § 240.14a-8.
68. Diane E. Lewis, "Unions Seek More Corporate Influence," *Boston Globe*, February 12, 2003, C1.
69. Stewart J. Schwab and Randall S. Thomas, "Realigning Corporate Governance: Shareholder Activism by Labor Unions," *Michigan Law Review* (1998), 1018 at 1045.
70. Diane E. Lewis, "Unions Take Fight Over CEOs' Pay to Shareholders," *Boston Globe*, April 11, 1999, F1.
71. David Cay Johnston, "Teamsters Are Challenging G.E. Chief's Compensation," *New York Times*, March 3, 1997, D2.
72. William M. Carley, "GE Chairman Defends Pay, Stresses Quality," *Wall Street Journal*, April 24, 1997, A4.
73. Amy Borrus, "Executive Pay: Labor Strikes Back," *Business Week*, May 26, 2003.
74. Stewart J. Schwab and Randall S. Thomas, "Realigning Corporate Governance: Shareholder Activism by Labor Unions," *Michigan Law Review*, 1018 at 1061 (1998).
75. Vineeta Anand, "Companies Opt for Peace: Shareholder Fighting Subdued in '96 Meeting Season," *Pension & Investments*, April 15, 1996, 19.

76. "Unions Wield Stock: Take Their Issues to Annual Meetings," *Bergen Record*, May 19, 1996, B1.

77. Ibid.

78. Dan Shope, "Teamsters Criticize Union Pacific's Lewis: Union Recently Won Elections to Organize Parts of Subsidiary Overnite," Allentown, Pa., *Morning Call*, March 13, 1996, B10.

79. Bill Menezes, "Grocery Union Throws Wide Net: Labor Organizers Pressure U.S. West, Other Companies," *Rocky Mountain News*, May 10, 1996, 1B.

80. Dan Piller, "Pier 1 Plans to Scuttle Clothing Sales," *Fort Worth Star-Telegram*, June 28, 1996, 1.

81. Ibid.

82. Marleen O'Connor, "Union Pension Power and the Shareholder Revolution," presented at the Second National Heartland Labor-Capital Conference, Washington, D.C., April 29–30, 1999.

83. Ibid.

84. Borrus, "Executive Pay."

85. AFL-CIO Proxy Voting Guidelines, 1997.

86. "The Lessons of Ullico," *Wall Street Journal*, June 14, 2003.

87. Charles Lewis, *The Buying of the Presidency 2004*, 108.

88. Ibid., 112.

89. "The Lessons of Ullico."

90. Lewis, *The Buying of the Presidency 2004*, 111–12.

91. "The Lessons of Ullico."

92. Allan Lengel, "Ex-Boss of Ironworkers Union Sentenced," *Washington Post*, October 29, 2003, A20.

93. "Panel Voices Concern on Ullico," Associated Press, October 29, 2003.

94. "The Lessons of Ullico."

95. O'Connor, "Union Pension Power and the Shareholder Revolution."

CHAPTER 9 Ending the Cycle of Corruption

1. John Fund, "Meany vs. Deanie," *Wall Street Journal*, January 19, 2004.

2. Philip Dine, "Labor Says It Will Support Challenge of Election," *St. Louis Post-Dispatch*, November 28, 2000.

3. Ibid.

4. See www.afl-cio.org/issuespolitics/votes/loader.cfm?url=/commonspot/security/getfile.cfm&PageID=14111 (visited February 16, 2004).

5. www.opensecrets.org/races/blio.asp?ID=MAS/&cycle=2000&special=N. Contributors include labor PACs, individual contributions from individuals who list unions as their employer.

6. Frank McMurray, "Initiative Would Shake Up Unions," *NY Hard Hat News*, Fall 1999.

7. The Davis-Bacon Act was enacted in 1931, unemployment insurance created in 1935, the National Labor Relations Act in 1935, the Fair Labor Standards Act in 1938, and the Labor-Management Relations Act in 1947.

8. U.S. Census Bureau, *Statistical Abstract of the United States, 2001*, 391.

9. U.S. Department of Commerce, Bureau of Economic Analysis, National Income and Product Tables, Table 1.1 (October 2003).

10. National Labor Relations Act, 9(a), 29 U.S.C. 159(a) 1935.

11. See, for example, Levitz Furniture Co., 333 NLRB No. 105 (March 29, 2001).

12. Samuel Gompers's address to the 1924 AFL convention.

13. Charles Baird, *Cato Handbook for the 107th Congress*, 399.

14. New Zealand Treasury Department, www.treasury.govt.nz/nzefo/2000/labour.asp.

15. Executive Order 12800, 57 Fed. Reg. 12. 985 (1992).

16. "Clinton Rescinds Executive Order on Beck Disclosure, 'Open Bidding,' " *Daily Labor Report*, February 3, 1993, AA1.

17. 320 NLRB 224 (1995).

18. "GOP Firm Issues Poll on Use of Union Dues," *National Journal*'s Congress Daily, May 2, 1996; Michael McMenamin, "Labor Lost: Why the AFL-CIO's Cynical Survival Strategy Is Doomed," *Reason*, November 2000.

19. Michael W. Lynch, "Union Blues," *Los Angeles Daily News*, September 5, 1999.

20. Prepared Statement of Kerry W. Gipe Before the House Education and the Workforce Committee, Subcommittee on Employer Employee Relations, March 18, 1997.

21. "That contractor has cheap colored labor that he transports, and he puts them in cabins, and it is labor of that sort that is in competition with white labor throughout the country." Remarks of Representative Miles Clayton Allgood, *Congressional Record* (February 28, 1931), 6,513.

22. Senate Committee on Manufactures, Hearings on S. 5904, 71st Congress, 3rd Session, February 3, 1931, p. 10.

23. www.dol.gov/esa/programs/dbra/faqs/trainees.htm.

24. Richard Vedder, "Michigan's Prevailing Wage Law and Its Effects on Government Spending and Construction Employment," Mackinac Center for Public Policy, September 1999.

25. Oklahoma Department of Labor, *Investigative Report: The Davis-Bacon Act and Fraudulent Wage Data Submitted to the U.S. Department of Labor*, July 11, 1995.

26. Remarks of Representative Ron Paul, *Congressional Record*, October 23, 1997, p. E2078.

27. "The Congress Should Consider Repeal of the Service Contract Act," U.S. General Accounting Office, 1983.

28. See Chapter 4, 10–11.

29. U.S. Census Bureau, *Statistical Abstract of the United States, 2001*, 380.

30. U.S. Census Bureau, "Money Income in the United States: 1999," Report No. P60-209, September 2000, 21.

31. In 1978 Congress passed the Federal Employees Flexible and Compressed Work Schedules Act as an experiment. It proved so successful that the measure was made permanent in 1985.

32. Princeton Survey Research Associates, "Worker Representation and Participation Survey, TopLine Results," October 1994; Penn and Schoen Associates,

Inc., "Flexible Scheduling and Compensatory Time Poll," conducted for the Employment Policy Foundation, October 27, 1995.

33. *Electromation, Inc. v. NLRB*, 35 F.3d 1148 (7th Cir. 1994).
34. U.S. Department of Labor, Commission on the Future of Worker-Management Relations, *Report and Recommendations*, December 1994, xvii.
35. NLRA sec. 8(a) (3), 29 U.S.C. 158(a)(3) (1935).
36. *N.L.R.B. v. Town & Country Electric, Inc.*, 516 U.S. 85 (1995).
37. The relevant Department of Labor forms are LM-2 and LM-3.
38. H.R. 1870, previously introduced as H.R. 5581/S.902 in the 107th Congress.

AFTERWORD FOR THE PAPERBACK EDITION Big Labor's Big Loss in 2004

1. Service Employees International Union, "Anatomy of an Election Strategy: The Facts on SEIU's Role in Bringing Home a Victory for America's Working Families," November 1, 2004.
2. Ibid.
3. Ibid.
4. Ibid.
5. Evergreen Freedom Foundation, "Organized Labor's Impact on the 2004 Election."
6. www.opensecrets.org/pacs/sector.asp?txt=P01&cycle=2004; Ronald Brownstein, "Democrats' Losses Go Far Beyond One Defeat," *Los Angeles Times*, November 4, 2004.
7. www.opensecrets.org/527s/527cmtes.asp.
8. www.opensecrets.org/527s/527contribs.asp?cycle=2004.
9. Brownstein, "Democrats' Losses Go Far Beyond One Defeat."
10. Bureau of Labor Statistics, "Union Members Summary: Union Members in 2004," January 27, 2005.
11. David S. Broder, "SEIU Chief Says the Democrats Lack Fresh Ideas," *Washington Post*, July 27, 2004. A full transcript of the conversation was briefly available on the *Post*'s website as well.
12. Ibid.
13. Stephen Franklin, "Dissidents Lose Key Votes on AFL-CIO Reforms," *Chicago Tribune*, March 3, 2005.
14. Harold Meyerson, "Labor's Inner War," *Washington Post*, March 4, 2005.
15. Matt Bai, "The New Boss," *New York Times*, January 30, 2005.
16. Bureau of Labor Statistics,

ACKNOWLEDGMENTS

My thanks go to our editor, Jed Donahue, who pushed us to keep digging for facts and whose careful editing helped smooth rough edges and turned the disparate styles of two writers into a coherent, readable whole. I'm also grateful to Crown Forum publisher Steve Ross, who believed in this book from the beginning. In addition, I'm grateful to all of the people at Crown Forum who worked so hard to accommodate a tight schedule, including production editor Mark McCauslin, managing editor Amy Boorstein, editorial assistant Mario Rojas, copy editor Toni Rachiele, production manager Leta Evanthes, and designer Barbara Sturman.

Thanks also to Eric Simonoff, my longtime agent at Janklow & Nesbit, who has consistently believed in my work. Nathan Paul Mehrens provided invaluable research assistance for this project. I am also indebted to other authors whose work on labor unions I consulted in writing this book, especially Max Green, Myron Lieberman, Peter Brimelow, and Richard Vigilante. And, as always, my husband, Chris Gersten, demonstrated patience and support through the long hours that went into this project.

—LINDA CHAVEZ

A surfeit of thanks go to Jed Donahue, whose uncanny skills were crucial, as well as to the rest of the staff at Crown Forum. Stan Greer of the National Institute for Labor Relations Research proved himself a walking encyclopedia of union knowledge in answering a number of difficult questions. Others who went above and beyond the call of duty were Mark Mix of the National Right to Work Committee, David Denholm at the Public Service Research Foundation, and Charlene Haar. Their years of dedication to restoring basic rights for American workers goes far beyond the scope of this book and should be appreciated by us all.

—DANIEL GRAY

INDEX

Acclaim for "Falling Uphill"

[Stoll] did something most of us would not do: He decided to ride his bicycle around the world. His impulse isn't as strange as it might sound. Humans have always sought answers to life's perplexing questions by undertaking long and arduous journeys.
    ~ San Francisco Chronicle

It was an exhausting yet exhilarating trip filled with both human kindness and treachery, with nature's beauty, challenge and danger.
    ~ Milwaukee Journal Sentinel

Stoll has some harrowing and heart-warming tales to tell.
    ~ San Diego Union Tribune

See! There's something else for us out there, we just have to dream a little bit. ~ WGN

The book is fascinating to read. ~ Showcase Minnesota

A bad day turned into an incredible adventure. ~ KION News

A book that makes me itch to get on the road again.... What surprised me was the style; not just another travelogue from A to B, but a whole philosophy of life and cycling. The best read since I read "Zen and the Art of Motorcycle Maintenance" over 10 years ago! ~ Andy G.

Scott's accomplishments and struggles reveal the beautiful and ugly sides of human nature, and his story gives us hope that we can all follow our dreams, no matter how foolish or impossible they seem. ~ Kate M.

A masterpiece on humanity. Thanks for not quitting so we can read about it and at the same time enrich our own lives. ~ Richard and Ingrid A.

It should be a primer for every child and on every home bookcase as ready relief for all adults. ~ Charles L.

If I had more money I would buy books for every library. The world needs people like Scott to show us what is possible, if you try. ~ Tony G.

I recognize the struggles you described, not so much because I traveled as far or as rough as you, but the struggle a lot of us have to be more appreciative of our lot in life, and to see the world with new eyes every day. ~ Chris D.

Through the author's words and experiences, I've had many self-realizations——See! He did make a difference. ~ Gerald H.

FALLING UPHILL

Dreams for the
young adventurer &
the young at heart

May the winds be with you

Scott Stoll

the Argonauts

STEM Academy
Randall Campus
Waukesha, WI 53186

Falling Uphill
Dreams for the young adventurer and the young at heart.

Published by The Argonauts. First edition © 2010. Printed in the United States.

Permissions: Center cover photo is thanks to Edwin Tucker's thoughtfulness. Thanks to Dennis Snader, Debbie M., Matt B. and everyone else that played impromptu photographers or models upon my request and whom I believe wish to remain anonymous. "Fried Crickets in the Chiang Mai Night Bazaar" photo courtesy of Alpha Lau. "Milestone, Jaisalmer" courtesy of Nevil Zaveri. "Maasai women and baby" courtesy of William Warby. Photo of Annie Londonderry courtesy of Mary Levy Goldiner. "American Bull" by artist Dwayne Wilcox, as photographed by Scott Stoll, courtesy of Sandy Conard. Thanks to the photographers and famous people whose images and life works have been granted to the public domain. Finally, thanks to Wikipedia, the free encyclopedia, for most of my fact checking. This is an amazing library by and for mankind.

Some names, places and events have been combined and/or changed to protect the identity of those involved and/or provide artistic clarity, but do not significantly alter the story's emotional authenticity as experienced by the author.

For up to date information on this title page, please visit:
http://www.theArgonauts.com/falling-uphill/copyright.shtml#dreams

Ordering information:
Falling Uphill is available at special bulk discounts upon request:
http://www.theArgonauts.com/falling-uphill/how-to-order.shtml

Library of Congress Control Number: 2009941988

ISBN: 978-0-615-33914-6

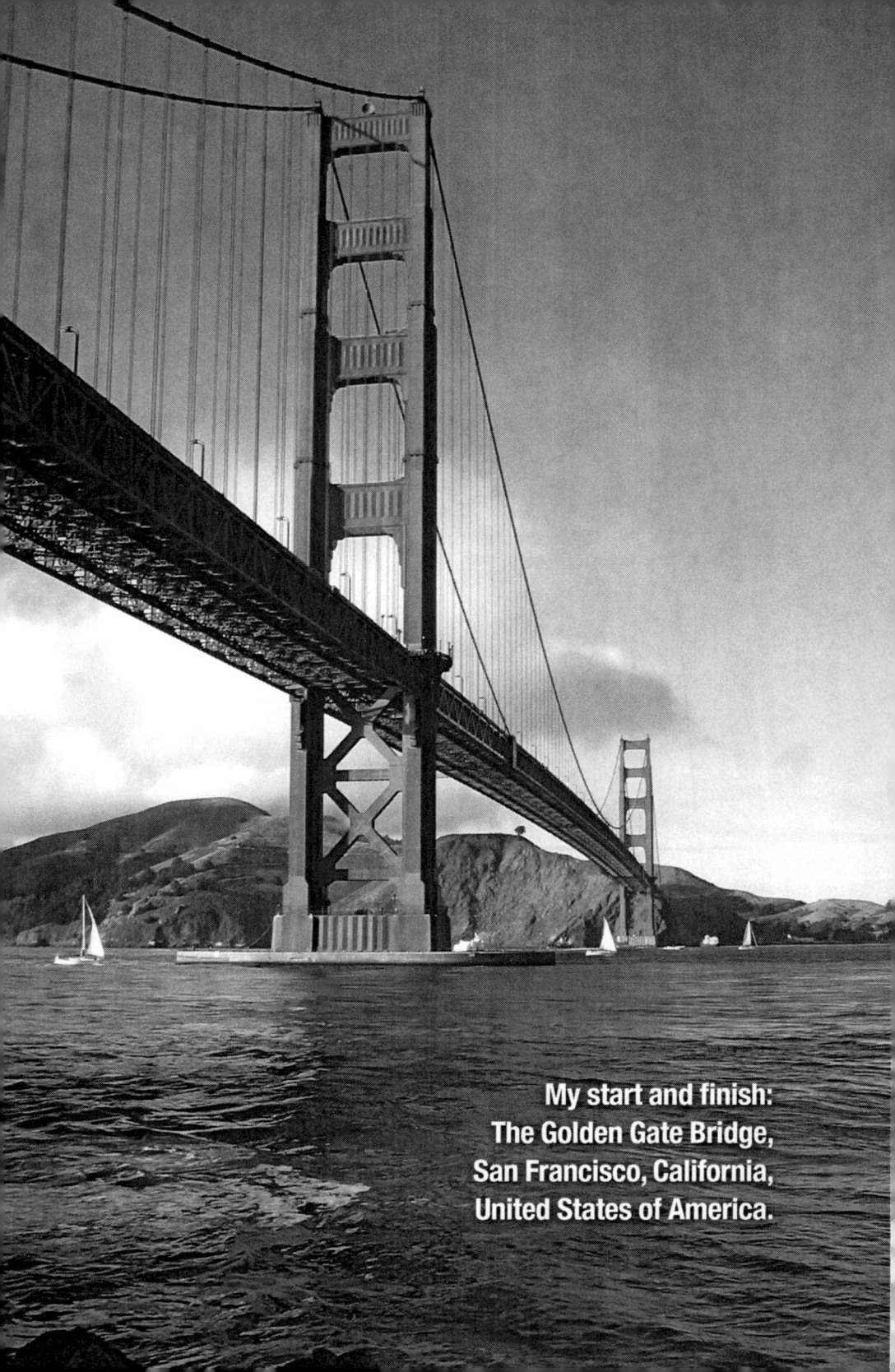

My start and finish:
The Golden Gate Bridge,
San Francisco, California,
United States of America.

Acknowledgements

It truly took me years to absorb the lessons I learned while I traveled, and one of the toughest lessons I learned was the lesson of coming home, not only to my country, but to myself. I feel I owe everyone a debt of gratitude for helping make my journey of self-discovery and my book possible. Specifically, thanks to my family (I am especially grateful to my mom for her unconditional support for this special edition) and Dennis for setting my wheels in motion and the tens of thousands of people that I met along the way who kept them spinning, your kindness and hospitality have been a tribute to humanity. Thanks to my armchair fans, many days I was inspired to keep going for everyone who said they never could. I even feel thankful for those people who fueled my passion by saying that I couldn't do it, and I was a fool for trying. Finally, thanks to all my future readers that will help bring Falling Uphill to life. I hope you find my adventures and misadventures entertaining, inspiring and somewhat enlightening.

May the winds be with you. ~ Scott

Table of contents

The gentle reader will never, never know what a consummate [donkey] he can become until he goes abroad.

~ Mark Twain

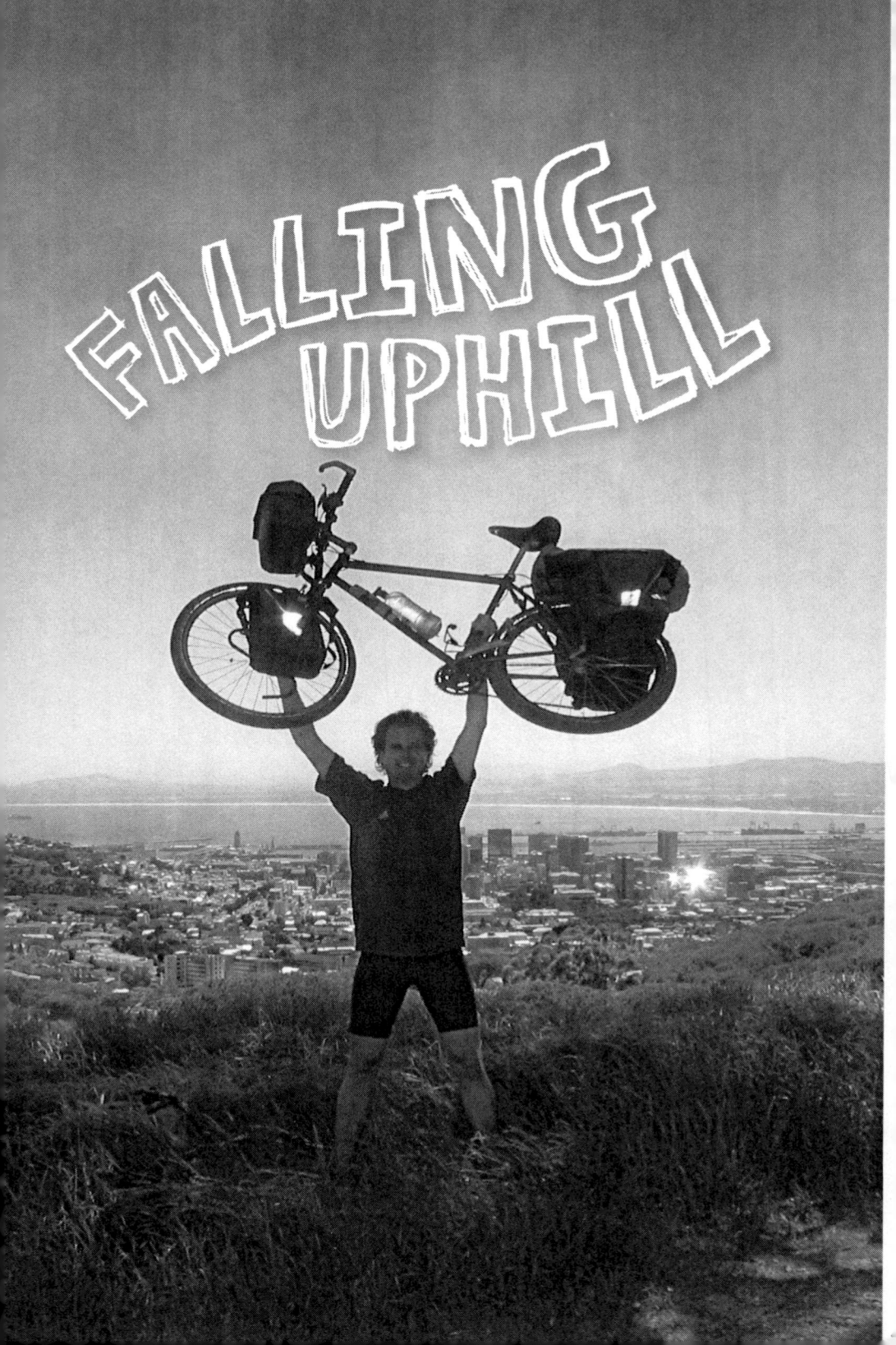

"Learn from yesterday,
live for today,
hope for tomorrow.
The important thing
is not to stop
questioning."

"I have no
particular
talent,
I am only
passionately
curious."

"Curiosity has its own
reason for existing."

"Life is like
riding a bicycle.
To keep your
balance you must
keep moving."

"Your imagination
is your preview
of life's coming
attractions."

~ Albert Einstein

Introduction:

Why would anyone read this book?

Albert Einstein was born at the age of 50 and is often regarded as the smartest person to have ever lived. I can't verify that because I never met Einstein, and I generally like to think of myself as the smartest person to ever live, but I can say that Einstein had some awfully interesting things to say. For example, Einstein, also known as the father of modern physics, once said, regarding his most famous discovery, the Theory of Relativity, "I thought of that while riding my bicycle."

As you may be wondering from the quotes on the opposite page, why did Einstein think questions were more important than answers? About 2400 years ago, the famous philosopher (questioner) Socrates said, "I know you won't believe me, but the highest form of human excellence is to question oneself and others." I think questions—the desire to solve mysteries and discover new curiosities—are what keeps people moving; and answers are what freezes them in place.

During my quest for happiness around the world on a bicycle, one mystery I discovered was that everywhere I went, sometimes dozens of times per day, people asked me the same questions. Most had never read a newspaper or watched television; some had never seen a foreigner, heard of America, or even knew in which country they lived. It was a fascinating mystery. How could all these people (regardless of age, race, gender, culture or any other factor) be asking the same questions in the same order? Then serendipity smiled and I realized that it was a key to human nature. People

A journey of a thousand miles must begin with a single step.

~ Lao Tzu

everywhere are fundamentally the same: we all have fears and doubts; and we all have hopes and dreams. The questions people asked me were evidence that we are all on a similar journey: struggling to survive, learning how to befriend our fears, questing for a purpose and ultimately seeking a creative, joyful, meaningful life.

This book is a collection of frequently asked questions that offer a small peek into my adventure around the world on a bicycle. The questions (chapters) flow in a similar order that the citizens of the world asked me, guiding you, the reader, through the creative process—from the mysterious unknown, into the misty realms of dreams, bursting into reality and one step beyond. However, my main goal isn't to answer questions, as if there is one way to do an adventure or one kind of an adventure. But I do hope it fires your passion, because your emotions are your power source, and if you can fuel your curiosity to find, solve and create mysteries, your passion can propel you along any adventure you can imagine.

For me bicycles are a metaphor for life; for example, if you stop pedaling your bicycle, you'll fall off. A metaphor means that one idea is substituted for another to help people think creatively (outside the box of their understanding). Metaphors are wonderful inventions because life is like a mirror—everything reflects everything else. I just used a simile, which is a variety of metaphor, to explain a metaphor. Are you confused yet? Don't worry confusion is the doorway to a new understanding.

This book is your metaphorical mirror. If I have done my job as an author, the curious reader will not only see a reflection of their dreams (and fears of their dreams), they will have also created a new image of themselves, full of new ideas, new hopes, new discoveries and they will have even taken the first few steps on their journey.

This book has essentially taken my whole life to write. It is the book I wish I had as a young lad.

What is your greatest passion in life?

How do you read this book?

Life isn't linear from birth to death. It is more like a spiral, sometimes spiralling up and sometimes spiralling down, and sometimes life spirals around giving you a new perspective on the past, and the possibilities of the future. That's why this book is an evolution and expansion, a new loop on the spiral, from the previous edition of *Falling Uphill*. Simultaneously, it is simpler and easier to understand; nonetheless, I don't believe in dumbing-down information. This book is intended to stretch your brain. It contains words and concepts that you might enjoy exploring and adding to your toolkit. It is a multi-dimensional book, like life and like my trip; so, I recommend you browse the questions that interest you first. While you read, I encourage you to imagine the impossibilities, and imagine that you are about to embark on your own quest and that you are asking the questions to prepare yourself. And, if you're an astute reader, having your unique vantage point in the universe and experiences, you'll learn things, correlate new information and make new discoveries from this book, that perhaps no one knows but you.

How many pictures did you take?

Not enough. I only have 3918 photographs remaining. I would have taken many more if I had a digital camera. I used film and it cost a lot of money. Unfortunately some photos got lost, stolen, confiscated or destroyed in the extreme heat and cold. Now these records of a few milliseconds of my trip are as valuable as gold to me. **Did you buy any souvenirs?** I didn't collect anything but photographs and the following memories in this book.

The Great Pyramid of Giza is possibly over 12,000 years old.

Question I:

How are you?

This is the most popular question in the world. It is the companion to the most popular word and gesture. Can you guess what those are?
[You'll find the answer hidden on the following pages.]

The above question comes in many variations that we'll explore in the first section, and they easily fall within **the top ten most common questions in the world**. They may be called icebreakers, because they help breakdown the icy wall that humans erect as a self-defense mechanism.[1]

At first glance, no one knows that I'm on an epic journey, and this question serves to satisfy one of our most powerful emotions—curiosity—and to open or close a door to a relationship, primarily business or friendship.

I've spent years bicycling and it has given me a lot of time to meditate and contemplate. After careful consideration and a new evolution of thought, I realized that the question: **Are you my friend?** is implied in every interaction we ever have—strangely, for some reason, probably fear of rejection, people almost never ask this question directly; yet, they are wondering: **Will you be my friend?** Sometimes, carefully and subtly interrogating the other and wondering: **Are you an enemy?**

I've also realized people everywhere want to relate to each other on an emotional level (rather than the impersonal business level), and the frequency of these icebreakers and hidden agendas of friendship has led me to conclude that we—people, human beings, homo sapiens, the bipedal hairless great apes—are primarily social pack animals, driven by feelings—the petrol in our gas tanks—to bond together like molecules in a crystal, which means that everyone you'll meet will join your adventure (and you'll join theirs), if only to say: **Hello. Bon Voyage. Goodbye** or even **Good riddance.**

---

1 *Self-defense mechanism* is a fancy phrase that I could define for you, but if you're going to be a world traveler, an adventurous businessperson or whatever your heart desires, you're going to need to learn to be resourceful; so, your next step in this adventure is to find a dictionary and encyclopedia to cross reference any new information.

What are you doing?

What are you doing? I'm riding my bicycle around the world. **What?** I'm riding my bicycle around the world. **You're doing what?!** *Sigh* I'm riding my bicycle.... **You're kidding me?** Nope. **Is that possible?** ...

Since, I'm more interested in why a person asks a question, rather than what they're asking, this frequent conversation helped me understand a bizarre fact—people literally can't hear an idea that is too foreign to their culturally "normal" experience. And, when they do *hear* the unusual idea of bicycling around the world, they often don't understand it, because it is an "impossible" idea. After all, the world is mostly water. It is said that when Columbus' ships arrived, they were invisible to the Native Americans. Re-discovering this phenomenon made me wonder how many sights and sounds and concepts were literally invisible to me. Perhaps this is why Marcel Proust, the famous French novelist, said: "The real voyage of discovery consists not in seeking new landscapes but in having new eyes."

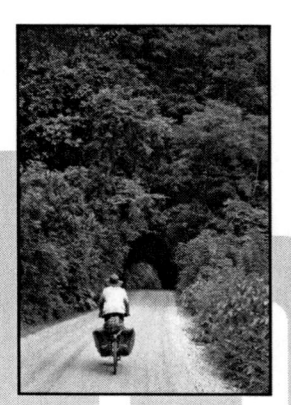

Above: The Western Wall is an important Jewish religious site in the Old City of Jerusalem, containing the "Foundation Stone" of the world. **Right:** A mysterious and dangerous tunnel in Bolivia. **Opposite:** Outback sunrise, Australia.

Where are you going?

One of the paradoxes of life is that no one ever really knows where they're going. Life is always different even if it appears the same; and, if you could know without a doubt where you are going, that means you've already been there, and that's unadventurous and boring.

One of the aspects that eluded my logical life for quite sometime is that people ask the same questions from different points of view and with different emotional intents, making the words almost meaningless or even exactly opposite what's being intended. The above question could be phrased as: **How did you navigate?** [pages 19-20] **Did you get lost?** [page 78] or **Where did you go?** [pages 22-23]. It's also a more specific variation of: **What are you doing?** And essentially an icebreaker: **How are you?** or **Are you a friend?**

The intent behind the question may indicate whether a person is a pessimist or an optimist, and that ironically indicates where the questioner is going with their life, because like a horse with blinders, people head in the direction they are emotionally focused on. For the record, it doesn't really matter where you are going, as long as you feel like you are going somewhere. So, **Where am I going?** The best answer comes from one of my childhood heroes, Speedy Gonzalez: *"¡Ándale! ¡Ándale! ¡Arriba! ¡Arriba!"*

hallo guten tag
hola hai 你好 jambo
salam salut नमस्ते

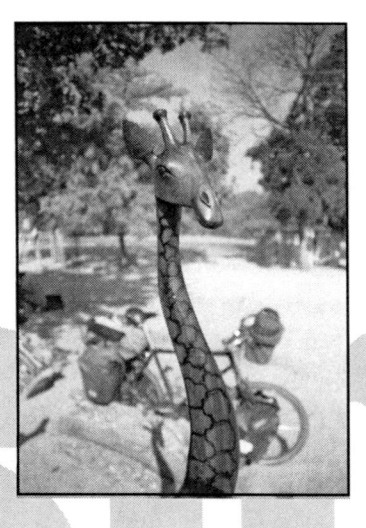

Can I help you?

Some people view everyone as a friend. It is immensely satisfying to help a person in need; furthermore, humans are like bricks in an immense foundation of humanity, and if one brick crumbles the whole foundation's integrity is weakened. I could fill an entire book with stories of how people helped me, fed me, boarded me, comforted and carried me when I couldn't carry myself. [For more about the kindness of strangers please see pages 90-91.]

Besides philanthropists: **Can I help you?** or: **What do you want?** is also the opening remark of a businessman. Ideally life is a symbiotic exchange; however, often the business world is run upon the illusion that there is a winner and a loser, and only the fittest survive. So, it's wise to be aware that often people aren't trying to help you as much as help themselves.

Left: There are more wooden giraffes in Africa than real giraffes. If you have enough money you can buy either kind, but not necessarily legally. **Above:** A mob of jellybean people sculptures for sale.

Does altruism exist?

Can you help me?

Hello, friend. Can you give me some money? This question was so common in some parts of the world that it made my ears ache by the end of the day. (Perhaps, this only seems like one of the world's most common questions, because I am perceived as a rich Westerner.) There are many icebreakers designed to gain rewards by preying upon your guilt and goodwill. Unfortunately, it originates more from a sense of entitlement and desperation than a sense of true need.

Even if you follow the advice of the ancient proverb, "Give a man a fish; feed him for a day. Teach a man to fish; feed him for a lifetime," I discovered one of the ironies of life is that the more you try to help someone, the more you teach them to be helpless and feel like a victim of misfortune [pages 56-57]. One exception is if the person truly needs your help, truly wants your help, and you truly want (have passion) to help them. The trick is finding the balancing point where you both benefit. Though I encountered many hucksters—they wouldn't call it stealing; they'd call it good business—I met many more honest, generous people, and fortunately one kind person or kind thought negates a hundred bad ones.

Above: My friend, Edwin, tries to teach a panhandling Tibetan shepherd that money doesn't grow on trees by exchanging a pen for a lamb. After a difficult barter, it's the shepherd who ends up teaching Edwin a lesson in international business when he wins both the pen and the lamb.

If you could do anything, what would you do?

Legend says that a traveler must answer a riddle to be granted safe passage or be devoured by the sphinx. Is this a metaphor for the perils of a spiritual journey if one does not answer their own riddle?

Question II:

Why did you ride a bicycle around the world?

This is the question with a million answers [as opposed to the million-dollar question page 113]. To find myself or to lose myself? I seemed to create a new answer every day to motivate myself. I'm still exploring why I cycled around the world; in fact, this whole book is an exploration of the best question of them all—**Why?**

My whole life had backfired. In one week, I lost my job, best friend, girlfriend, faith in my self and the world. I remember thinking, "This is *not* how my life was supposed to turn out. I did everything *right*, everything everyone told me to do." I realized that I'd been running the rat race to accumulate all the cultural symbols of success advertised by television, considered cool by friends, inherited misconceptions, cultural baggage... too many things to list for such a short book. Things I didn't necessarily want, but feared I needed in order to be accepted and loved. I had been living a delusional illusion of what I thought society thought I was supposed to be.

I realized that I only have one life, one chance, and I didn't want to be the guy lying on his deathbed full of regrets and what-ifs. I wondered, "If I could do anything, what would I do?" I rolled this thought around inside my head, listing all my dreams and fears, the things I enjoyed and didn't enjoy, and imagined possible and impossible. After hours, when the meaning of my life still eluded me, I resigned myself to a life of mediocrity, and suddenly the "impossible" answer popped into my head with an explosion of tingles: **"Why not ride a bicycle around the world?"** Surprised, I thought, "Yes. Why not just experience life for myself? Why not find the answers? Why not go find happiness and the meaning of life? If there is rhyme or reason to the universe, why would it be a secret?"

After that the idea grew out of control, like a virus with its own mind. I could say my trip took me around the world. Besides, being disillusioned with society and full of angst and stubbornness, I felt I had nothing to lose.

*He who has a **why** to live for can bear with almost any how.*

~ Friedrich Nietzsche

Are you on a spiritual journey?

Of course, silly me, I made a big deal about going on a spiritual journey without realizing I was already on a spiritual journey.

The reason I consider this a spiritual journey—a bikeabout—rather than a simple adventure is because I want to live the best life I can, and to me that meant traveling the world to answer the fundamental questions of philosophy: **What's the meaning of life? Is there a God? What's the nature of the universe? Where did it all come from? Who am I? Do I have a soul? Do I have free will? How do I know what I know? What is good and evil? What's my moral and ethical duty? What happens when I die?** And, most importantly from a practical standpoint: **How can I find peace, love and happiness?**

According to the Hindu tradition, I've been following the path of knowledge, one of many paths to enlightenment. For example, in one week: I climbed mountains and temple stairs; rang bells; was anointed with ash and colored powders; wore sacred coconut hats; was sprinkled in holy water; prayed for world peace; ate dirty sacraments of puffed rice; bounced up and down; bent myself into yogic shapes; set sail ships of marigolds and candles; cleansed my sins by swimming the Ganges; donated money to God's representatives; chanted and hummed mantras; and, generally drowned myself in books and thought myself sick. No wonder Hindus consider the path of knowledge the least effective.

I don't know what I'm looking for,
but I'll know it when I see it.

My friends often say that I think too much and ask too many questions, making myself unhappy. However, I think the plethora of questions people have asked me proves that everyone, to some degree, is a philosopher. Because our world constantly presents us with a multitude of challenges and experiences, the mind instinctually sorts through this mass of information, questioning and creating patterns, some sense of life, so that we may survive if not thrive. Our philosophy is our interpretation of the world, our meaning of life, our survival strategy, and the more accurate our philosophy, the more fulfilling our lives.

Even if my ambitions were more mundane and this were a simple adventure in my mind's eye, it would still be a spiritual journey because we are all essentially magicians in a magic kingdom. Everything we do is an act of magic. Unfortunately some peoples' magical acts are very mundane due to fear, ignorance, lack of skill or a failure of imagination, like the school yard bully.

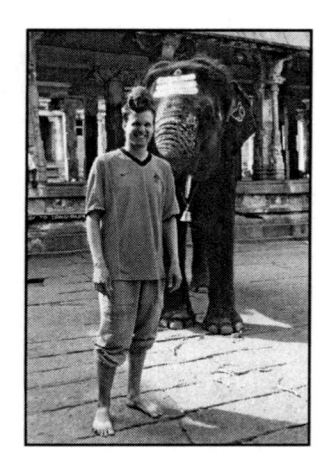

Opposite: A Hindu holy man, called a sadhu, on his personal quest. Since I wore the same saffron colored clothes, I was often called the bicycling sadhu. **Right:** Elephant blessing. **Above:** Pilgrims bathing in the holy waters of India's most holy river, the Ganges.

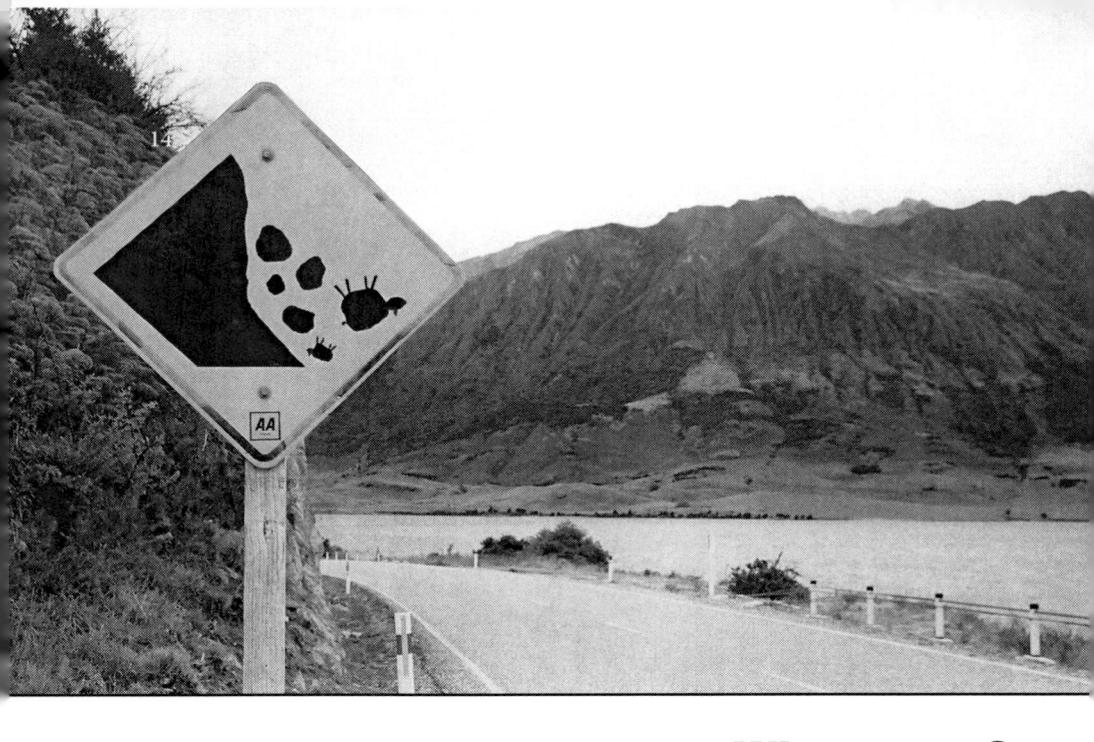

Who cares?

Call me egotistical, but I thought what I was doing was the most spectacular thing I could imagine, and I admit that I was surprised to discover that no one really cared. They might care for a few moments, or a few days, or off and on through the years, but sooner or later, they'll get on with their life, and you'll have to get on with yours.

At the risk of sounding cynical, I must tell you about one of my greatest discoveries, because I feel we all must learn the truths of reality, even if they appear to be negative, so that we may swim with the river of life. So, I encourage you to bear with this abstract discussion.

A mystery puzzled me for a long time. When I told friends and strangers what I was doing, I was often ridiculed. People called me a liar and a fool. I became reluctant to mention my trip, because I was tired of explaining (defending) myself to naysayers, and couldn't endure the backlash [page 47]. It was very hard for me to accept, but there was no other explanation—some people wanted me to fail. In fact, I have evidence that some were actually sabotaging me. They would rather ensure I failed to further their own agendas, even if their agenda was simply to preserve their self-image and ego-importance. Call me naïve or pessimistic, or perhaps I needed the arrogance knocked out of me, but

it was the single most discouraging thing I've ever encountered.

The silver lining is that I discovered one of the secrets of life—people are driven by their emotions. People do and say a lot of things. They may look beautiful and own a lot of fancy things. They might be smart and funny and have all the other enviable qualities that make you wish you were them or with them. But that's all meaningless compared to the intent behind their actions—what motivates them? For example, someone says they want a relationship, but are they motivated because they love you? Or because they need your love? There are infinite motivations, but they can be classified as joy, fear or confusion.

That may sound obvious, but it wasn't obvious to me. I thought I wanted to conquer the world on a bicycle, but what I really wanted was to discover myself so I could belong to the world. This all led to **my most important discovery to understanding human nature** which explains the pitfall of being human. Psychologists call it cognitive dissonance, and Æsop (a Greek slave) described it in his fable "The Fox and the Grapes" 2600 years ago, a concept colloquially known as *sour grapes.* Everyone has multiple motivations, conflicting thoughts, crossed purposes, wanting versus can't having, needs versus desires, fears versus imaginations, dreams versus reality. The list is endless. And these multiple motivations essentially cancel each other out. It leaves most people feeling confused and stuck, and many will go through all kinds of weird rationalizations, justifications, denials, and even erase their own memories by throwing away any experience that doesn't fit their box—all to ease their troubled minds. This explains why people would often pooh-pooh my trip. It also explains my own doubts and confusion, which before I knew better, often spiraled into depression.

Despite all I've said, this is a 100% normal state of affairs. Anyone who is exploring the frontier of their life is essentially dancing on the edge of the unknown. Life is an art; and it would be an extraordinary artist who learned the skill to align their feelings, thoughts and actions to paint timeless masterpieces. [Learn the magical spell to turn your dream into reality. Page 136.]

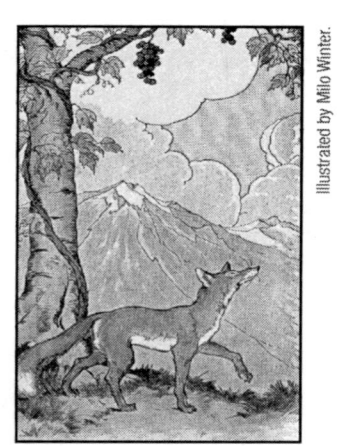

Illustrated by Milo Winter.

Opposite: New Zealand road sign graffiti:
"Beware falling sheep."
Right: The Fox and the Grapes.

What are you trying to prove?

Everything in life is a mirror. So, not only is this questioner questioning whether I am driven to prove myself better than others, perhaps they are blaming me of being just like themselves (more *sour grapes*); and, if not, this question still mirrors the importance of this issue for the questioner from the other infinite questions that could have been asked. Either way it is still a good question.

Do I have a big ego, meaning a little ego? Yes. I was trying to prove that I could be big when I felt little. I wasn't trying to demean others to appear important, but I did judge myself, and let my happiness be based upon other people's opinions.

Did bicycling around the world cure my ego-importance? No. You can achieve all the awards society has to offer and still not win any long-lasting fulfillment. The true path to happiness, so it is said, and as far as I can tell, is the inner journey. So, yes, my trip did begin the cure to my ego-importance, because it taught me to look inside.

Above: New Zealand's Franz Josef Glacier.
Right: The world cyclist is the last one to finish climbing the glacier and limp back.
Opposite: A group of hikers appear like ants upon the glacier.

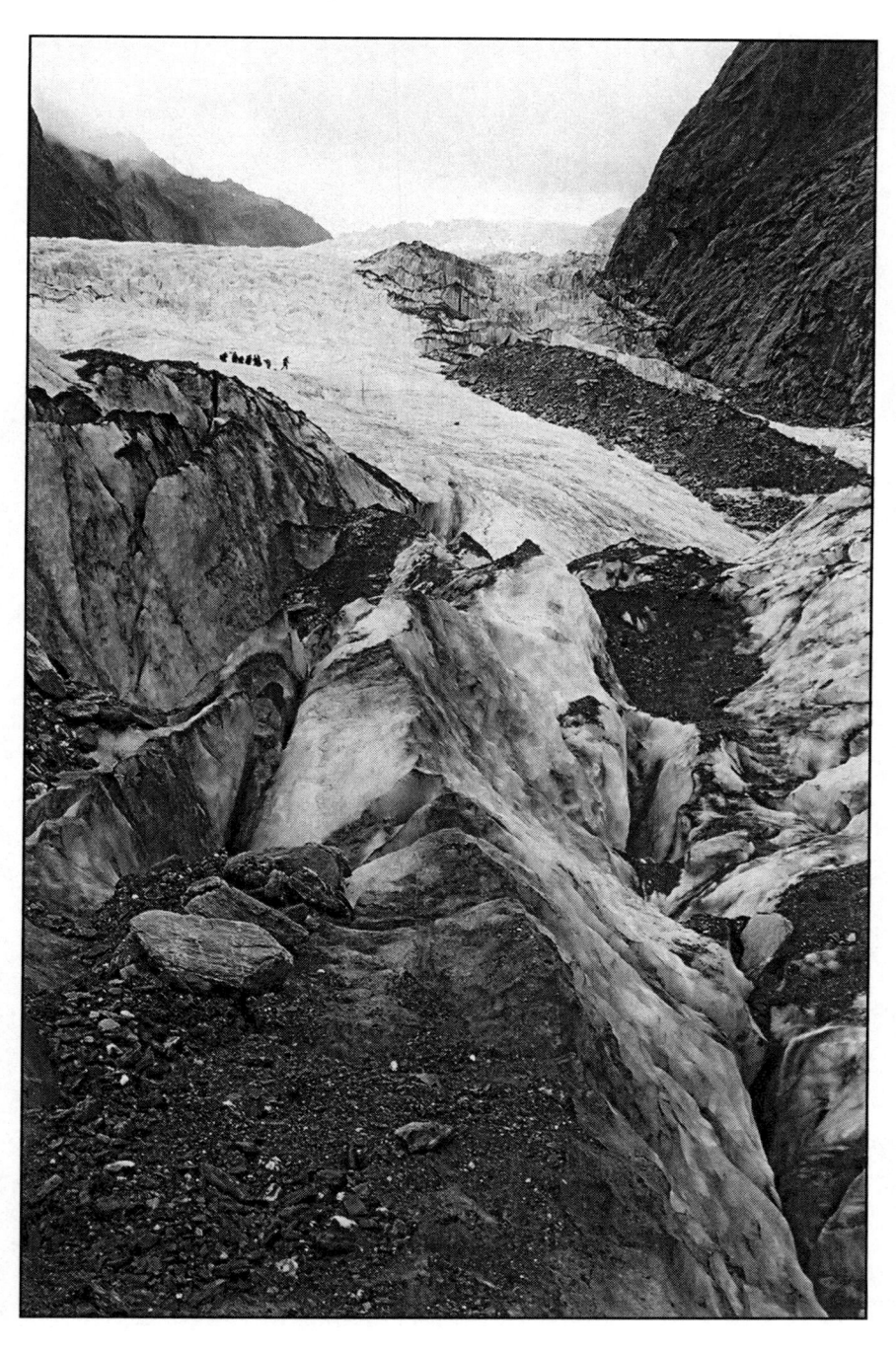

18

29,220
Estimated times
I asked for directions.

How do you ride a bicycle around the world?

Every adventure can be reduced to a couple clichés: **one day at a time** and **enjoy the moment**. If you have a bicycle, basic camping gear, a passport, a little money, a lot of passion and little patience, all you have to do is start pedaling—you'll figure the rest out very fast. The first question is: **How does one define bicycling around the world?** You wouldn't get very far trying to bicycle around the equator since it is mostly water. However, you could try lugging your bicycle to the North or South Pole, once there you could finish the trip in minutes. Or, you could join the astronauts as they pedal a stationary bicycle while their ship orbits the earth every 90 minutes. Maybe a more practical definition would involve bicycling every continent or every country. As it turns out, these aren't practical options. The definition between continent, continental plate and island are not clearly defined; while zigzagging between the invisible and often disputed political borders seems silly. Therefore, I defined bicycling around the world as cycling the equivalent of the Earth's circumference (40,075 kilometers as measured around the equator; the Earth's a little fatter around the middle like most people) without treading the same ground twice (otherwise I could have stayed home and bicycled circles around the local pub) while visiting as many cultures and world wonders as practical. My friend, Dennis, re-discovered the bizarre fact that one can travel around the world following a **perpetual summer** by crisscrossing the equator (the seasons are in opposition). For example, only at the speed of a bicycle can one travel from the tip of Anchorage, Alaska to the tail of Tierra del Fuego, Argentina; a car would be too fast and walking too slow. As you can see from the map [pages 22-23] **my route** was a compromise

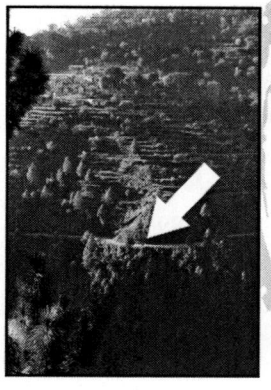

between all these considerations, additionally: avoiding prevailing headwinds, rainy seasons, cold winters (some winters are pleasantly warm like India), plague, war, famine, pestilence (I was rather unsuccessful at the last four) and, of course, Death, who only peeked in my direction a couple times. All the while, I constantly pushed forward, never counting the same kilometer twice.

Opposite: A muddy "short" cut to the Bolivian border.
Left: Cycling up the Himalaya foothills.

How did you plan your trip?

A wise approach would be to research and correlate the dozens of significant variables of expedition planning, while understanding that there is no perfect solution and that as soon as you begin everything will change, yet knowing you have prepared for the worst and are expecting the best. Or, if you're like me, you'll try to do everything perfectly, become overwhelmed, sick with stress, procrastinate until the last moment, and begin the journey feeling frazzled and unprepared. Fortunately, I discovered the best plans were often fortune, whims, the advice of locals, the toss of a coin and following the weather hither thither. [Also see: Did you get lost? Page 78.]

As for the incidental daunting details—**vaccinations, passports, visas, planes, trains, automobiles, boats and donkey carts**—you'll figure all that stuff out as you go. It is impossible to plan for a four-year journey in advance because the world is a constantly changing place. You'll learn to adapt if you're motivated, but I do recommend that you read your **guidebook** before bush camping in a potential Croatian landmine field like I did!

Did you do any training? It's not a race; you can train slowly when you begin your journey. If you listen, your body will tell you when to rest and what to eat. If this counts as training, I did have: laser eye surgery and arthroscopic knee surgery; plus, physical therapy, chiropractics, and some weight training to strengthen my broken knee, but the best cure—luckily or fatefully—was riding a bike. But, mostly, I practiced a lot of denial as a form of mental preparation.

How do you ride a bicycle across the ocean?

I put extra air in my tires.

This is one of the most popular questions, and one of my favorites.

Where did you go?

Milwaukee

Washington, DC (Start)

San Francisco

——————— **Warm-up**

——————— **Route**

················· **Plane, train, boat, auto**

Ⓐ **Antipodes**

I've traveled to 57 countries: USA. Canada. Mexico. Guatemala. El Salvador. Honduras. Nicaragua. Costa Rica. Ecuador. Peru. Bolivia. Uruguay. Argentina. England. Wales. Ireland. Northern Ireland. Scotland. Belgium. Holland. Germany. Czech Republic. Austria. Slovenia. Italy. Croatia. Bosnia and Herzegovina. Greece. Turkey. Egypt. Israel. Palestine. India. Nepal. Tibet. China. Thailand. Myanmar. Malaysia. Laos. Vietnam. Australia. New Zealand. Kenya. Tanzania. Zanzibar. Malawi. Zambia. Zimbabwe. Botswana. Lesotho. South Africa. On separate trips I visited: France. Spain. San Marino. Monaco. Indonesia. And I attended university in England for a semester. Note: Some countries listed are given the benefit of the doubt, such as Tibet. Also, I don't count airports in transit, such as Chile and The United Arab Emirates, though I did get a great look at these countries.

Cape Town

Where do you want to go?

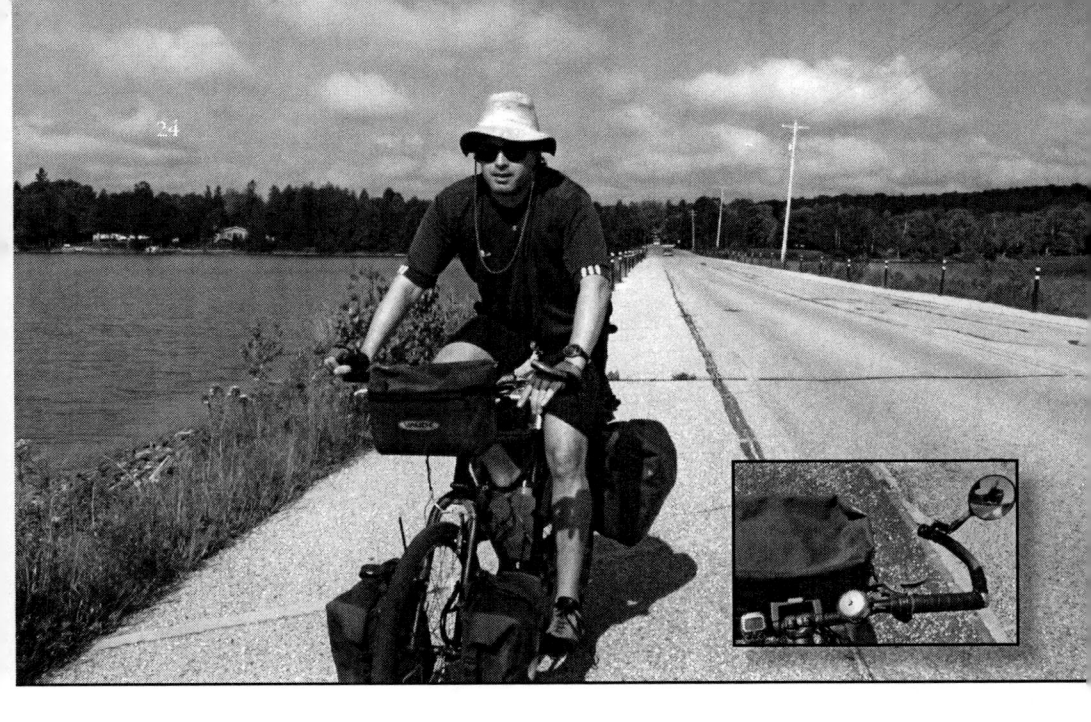

How many miles did you ride?

I cycled 41,444 Kilometers[1] (25,752 miles), not including mass transit such as donkeys or camels. If I include my warm up ride across the United States (ocean to ocean and border to border) that's another 10,609 kilometers. In my lifetime, I've cycled about 122,000 kilometers—the equivalent of 3 laps around the earth's equator or 11 laps around the moon or 0.08% of the average distance to the sun. **How many countries?** 50 by bicycle. **How many continents?** Six. **How many miles do you ride in one day?** My goal was to average 80 kilometers per day. **How fast did you go?** My top speed was 79 kilometers per hour for a few seconds, and my average speed was about 10 kilometer per hour. My best day was only 187 kilometers in about 6 hours in Australia with a blistering tailwind on pancake-flat roads. There were many "worst" days when I couldn't cycle due to illness, fatigue or weather, and some days where I averaged less than 1 KPH. (The average person walks 5 KPH.) **Did you hitchhike?** Yes. I decided it was another kind of adventure, but I didn't count those miles. **What was your highest and lowest elevation?** I ranged from -2 meters to 5400 meters. **How long did it take to bicycle around the world?** It took me 1461 days. I could have gone faster, but I liked to watch the scenery. **When did you start and end your journey?** I began pedaling September 6, 2001 (five days before the terrorist attack in New York City) and returned to my starting point exactly 4 years later.... On second thought, the journey never ends.

---

1   If you're going to be a world traveler you need to learn the metric system. See page 144.

40,007.86 Earth's polar circumference in kilometers

How much did it cost?

Are you rich? By American standards, I have lived many years below the poverty line (as I am now writing this book), but for a world citizen I am rich beyond most peoples' imaginations. Like everything, cost is relative. Some calculate cost by money, and some calculate cost in man-hours (the amount of hours it takes a person to earn the money to purchase a commodity). The richest person in the world could exchange a few seconds of effort for my bicycle, whereas it cost me 6 days of labor, and it would take my Indian friends working in a Mumbai hotel over eight years to purchase my bicycle (minus all the gear, and assuming they had no other expenses except rice and beans). My trip averaged about 20 United States Dollars per day, including airfare, equipment and enough money to visit the local attractions. It was possible to tour for as little as 3 USD per day, if I camped in the bush, cooked my food, filtered my drinking water, and washed my laundry by hand. (As an extreme adventurer, you have to do these things.) **How did you afford it?** For about 4 years, my adventure was simply earning the money. I worked all the time and never purchased anything that I didn't need to survive, e.g. no music, movies, or restaurants. I rode a bicycle to work and brought a bag lunch everyday. And, my friends helped me invest my money. **Did you work along the way?** I stopped to help people plant food, build roads, fix cars, etc., but never for money. Occasionally, I traded my handiwork like plumbing, cleaning, or drawing pictures for a bed. **Did you ride for a charity?** No, I philosophized that if I could change myself, I would change the world. **Did you have sponsors?** No, I didn't want to be responsible to any corporations or media. An interesting question that no one asked is: **What was the cost of my trip to the environment?**

What's the cost of not living your dream?

What kind of bicycle did you ride?

I rode a basic steel mountain bike (steel can be welded by any auto mechanic or farmer, and the simple design avoids mechanical problems) with downhill racing rims with extra spokes, bulletproof tires and a leather saddle—an all-terrain workhorse.

I'm in love with my bicycle. I've been constantly tinkering, rebuilding and repairing my bike ever since it was born, fine tuning everything down to the millimeter. I've molded the bike to my body and vice versa: By brute determination and sheer human power, I've worn down steel, cracked aluminum, snapped titanium, and rubbed my handlebars smooth as glass with my hands, leaving a trail of human and metal dust around the world.

I love the feel of my bike buzzing down the road, and listening to it whistle in the wind. I can't explain it. It's called cathexis (love of an inanimate object), but I'm convinced my bike has a life of its own. It's enormously popular. Everywhere I go people want me to bring my bike. They *ooh* and *aah* and run their hands down the frames, caressing the nicks and scratches. It's been photographed thousands of times, requested to be on television and featured in newspapers and magazines (without me). It was even honored on the race podium without winning a race. And, she likes to be called Yerba.

What is the metaphorical
bicycle of your journey?

Did you have any major breakdowns? 1 warped wheel, numerous broken spokes, 9 welds (broken braze-ons), 2 snapped chains, 1 mangled derailleur (I learned to shift gears with my foot), 2 broken seats, 1 snapped rear cog set (rode through India minus my easiest gears), two broken racks, 2 broken odometers (makes finding food and water dangerous), and many minor breakdowns, like bolts falling out due to the vibration and attrition.

How many flat tires (punctures) did you get? Over 100. How many times have people asked me this question? 10,000. **How many tires did you wear out?** About 20. In South America, I had to use the generic local brands, and those tires exploded like gunshots about once a week from the weight of my bicycle. I also wore out six rims, several hubs, five drive trains, three times as many chains, three sets of pedals, a dozen brake pads, and more. In fact, everything on my bike has been replaced but the frame, handlebars and surprisingly the aluminum rear rack, which is almost worn in half. The frame is more or less okay, except for some potential corrosion, but if that gets replaced, will it still be the same bike? My body has undergone similar replacements. I estimate that I have regenerated my eyes 2700 times.

How much did your bike weigh? The bicycle alone weighs 16 kilograms. My gear weighed an additional 18-kilos. Plus, I carried about 2-5 kilos of food and 5-10 kilos of water. Including me, I was pushing 124 kilos (273 pounds). **Did you bring any luxuries?** If my bike got too heavy, I risked injuring my knees or not being able to cycle far enough to find food or water. I carried over 200 items [next page]. My only luxuries were a shortwave radio, camera, book, journal, coffee, cookies, and, occasionally, I included deodorant if I was trying to impress the locals. My biggest luxuries were hot showers and Internet cafés. **Was it hard to ride with the extra weight?** Yes and no. It's surprising how the human body can adapt. It took more energy to pedal, but it had better balance and traction.

Do you still have the same bike? Yes. It brought tears to my eyes when I recently snapped the front axel and cracked the fork. (Luckily I still have my front teeth.) I plan to hang Yerba on the wall like a piece of artwork.

Opposite: Yerba perched on the edge of a cliff. This is the same location as the photo on page 127, but 5 days prior.

Right: Emergency repair. I used a door hinge as a bracket on my cracked rack.

passport
28
with extra pages * Visas * **Drivers license** * Medical em

Blood type + Allergies + Yellow Fever inoculation + Health history + Physician contact +

Photocopy of all documents placed in separate pannier • Money: **Debit Card** (Masterca

Bribe money (in small wallet) * Emergency stash of dollars hidden in clever places *

Malaria medication * Diarrhea medication * medicine * aspirin * Ibuprofen (kept ir

* Insect repellent • Cooking supplies: **Stove** and repair kit * Fuel Bo

16 Oz. nylon **coffee** cup • Bicycle gear: Bar ends * 2 Bottle cages * 2 Water bot

* Racks * **panniers** * handlebar bag with map case *

* Combination chain lock * rear view mirror * Heavy duty tires * Warning fla

Chain whip • Lock ring remover • Adjustable wrench • Needle nose pliers • Swiss Army

What did you bring with you?

Supply lists are forever incomplete and outdated. That's because one rule of the universe is: **The only constant is change.** Thus, by definition it's impossible to prepare for the unexpected, while paradoxically you are preparing to expect the unexpected; therefore, there is no perfect travel kit. So, have faith that if you are missing the resources, you'll find your resourcefulness. And remember the rule of thumb—leave half of everything at home and you'll still be carrying too much.

Gloves * Cold weather gloves * Hemet with a visor * Knee warmers • Street Clothes * Sca

Shoes * Wool socks * Foldable full-brim hat • Toiletries: **ear plugs** *

balm * Deodorant * Mirror * Razor/blades * **Wash cloth** * Towel * Nail clippers * tweeze

Bunji cords * Ground cloth • Electronics • Camera * Film * **Video camer**

* Journal * Ball-point pens * **sunglasses** * Eyeglass strap * Compass + W

and **guidebooks** * 3 days of FOOD & 1 day of WATER: * Water purification tablets (ic

salt * *Chili powder* * Rice * Bananas * Vegetables * Lemons * Vitami

info: • Health insurance card and info • World Health Organization Vaccination Card +

cy and Power of Attorney contact * Banking and money info * Consulate/embassy info *

dit Card (Visa) * Local currency * Stable foreign currency (American dollars or Euros) *

of document holder * Money belt * Address book * First aid kit: aloe vera *

of Nalgene bottles) * Bandages * Eye drops * Anti-bacterial ointment * Sunburn medication

nless steel pots and lid * Matches and lighter * Stainless steel spoon *

as many soda bottles as needed) * Pedal clips * Bicycle shoes

saddle with cushy springs * Bicycle computer: Altimeter / Odometer / Thermometer

* Rims (downhill, double-rimmed with at least 36 spokes) * Tools & repair kits:

Allen Wrenches • Chain cracker • Spoke wrench • Nylon spoons * Wire * knife *

ician's tape • Grease * Oil • Presta adapter • Plastic zip ties • Rubber

ds • Plastic grocery bags • Ziploc bags * spare parts * Super

• Brake and shift cables • Two spare chains and extra links • Brake pads • Nylon rope

* 4 inner tubes * 6 Spare spokes • 1-2 Spare tires • Spare nuts, bolts and

ers • Regular patch kit & rubber cement. • Maintenance kit and spare parts (air

ss repair kit, air pump, water filter, stove) • Bicycle Clothes * 3 pair bicycle

s * 1 pair bicycle underwear * Bicycle socks * Booties * 3 bicycle jerseys. * Cold/rainy

er jersey * Cold/rainy weather pants * Yellow wind/sun breaker. * Rain jacket * Riding

* Shorts * Shirts * Blue Jeans * Underwear * Sandals or flip flops * Hiking

shampoo * Needle and thread * Floss * Toothpaste * Toothbrush * Comb * Lip

mping supplies * Silk sleeping bag insert * Air matress *

atch * Alarm clock * Spanish dictionary • Misc * Backpack * Binoculars

ap (to show locals what I was doing) + Regional topographical and political road map

eramic water filter * peanut butter * Do you believe I pedaled all this

inerals * And me :) stuff around the world on a bicycle?

Where did you find water?

Did you ever run out of food or water? A human being can go 3 days without water in average conditions, but in a desert you can die in a matter of hours. Before I learned how to read a map to identify sources of water [page 78] and judge my physical limits, I ran out of water in the baking furnace of Baja California, Mexico in the Sonoran Desert, where it's surprising the cacti didn't turn to dust. I remember resting in a small patch of shade, careful not to touch the burning rocks. I was so dehydrated my eyelids were sticking to my eyeballs, and the veins in my temple pounded painfully. One of the dangers of heat stroke and dehydration is dying of a heart attack because your blood becomes too thick to pump. I was so thirsty, I scanned the road for bottles of urine the truck drivers might have tossed out the window. I watched ranks of saguaro cacti, like Martians with arms raised in salute, march up the flanks of the candy-striped volcanoes. **Am I hallucinating?** After 15 minutes in the shade, my thermometer still registered over halfway to boiling; yet, I was shivering cold and delirious, telltale symptoms of heat stroke. I didn't have long to live. I needed to make a decision: **Wait for rescue or find help?** Cycling can actually be cooler than sitting in the stagnant hot air; so, despite common sense urging me to wait for help, I entered the baking sun. Vultures circled above. "I'm not dead yet," I taunted. Fortunately, I found the next town sooner than expected. I purchase a gallon of water, prepared to trade my bicycle for a glass of water if necessary. The first few gulps of water felt like swallowing lumps of ice, then my body spasmed and my pores opened like a 100,000 floodgates. Heaven is a cool glass of water in a hot desert.

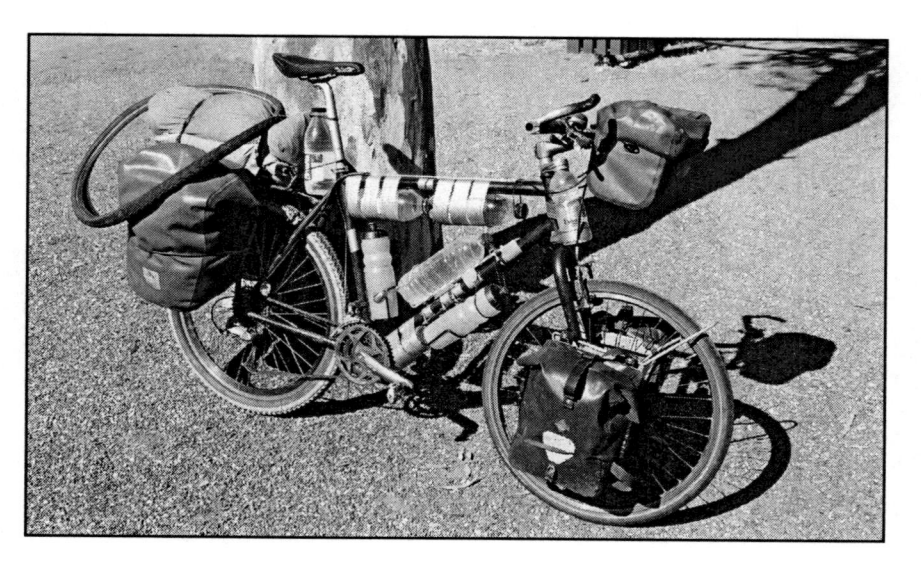

What did you eat?

Besides curiosity and pragmatism, the intent behind this common question implies that majority of the world's inhabitants haven't met their basic needs, or haven't overcome their fear of survival despite having more exotic food choices in the average supermarket than all of the ancient kings and queens combined.

Basically, I ate three times whatever the locals ate, except I cooked nearly the same thing every night. It made lugging my stove and pots up the mountains seem worthwhile. My all-purpose recipe, kind of a rice casserole, was to throw the local foods in a pot, boil the bacteria to death, and depending on how rotten the ingredients were, I added more or less chili powder and turmeric to kill the smell and taste—I learned that cooking tip in India.

Opposite: The beautiful cacti forests of Baja, Mexico. **Right:** Finding and filtering an average of 12 liters of water per day could take hours. Eventually I discovered that I could siphon water through my filter, which took even longer but at least I could conserve my energy for cycling. **Top:** Preparing for an Outback adventure. Carrying 26 liters (57 pounds) of water through the Australian Outback. I needed special permission from the Aborigine Land Council for this adventure. Basically, I had to convince them I wouldn't make a nuisance of myself by dying.

What is the grossest thing you ever ate?

Warning: this story is grosser than gross, *C'est la vie* (such is life), say the French, but the faint-hearted may wish to skip ahead.

My cycling companion Dennis and I had just arrived in Guatemala. We cycled 12% of the way around the world as measured by a wobbly bicycle from San Francisco, California. Life is short and Planet Earth is small when I think of it this way; however, most days seem a week long, as we output the same amount of energy as climbing the Empire State Building 5-10 times (depending on terrain and weather) while carrying a 45 kilogram backpack, which is even heavier, psychologically anyway, in the empirical system—99 pounds.

To celebrate our third country (fourth including Canada from a previous trip), Dennis and I visit a restaurant, like a cement bunker with one wall open to the war zone on the street: backfires of vehicles, screams of vendors, catcalls and whispers. We're in a border town that preys on rich Mexicans and naïve tourists, and caters to the vices of less scrupulous people. The furniture in the bar is decrepit plastic and wood. The walls are urine yellow and the cracks are papered with posters and calendars that advertise vices with other vices.

We meet Felipe and Umberto, and they're quick to treat us to a cold drink. The

sugar swims unimpeded through my depleted blood stream and steeps my brain in giddiness. While enjoying our cold beverages (ice cubes have become a luxury item) an 18-inch rat runs sideways up the wall and upside down across the ceiling along the rafters. I gasp, but Umberto laughs and pooh-poohs, "That's a little rat."

Note: this conversation takes place in Spanish with informal sign language to help translation. I've learned Spanish by reading a book in my tent at night as I massage my aching legs to sleep. I figured Spanish would be easy compared to physics, but perhaps it's the wrong side of my brain, because I'm a dullard when it comes to anything requiring interpreting sounds. I speak Spanish like playing horseshoes, thinking close enough is good enough. For example, I generally ignore the masculine or feminine articles and nouns, which occasionally results in referring to myself as a pretty girl, or telling a woman she looks fat when I'm speaking about myself. I also generally ignore the verb forms (there are over 100 different forms of the same verb, whereas English regular verbs have only one basic part, and you just glue on a different ending, e.g. talk, talks, talked, talking...) I use only the root verb (or whatever verb form I happen to know), so apparently I've been telling people that I love them in a local idiom. A translation of my trip to the market probably sounds something like: "Why you not love me sweet apple. Thank you very much.")

Umberto continues, "In Guatemala City, they eat rats. You must be careful." Dennis and I express amazement. "Si, si. It is true. People will say it is the meat of the cow, but—" a mischievous smile cuts off his words momentarily— "it's not the

meat of the cow...." Umberto pauses and relishes our amazement as we hang on his words. "The truth—it is the meat of the dog."

"Perro?" I say, unsure if I understand. (Dennis and I would notice far fewer dogs in Guatemala than Mexico.) At that moment, a cute shih tzu, the family dog, walks through the restaurant and I point and say, "Meat of the cow?"

Everyone laughs. "Si. That is dinner. Are you hungry?" Felipe asks.

"No, no. I'm not hungry."

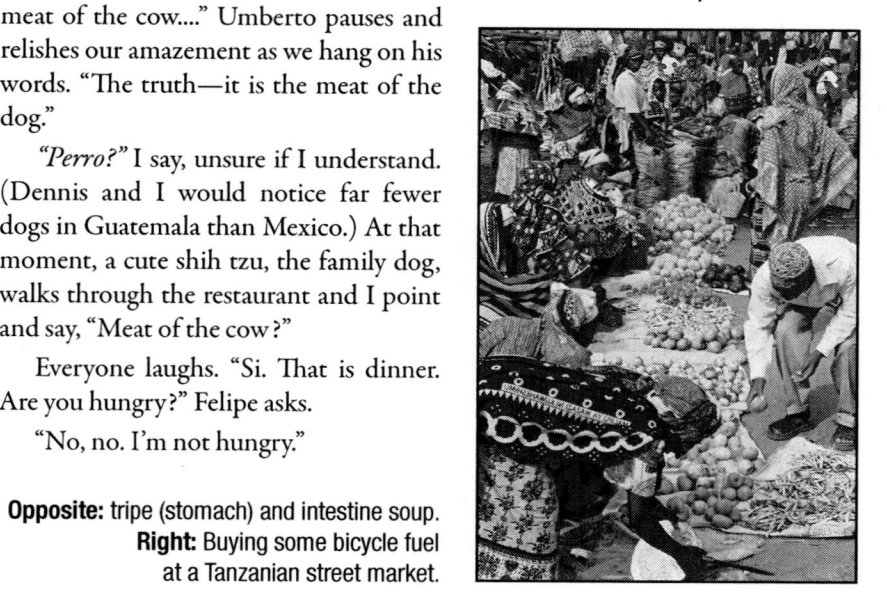

Opposite: tripe (stomach) and intestine soup.
Right: Buying some bicycle fuel at a Tanzanian street market.

"We had dog for lunch," Dennis jokes.

"Burrito con carne de perro," I say practicing my Spanish.

Umberto continues to advise us of all the potential hazards and lists the disguised food: old horses, rabbits, cats, snakes, iguanas, lizards....

I'm reminded of strolling through a Mexican plaza sampling all the local foods with Dennis—our favorite thing to do at the end of eight hours of pedaling. We ordered some *meat tacos.* The word for *meat* often implies *beef.* Our tacos seemed slimy, undercooked and tasteless compared to normal. Only after we walked to the front of the booth and saw the sign and the severed head lying on the bloody block with its skull cracked open, did we realize that we had eaten cow brain tacos. "You are what you eat," Dennis said in his pragmatic way.

"Well, Umberto," I ask the obvious question, "how do you know the difference between a dog and a cow?"

Umberto should have been an actor instead of a truck driver; after a dramatic pause and swoop of the hand, he touches his tongue, "Taste," he says with a grin.

Everyone in the restaurant laughs. Of course, by then it is too late.

Bicycling for eight hours per day not only requires a lot of raw energy, but staying nourished to rebuild my body is extra challenging. I've eaten some strange things to satisfy my cravings for vitamins and minerals, like: rancid Yak butter tea, kangaroo steaks, impala legs, barbecued cactus, crocodile burgers [picture page 119], pig's knees, chicken foot soup, goat ribcages, cow bone broth, chicken liver shish kebab, tongue omelets, octopus tentacles, eggs of various and unknown creatures.... The list is long. Unfortunately, I don't know the names of most of the creatures I consumed because I couldn't read or speak the languages. I simply pointed to items on the menu or in the cart; and, for example, was rewarded with something looking like squid jerky that had been run over by a truck and dried in the sun. I also enjoyed testing my survival skills. I've harvested wild apples, berries, pomegranates, figs, et cetera. The caveman inside of me is proud to have claimed some fish. I extended my foraging to mussels that I gathered during low tide (those made my insides turn a little juicy). And I've spent considerable effort hunting Australian rabbits with a slingshot, but the closest I ever came to killing a rabbit was running one over with my bike. So far, I've declined hospitable offers to eat guinea pigs, hamsters, mice on a stick, chicken fetuses, and a freshly excised cobra heart beating a glass of rice wine red. While I'm on the subject, I'd prefer not to eat pigs. They are like vacuum cleaners of human filth in the villages (and dogs to a lesser degree), which means the meat possibly contains many diseases and parasites, and since a human's metabolism is very similar to a pig, these parasites would love to dine on us too. (I believe

the taboo against eating pigs, shellfish and dogs originated in ancient times, during less sanitary conditions without refrigeration, when eating undercooked meat resulted in a lot of illness and death.) Nor do I enjoy eating: ants, mosquitoes, flies, maggots and worms. I prefer to keep the bacteria (plus their toxic by-products) and parasites to a minimum, even if they have had the life cooked out of them. As a general rule, I don't like to eat anything that moves, but once again I'm sounding like a finicky eater. And, finally, for the record, I've accidentally and quite regularly ingested: smoke, fumes, oil, diesel, gasoline, ash, exhaust soot, mud, dust, dirt, sand and pretty much anything else organic or inorganic that flies down the road.

Thanks to Umberto, I have turned down various suspicious dishes, such as some "beef" tacos made out of a white meat, before the chef could hide it under some "sauce of the tomato". However, considering I still didn't know what a dog tastes like, I must have eaten a lot of dogs without knowing any better.

Before I go any further I should mention that I'm an animal lover extraordinaire—besides being tasty—I mean I fully respect an animal's right to life, liberty and the pursuit of happiness. It breaks my heart to even think of some things I've seen, much less write about them. However, we do live in a world where everything is food to something else—even you and me—and we all need to eat.

In vegetarian India, there was a wonderful variety of wildlife running around, including flocks of butterball peacocks. In contrast, from the seat of a bicycle, it was easy to deduce the Vietnamese, like Guatemalans, seemed to eat anything that moves, which sounds somewhat disparaging, though I think it has a lot to do with a culture of gourmet delicacies combined with over-population and diminishing resources. From an objective point of view, what's worse about eating a dog than anything else? Contemplating that question too long might turn you into a vegetarian. For that matter, it's best not to think about a plant's right to life either.

During a pit stop in Vietnam to refuel my bicycle—meaning me—I used my keen instincts to find lunch by honing in on the smell of roasting meat. Luckily, the women refused to serve me communicating, by pointing to their pet

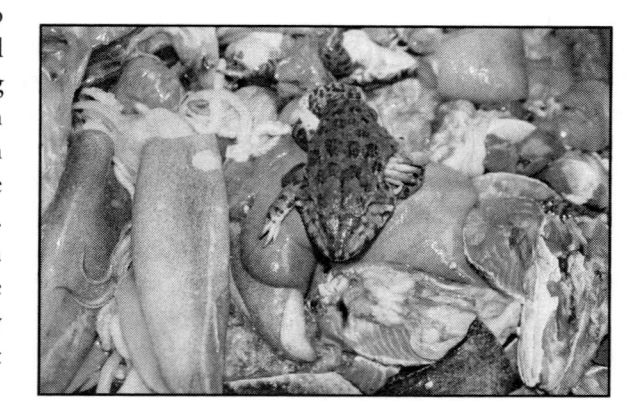

dog, what was on the menu. In Vietnam, a male-bonding ritual involves eating *thit cho* (roast dog meat) during the end of the lunar month. Dining on dog—giving a new meaning to *puppy chow*—is supposed to bring good luck during the beginning of the month and raise the libido.

Ordering food in Vietnam is very difficult. Once, without the help of a chalk menu to point at, I tried to order cơm or phở (rice or noodles). The waitress was bewildered as I kept repeating, "cơm phở," using every tonal variation I could imagine, trying to get the singsong inflection right. "Aha!" she seemed to say and ran down the road. It is common for restaurateurs to buy ingredients only when they need them. She returned a few moments later—looking exceptionally proud—with a box of laundry soap.

During another visit to a Vietnamese roadside restaurant, the hostess wasn't inclined to be informative or helpful with my laundry. When I was served my dish, despite having taken precautions, I was suspicious. It was a white meat similar to pork but sweeter and tenderer. Afterwards, outside the restaurant when I saw the sign, *"Thit Cho,"* I realized I had just eaten barbecued dog, and probably a side dish of stray dog noodle soup. Unfortunately, I didn't receive any good luck. In fact, fourteen kilometers later, I snapped my chain and ripped my front derailleur in half, after which I had to switch gears with my foot all the way to Australia.

I wonder how dogs lost their dignified status as man's best friend? Dogs, one of the first domesticated animals, were originally wolves, cajoled out of the wilds for a few scraps of leftovers in exchange for keeping guard outside the cave, a symbiotic arrangement that would last tens of thousands of years. However, the average Third World dog is a mongrel. (For the record, the more politically correct term is Underdeveloped World, according to the Human Development Index, which I find even more insulting; villages are often much more civilized than cities.) All the adaptations for beauty, running or hunting have been mixed into nothing; what remains is the lowest common denominator dog able to survive in the corner of humanity's eye. It is an average-sized dog with motley, short, brown hair, a slender body, rat-like snout, pointy teeth and ears, and a stiff tail. As cute pups, they're coddled, but as adults they're teased, beaten and stoned, probably because locals don't want their mangy fur or rabid teeth anywhere near them. Third World dogs, aching to be loved once again, rather than return to the wilds, must fend for themselves on the dregs of humanity. This is the average Laotian stray dog that I personally witnessed being harvested and sold to the Vietnamese—and I have to admit, they don't taste bad, a lot like sweet chicken, a little tough and wormy, but better than the average, unhappy, industrially-grown chicken pumped full of hor-

mones and antibiotics. Unfortunately, the roadside chefs often fail to execute their dishes without a smoggy taste and sprinkling of sand and peppering of flies.

The Third World mongrel is quite a contrast to the pampered pets of the West like California where cats are fed vegan diets and dogs have personal dieticians, masseurs and psychologists. An acquaintance of mine teaches "doga" (dog yoga) and another does crystal energy healing for pets. I think Californian dogs would make wonderful delicacies. How about a gourmet Chicago-style wiener dog? Or Saint Bernard chops marinated in whiskey? Or spicy Chihuahua kebabs?

I'm being facetious to make a point that I wish the human beings of the world were treated with as much respect as a Californian dog. I would never eat one. It's too much like a friend. In fact, I don't think I could ever eat anything that I knew on a personal basis. The thought of eating my pet parakeet horrifies me. In fact I'm afraid to name my vegetables.

On the other hand, I wouldn't feel one bit bad about eating a hillbilly dog. Those dogs are bred to kill bicyclists. I remember riding through the Appalachian Mountains. When one dog saw me coming, he howled to his neighbor dog, and so on, until the whole valley was a howling dog gauntlet. Most of the time they went for my front wheel, instinctively attacking my most vulnerable spot, and sometimes they've herded me into the opposite lane where I was nearly run over by a hillbilly truck. If it weren't for my squirt gun full of flea spray, I would have surely been eaten by a pack of hillbilly dogs.

I wonder, "Do I taste like chicken?"

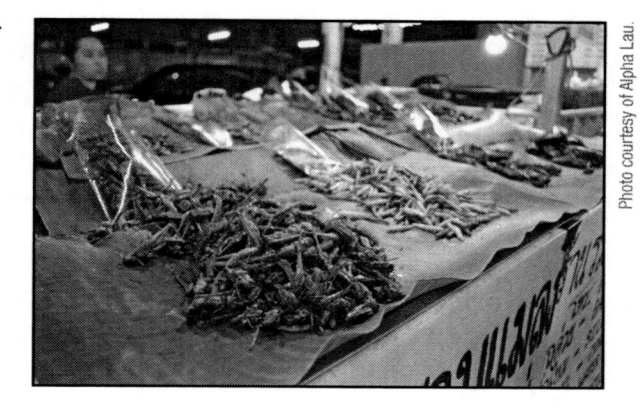

Photo courtesy of Alpha Lau.

Fried crickets in the Chiang Mai Night Bazaar served on a banana leaf in Thailand along with some other maggots and six-legged tasty tidbits. I never was brave enough to try a fried cockroach or waterbug, but I can say I prefer my grasshoppers dipped in chocolate. **Previous:** Frog, squid, fish, chicken, liver and other unidentified meats from a Thai street-food vendor.

Where did you sleep?

I carried all my camping supplies with me (tent, sleeping bag, air mattress, flashlight, et cetera pages 28-29) so that I could camp in some of the most beautiful places in the world like the World's Highest Monastery near Mt. Everest Base Camp; and many kind strangers hosted me in their yard, often treating me to a home-cooked meal [pages 88-89].

Of course, sometimes I couldn't find a nice place to sleep, and was forced to hide in a garbage dump, or in the woods near a herd of goats that a local lion had been preying on (I prayed the lion preferred goats to bicyclists). The safest places to camp were cemeteries, because everyone is afraid of waking the dead; however, if I couldn't find a safe place, I would tie a rope around my bicycle to my wrist. And if people bothered me, which was rare, I often acted like a crazy old bear to scare them away. Sometimes it got lonely, or wild pigs surrounded me, or it got so cold my water bottles froze; but, nonetheless, I loved my tent. It was my home away from home.

bush camp couch surf

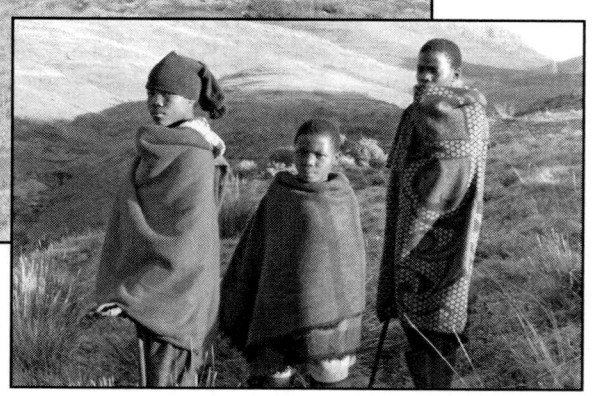

Most artificial urban ecosystems: campground graveyard jail cell hospital fire station police station park bench hostel motel airport. And most earthly ecosystems. See page 103.

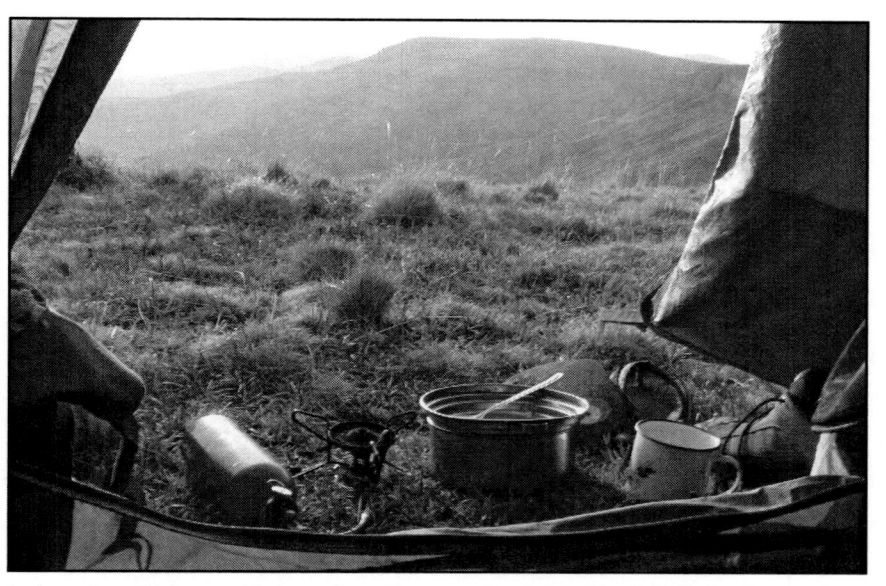

A view of my kitchen and balcony from the campsite pictured top left. Notice the small village barely visible in the valley near the river. The three shepherd boys from this village pictured above came to visit me.

Where did you go to the toilet?

The same place a bear does—anywhere he darn well pleases.

Every traveler has their grosser than gross bathroom story that they wear like a badge of honor; it's an initiation rite we all have to pass. Unfortunately I have more than one story, which fortunately must make me more of a worldly traveler. **My most embarrassing moment** was in Mexico. When the emergency bells began ringing in my lower intestine, I zoomed down a mountain until I found the perfect spot, screeched to a halt, propped my bike up against a shrine, prayed for the best, ran through the woods, and into an impromptu garbage dump. I desperately kicked my clothes off, unaware that the road had switched back, and suddenly a truckload of Mexican sugarcane workers came around the corner and started hooting and hollering, "Look. Look. An American with no clothes!"

Where did you take a bath?

I got used to being dirtier than I ever imagined could be comfortable; in fact, I proved that mud is a good sunscreen. I took a cold sponge bath every evening, and once a week, I would rent a hotel just to take a hot shower, shave and hand wash my laundry in a waterproof pannier.

Some of the world's most dangerous toilets. **Opposite:** An outhouse leaning precariously over the edge of a cliff. **Bottom:** A Turkish toilet (also known as a squat toilet). This bathroom in India was one of dirtiest and most dangerous. The tile was falling off the wall and clogging the drain. The doorway was so small I had to stoop and be extremely cautious of slipping on the slimy, moldy, fecal-coated floor and gouging out my eyeballs on the rusty nails above the door. However, I could entertain myself by watching a line of ants marching to the drippy faucet for a drink, and the monkeys hanging on the window bars outside. **Left:** A latrine pretending to be a third story balcony. In the

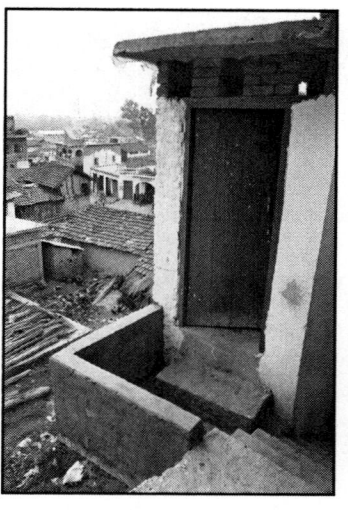

middle of the night with no lights, I slipped in the urine in my slippery flip-flops and nearly fell off. Luckily when I grabbed the door, the molding cracked but didn't snap. **Right:** Doing weekly maintenance and laundry in a hotel room.

What about the cars and roads?

As a bicyclist the road conditions are your biggest concern. It can make the difference between the time of your life and risking your life. It's a big topic that doesn't have much general interest to non-cyclists, but I did find the roads to be much better than expected. (In fact, except for returning home, every aspect of my trip was better than expected.) The few times that I had long stretches of gravel, it was a relief because it meant fewer cars and less pollution, therefore more wildlife and scenery. And, the one rule of the road that overrules everything else is: **might is right** or the **bigger the better**. If you obey the hidden rules of the road (or society) and find your proper place as a bicycle in the hierarchy (somewhere beneath a rickshaw, equal to a motor scooter and above a cow, except for India), you'll find most countries to be very bicycle friendly. And once you understand the rules, you can rewrite them.

Pictured above an Indian traffic jam. Cows are considered a sacred animal and always have the right of way. Sometimes they sleep in the middle of the road, while waiting for someone to drop a banana peel.

Where do you fit in the hierarchy of your world?

What did you do in bad weather?

I hunkered in my tent or tried to find shelter, but there is no avoiding weather—I got cold and wet. Despite following the pleasant weather and the wind, I saw my fair share of blizzards and floods. When I was in the Czech Republic it rained so much the manatees simply swam away and the zookeepers let the gorilla out of the cage so it wouldn't drown. I think I glimpsed him somewhere near the Austrian border.

Top: Record floods in Argentina submerge a park. **Bottom:** German church spire peaking over picturesque sunflowers. Churches always made a perfect refuge in bad weather and late nights. I would camp behind the church, sometimes in the cemetery, and be gone before anyone arose, leaving no trace.

How did you communicate?

People, like animals, have a sixth sense, so with a smile, an open mind and open heart, you can communicate mountains of information. And, fortunately or unfortunately, depending whether you think cultural homogenization is beneficial, English became the *lingua franca* (common language) of the world, due, in my opinion, primarily to the English Empire, American movies, television and the Internet.

How many languages did you learn?

Being multi-lingual isn't my forte. I learned a little conversational Spanish by reading a book and making a lot of mistakes. I also learned the basics words in every country, and a few hundred words of my favorite languages [next page]. And, I became fairly good at conveying meaning through basic sign language, for example: Rest head on hands in prayer position, then gesture in each direction and look inquisitive. ("Can you show me a place to sleep?") **Did you hire a translator?** Since I was usually surrounded by curious kids, there was often someone eager to help translate (kids speak more English than the older generations) and escort me to the hotel, market or restaurant.

What was your favorite language?

I loved rhyming Swahili. *Habari safari?* (How is your journey?) And the singsong of Thai was delightful. The phrase below, which is also visually beautiful, is written phonetically in English as: *Mai mai mai mai mai.* It's pronounced with five different tonal inflections as if a mother is scolding her child in English, and it means, "Green wood doesn't burn, does it?"

ไม้ ใหม่ ไม่ ไหม้ ไหม

The world's favorite words

I discovered that learning some basic words could literally open a lot of doors in any country. I found it interesting that the most commonly used words and phrases are the same in every country: *hello, goodbye, very, good, bad, okay, thank you, please,* [numbers], *hotel, restaurant, taxi, stop, go, wow. I don't understand. Excuse me. How are you? Can you help me? How much? Where? What?* And my favorite—*no problemo* [Spanish], *it's cool* [Californian], *no worries mate* [English English and Australian], *hakuna matata* [Swahili], *mâi pen rai* [Thai].

And if that all fails—smile.

Did you have any communication devices?

No. I wanted to get away from modern civilization and follow my primal instincts. Besides, a mobile phone wouldn't get a signal in most places I traveled. I would have also needed to carry solar panels to charge my phone, computer or navigation device. A great way to communicate with locals is to take a photograph with your digital camera and show them their image. Many people have never seen such a magical device; and some don't even recognize their own picture.

Opposite: Communing with a newfound friend. **Right:** My friend Debbie lost in a crowd in India during a common event: a group of people wanting their picture taken, some for the first time.

Karlu Karlu.
(Devils Marbles)
Australia

Question IV:

Who are you?

Does anyone know who they are? Isn't that why we travel? To find out who we are? To re-create ourselves? To grow in ways unimaginable and previously believed to be impossible?

After getting the basics answered, strangers start to wonder: **Who the heck is this guy?** or sometimes: **What makes him so special?** It seems that forevermore I will be known as The Man Who Rode A Bicycle Around The World. I'm not sure that's how I would have labeled myself, or if any label really describes who I am or who I think I would like to be, but it does have a nice ring, "And, now introducing The Man...." The problem with labels is that they create a lofty unrealistic image, which often backfires, because like the tale of Rumplestiltskin, your name—your self-identity—gives people a certain power over you, and it's human nature to throw stones and pop bubbles. For example, once I had a girlfriend who said, "For a guy who rode a bicycle around the world, you're not very worldly," which was painfully true. I have a lot left to discover, and though I think it is normal, I still fear being forever naïve.

Once again this question asks the hidden question behind all the questions people ask: **Are you my friend?** But, despite what I've just said, I don't think people are as interested in friendship as they are interested in my quest. So, the

other hidden questions people are asking themselves are: **Who am I?** Or: **If I could do anything, what would I do?** In other words, by exploring me, people are actually exploring themselves (which is good because I find myself quite boring).

You must be the change
you wish to see in the world.

~ Mohandas Gandhi

Where you alone?

We aren't just flesh and blood creatures; we are an entire web of relationships, so, one of the definitive qualities of who you are is who your friends are.

I theorize this question is common while traveling because being ostracized from your community is one of the greatest punishments possible, thus many villagers asked me: **Why would you ever leave your family?** So naturally people are suspicious of lone rangers.

Through a serendipitous string of coincidences, I've had many dozens of friends, if not thousands, join my adventure as if to guide, protect, teach and carry me when I couldn't carry myself. I would never have finished if not for their generous companionship. Nonetheless I was alone for months on and off for years; but: **Was I truly alone?** Someone built my bicycle. Someone built the roads. Someone drove past and waved hello. Someone grew the food I ate in their backyard. Another shipped the food to the market. And another cooked the food. And another shared the meal with me. And another....

Above: Standing in a Bolivian saltpan. **Opposite page:** This is the first photograph of the Earth from the surface of another planet—Mars. The Mars Exploration Rover Spirit made this photo one hour before sunrise on the 63rd martian day of its mission.

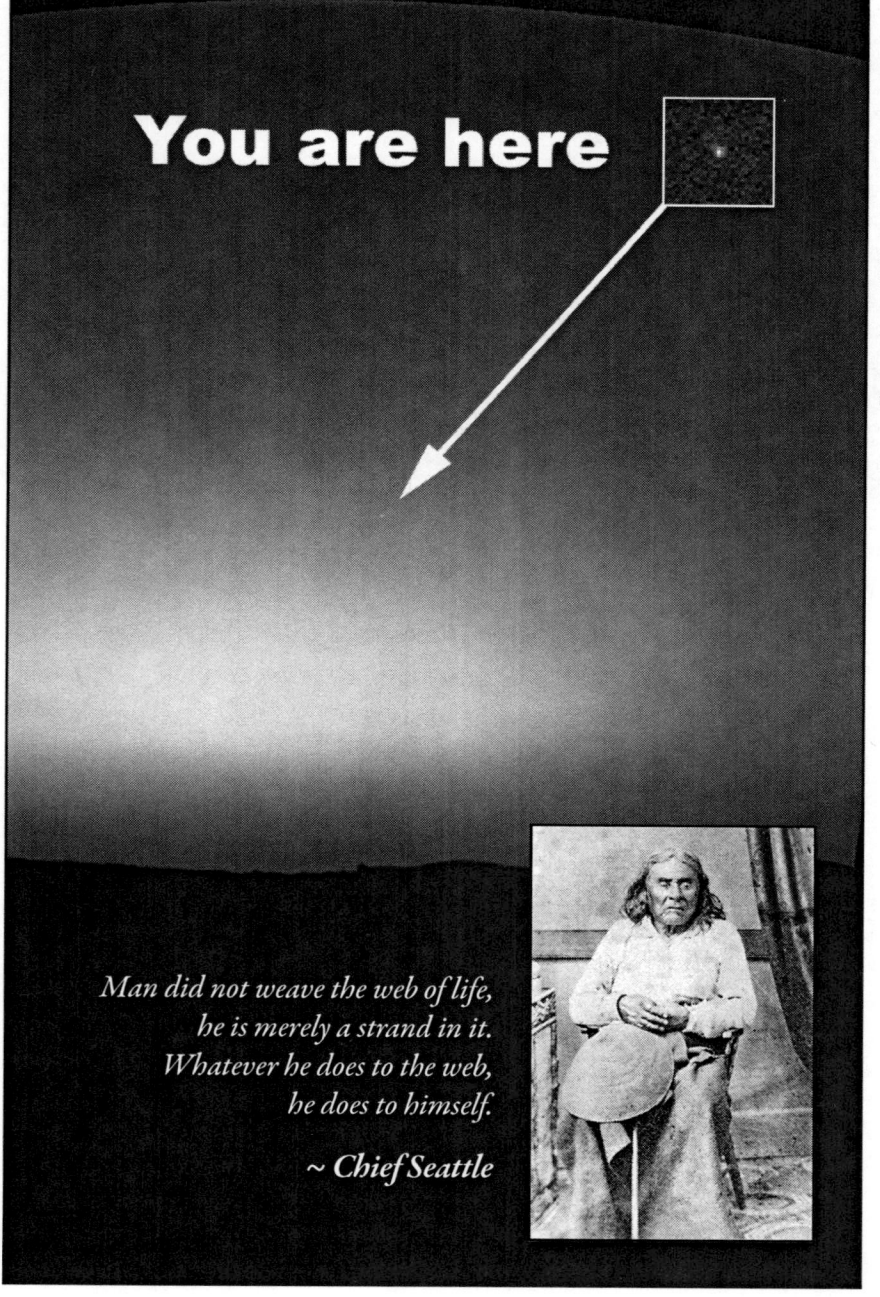

What is your tribe?

In Africa, I used to say, "I'm from America. We don't have tribes." Then I realized that Americans have a much more complicated tribal system, like an invisible, nameless caste society revolving around power and popularity—the Cool Factor.

Given enough time, people ask many surreptitious questions to determine who I am: name, age, nationality, race, status, income, politics, religion, family, career.... Often they are wondering: **Do I want to include you or exclude you from my tribe?** Again they are essentially asking: **Are you a friend or enemy?**

Human beings are pack animals much like wolves or lions. We band together and cooperate in the hunt so that we can eat rather than be eaten. The us-versus-them mentality is instinctual, which is one of the reasons why fear is our most powerful emotion, and that our first action is often a fight or flight reaction. It takes skill to be proactive in life, meaning to view every situation with creative, loving, joyful eyes.

Above: A tiny village under a baobab tree. **Opposite:** "Power to the people" is a common theme all over the world. El Che, the world famous counterculture symbol, advertised on the back of a road sign in Argentina. **Inset:** Chinese truck in East Africa advertising America's War on Terrorism in the Middle East.

How often are your actions reactive or instinctual?

Where are you from?

I was born in Milwaukee, Wisconsin, USA, Planet Earth, Sol System, Milky Way Galaxy, the Known Universe, and have lived in various places, for extended periods, including: England, Washington DC, San Francisco, Mexico, Guatemala, Australia, and overnight in over 1000 cities in 57 countries. I have been called and like to think of myself as a citizen of the world.

Often another litmus test for friendship is being from the same place and having similar views, such as political beliefs. So, this question is often a subtle way of asking: **Are you an *us* or a *them*?** or: **Are you for or against the war?** I like to think of myself as apolitical, meaning the Switzerland of people. I like to remain neutral, keep my mind and options open. I vote for the issue not the person or the label; and I vote with my dollar, opinion and companionship. But since America was at war during my travels, I often had to defend my country; and, people would often try to anger me to help prove their point, but I was always proud to remind myself, that many citizens of different nations called me: "The Bicycling Ambassador." So, I felt like I was on a diplomatic mission to teach people that not all Americans were the same, that our country like every country, has its pros and cons, and most importantly—that the people in America—and every country whether they realize it or not—are the government.

If you were born in Iran, Iraq or Afghanistan who would you be?

Are you married?

I had about 8 informal marriage proposals while I traveled.

Most cultures have very strong family values. So, when they see a single man, they can't believe it. Often they assume that if I don't have a wife, no woman must want me; and, therefore, especially being an adult Westerner riding a bicycle, they conclude something must be wrong with me. Contrarily, families are often thinking they might like to marry me, because of the stereotypes of being a rich American living in a land of luxury—Yes!—I did mean families wanting to marry me. In many cultures, marriage is more a matter of survival of the tribe, or family honor, so romantic love isn't much of a factor, and it is quite often decided by the parents. By the way, no, I'm not married; and as far as I understand, though translation can be problematic, I'm still not married or engaged.

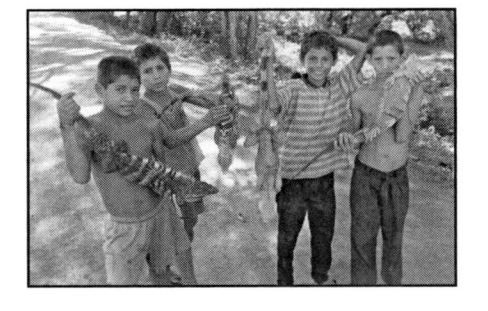

Above: Mountain bicycle yoga in the Himalayas. **Right:** Guatemalan boys sell iguanas for food. In many cultures, if you don't have children you are considered a poor person, because they will work to support the family, especially when the parents age or become sick.

Do you have children?

Because I'm not married, the next questions are: **Why not? Do you have a girlfriend? Do you want a girlfriend? Is something wrong with you?** Which illustrates how if you are doing something outside the cultural norm you are therefore abnormal. And, **Do you have children?** This last popular question illustrates that there must be a lot of single parents in the world.

Even though I was 31, I felt too immature to make a lifelong commitment, especially if that person happened to be a child depending on me to guide them through life's journey. I needed to go on my own vision quest or walkabout, similar to some Native Americans or Australian aborigine. I wonder why the modern "civilized" world has forgotten most rites of passage, like a coming-of-age journey to explore and find your path through life, leaving many people to wander aimlessly trying to reinvent the Wheel of Life? [Page 112.]

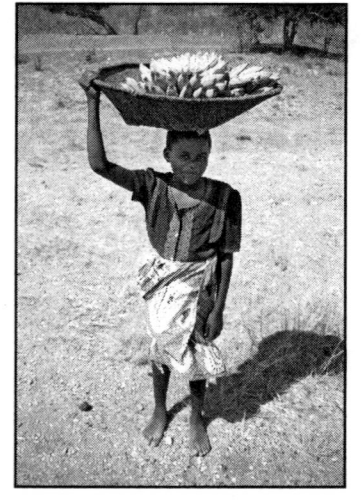

Top: Curious Tanzanian village boys flock to watch a foreigner eat African food. **Right:** Ragged Zimbabwe girl selling bananas to support her family.

What is your religion?

I could say that I rode around the world to answer this single question—to find faith. Faith in god. Faith in the universe. And mostly faith in myself. I thought if I could find God I could find happiness.

This question is one of the first things people want to know, but don't want to ask, because it can be a friend breaker. For many people, religion is a matter of life or death, and it's an important qualification in whether they want to include or exclude you from their community. It was my goal to meet the world on equal terms. So even if I didn't believe or understand someone's religion, I suspended my disbelief, because I knew one thing for certain, the people believed they were right and they believed because they knew something I didn't know.

I considered it my job to investigate all the cultures and religions of the world. I've read hundreds of books on religion and philosophy. Talked to priests, rabbis, imams, gurus, buddhas and more. They all contributed something useful to who I am, therefore I believe religions are like road maps. As every good traveler learns, you need more than one map to find your way. And often the best map is simply the advice and friendly encouragement of a stranger. [For religious metaphor see pages 78-79.]

If you were raised with a different religion how would you view the world?

*The essence of all religions is one.
Only their approaches are different.*

~ Mohandas Gandhi

Do you believe in God?

I don't like to answer this question, mostly because my answer keeps evolving as I grow wiser, and describing God must be similar to counting to infinity, besides I don't want to imply my answer is better than anyone else's. One of the general rules I've created for myself, called a personal ethic, is to never pretend to know something I don't, or criticize someone for a belief that gives them hope. I'm also paranoid of being ostracized if my words are misconstrued.

I've always known there was more happening behind the curtain of reality than could be explained in logical scientific terms. Call it: destiny, fate, coincidence, serendipity, miracles, magic [page 117], synchronicity, synergy, or good fortune. I could sense it. (Especially, after bicycling to the point where I was so exhausted my mind stopped defending itself.) So—yes—I did re-discover God, Allah, Brahman, Tao, Qi, oneness, the Great Spirit or whatever you want to call him, her, it or not it. In other words, I had a heartfelt experience of the miraculous energy flow of life; but I still can't put a label on my religion.

Opposite: That's a photograph by the Hubble Space Telescope, but those aren't stars. This is a photo of nearly 10,000 galaxies in a swath of sky billions of light-years wide. It is the deepest visible-light image of the cosmos, called the Hubble Ultra Deep Field. The Qu'ran, the holy book of Islam, states: "There is nothing comparable to [Allah]." Imagine that!—this mind-boggling, magnificent photo doesn't even compare to God.

How did you get so lucky?

I'm not sure I can answer this question. **Am I lucky?** Or: **Was it just hard work?** Or, as some people suggest: **Maybe I am unlucky and squandered my life force riding around the world?** Contrarily, if you're asking this question: **Why do you consider yourself unlucky?** After people asked me variations of this question a few hundred times, I realized feeling lucky illustrates how people feel helpless, and wonder how to create meaning to their lives in a seemingly random universe. To illustrate this question, here is a clip from one of my favorite stories:

I passed 86 Greek roadside memorials today—86 carloads of people killed. Most shrines were clustered around the curves. If the cars couldn't negotiate a turn, I wonder how they've managed to miss me.... On second thought, they haven't all missed me. Many people outright state, "You should be dead," or ask, "Do you have a death wish?" And judging by more innocuous questions, most people reckon we should've perished long ago: succumbing to microscopic monsters, thirsting or starving in the wilderness, stoned by fanatics, beaten by overzealous bandits, or, most likely, crushed underneath a truck—there are a million ways to die. A million to one odds, yet I survive. I wonder—and many people ask—**what motivates me to keep cycling when I've been inches from death so many times?** I feel I have nothing to lose. I'm more frightened of dying from boredom back home.

I'm reminded of cycling a Mexican mountain, back when I complained all the way up a hill and daydreamed all the way down, missing the whole point of touring. It was a steep, rutted dirt road full of rubble the size of oranges and grapefruit. I was pedaling hard enough to risk ripping the tendons from my bones to maintain my momentum. (If I had stopped, I wouldn't have been able to start again, and I would've had to walk my bike.) I hit a stone and nearly fell, but I zigged right, steering into the fall, to recover my balance, yet couldn't regain control before hitting another stone and zagged left. (One of the tricks to riding a bike is letting the bike decide where it wants to go.) At one point, I nearly zigged off the cliff, but a square rock caught and held my front wheel. Some say it's only blind luck, but if it was only luck, as if I kept doubling down my life on a roulette table, I would be dead a dozen times over. Feeling lucky leaves me wondering if I could do it again—a victim of luck. Others call luck being in the zone, the synchronous signs that reveal you're traveling your true path. Deep inside me, I believe a force greater than what I'm aware of as myself, propels me forward despite the odds.

And so zigzagging, bouncing off rocks, spinning my wheels in dust, caught in ruts, I realized I was falling—falling uphill—falling all the way to the top of the mountain. Every dying heartbeat buying me a moment of joy. And when I crested the mountain, my epiphany must've rewired my brain, because my attitude changed. Coasting down the other side of the mountain—creatively falling—I felt as if I grew wings and could soar off the cliffs, and seemingly I gracefully flew all the way to the valley floor. It was the second moment of enlightenment I've experienced—or should I say?—it was the second moment of enlightenment that I noticed.

[For more falling uphill moments see pages 108-109.]

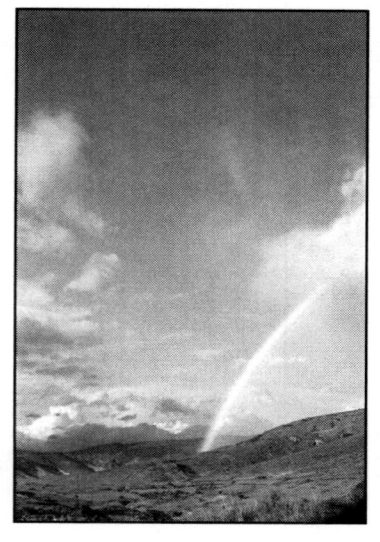

Right: A rainbow and sunny skies in Mexico.

Opposite: Μετέωρα (Metéora Monastery, Greece.) Some monks honored in the ossuary.

Are you crazy?[1]

Is it me or the rest of the world that's crazy? Once, I was surrounded by a group of Tanzanian boxers that were two meters tall and rippling with muscles. The leader said, after feinting a punch, "Do you know why we would never fight you? You must be a very brave man—a very strong man—a very crazy man to ride your bike here. I am African, and I would never do this." And all his friends agreed.

Insanity may manifest as violations of societal norms (the behavioral expectations and cues within a society or group).[2] That is an informal definition, but a societally held belief, meaning that anything outside of the cultural norm is labeled crazy. The word "culture" is derived from the Latin word *cultura,* meaning *to cultivate.* For example, wine is cultivated from a culture of yeast (fungus), which breeds off the surrounding material (fresh grapes), until either there's nothing left to eat, or it dies in it's own excrement (alcohol). So, labeling someone as *crazy* is often a defense mechanism against anyone who threatens our self-image or cultural belief structure. Ironically, another case of *sour grapes.* Some, if not all, of history's greatest scientists and creative thinkers were considered to be crazy by their peers: Socrates, Jesus, Joan of Arc, Galileo, Martin Luther King, Jr. All of them were persecuted, and most became martyrs, meaning they were so different that society killed them to kill their beliefs. Now that doesn't prove I'm sane, but it does prove there is a fine line between crazy and genius.

---

1   This rarely used punctuation mark ؟ is called an irony mark.
2   "Insanity." Wikipedia. November 2009.

What is your job?

I've had hundreds of jobs. Primarily, I used to be a graphic designer, art director, artist, photographer and copywriter. Then I rode a bike. Now I am a graphic designer and author... well, I like to think I'm an author. Whether they're good or bad, I write books, because I feel fulfilled.

Did you go to school?

I enjoy educating myself; I think of it more as exploring. Many people in the world don't even have a third grade education; instead they are apprentices to their family businesses. Having a college education is relatively rare. Even though I have a bachelor's degree in fine art and commercial art, I didn't consider myself educated until I traveled the world. My bicycle trip was my master's degree in life, and this book is my thesis on social studies and human consciousness. In fact, we are all students of the world, learning all the time, and creating our self-image from what we observe in our environments.

How old were you?

I had the idea when I was 25. I worked to earn money and went on a training ride across the North American continent during my 27th year. I spent the next four years working to save more money, and I traveled the world by bicycle from 31-34 years of age. Since my return I've experienced a lot of culture shock, and spent years reevaluating my life, digesting my trip and writing this book.

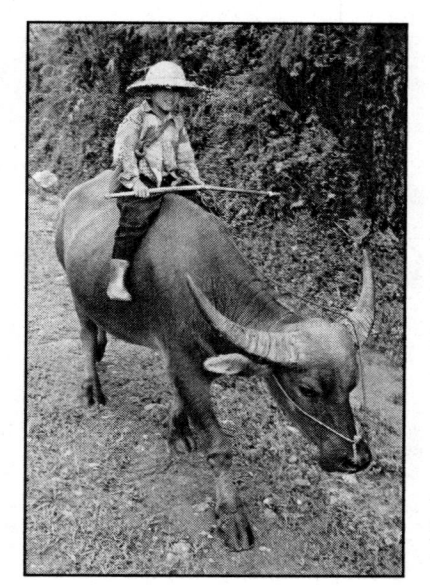

Opposite: Riding through the edge of Australia's Maralinga atomic bomb testing grounds.

Right: Children in South East Asia are often in charge of the family water buffalo.

Yak framing the
North Face of Mount Everest.

What was it like to ride a bicycle around the world?

It was the worst of times; it was the best of times; it was the ugliest of experiences; it was the most beautiful of memories; it was the winter of ignorance; it was the spring enlightenment; it was the epoch of doubting myself; it was the epoch of hope in the world; it was the mountain of my foolishness; it was the summit of my wisdom; I lost my material possessions; I gained my soulful self; I experienced the follies of mankind; I experienced heaven on earth; in short, the trip was so much like life in general, that rather than be understood as absolute good or evil, it can only be understood in the irony of the superlative degree of comparison.[1]

What did you do every day? Traveling is perhaps the ultimate freedom and adventure; however, my average daily life still had it's boring routine. I spent the majority of my time pedaling and looking for water, food and a place to sleep and sleeping. And when I wasn't looking, I had the best and worst times of my life.

This section could be called: **What were your best and worst experiences?** or **Is the world good or bad?** Both, and it's people who determine which is which, and that's reflected in the questions people ask. If someone has a passion about architecture, they might ask about the cathedrals of Europe or the mud huts of Africa. Or if they have a fear of the strangers, they might focus on all the possibilities of being robbed or run over. Beside being motivated by curiosity (sometimes a morbid curiosity), the underlying question people are asking is: **What kind of adventures might I want (or not want)?**

This category of questions is the largest, so I've broken it down into: **Was it dangerous?** [following page] **Was it a difficult?** [page 75] **Are people good or bad?** [page 83] and **What was your favorite___?** [page 93].

---

1   A tribute to Charles Dickens, *A Tale of Two Cities*, one of my favorite authors and books.

One person's good is another person's boring; one person's bad is another person's exciting. **Is living your life risky?** Yes, we live in a world that can bite and scratch. **Is not living your life risky?** Yes, if we put ourselves on automatic pilot, the vacuum of life seems to guarantee that "bad" things happen at the "worst" time.

Certainly some people are wondering: **Is the world safe?** However, maybe the more interesting questions is: **Why do people enjoy horror stories?** Perhaps, fear is nothing to be afraid of, but an emotion to be savored.

I theorize that people are playing with their uncomfortable emotions like fear, trying to normalize a seemingly random and senseless world. Another theory is that the difference between fear and excitement is a very thin line. For example, jumping out of an airplane is exciting; forgetting your parachute is horrifying. So not only is fear like a friend protecting us from danger, but also guiding us in the direction of our greatest opportunity for growth by highlighting our desires and weaknesses. In this case, our desire to fly and our fear of heights. If we ignore or are ignorant of the dangers of life than it's impossible to change them, and we give them the opportunity to sneak up on us. For the record, I've proven most stereotypes and gossip wrong, and my bad experiences were very rare, helped along by a healthy dose of ignorance and arrogance. So, at the risk of dwelling on the negative, the following section is here to portray a thrilling, full-bodied aroma of life on Planet Earth as I experienced it. [Also see dangerous humans. Pages 85-87.]

Opposite top: A skull and crossbones sign warns of the imminent danger of being run over by a truck. "Right is might" rules the roads in India. **Bottom:** If this hotel catches fires, you have a choice of putting out the flames with buckets of sand or bottles of soda. **Above:** "Bad" weather sculpts world-class scenery in New Zealand's Southern Alps.

What was the worst thing that happened?

I've experienced a lot of natural disasters during my short time on earth: avalanches, earthquakes, mudslides, sinkholes, volcanic eruptions, floods, tornadoes, blizzards, hailstorms, ice storms, drought, thunderstorms, lightning storms, firestorms, pestilence, famine, death. And some not-so natural disasters: greed, war, wrath, accidents, jealousy, economies failing, governments falling, societies crumbling, terrorism, bombings, riots, mobs and mayhem.... But I never imagined how bad the worst thing would really be!

Most people think that the worst aspect of my trip would be something physical like climbing the Himalaya Mountains with intestinitis and strep throat; or being mugged and beaten; or robbed and thrown in prison; maybe even the perpetual hunger and headwinds.

I've always been discouraged that this question is so common; however, I think I am in a unique position, having experienced such a wide gamut, to unequivocally say that I experienced the worst thing that could ever happen to me or anyone.

It happened in Guatemala. I had my heartbroken from afar by the woman of my dreams who I met in New Zealand through an impossible chain of events that could have been nothing but the magnetic attraction of true love. And I realized when I sat down with shaking hands to eat the breakfast that I had eaten a hundred times before—my eggs had no flavor; my coffee was bitter even with a tablespoon of sugar; and my *pico de gallo* had no *pico*. It even vaguely occurred to me that the birds were singing, music playing, people laughing, but I didn't care. Ironically the worst thing was also the best thing that ever happened to me—her parting gift was the greatest lesson in life: that it doesn't matter what you do, if you feel nothing, if you become indifferent to living.

Opposite: The ironically named "Volcano of Water" looms over Antigua. When this volcano erupted in 1541 it caused a flood and mudslide which destroyed the original capital of Guatemala. **Top:** A volcano erupts in Ecuador. The locals didn't seem to notice this every-day event. Note: in the second picture all the snow has melted off the top. **Bottom:** A mudslide, like wet cement, floated a car out of a parking lot and jammed it underneath a bridge.

Did you ever get in an accident?

Did you get run over? I've been run into, over, knocked aside and blown off the road by the wind of a passing truck more times than I can remember, but I kept going. I loved feeling free as a bird and the mystery around every corner—I earned it. [Rules of the road page 42.]

What was the most dangerous thing that happened? The worst time was in California when a pink-haired hippy ran a stop sign and knocked me off my bicycle. It was very undramatic, but permanently damaged the cartilage in my knee. And once in Vietnam some over-zealous and xenophobic teenagers on a motor scooter were trying to frighten me (playing chicken). The driver turned too sharp and lost control of the scooter. Here's the melodramatic reenactment:

Colors flash in my peripheral vision. His scooter rips through my front pannier, crushes my fuel bottle, breaks my pump, resets the combination on my lock, wraps my rack around my front axle like a wet noodle, rips my shoe, snaps my pedal.... "Is this a nightmare?" I wonder. The driver's face and his two companions smash into my outstretched arm just below the elbow. I pinwheel off my bike. My thighs catch the seat and the titanium strut snaps with a sound like breaking glass; simultaneously, I land on my tailbone. Agony whitewashes my vision, and I crumple on the ground believing I've broken my back. "It was only a matter of time...."

Did you ever have a near-death experience?

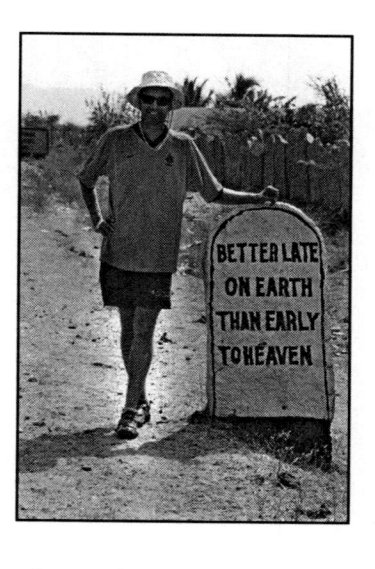

BETTER LATE
ON EARTH
THAN EARLY
TO HEAVEN

I haven't had any paranormal near-death experiences yet, but I have had a lot of normal near-death experiences: people regularly die from dengue fever, and even salmonella poisoning. I nearly ran off a cliff several times. I was shot at a couple times (once by accident and once as a bad joke or warning). Armed bandits have threatened to kill me twice. I've slid across ice into oncoming traffic. If parallel universes really do exist, I've been killed by trucks a thousand times. But the closest to death I've been in this universe is dehydration. [See pages 30-31.] There is nothing like the taste of death to make life seem sweet. That's why people ride roller coasters and jump out of airplanes.

How many times did you fall off (crash) your bike?

Dozens of times. Almost all very minor. A couple crashes took some time to recover, but nothing that one doesn't expect doing this kind of thing. So, it is important to practice crashing. Landing an airplane is simply a controlled crash. And remember the adage: if you fall off your steel horse, get right back in the saddle—don't let that fearful emotional seed grow into a redwood tree.

Right: A daily sight: a Mexican roadside memorial for Hector the truck driver. In Greece, I passed 86 shrines and memorials in one day [story page 56]. **Opposite:** A Hindu shrine on wheels overturned.

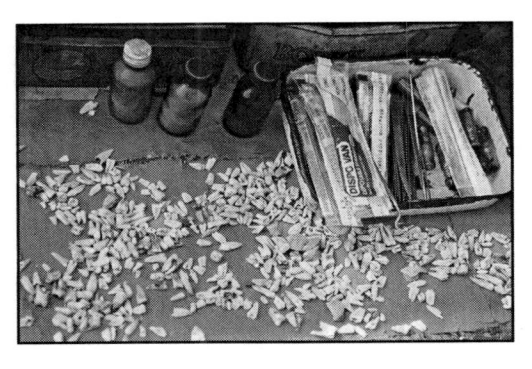

Did you get sick?

After hearing stories about tapeworms 10 meters long, viruses that eat you alive in a matter of hours, bullets knocking the arms off people, monstrous trucks blowing cyclists off cliffs... it didn't take long to realize health is my number one priority.

Life on the road, exposed to the elements and indigenous microscopic bugs, combined with the fatigue of cycling, wears your body out quickly. The worst illness was being cursed with Montezuma's Revenge over and over again, including acute intestinitis (salmonella poisoning), combined with some parasites hiding in my clogged intestines, which mutated into irritable bowel syndrome

Above: An Indian street dentist extracting a tooth from a patient sitting astride an open gutter to the sewer. **Left:** Close up of pulled teeth and dental equipment displayed on a red carpet advertising his successful business.

and plagued me for years. I was also infected by giardia, dengue fever, boils, strep throat, conjunctivitis, prickly heat rash and some other things you'd not care to imagine [page 80]. **Did you go to a doctor?** One of the planet's most dangerous critters is a mosquito, luckily I didn't get malaria (the malaria pills made me ill enough), though I was so sick in Malawi the doctors investigated my blood for the parasite. And fortunately, I was never bit by a dog (a big menace to cyclists). I skipped my rabbies **vaccination**, because the doctor told me I'd only have 12-36 hours to get to a hospital, and I said, "I'd rather save the money, because if I get bit by a rabid dog, I'll probably die anyways." Medical care was extremely poor in the villages and small cities. Doctors, and sometimes witch doctors, often worked in a roadside shack full of shelves with bottles like a medieval alchemist. Fortunately the number one cure is prevention. And since one of the leading causes of disease is stress, one of the leading cures is relaxation, which includes riding a bicycle. Generally, my health was far greater than when I sat in a chair and worked on the computer all day.

Were you injured?

The trick to playing with snakes is knowing which end is the pointy end, which means I expect life to give me a few bumps and bruises, but I intend to minimize the risk.

Most of my injuries were minor to medium scratches and bruises, except being run over a couple times [page 66], which damaged the cartilage in my knee, causing reoccurring tendonitis, preventing me from cycling. I'm embarrassed to admit I dislocated my wrist hand-washing my laundry. In addition, I incurred facet syndrome (caused by whiplash of the back), bruised tailbone, hyper-extended elbow, heat exhaustion and heat stroke [page 30], sunburn, frostbite, saddle sores, nappy rash and a broken heart.

Scars from repeatedly jamming the chainring into my leg. I liked to tell the boys in Central America that I was bitten by a shark.
"Un tiburón morderme."

Were you attacked by animals?

If an animal feels threatened and has nowhere to run, even a chipmunk can be frightening.

In South East Asia, I ran over a cobra, one of the world's most venomous snakes, that should have zigged instead of zagged. The cobra slithered away so fast that it didn't have time to think about biting me. I found that almost all animals were more scared of me than I was scared of them. Humans have few predators, like: lions and crocodiles, and that's only if they're hungry. You're probably thinking what I often thought: **How can I tell if a lion is hungry?** I'm not sure, but I wasn't accepting any dinner invitations.

Elephants were my favorite; perhaps it's their humorous nose combined with their noble jungle standing. Not even the king of the jungle—*simba*[1] the lion—will attempt to hunt an elephant. However, once in Nepal and again in Tanzania, I was almost trampled

---

1   "Simba" means "lion" in Swahili, one of the main languages of East Africa.

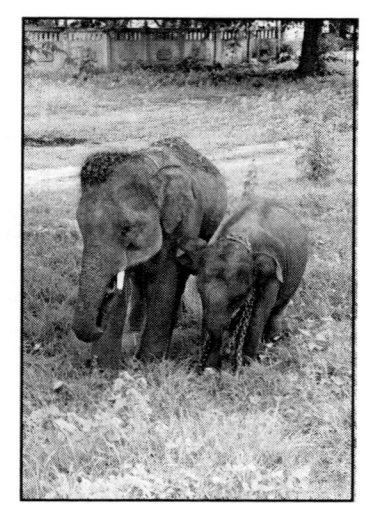

This page. Top: A hand-painted road sign in Tanzania warns of wild elephants. **Bottom left:** A shaky photo of a bull elephant crossing the road in Mikumi National Park, Tanzania. This elephant is so enormous, I could have cycled between it's legs. **Bottom right:** Asian elephant mother and child chained alongside the road in Thailand.

Opposite page. Top: Eleven wild Asian elephants cross the road in Nepal. **Bottom:** Captive Nepalese elephant with weeping eyes.

by an elephant because I accidentally scared a mother guarding her baby. I never believed it possible to miss seeing a six-ton animal standing next to the road.

Were you ever attacked by animals? If you watch television a lot, you might think there are dangerous animals lurking around every corner. Unfortunately, that's not true, especially in this over-crowded world, where people eat almost everything, even "artificial" food. Except for humans, dogs, flies, mosquitoes and the microscopic animals lurking everywhere, I was rarely bothered. However, one of my scariest moments was on the border of Austria, when my tent was surrounded by aggressive wild boar that can gouge a hole in a car with their tusks. I'm fortunate they could only smell me but not see me.

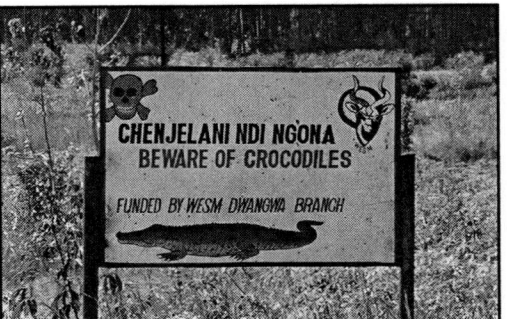

This page. **Top:** A sign warning people not to bath or do their laundry in the river. **Right:** Vietnamese snake hunter. He has a giant rake to comb the snakes out of the grass, a rifle and machete. He's holding dinner—a beheaded cobra.

Opposite page. Glad none of this stuff ever crawled in my tent or shoes. **Top:** Some **freshwater crocodiles.** The safe kind of crocodile as opposed to the saltwalter croc. But, then again, you can never be too sure. **Bottom clockwise from top left:** It looks like a **miniature alligator,** but who knows? That is one of the major flaws of traveling: most of the time I didn't know what I was looking at and no one could tell me. **Outback spider.** Australia has the most venomous creatures on earth. I went swimming with the **Great white sharks** in South Africa. Luckily I was in a steel cage. **Baby scorpion** on my nose. I got stung three times in Argentina when one decided to crawl in my bed. An Australian **baby brown snake** the second most venomous land snake in the world; babies are even more dangerous than adults because they panic easier and can't control how much venom they inject into their victims. **Male tarantula** crossing the road in Bolivia seeking a mate. The photo is a little blurry because he kept jumping at me.

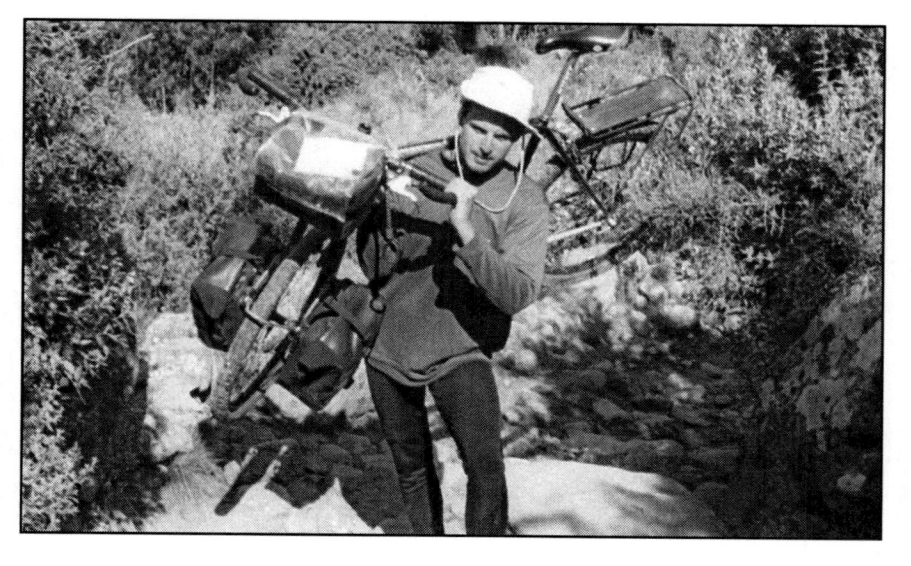

I admit my frustration makes me seem very ungrateful for having the resources to travel the world when some people are sleeping in beds of newspaper. I met a Scotsman that helped adjust my attitude. He said, referring to my doubts, "Well, ya can always go sit on your arse back home, can't ya? Or ya can roll the dice. Have some fun."

Most people think the most dangerous and difficult aspects of cycling would be something like cycling through the monsoons of Asia, or through the Atacama Desert, the driest desert in the world. Indeed some days were so physically gruelling that I lost bladder control because my body was so exhausted; nonetheless, the most difficult aspect for me was not physical but emotional.

The previous section was more about facing the dangers of the external world. This section deals more with the personal physical challenges and the emotional dangers of the inner world such as fear and doubt. One thing I've discovered is that everyone has their inner demons they struggle to tame, so these negative things are really not so negative, but normal consequences of building your emotional muscles; in other words, they are opportunities to grow. [Is fear your friend? Page 63. What is happiness? Page 115.]

Opposite: My friend, Dennis, finds a cozy place to hide from the sun. In Baja, Mexico the temperature was 50°C (120°F) in the shade, probably more but our thermometers didn't go any higher; the road surface can go over 160°F—hot enough to cook an egg.

Can you think of something painfully difficult but even more rewarding?

What was the hardest part?

Loneliness, boredom, doubt, depression, headwinds, aches and pains.

People must have suspected these were my biggest challenges, because often they ask: **Did you get lonely?** Painfully. I often traveled months alone, sometimes not being able to speak the same language as the locals, feeling like an alien, or an explorer of strange parallel universe. **Did you miss your friends and family?** More than I imagined. Sometimes I would ride many miles out of my way to find an Internet café and read my email. **How did they feel about you leaving?** They thought I was crazy, but afterwords everyone was glad that I survived and very proud to tell the story about their friend who rode a bicycle around the world. **Were you scared to be by yourself?** Sometimes it was unsafe. **Did you make any friends?** I made more friends than I can count, and some of the best friends of my life. **Did you get bored?** I was so bored, sometimes I read a book while I rode my bicycle.

I'm not superman, and we all have our challenges, mine is a predisposition towards depression, which made traveling alone difficult. Despite driving me a little crazy, being alone helped purge my spirit and reset my frame of reality from the cultural illusions of materialism to a much more instinctual level. In other words, being isolated gave me the opportunity to separate myself from society enough to see who I think I am, who I really am, and who I want to be.

Why didn't you quit?

I did quit dozens of times. The American culture, like all cultures, has many myths, misconceptions, beliefs and moral values that aren't necessarily true. One of them is: Winners never quit. Here's another: Failure isn't an option. In my opinion, failure is an excellent option (the only true failure is never trying) and resigning a losing battle is considered honorable in some countries—the only way to survive to fight another battle. That being said, you have to choose your battles wisely. (Aren't clichés wonderful shortcuts?) Nonetheless, I'm glad I was never next to an airport when I decided to quit, because by the time I found one, I got my motivation back. I'm glad I persevered, because now I realize that my doubts and other weaknesses were part of the answer to what I was seeking [pages 113]. It helped to put my decisions into perspective by asking myself: **It may be lonely and painful now, but do I really want to live with the regret of quitting for the rest of my life?**

Opposite: A picture perfect road aiming for the Olgas or Kata Tjuta, an Australian aboriginal sacred site neighboring the more famous Uluru [page 95].
Above: Salar de Uyuni, Bolivia. A surreal salt desert.

Did you ever get lost?

As much as I tried to get lost, everywhere I went, there I was.

I usually carried several maps (road, political, topographical), so I almost always knew where I was; it was getting where I wanted to go that was the problem. The maps contained many errors (sometimes the errors were intentional to lead potential invaders astray, but mostly the people who drew the maps weren't very skilled) and often the maps weren't detailed enough to tell me anything except I was on a line halfway between two dots, generally heading in the right direction. In Mexico, it took me all day to go a few centimeters on the map. If I couldn't pinpoint my location, I soon learned that I had to ask three people for directions, because the first two usually didn't agree. And I learned that the best maps and guides that existed were actually the nebulous network of ideas contained within the group mind of the people I met, kind of like a "peoplenet".

After running out of water a couple times, I learned how to read maps to predict where the food and water would be. For example, if two major roads intersected, it would almost guarantee services for the vehicles and their drivers. Or, if my map had topography, I could predict there would be small streams in the valleys, and that the water was fresh and clean, since there are few farms and

My question is: What's my question?

factories on top of mountains to pollute the water. I could even expect a chilly headwind, as cold air flows downhill.

Even if I had all the best maps in the world, they couldn't describe something infinite and ever-changing like Planet Earth—they aren't the same thing as actually traveling the road. My ultimate goal was to throw away my maps, trust my inner compass, feel the grass between my toes, get lost in the woods and discover panoramas never seen by any cartographer.

Physically, I was rarely lost, but emotionally, I almost always felt lost. That's another reason why I rode around the world—because I wanted to find myself. Once I told a wise man I was confused. And he surprised me by saying, "Good. You can't create a new order until you disorder who you are." So being lost is the essence of being a good adventurer in life. Most people are afraid of getting lost, consequently they get stuck traveling the same path everyday because it seems the easiest path to pleasure (body) and joy (soul). But in my opinion it is the easiest path to boredom. So the next time you find yourself lost, congratulate yourself; you might not want to go where you were going anyway.

Photo courtesy of Nevil Zaveri

Opposite: A bridge washed out in the Czech Republic. Now what? **Above:** In India, "milestone" is not just an expression. Here is a road sign hand carved out of rock half buried in the sand and marking the way to Jaisalmer. Well... I think it says Jaisalmer, and it's actually a "kilometerstone" to coin a word.

If you want to get found, first you have to get lost!

Don't your legs get tired?

People love pleasure and sometimes love stories of pain even more. **Did it hurt?** Yes! Both mentally and physically. **Did you ever cry?** A regular drippy faucet. **Didn't you get tired?** Once I feel asleep next to the road, and woke up the next day. **Are you sick of riding your bike?** I still enjoy riding, but I am tired of competing with cars and inhaling exhaust. My body is a bit worn out and I've reached the point of diminishing returns as far as bicycling is concerned. **Are you afraid you won't be able to have kids?** It crossed my mind. **Did your bum hurt?** Yes. Frequently, I got crotch abrasions, crotch rot or saddle sores. Saddle sores are pressure ulcers, which are wounds that result from the pressure cutting off blood circulation and your flesh dying. It hurts! Before I got my beloved Brooks Saddle, I rode through the Australian Outback with a bleeding bottom.

Top: Barely visible is the winding road I rode through the conical limestone mountains in north Vietnam. **Left:** A Mexican shortcut. **Opposite page middle:** A repetitively redundant sign. **Bottom:** A beautifully ironic piece of art by Native American artist, Dwayne Wilcox.

PLEASE KEEP GATE CLOSED AT ALL TIMES

What was the most difficult country?

Ironically or not so ironically, the good ol' United States of America is one of the hardest countries to travel by bicycle, especially East of the Mississippi. I'm never one to stereotype; so generally speaking, American's are very bullheaded and prudish when compared to other countries. Being "the land of the free" also makes it the land of freely telling a person what they should and shouldn't do. In my book of opinions (subject to change without notice) America holds the record for road rage (especially towards bicyclists), fences, no trespassing signs, rules, regulations, and prosecuting violators. Mind you, it is my country, and I tend be more critical of anything related directly to me, especially if it happens to be me. However, **there's a more important reason why the USA was the most difficult—it's too easy.** Your home country doesn't provide the perspective that reality is a frame of mind. For example, if you witness people in Bangladesh surviving in a shockingly different way, maybe your way of doing things isn't the absolutely right way of doing things, and maybe if one doesn't like their reality, they can literally change their mind—that's one of my biggest lessons learned.

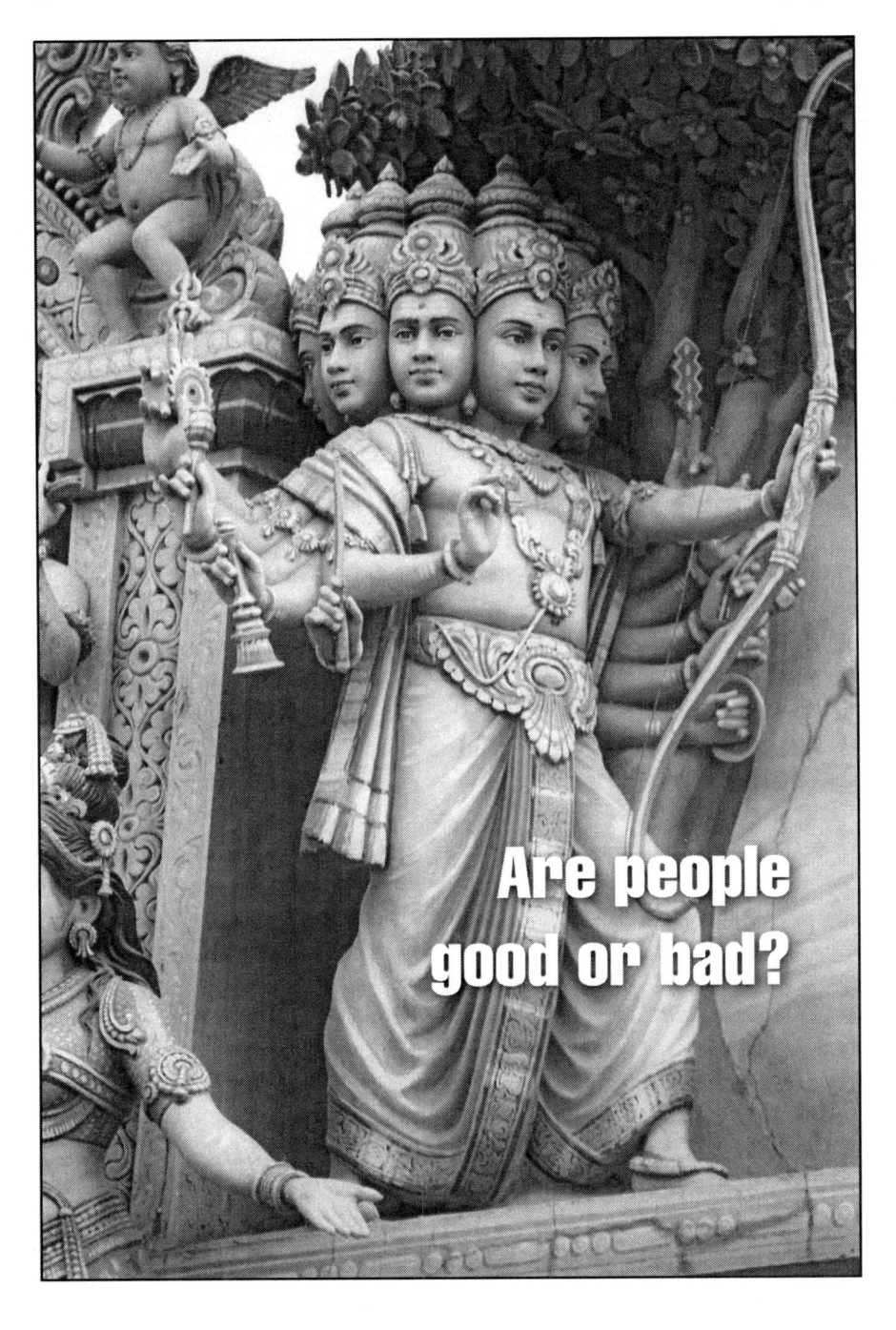

From a third-person perspective, people are both good and bad or neutral; from a first-person perspective they are always good.

I've met over a million people and the common denominator is that we all feel fear and joy and everything between mixed in infinite variations. I've concluded from the questions people asked during my journey, that, more or less in order of importance, we are all needing to survive, afraid of dying, even more afraid of not having an influence in life, wanting to thrive and grow, and love and be loved, gently accepting the unknown with a sense of hope and faith, questioning if there's something more, dreaming of realizing our fullest potential, and, occasionally, living life beyond our wildest imaginations.

I've never met anyone that intentionally makes mistakes or intentionally tries to live a bad life; therefore, everyone is following their path towards the greatest possible joy, though sometimes that path isn't very proactive, and even so it can still be covered in broken glass.

Almost everyone I've met with an open heart and open mind, has been kind and generous, valuing their friends and family almost more than anything. I believe people always make the best decision for themselves, with some unfortunate, unforeseeable consequences if they're being reactive, meaning fearful. Fear is almost always imagined, which grows into anger, and sometimes mutates into violence. I've never encountered someone trying to harm me as much as protect themselves. I think if I

Opposite: A temple detail in India. The Hindu pantheon has over 330,000,000 gods, which are really 330,000,000 aspects of (ways of describing) the same god Brahman. Young boys in India would often ask: "What is your favorite god?" **Above:** Some curious Vietnamese girls selling homemade necklaces alongside the road.

truly understood someone else's point of view, I wouldn't be able to blame them for anything; therefore, I remind myself to have compassion for my fellow human beings, because their answers to life work perfectly for them (otherwise they wouldn't feel a need to do them) and are often better than mine. And, whenever we've combined our views, we've discovered an even better answer.

I can also say with certainty—not because it's a belief or myth, but because I experienced it to be true—everyone loves somebody and something, and everyone feels safe because they love and are loved. And as a whole people are far more capable of creatively changing for their benefit than they give themselves credit.

What was it like to visit all those different cultures?

People are the most valuable resource on the planet. I often felt like an ambassador or anthropologist, and even an astronomer or gemologist, investigating people and cultures as if they were beautiful stars and jewels. There are many fields of study dedicated to the different cultures and the differences between cultures. However, I'm more interested in the similarities between culture because it reveals the patterns of life, which help me to understand who I am, how I fit into society, and how we can all cooperate to achieve unimaginable, seemingly impossible goals like walking on the moon, or even someday—living on Mars.

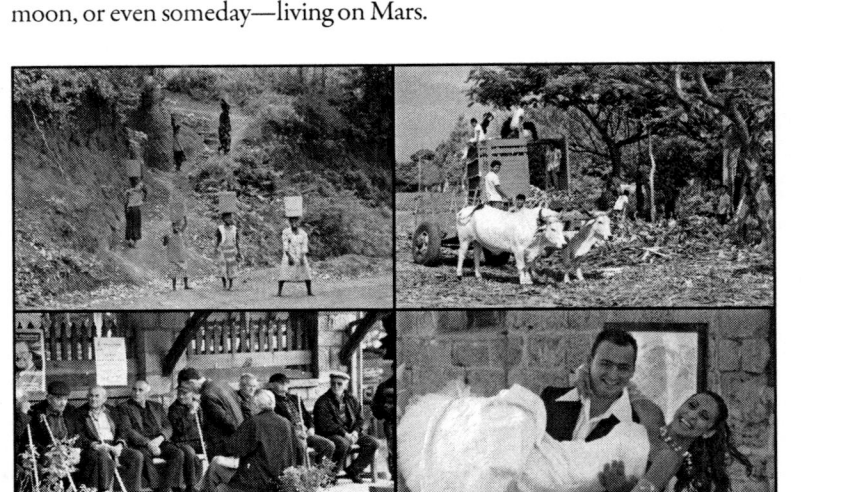

Clockwise from top left: Some young **Tanzanian women** fetching their daily bucket of water. **Young men in Nicaragua** harvest green bananas with the help of an ox drawn cart. Happy **newlyweds** in Tel Aviv, Israel. Distinguished **Greek gentlemen** chat about the day's affairs in the town plaza.

Were you attacked by people?

I was never attacked physically, but I often joke that the only animal I'm afraid of is a human being. I'm not really afraid of people, maybe more afraid of what they think of me, then what they will do to me. Certainly, I have a great respect for people and have learned that it's very dangerous to back a human into a corner either physically, mentally or emotionally. In other words, a person will guard an idea or their pride as if it's an arm or leg. So when some poachers and a witch doctor threatened me with a magic crocodile, I smiled my biggest smile and slowly backed away.

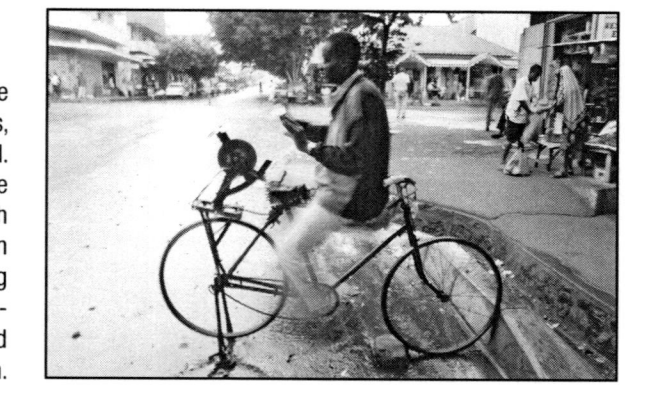

Above: Children are almost always curious, kind and good humored. Here some Zimbabwe boys are playing tough guys. **Right:** Tanzanian entrepreneur sharpening my machete on a home-made bicycle-powered grinding wheel in the rain.

Were you ever robbed?

There is something about dogs snapping at your heels that makes me feel wonderfully alive, and being robbed makes a much more interesting story than sipping café au lait in the Eiffel Tower in France.

Most of the time I was as safe or safer while traveling abroad than at home; I often left my bicycle unattended in the small villages of the world's poorest people, but in big cities among the world's richest people, the backpacks of some of my travel companions disappeared in a few seconds of distraction. The hazard of being a tourist with a camera, wallet full of cash, and a passport glued to my sweaty butt was my biggest peeve.

My tent and panniers were burglarized a few times. The thieves usually stole small items hoping I wouldn't notice, like: toothbrush, lighter, pen or water bottle. In Tibet, some locals stole a bag of food from my tent, but left all the valuables. It is difficult to label people as criminals, because some societies have a sense of communal property, where items like tools belong to everyone. So, it is more like borrowing then stealing. Likewise, if it comes to food, it's not so much stealing as it is surviving.

Pictured above is the road up to the Tibetan plateau, thrice a gang of highway bandits wanted money for safe passage, veiled as a tip for their efforts to fill the potholes in the road. They were mischievous but meant little harm. I was more of an oddball attraction than a source of income. For example, when I was pulled over by a policeman in Mexico, I thought I was going to be blackmailed as was prevalent on the gossip grapevine, but he simply wanted to know where I was going and why was I riding a bicycle.

In Guatemala, I was mugged while jogging down a street closed for construction. The men had a shotgun and revolver and echoed the classic line: "Your money or your life." I was in a sour mood and opted to run. They beat me with sticks while I ran, until I dropped my valuables. To be fair I should state for the record, I was also mugged by knife once in my hometown of Milwaukee. I had nothing but bus fare, and my assailant told me that I'd have to walk home. Overwhelmed by curiosity I asked him if he would really stab me for 75 cents. He was flabbergasted for a moment then laughed and said, "You are a brave but stupid man," and walked away. People say that a lot.

Confidence men (con men), swindlers and hucksters, or from their point of view, clever businessman, would approach me dozens of times per day in tourist traps like the Pyramids of Giza or the streets of Mumbai. Quite often they succeeded in getting a few extra pennies, but in Zimbabwe they got a hundred dollars. Because the government and economy were collapsing and the extreme deflation of the Zimbabwe dollar, I attempted to change money on the back streets of the black market. When I exchanged my 100-dollar bill for a fistful of several million Zimbabwe dollars, I discovered that all the bills except the one on the outside was worthless—the bait-and-switch scam. The corrupt government, economic crash, genocide and war made Zimbabwe **the most dangerous country I cycled.**

How did you like prison?

When I reported that I had been robbed to the Zimbabwe police, they told me it was illegal to change money on the streets. It is a long and complicated story, and the pinnacle of my arrogance, but eventually I ended up in prison with some of the men who had robbed me. Despite being behind a barbwire fence, guarded with a shotgun and very scared, it was quite nice—sunshine, fresh air and a pleasant view. Luckily, I didn't have to eat the food, which would have been boiled cabbage three times a day. The Zimbabwe authorities treated me with a lot of courtesy and some good humor. After going to court and paying my fine, I was released later the same day. I had a choice between 2 months in prison or 18 US dollars.

In retrospect, it's one of my favorite stories. That's the odd thing about travel, it seems the most physically and emotionally grueling events, where my entire survival was at risk, situations for which I would never have volunteered, and the most humiliating to retell, were the most rewarding in terms of my growth as a person.

Opposite: The Himalayas.
Right: Giraffe statues left to rot. One could argue the Zimbabweans were robbed of their businesses by their corrupt government.

Did anyone invite you home?

One of the great honors of being a traveler is being invited to someone's home; it's also the best way to learn about a new culture. I've been welcomed everywhere I went. Here are a few examples:

Top: A mud-brick hut on the Altiplano in Bolivia. The family, who literally didn't have even one boliviano (money worth about 0.14 US dollars), treated us to a hot cup of coca tea and a bowl of dried potato soup in their warm earthy home. **Bottom:** I was the guest of honor at an important ceremony in Thailand to welcome a new buddha. All the families invited me home for dinner, and to stay as long as I wished. **Opposite clockwise from top left.** Some self-appointed guides and friends escorted me to the top of a small mountain and ancient fortress. Here I'm the guest of honor in the **Maharaja's elephant throne**. A group of **Tibetan farmer's** invite me to lunch while they take a break from tilling the spring fields with their yaks. The **Greek fire department** that rescued me from torrential rains and showed me their hometown and treated me to one of the finest meals of my life. **A family in Rajasthan India** that hosted me for lunch. Sharing a traditional dinner with new friends in a **small village near Cairo**, Egypt. A group of young fans from my night sleeping outside the chiefs hut in a **Malawi village.** The chief treated me to a great luxury, a warm bowl of water for a bath.

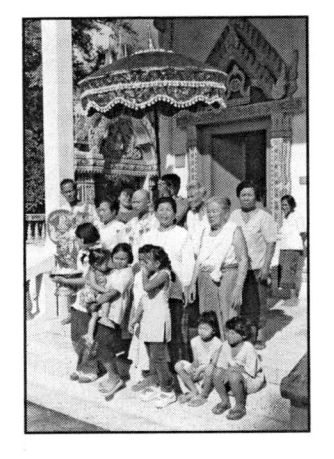

Did anyone ever feed you?

In every country I was invited to share a meal, ironically the poorest of poor people were most often my hosts.

Many people who hosted me literally had no money, but relied on trading and gifting goods and services. At first, I felt embarrassed and guilty to accept people's hospitality, until I realized that we both benefited from the cultural exchange and that these people would regale their neighbors with stories of the "crazy" bicyclist that passed through their village and honored their home with a visit. I also learned that in many countries, especially in the Middle East and Asia, it is polite to refuse an invitation three times, but rude and insulting to refuse it a fourth time.

Have you ever invited anyone
into your home or to share a meal?

Photo courtesy of Dennis Snader

Did anyone help you?

Even if I wasn't in need people offered help just to be part of the journey. Citizens of every country were so kind and generous that it was a personal challenge to graciously accept so much hospitality.

One of my favorite memories began in The Gran Chaco, a vast desert spanning Bolivia, Paraguay, and Argentina. When it rains in the Chaco, the gravel and dirt roads turn into mud that either sticks to everything or melts into the desert. During the rainy season, it's impenetrable. It had been raining for two days, and I was walking my bicycle through miles of puddles and slime. I was straining to average 1 KPH, and wouldn't reach the next village for several days, long after I ran out of food, and forced to drink mud.

The only truck to pass me all day, spun into the ditch before me as he attempted to slow down and say, *"Hola."* When I approached, the driver, Romiro, realizing my plight, didn't just offer me a ride—he began throwing my panniers into the back of his truck and easily lifted my mud-coated bicycle over his head; simultaneously his son (families often live and work in their trucks) threw down gifts of fruit and soda. Further down the road, we picked up my friend Dennis. It took us the remaining day and all night to drive and push his truck through the mud to his home about 100 kilometers down the road. "You must think it was easier to bicycle," Romiro joked during a tea break in the middle of the night.

Have you ever helped anyone in need?

We arrived at Romiro's ramshackle house on an "aboriginal community" and had a very late dinner (or early breakfast) with his family. "You're like my sons. Eat. Drink. *No problemo.*" Romiro said, despite the fact that Argentina's economy was crashing, and his pesos were only worth a third of their value as three months ago. Romiro was accustomed to poverty. He built his life in a similar ramshackle manner to his house. During his first few years he lived on the streets and owned nothing, not even clothes. At this young age, Romiro decided he wanted a better life. From the ages of 3–14, he only owned one set of clothes and one pair of shoes and worked in his uncle's garage as an unpaid apprentice, watching and learning everything. At 15, he began to earn small tips and wages. Now, Romiro is a community leader, with two businesses, two houses, four trucks, and provides for his wife, five children—two with plans to attend college in the big city—one grandchild and two ravenous bicyclists.

We're stranded for days. On the first day, we met the community elders, teachers and priests; the second day is filled with local businessmen and students; and the third day, a group of young, single women arrived; and the whole time we're surrounded by children. Some people, too shy to venture inside the house, waited outside for a glimpse of us strangers. If our visitors didn't ask about our bicycle trip, Romiro joked about how pathetic we looked drenched in mud. He also enjoyed telling stories about the gringos who escaped being eaten by anacondas so big that a truck could run over them and they wouldn't even wake. We also had many appointments: running errands with Romiro's daughter to meet the community; participating in bicycle races with the kids; watching the local football game; lecturing to the high school students; visiting a charity organization that is building houses for the locals despite what the locals really need and want are jobs; and going catfishing to feed the family.

When the roads are dry enough to risk taking a bus to Juarez, we profusely thanked Romiro. Grinning as usual, he said, "No, thank you for showing my village and my children that the impossible is possible." I'll never forget as the bus passed the school, seeing Romiro's youngest son, Pablo leading the charge as the whole school threw themselves over the fence and chased us down the road, just to wave goodbye one last time.

Opposite: Romiro extracts a broken bolt from my bike while Pablo watches and learns. **Above:** Stuck in the mud in Argentina. **Right:** Some Indian men are so excited to help me filter water, they don't let the kids help. Gathering water is traditionally children's work.

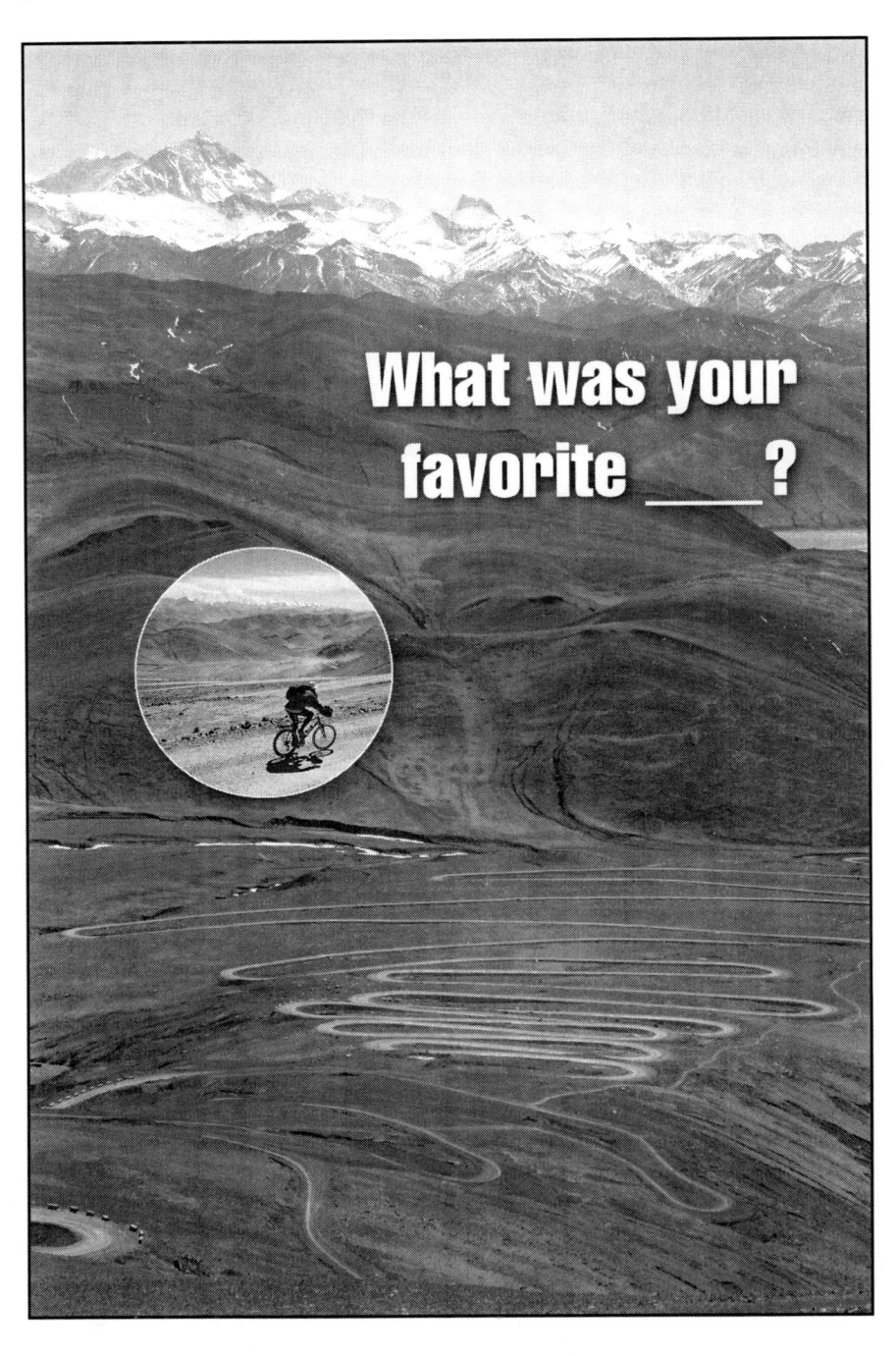

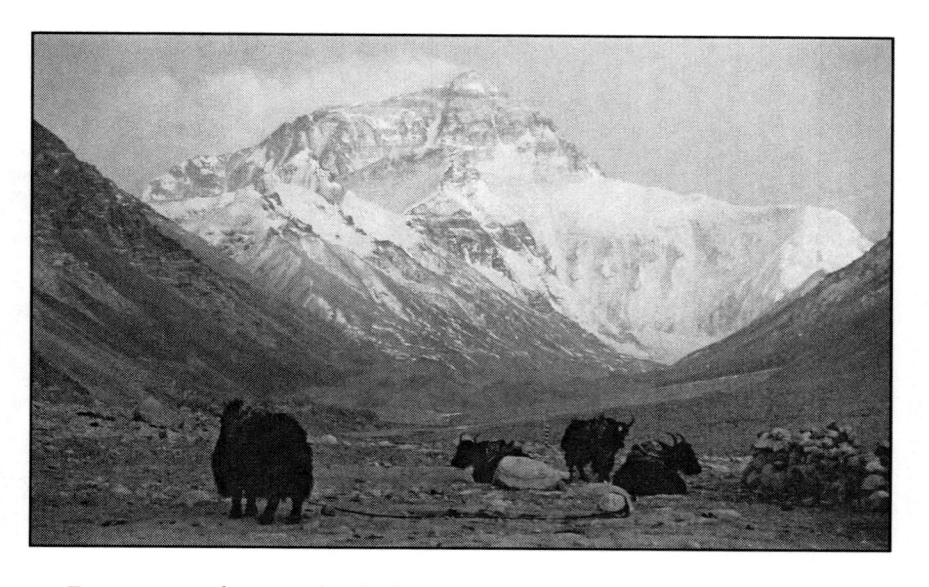

For years, people primarily asked me more pessimistic questions, like: **Why would you do that?** Now, people suddenly are much more optimistic, and ask questions, like: **What did you discover?** I guess people are inherently pessimistic beforehand and optimistically curious after the fact. And then there are those people, like myself, who are just optimistically pessimistic. Another oddity of being a human being is that the more time that passes the more favorite experiences I remember. It's as if my experiences are rough stones in the mud, that once cleaned and polished and held in the sun are revealed to be rainbow-colored diamonds.

You can consider everything in this book a favorite experience—a small taste of the infinite flavors in the world, such as: **What is your favorite bicycle ride or road?** North America has one of the most beautiful bike rides in the world with a network of roads thousands of miles long that run along the Pacific Ring of Fire, from Canada through the United States and into Mexico. One of the most beautiful sections is Highway 1, Big Sur, California [photo page 21 and redwood trees page 95]. **What was your favorite food?** [Can gross food be your favorite? See pages 32-37]. Or: **What was your favorite language?** [page 45]. **Inspirations** and **inspirational people** [see the quotes peppered throughout]. Subjects like psychology [pages 14-16] **philosophy** [this whole book]. And all the **multi-layered stories** and **ideas** that you get to discover for yourself. The following section presents a few more highlights. If I listed them all, this book might take four years to read.

Opposite: The road to Everest Base Camp. Mount Everest in the distance.
Photos courtesy of Edwin Tucker.

Natural wonders of the world

Victoria Falls. Above is a scene from a Tarzan movie. Victoria Falls or Mosi-oa-Tunya (the Mist that Thunders) is often listed as one of the Natural Wonders of the World. It's the biggest waterfall in the world about one kilometer wide separating Zimbabwe and Zambia. How many crocodiles and hippopotamuses do you think have accidentally gone over the falls?

Butterfly sanctuary. Mariposa Monarca Biosphere Reserve in Mexico is the winter home to hundreds of millions of migratory Monarch butterflies. It takes 4 generations to make the return journey. The weight of so many butterflies sometimes breaks the branches off the trees.

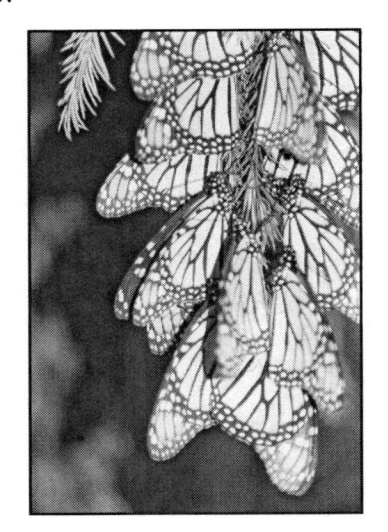

Misc. wonders. I'm embarrassed to admit I didn't take photos of the **Grand Canyon** or the **Aurora Borealis**, and I rode past **Parícutin Volcano**, which sprang up in Mexican's cornfield while he was plowing, not realizing it was a Natural World Wonder. Also see See **Mount Everest** [pages 60, 92-93, 106].

The oldest, fattest and tallest trees in the world

Cycling through the redwood groves of the Pacific Coast with the world's most massive trees, thousands of years old is like traveling back in time and one of my favorite places on earth. I also visited the world's tallest tree, General Sherman, a giant Sequoia in the Sierra Nevadas. Nearby in California, I rode past the world's oldest tree, Methuselah, a bristlecone pine. And in Oaxaca, Mexico I saw the world's fattest tree, "El Arbol del Tule," a Montezuma Cypress.

Massive monoliths

Australia is the flattest and most boring continent (the government actually rebuilt some outback highways, adding slight curves so that drivers wouldn't fall asleep from boredom), which makes Uluru (Ayers Rock) one of the world's most massive and most col-orful monoliths, even more massively fascinating. Pic-tured here is a close up of the Red Rock, in the distance you can see another sand-stone monolith Kata Tjuta [Also page 76].

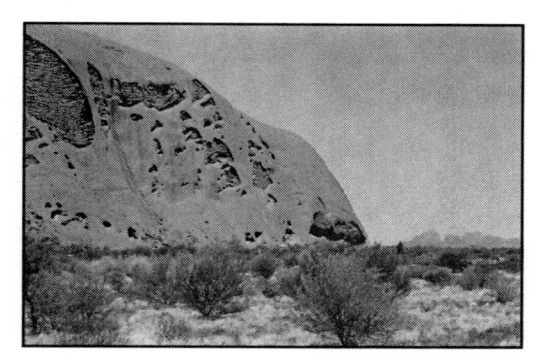

Ancient wonders

Parthenon, Athens, Greece

The most important building remaining from the classical Greek era, temple of the Greek goddess Athena, constructed between 447-432 BC. Below, from the same era, the **Temple of Apollo, Delphi** home of one of histories most famous oracles.

The Giza Necropolis & Jerusalem

Near Cairo, Egypt, the Great Pyramid of Giza [page 4] is the only one of the Seven Wonders of the Ancient World that survives. Also from the same location see the **sphinx** [page 10]. And a few hundred kilometers away, **the Old City of Jerusalem** another Ancient Wonder containing the **Western Wall** [page 6].

The Lost City of the Incas, Machu Picchu

[Opposite top.] Skeptical of all world wonders as potential tourist traps, even I was amazed by the beauty and craftsmanship of this Sacred City of the Sun hidden in the Andes Mountains in Peru.

Tzintzuntzan

Tzintzuntzan means "Place of the hummingbirds". (Try saying it.) A Mesoamerican archaeological site in Mexico. Another famous Pre-Columbian site that I recommend you discover is Tikal, built by the astronomical wonders, the ancient Mayan civilization.

Coliseum

The Pula Arena, an ancient coliseum or amphitheatre in Croatia. It was constructed by the Romans about 2000 years ago. Imagine bicycling down the road and seeing this unexpected marvel or having a tailgate party at these games!

Government, History & Architecture.

I experienced all kinds of systems for governing (managing) people, including: socialism, capitalism, aristocracy, dictatorship, theocracy, anarchy and tribal. I'm not an expert, and even the experts disagree, so I can't say which government works best, but I can say that government starts by governing yourself. [See page 51.]

I've spent a lot of time in London, and despite or in spite of the dreary weather, it's an *absolutely fabulous* **city**. Pictured above the **architecture** of Big Ben and the Parliament Building are contrasted beautifully by the **modern marvel** of the Millennium Wheel. The center of the British Empire, once called, "the empire on which the sun never sets," was one of the most influential forces on the planet until the television was invented. London and Paris (I have a picture of the Eiffel Tower around

here somewhere) and Europe in general seems to be on every traveler's checklist. There's **history** around every corner, after a couple months, you'll think, "Ten thousand cathedrals, and all I want is one McDonald's."

Continent, Nation, City, State, People

I can't say what my favorite **continent** is except that I'm pretty sure Antarctica is not it. As for a **nation** or **country**, I have my likes and dislikes, but I can't pick an overall favorite. I can objectively say that taste is largely subjective, and there's only one way to tell, and that's to experience it yourself. After traveling the world, I'm honored and relieved that my favorite **city** is still San Francisco. The Golden Gate Bridge [front cover and page v] is also one of the **modern marvels of the world.** Above is a picture-perfect village in Lesotho, the island country floating in South Africa. The door is the most beautiful cobalt blue. The occupants must have walked many miles and exchanged many hours of labor to buy that paint. [See color photos online. More info page 145] The mud, stone and thatch huts create a soothing, womb-like atmosphere. The owners hand-sculpt the house and furniture with fistfuls of mud and straw to match their personal physical dimensions. So often the door is slightly bigger than the occupants, and the table is the perfect height to reach out and rest their hands. The most beautiful African villages and **architecture** flow like a wave of earth from hut to hut making a gigantic handmade sculpture decorated in colorful geometric paintings. Pictured on the left is a beautiful red barn, minty green grass and some black and white heifers in my favorite **state**—Wisconsin, USA. I've proved another cliché—there's no place like home. This classic pastoral image may seem so normal that you didn't even notice it; however, after traveling the world, I can say this photo is as unusual and extra-ordinary to the citizens of another country as any oddball image you may find in this book. The Maasai of East Africa is one of the few **tribes** that continues to practice their traditional lifestyle, and they have a mysterious majestic almost magical presence. I don't have a favorite **people.** My experience has proven that everyone everywhere is fundamentally the same, even if that means we're equally different; it's the cultural adaptations that makes us significantly different. So what is my favorite **culture?** To be honest, I can't be honest, I've already said too much, and someone somewhere will get mad at me.

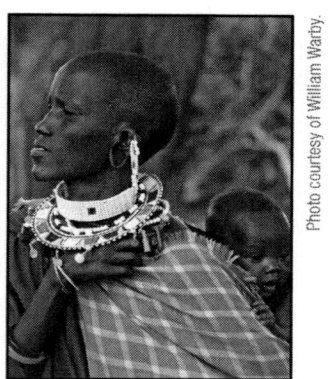

Labor

I was amazed to see how resourceful and industrious people were, especially in India. India was a **country** that I loved and hated. At times it was **the most beautiful place**, and at times because of the poverty it was **the most ugly place**. It was a shock that people still did everything by hand. I remember riding past a three story building being constructed. The people appeared like ants as they filed into the building carrying baskets of bricks and sand on their heads. The building didn't even use scaffolding. They simply piled dirt around the walls and used that as both a brace and ladder. The potential of the human race—if we all cooperated—is mind-boggling.

Above: Indian women in rainbow-colored saris plant rice. **Left:** women walk many miles to harvest grass for their goats and cattle.

Opposite page top: A man sells toy windmills and cars that he made from scraps and garbage.

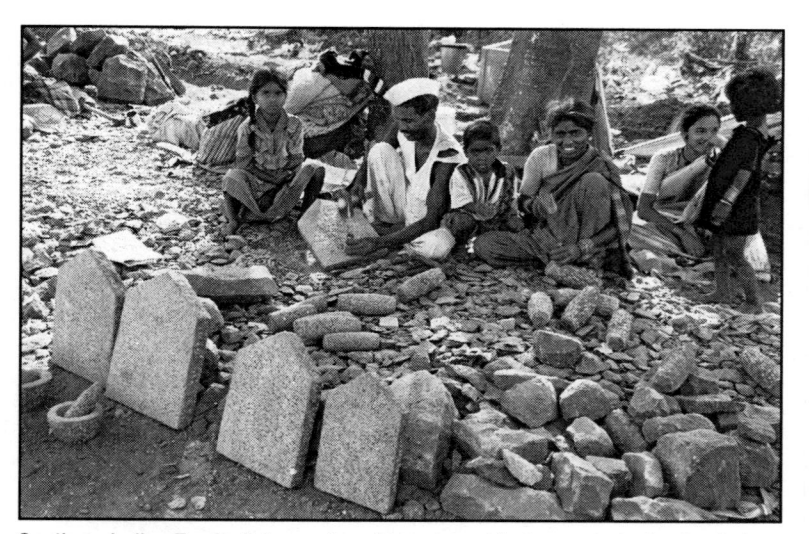

Economy

One of the retrospective benefits of bicycling, though in the moment seeing so much poverty and waste was heartbreaking, was that I witnessed the blood and guts of how a city works. Bicycling around Mexico City, one of the biggest cities in the world, took weeks. From the seat of my bicycle, I could literally see money or wealth being made: sugars pressed from fields of cane, cattle transformed into hamburgers and shoes, ores being stripped from extinct volcanos, factories stamping out millions of tortillas.... In short, I witnessed a thousand examples of the energy of the sun, mineral wealth of the earth and bounties of the plant and animal kingdom being harvested by mankind, manufactured into objects of need or desire, transported in trucks (the platelets of the cities arterial system, constantly shipping in supplies and carting out waste) and traded for colorful pieces of paper called **money**. In Zimbabwe the economy crashed and the cliché came true when the money was worth less than the paper it was printed on and people became desperate with hunger as their material wealth somehow disappeared. In Argentina, a similar thing happened and the generosity of strangers was a tribute to humanity.

Southern Indian Family living and working alongside the road carving tombstones for people who make their one true mistake. Notice the variety of reactions to me.

Sacred places

One thing the world religions agree upon (as far as I can tell and believe me I've spent years studying this stuff) is that you can see the handiwork of God in anything. So, in a sense everyplace and everyone is sacred. But being human beings, we like to label some things more sacred than others, and from our mere mortal perspective some things are better than others. **Above** is Istanbul's Blue Mosque. [Also see the front cover.] **Middle:** The Church of the Holy Sepulcher in the Old City of Jerusalem. **Bottom:** Dinant river, bridge, cathedral & castle in Belgium. Some other hide-and-seek sacred places (according to various authorities) pictured in this book are: everything but one [pages 96-97], two Buddhist temples and the Wheel of Life, church spire in Germany, Ganges River, Hindu temple, Uluru, Karlu Karlu, Kata Tjuta, Metéora Monastery. Miscellaneous sacred things: shrine, wedding, flower, ox, cow, elephant, sadhu, the reader [not pictured], and more.

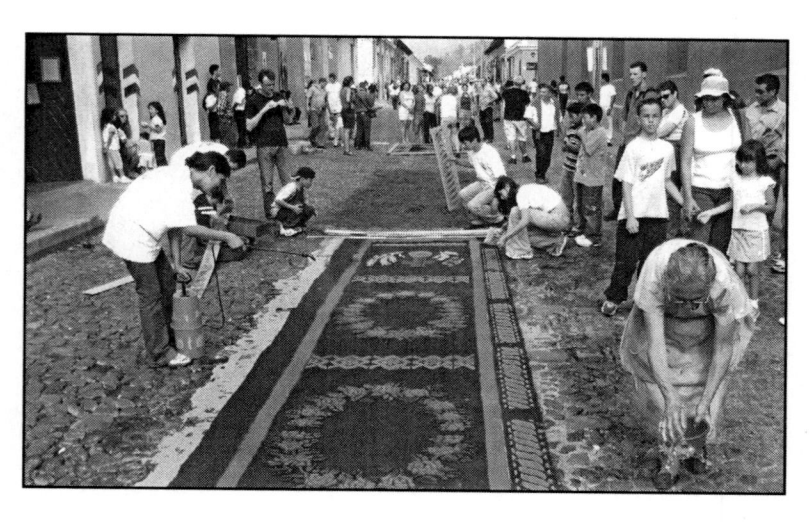

Festivals & Holidays

People love celebrating so much that sometimes they celebrate celebrating. Above people are creating very colorful carpets of sawdust that will soon be trampled in a parade during the largest Easter celebration in the world in Antigua, Guatemala. This celebration is called Semana Santa which means "holy week" but the celebration lasts over a month. [Back cover: Nepalese children celebrate the spring Festival of Colors, Holi, by soaking each other in colored pigments.]

Geography & Weather

Geography: I've camped in most ecosystems: urban, farmland, shrubland, mountain, swamp, rainforest, forest, prairie, desert, tundra, savanna, oceans, lakes, beaches, even in a tree. Perhaps my favorite is a mountain on a beach. But what really fascinated me was feeling the geography beneath my wheels as if my bicycle was sculpting the land, and to witness how the land was both shaped by the weather, and shaping the **Weather:** For the record, I've never had the wind with me—it's always been against me or I'm having a good day. I can say, when it's sunny I'd prefer a little cloudy; and when it's cloudy, I'd prefer some sunny.

Agriculture

How do you feed a world? Looking back at the snaking road in the Nepalese Himalayas and hand carved terraces in the undulating foothills. The colorful patchwork contains hundreds of mini plantations of various crops helping to create a symbiotic growing environment.

Artwork

I was always impressed with the craftsmanship and resourcefulness of some artists, especially in Zimbabwe and Bali, Indonesia. Here are some busts taller than me. [Also see page 8 and 101.]

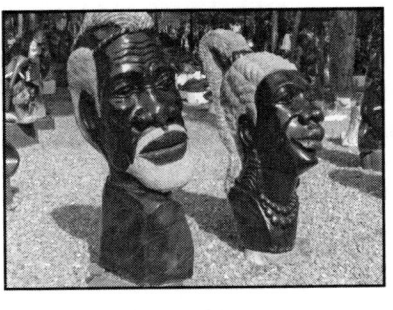

Animals

I always thought I was a monkey and dolphin guy, but what amazed me when I returned was the amount of photos and stories about butterflies and elephants that I collected. One of my favorite experiences was seeing a wild Bengal tiger take a sip of water from a river. Pictured here is butterfly with tiger eyes. [More **animal encounters** on pages 70-73]

Experience

My trip was more about collecting experiences than seeing things. On my first flying lesson over the glaciers

of Squamish, Canada, courtesy of my test pilot friend, François, I got to take off and land doing a simulated power failure. It was as scary as riding down a mountain with no brakes in the rain, when I panicked just a few feet above the runway, calm and cool François took control.

Weird Places

Sedona, Arizona, USA

Described as one of the earth's chakra points, you gotta feel it to believe it. Even if you're a skeptic, Sedona boasts some of the most spectacular scenery I've ever seen. This is the Bell Rock Vortex; this type of vortex is like an invisible tornado of the subtle energies that create the physical universe as we experience it, and has carved this rock into a bell shape.

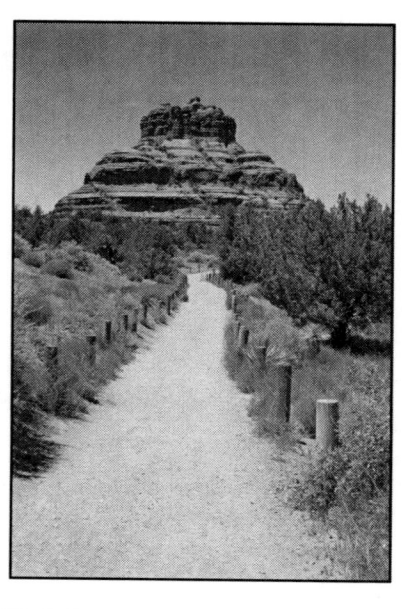

Wycliffe Well, UFO Capital of Australia

UFO sightings are so common that if you stayed up all night you'd be considered lucky *not* to see one. If you're an alien, what better place to set up residency than the Australian Outback. Pictured on the right is a spaceship that I happened to stumble upon one day.

Writing of alien creatures reminds me of **the most annoying creature on the planet**—the outback bush fly. Aliens and flies or alien flies? You decide.

What's your top 10 list of places to visit?

What was the highlight of your trip?

The highlight of my trip, despite or because of the challenges, was the epitome of superlatives, Mount Everest, Qomolangma, the Tibetan mother goddess of the Earth, the mountain so high birds cannot fly over it. [See photos on the pages 60, 92-93, 106]

My friend, Edwin, and I cycled from sea level to Mount Everest Base Camp at 5180 meters, about 5% of the distance to outer space, with air half as thick as sea level and the oxygen level about 40%. If you were suddenly teleported from sea level to Everest Base Camp you'd probably die of asphyxiation. We were cycling at a greater elevation than almost all the mountain peaks in North America, yet the summit was still another 3668 meters above us.

At Base Camp, we met two climbers acclimatizing themselves for their attempt to summit the mountain. For a few moments, we all stood in awe of each other, "That's amazing. I could never do that," we all seemed to say.

As we left, I asked Edwin: **Why couldn't we climb Everest?**

Why not? he said.

Qomolangma must certainly be magic, because unbeknownst to us we had re-discovered the same secret of life George Mallory eloquently stated in one of the **world's most awesome quotes**, especially considering Mallory might have been the first person to summit Mount Everest. He died in 1924 during his attempt. His body was found 75 years later. The photo of his wife was missing from his pocket; I like to believe he left it on the peak of Everest as an offering and a tribute.

The first question you will ask and which I must try to answer is this, 'what is the use of climbing Mount Everest?' and my answer at once must be, 'It is no use.' There is not the slightest prospect of any gain whatsoever. Oh, we may learn a little about the behaviour of the human body at high altitudes, and possibly medical men may turn our observation to some account for the purposes of aviation. But otherwise nothing will come of it. We shall not bring back a single bit of gold or silver, not a gem, nor any coal or iron. We shall not find a single foot of earth that can be planted with crops to raise food. It's no use. So, if you cannot understand that there is something in man which responds to the challenge of this mountain and goes out to meet it, that the struggle is the struggle of life itself upward and forever upward, then you won't see why we go. What we get from this adventure is just sheer joy. And joy is, after all, the end of life. We do not live to eat and make money. We eat and make money to be able to live. That is what life means and what life is for.

What was your least favorite ___?

This is a common question, perhaps people want to know where not to go; however, my least favorite experiences don't make a very interesting book. But I will say, generally speaking, the most depressing places were where humans had pillaged the environment or other humans, including places that seemed (from my perspective) to lack or oppress basic human rights. Especially heart-wrenching was seeing so many young children, barefoot, streaked in filth, dressed in rags, begging for money. [Photos of working kids pages: 39, 52, 53, 59, 83, 84, 101]. I could never find a good solution: give them money and perpetuate the problem by encouraging the parents to enslave their children, or don't give them money and witness the parent's beat their poor "employees". I developed a tough skin while traveling. I've done things I would have argued I'd never do, like step over people lying in the street that perhaps weren't even alive, and think things about those cruel parents I'd rather not think. A cliché I've proven true—ignorance is bliss.

Top: A truck chugs up a mountain in Ecuador with a contrail of exhaust, making me gag for a kilometer. **Bottom:** Often young street urchins would adopt me for an afternoon. This vivacious Vietnamese girl "Chewy" adopted me for a week.

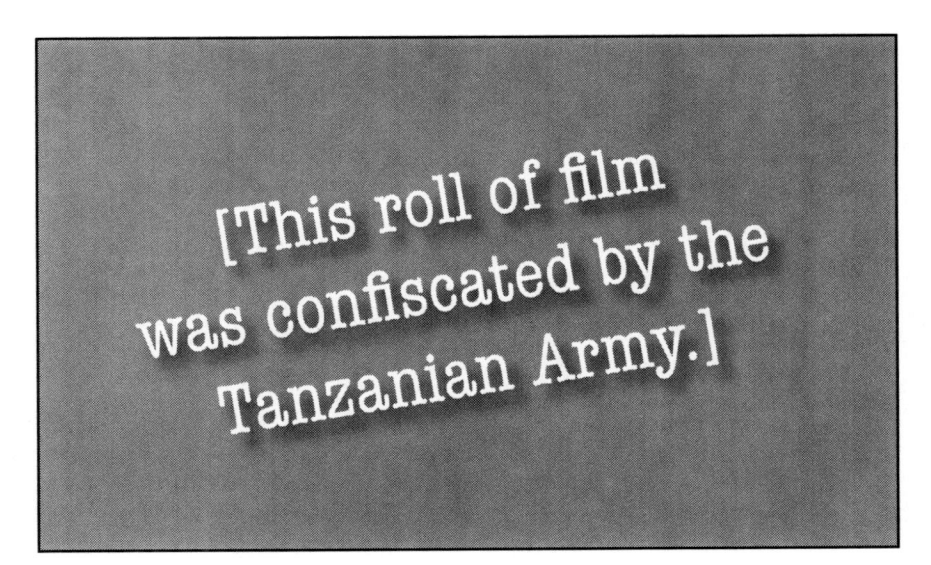

Don't you just love to hate?

Okay no one seriously asked me this question, but it does illustrate a common human trait—sometimes our "worst" experiences are our most fruitful. How boring would a perfect life be? Most clichés contain a grain of truth to them; I think the cliché of dying of boredom has a whole avalanche of truth. The following is a short story of my favorite least favorite moments:

Now that I've survived unscathed I have many fond memories of suffering. As my bicycling companion, Dennis said, "It's funny now." He referred to these moments as *menudoes* (I call it *falling uphill*) after purchasing a can of *menudo* in Mexico (like minestrone but with beef tripe) that was so old the label was faded blue and the can rusted. That was the first time Montezuma gave us a swift kick in the guts. Other *menudoes* include: Dennis pitching his tent in our Central American hotel room because there were more mosquitoes and creepy crawlies inside than out; camping in a swamp during a storm, a tree falling beside our tents, nearly crushing us; awaking in ten centimeters of water, floating on our air mattresses like rafts; being eaten alive by a swarm of fire ants; crawling into bed with a scorpion; getting caught in a riptide, nearly drowning and bumping into a shark while surfing in El Salvador; being so exhausted, that I fell asleep three

meters away from the road and didn't wake until the next morning; rotating in the shade of a saguaro cactus like a sundial; making a poncho out of plastic bags and duct tape to survive the icy rain and wind; being stoned out of a village in India by some children; waiting for a bus in Nepal alongside a corpse (still wondering if that counts as baggage or if the relatives had to buy an extra ticket)....

Sometimes I wish I could bottle and sell my *menudoes*, like a happy pill: jamming my chainring into my calf and telling the Mexican children that I was bitten by a shark; Montezuma's Revenge, a reason to stop and admire the scenery (from behind a bush); the burning pain of cycling up the Andes mountains, and the exhilarating descent; being so hungry and thirsty that rice tastes like ambrosia and water seems like nectar; camping less than 100 meters away from a plantation that was burned by the farmers during the middle of the night, and listening to their eerie Hindi music while watching a firestorm sweep through the banana trees like an orange tornado; over-exerting myself chasing some fishmonger bicyclists, and racing through a small village, being cheered by a hundred people as if it was the Tour de Tanzania; being startled awake by the haunting rhythm of African drums; hearing the gut-wrenching caterwauls of two women groveling, sand running through their hands like an hourglass, as they mourned their relative; sliding through gravel, around a curve and nearly off a Guatemalan cliff, and grateful for a simple sunset; being heartbroken, and spending a morning giving coins to every homeless person, who didn't and may never have anyone....

Moments like these made me feel alive. Perhaps suffering is a small taste of the possibility of success. Certainly, an absence of pain does not make a meaningful and happy life.

Every traveler has stories that they love to tell but hated to experience. Here's one of mine: In Thailand, a giant cockroach ran across the ceiling and fell into my bed. Somehow, while I was sleeping I beheaded the menace and woke to find the roach's remains just a few inches from my nose and a bad taste in my mouth.

Question VI:

What was it like to return home?

It turned my world upside down.

Magnify your confusion of seeing this upside down page by about one million and that might be close to my experience of returning home.

Flying from one hemisphere to another physically turned my world upside down, and it felt like my emotional and mental state also flipped upside down and inside out. It was the biggest cultural shock of them all, and the hardest part of my journey.

While traveling abroad, it was easy think I was the normal one, and everyone else was curiously abnormal, but submersed in my own culture again was like being in a funhouse, seeing hundreds of reflections of myself in the warped mirrors. Therefore, my major realization—more like an obvious fact that I could no longer runaway from—is that I've been programmed—culturally brainwashed to talk and walk and think a certain way, to believe that what I heard and witnessed in society was the only truth—the right way to do things—what needs to be done to be loved and accepted.

It suddenly felt as if I had been a zombie my whole life, feeding off the ideas from my peers, television, magazines, movies, music, video games; and, in an effort to prove my self-worth (importance) was regurgitating even more distorted ideas into the population infecting them with my dis-ease of dis-content.

Is it a coincidence that our culture is obsessed with brain-eating zombies and blood-sucking vampires? I counted hundreds of movies, books and TV shows about the horrors. **Was this a subconscious rebellion?** In biblical times the word *sin* was an archery term, which has been variously translated as: *to miss the mark, to miss the target, to err, to go astray, to fall short*. I wondered, is this what is meant by original sin? Have we all been born and brainwashed by a culture that has missed the mark?

Who was I? How do I fit into society? It boggled my mind. Suddenly I was living in an illusion. I had jumped into the rabbit hole and fell into Wonderland.

A saguaro cactus about
100 years old. The Sonoran
Desert in North America
is a surreal landscape
unseen anywhere else.

Question VII:

Did you find what you were looking for?

This is the million-dollar question. Ironically, I couldn't find what I was looking for or integrate what I had learned until I turned my world upside down and returned home, meaning the biggest unforeseen consequence of my trip was learning that first I had to deconstruct who I thought I was, before I could reconstruct who I wanted to be.

Though I believed it impossible, I found answers to all my questions, proving the biblical wisdom: "Seek and ye shall find." (Ironically, it raised even more questions.) When people ask me if I found what I was looking for, they are essentially asking: **Was it rewarding?** And they are essentially wondering if they will benefit from following their own dream. I am not qualified to answer whether you will benefit from following your dream, but consider this: What is the benefit to not trying?

What did you find? I found moments of truly living my life. **Did you find the secret of life?** Yes and no. Life is mysterious, ever-changing and waiting to be discovered, if not created, but it doesn't keep secrets. There is no one big secret, there is no perfect answer to make a perfect life, but here is a small secret: Focus on what you enjoy rather than what you don't.

What did you learn? Maybe instead of saying *learn*, it would be more accurate to say: **What did you earn?** I thought I would simply find the meaning of life, but I got much more than I bargained for—or maybe I got exactly what I wanted. I learned how to do my laundry in the sun, and how to talk with my hands. I learned to smile when things go bad, and that you can ride your bicycle to the moon, and still not get away from yourself. My trip taught me thousands of things, maybe millions, depending on your definition of *things*. And, as my picture of the world keeps growing and the puzzle pieces fall into place, I keep learning, keep finding new discoveries; therefore, the following section is a retrospective look from my new perspective at my biggest earnings of cycling around the world.

Left: The Buddhist Wheel of Life, symbolizing the Big Bang of creation.

Did you find peace?

In Zambia, I was hypnotized by a giant, bone-breaking pothole. Frozen with fear, my wheels caught the broken ripples of the road and I was sucked into the blackhole. The shock flung me and all my panniers off the bicycle. As I laid on the ground listening to the laughing monkeys, I chastised myself for forgetting to look where I wanted to go—at the path around the pothole. Or if I simply had ridden slow but steady through the pothole, I would have only have rattled my teeth instead of nearly knocking them out. It occurred to me, that my emotions are like riding a bicycle; and so, I learned to accept peace by learning not to fight or deny the blackhole of my fear and doubt and the infinite varieties of "negative" emotions, but to allow them as being a valuable and curious part of who I am.

Zanzibar fishermen mending their fishing nets on their dhow, a traditional Arab sailing vessel. **Right:** Some of the happiest kids were the poorest of poor. These curious guys are from Lesotho.

Did you find happiness?

Are you happy? is a common question, which implies happiness is a relatively rare commodity everyone is seeking. I also suspect people ask me this question because they are wondering if they followed their dream, would they find happiness?

The path to discovering happiness was an arduous road up a steep mountain in bad weather, but now that I have arrived it seems simple. Is it the absolute secret that will work for everyone? Generally speaking, yes, but effectively speaking, no. Happiness is relative. I remember a "slumdog" following me through Mumbai, India tugging on my pants, begging me—the rich and happy American—for money. I asked him why he thought I was happy? "You have shoes!" he exclaimed. "Look no shoes." He showed me his cracked, blackened feet and demonstrated the broken zipper and missing pockets in his shorts. It was sad, but happiness isn't simply a matter of satisfying survival needs. There are a lot of people physically suffering that are happy to be alive; and others living in perfect comfort that are perfectly miserable. One thing can make one person happy and another person sad; in fact, one thing can make one person happy today and sad tomorrow.

And now to contradict myself: the real secret to being happy is realizing that you aren't meant to be happy all the time. Happiness, peace and every other emotion look like the illustration on page 125. If every day is a happy day, you don't have any reference point to tell whether it is happy or sad, and you become bored with happiness. I'm not saying I fully understand it or I'm happy about it, but suffering does open the door to knowing pleasure. (The ironic part is that if you are suffering, it is still the happiest you know how to be at that moment.)

Happiness is like weight training: occasionally you must break down the emotional muscles so they can grow back stronger and you can accomplish more with life. Besides, we have been gifted with an enormous palette: **Why not enjoy all of life's emotions?** Why live only a black life or only a white life when you could live a black and white life, or a life full of shades of gray? In fact, there are infinite rainbow hues waiting to be discovered, waiting to help paint your multi-dimensional picture of life. A grand paradox of life: one must suffer to enjoy it. Try it. Try enjoy feeling miserable for a moment and feel the weight lift off your shoulders.

Did you fall in love?

I fell in love everyday. And sometimes I landed pretty hard.

First I had to ask myself: **What is true love?** And **Why do I feel I'm missing love?** And **Why do I fail (fall) so often?** I discovered that love unites two things, creating a sense of at-one-ment, which opens a door to realizing your connection to the web of life. Conversely, tough love highlights the differences between two people, and it's that contrast between two people that creates a whole new thing, like blue and yellow creating green. Love isn't a helpless feeling of falling, hoping you don't land. Love is a creative act, like sowing seeds that blossom into groves of cherry trees and tables of cherry pies. And the answer is—yes. [Read my love story on pages 26-27.]

Top: The toothy grin of a saltwater crocodile.
Left: Termite hill in Australia's Outback.
Opposite: Giraffes during a magical moment on a bicycle safari with the setting sun and rising lions.

Do you believe in magic?

I certainly have experienced a lot of seemingly strange events and impossible coincidences. Sometimes I think just surviving my trip is a miracle. I've met many people on pilgrimages for the magical sacred mysteries of life. Magic gives us a sense of hope and faith that our lives mean something and that tomorrow is going to bring something unimaginable rather than predictable.

I like to think of magic as a science not yet discovered, and I think there's enough science left to be discovered to keep humanity busy for several billion years and possibly infinity. Emotions are the closest thing to magic that I've discovered; I think if you have the passion, nothing is impossible. Certainly, two things are almost always true: If someone says something is impossible they are almost always wrong from a universal perspective; and, paradoxically, if someone says something is impossible from a personal perspective, they are almost always right. That's why emotions becomes a self-fulling prophecy— if you don't believe you can do it, you won't even try. If you want to hear an impossible idea, here's a whacky hypothesis—a science waiting to be discovered—I hypothesize that emotions are like a super subatomic particle or energy that makes up the universe. For example, how many times have you *woke up on the wrong side of the bed* and everything went wrong; and how many times have you smiled and the world smiled with you? [See: "The Magical Exercise to make your dream a reality." Page 136-143.]

Did the world change you?

Or: **Did your trip change you?** Everything, no matter how seemingly small, changes us. At first I didn't think I changed much, but in retrospect, I learned so many thousands of lessons—or should I say?—I discovered so many thousands of mysteries that my trip still continues to teach me and change me. Maybe better questions are: **Why do I think I'm still the same?** Or: **Why didn't I change the way I thought I should?** It is difficult to see ourselves, that's why our friends or the world are our best mirrors. The following example, shows how the reflection of two ants and one idea can make a lifetime difference.

In a German forest, amid the throes of loneliness and sadness, I was contemplating two ants that had been fighting over a crumb, both with the same purpose of taking it back to the anthill to feed the family. Suddenly I realized that my thoughts were fighting themselves, like the fox in Æsop's fable [page 14-15]. I was grateful that my artificial beliefs and bad habits were falling alongside the road, and it occurred to me that my trip was like a white-hot furnace burning out my impurities and forging my spirit. I was reminded of how the Mexicans used to call my bicycle: *"El caballo de acero."* (The Steel Horse.) My fog of depression blew away in great wind when I realized that made me: *"El caballero de acero."* (The Steel Cowboy.)

Above: The before and after picture. Is the internal change as big as the external? **Opposite:** A crocodile cheeseburger.

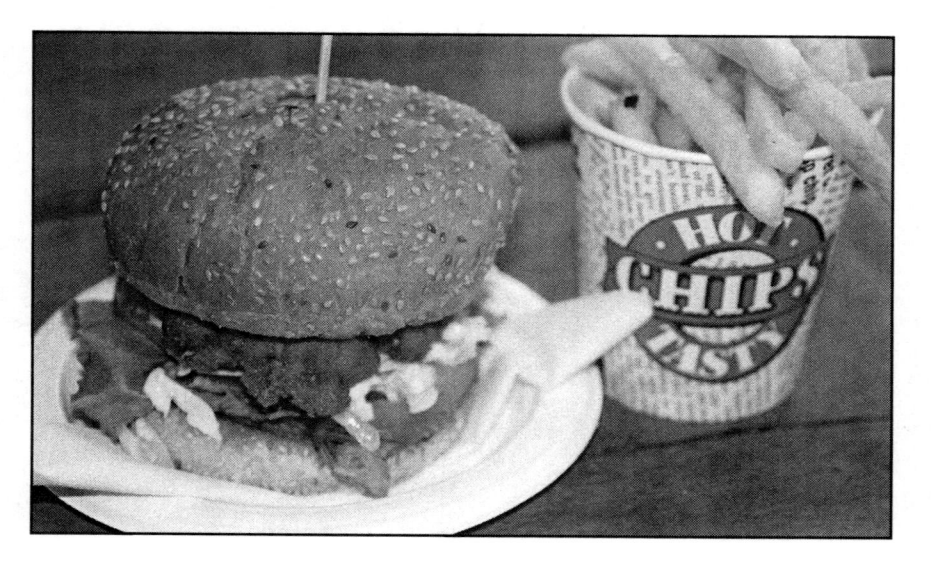

How much weight did you lose?

Riding a bicycle over the Andes Mountains with severe salmonella poisoning while only being able to stomach bananas and Coca-cola is a guaranteed weight loss program. Even when I wasn't sick, it was hard to find nourishing food. My body burned through my fat and then ate the muscles right off my bones to fuel that bicycle.

I started at 222 pounds and lost 65 pounds of fat and gained 15 pounds of muscle (after I learned how to eat properly). **How did you lose so much weight?** Being physically fit isn't a big secret—it's a little self-discipline, including moderate exercise and a sensible diet, but mostly physical (and mental) fitness starts with being kind and gentle to yourself, and finding something you love to do. My passion for bicycling overruled my passion for lazy days, junk food and my excuse of having bad knees, which I do. By the way, if your passion happens to be junk food and television, that's okay—the key is to accept the benefits and consequences. One of the consequences of my trip was though I may have been in Olympic fitness, I also wore my body out twice as fast [pages 68-69].

Is this crocodile cheeseburger the door to my greatest joy?

120

Photo courtesy of Dennis Snader.

Did you change the world?

I influenced the world both "good" and "bad" a million times more than I am capable of imagining; but as some of my critics ask: **Did you make a difference?** meaning: **Is the world better for me and my trip?** I wonder: **How does one know what is best for the world?** Once I asked a great buddha: **How did my bicycle trip change the world?** He said:

> *Doing the apparently not useful thing and doing it in a very big way, gave a lot of people a sense of hope and a state of wonder of why it is that someone would travel so far from their home for nothing more than to simply see the sites. Having done this some of the people that you interacted with grew a sense of faith that it's possible. In the scope of world events, it was an event not unlike events that have occurred before. What made it special is—you did it. How did it affect the world? As anything that human endeavors have ever done for a state of passion and a state of curiosity, very highly. Did it bring world peace? No. Did governments look at it with a sense of this is the power of a man? No. But the people that you interacted with will remember, and they will tell stories to their children and their children's children of the day you passed through their village. In some places, yours is a legend to tell children: "Conquer the world." And in other places, it's a legend to say: "What a silly thing to do. Why would anyone wish to go more than ten miles?" Once you are gone, what you will have lent to the world is simply a sense of possibility and hope.*

Did you change anyone's life?

Sometimes people even ask: **Have you ever saved anyone's life?** Perhaps these are rhetorical question meant to put the relative importance or unimportance of one's life into perspective; one thing is for certain, we all wish to influence and be influenced by the world—it is how we feel alive—maybe it is even why we live.

In fact, I have changed millions of lives, though perhaps that was just because my bicycle happened to be impeding someone else's car. I've also saved dozens of turtles from being squashed in the middle of the road; in fact, I saved a giant snapper just the other day, when his home was drained away by construction. Thoughts are like seeds and my guilt for accidentally killing a turtle when I was a child has grown like a weed in my mind, and I admit saving dozens of turtles has not uprooted this guilt. Contrarily, one action or memory that I planted has produced much fruit: Once in Kentucky, I saved an old school teacher who fell down in her driveway in the middle of the summer sun. My friend Forrest and I circled back, unlike the cars, and carried her into her home like a sack of potatoes and nursed her back to consciousness with glasses of ice water.

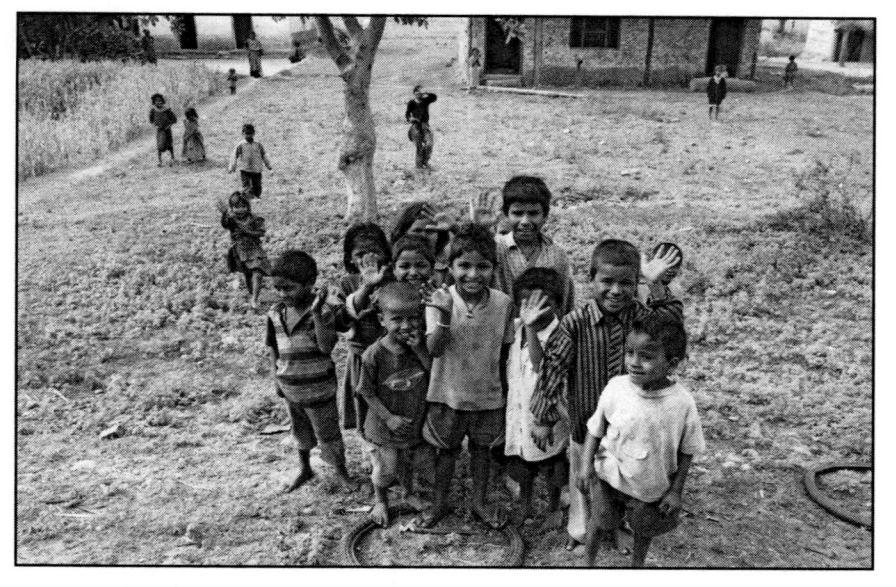

Above: I believe that I inspired the thousands of children that I met. My voice went hoarse so many days from saying hello, that I bought a bell just to ring a friendly greeting. Is it a coincidence that these Nepalese kids are standing on a bicycle tire?
Opposite: Some Bolivian school boys supervising a repair.

What is the meaning of life?

Wise people often ask: **What's the biggest lesson you learned?** I have to admit that it makes me jealous that I spent all those years and all those tears to discover what I can say in a few words. Then again, one of the things I learned is that information is just a thought, and thoughts don't have much emotional reality, and emotions are what govern a person. So, fortunately or unfortunately everyone must make their own journey in life. While I'm being honest, I should also admit that I find it humorous that instead of people asking me: **Are you crazy?** [page 58] they now ask things like: **So what do you think it all means?**

The meaning of life as described to me by a great buddha, the wisest person I ever met, is: "To create quickly and impeccably and with the greatest joy possible." He also said: "Everything you do as a human has a special purpose and intention. There is no one thing. The meaning of life is to be committed to living it, and not be vested in living it exactly a certain way. Have the passion to live, and have the purpose to know it is yours." He also said, the meaning of life is different for every person, and has to do with their sense of participation and ownership of their life. "If you retreat into the wilderness you will find the meaning of life, simply because you will no longer be trying to fulfill other people's expectations of you. But it is your meaning of life, and you can only use that meaning of life when you enter relationships with others. If you hold your

What is the meaningless of life?

meaning of life as an absolute truth, you become like a rock, not moving, not relating, and you will view anything different as an attack."

What all that means is that we create the meaning to our life in every moment of every day. So, the basic default meaning of life is very simple—it means whatever you think it means. It's so simple it took me almost two decades to find it. In other words, if you think life is hard work and then you die—you get a life of drudgery, or at least life feels like drudgery. If you think life is an adventure around every corner—you get a life full of mysteries and discoveries. This creates a phenomenon known as a self-fulfilling prophecy because you filter life through your understanding.

Here's the good news. Every thought you have is a molecule of who you believe you are. Now I'd like to add another molecule to who you think you are. As I exampled on the previous page, thoughts are like seeds: most die on infertile ground, some grow and blossom and produce heavenly fruit, and others are like weeds choking your garden. So, here is another seed. Careful. Are you ready? Some seeds take germination against your better judgement. If you still feel ready, turn the book upside down and read the seed.

If you don't like who you are, if you don't like what your life means—you can create a new meaning of life. Start right now. Plant a new seed. Who do you want to be?

Philosopher in meditation.
The philosopher sits beneath a double helix staircase resembling DNA, the basic blueprint of life, which was discovered hundreds of years after this painting.

Rembrandt van Rijn. 1632.

How does it feel to cycle round the world?

I felt like a prince of the universe, and sometimes I felt like a frog.

Nine years after the idea possessed me, it was difficult to believe I had finished. My last day seemed like any other. There was no yellow tape at the finish line, no journalists, friends or family. The woman of my dreams wasn't waiting to wrap her arms around me. When I checked into a hostel, I told the receptionist, "I just rode my bicycle around the world," which were the words I'd envisioned would be a magic spell transforming the Wisconsin frog into a prince of the universe. Nothing happened. I didn't feel anything; not like the Marco Polo of cyclists or anything but my same old self. I wondered, "Did I do something wrong? Have I worn out my emotions? Did I miss something along the way?" It was painful proof of the proverb: **It's the journey not the destination.**

I had finished cycling around the world, but had I finished the inner journey as well? (It would actually take me many years if not my whole life to digest all the lessons I learned during my travels.) It feels naive to say this, but it didn't solve my life. In fact, suddenly the rest of my life was facing me like a giant tire-eating pothole. **Now what?**

Happiness Graph

(Hint: Look at this illustration upside down in a mirror.)

Emotion ⇧⇩   Time ⇨

Sadness Graph

The postpartum bicycle blues began to circle my subconscious. For two weeks, I was in shock: weeping at silly things and laughing at serious things. I felt wise and naïve. I felt proud and humble; and, my ego desperately tried to interpret my life as a prince.

Then for no particular reason other than I could, I did a favor for a grouchy woman dying of cancer. She was unexpectedly grateful and her warbling voice and teary eyes flooded over to me, and I thought, "So, this is what it feels like to cycle around the world." And, I realized that I found what I was looking for—not an answer to a question—but a feeling of being alive—and that I didn't have to ride all the way around the world to find it... or did I? The irony made me laugh and cry at the same time, which I didn't know was possible. I was free to be whatever I may be—the frog or the prince, or both, or neither.

Top: What would a graph look like for being happy 100% of the time. Hint: Make an experiment of eating your favorite food for as long as you want. Eat as much as you want, but only eat your favorite food. Watch what happens.
Middle and bottom: Beautiful examples of life and death: the pincushion flower and an impala skull disintegrating in the South African sun.
Opposite: Whale.

Do you have any regrets?

Everything has a benefit and a cost, and it depends entirely on your point of view. I've rephrased this numerous times, because it is one of the top lessons I learned. This may sound obvious, but understanding a concept and living it are on opposites sides of the universe.

The benefit of regrets is that they teach you what you value, and how you can improve your future; therefore, a pragmatic optimist might rephrase this question as: **What would you do differently?** I did set an over-ambitious goal to bicycle the world and find the meaning of life, so frequently I was racing the weather and visas. Next time, I would set no goals, because life has a way of opening doors for you, and too often I just rode past them with my head down. I'd practice enjoying the moment, meaning to really internalize the cliché: Life is a journey, not a destination. I'd settle down for long periods to learn the language, make friends and work, and become an intimate part of their community and culture. Mostly, I wish I had less angst and spent more time to create meaning in my life and the lives of the people I befriended, rather than thinking there was some external solution to happiness. I also wish I had documented the trip better. Then again, I don't regret anything and wouldn't change anything, because if I didn't have the angst and the soul-searching drive, if I wasn't who I was, I would never have left my comfy couch.

What was your reward?

Ironically this question is much more rare than it's opposite: What was the worst thing that happened? And, it's more difficult to quantify.

During my trip, I would have said my reward was all the new experiences, but years later my overwhelming impression of my greatest reward wasn't what happened to me on the trip—I feel my reward was the cumulative effect of the whole trip, that still seems to grow inside me. Somehow through pure passion and pure stubbornness, I found the gumption to just do it, despite my doubts and fears, and I didn't quit, and I can always treasure my library of memories. And the really best thing is that I earned a lifetime credit of faith and hope knowing that I can always exceed what I think is impossible.

Opposite and right: Buddhist temple in Thailand. A monk hiding his smile while posing stoically for a photo.
Above: Caught in blizzard in Lesotho.

Did you break a world record?

To me riding a bicycle was just the vehicle of my spiritual journey— my bikeabout—not a race around the world.

I had never heard of anyone riding a bicycle around the world when I had the idea six years before I started, before the Internet made things relatively to research. I didn't even think it was possible. I did want to do something great for me and everyone that I met along the way. Of course, being great is a matter of definition. One of the tricks to being great is to define greatness internally instead of letting the external world define who you should be. But, no, it's not a world record, though it is relatively rare. I estimate that about 00.0000000285% of the population attempts to cycle around the world in any one year, and far less succeed. I truly believe everyone is capable of doing amazing things, and setting their own personal records. And since another rule of the universe is that nothing can ever be repeated—it may look similar, but it's not exactly the same—everyone is setting a Universe Record every moment.

Above: Cycling fully-loaded up the "World's Steepest Hill" according to the Guinness World Records in Dunedin, New Zealand. Note: the camera is angled down about 19° making the road appear flat. I have cycled up much steeper unpaved roads that aren't in any record book, and in places where I don't think the locals have ever seen a foreigner on a bicycle.

What Universe Record do you want to set?

The most extraordinary journey ever undertaken by a woman.

~ New York World October 20, 1895

Photo courtesy of Annie's granddaughter Mary Levy Goldiner.

The first women to ride a bicycle around the world.

Annie "Londonderry" Kopchovsky was an immigrant Jewish mother in Boston that bicycled around the world on a dare. She began penniless with nothing but a bicycle, revolver and a change of underwear.

The bicycle has done more for the emancipation of women than anything else in the world.

~ Susan B. Anthony. 1896

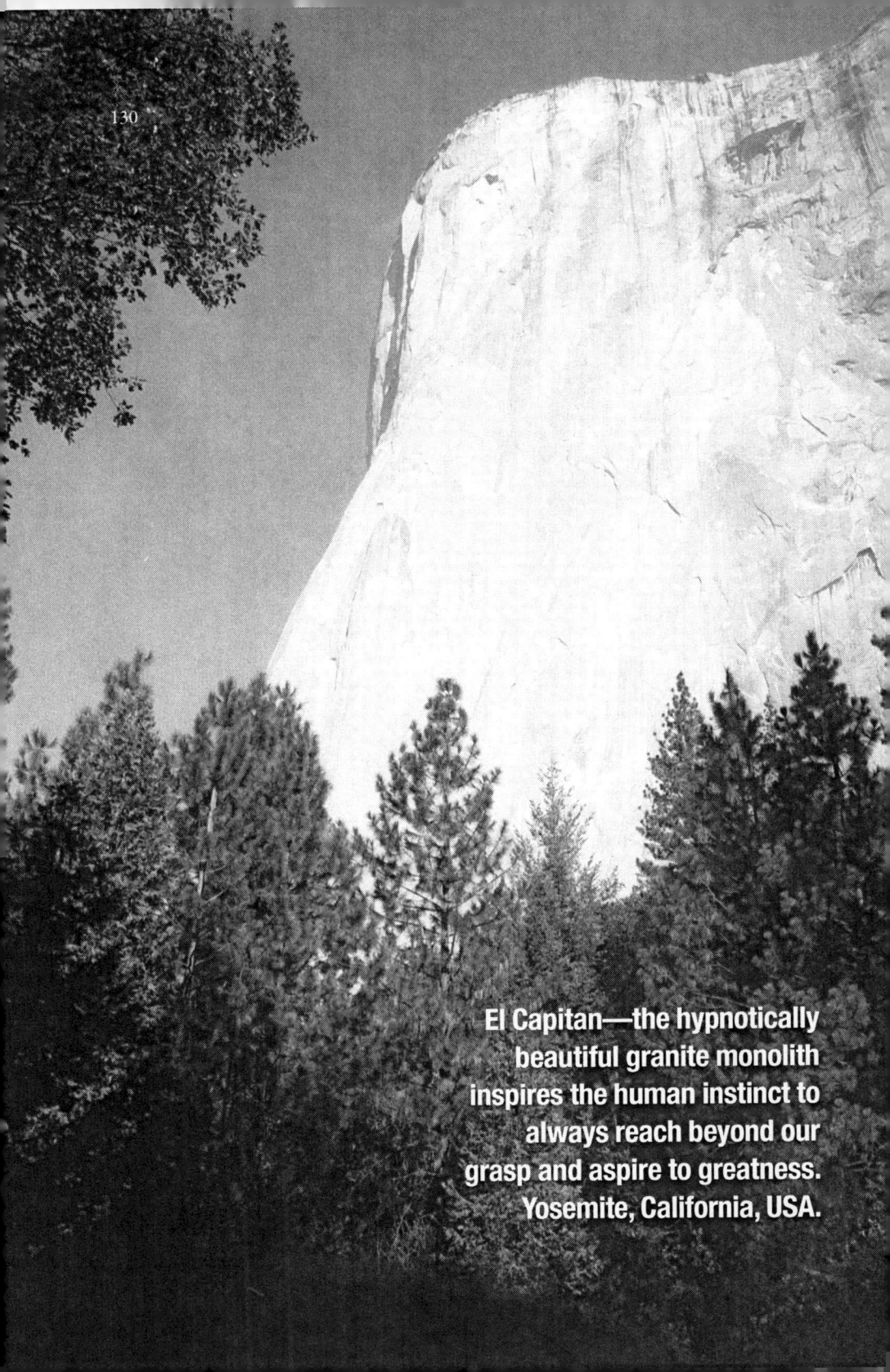

El Capitan—the hypnotically beautiful granite monolith inspires the human instinct to always reach beyond our grasp and aspire to greatness. Yosemite, California, USA.

Question VIII:

What is your next adventure?

The Wheel of Life has turned full circle. **Now what? What's bigger and better than riding a bicycle around the world?** That's a tough question. **What do you think is the answer?** Try to set a world record? Ride a unicycle around the world? Bicycle the moon?

After thinking about this question for years, I finally decided that there isn't anything bigger and better than riding a bicycle around the world. I also realized that no matter how much you achieve (physical) in life and no matter how much you accomplish (emotions) you will always seek to create more. That's another truth of the universe—there are no limitations. Therefore, you'll never reach a peak and feel perfectly, eternally happy. Consequently I felt stuck halfway up an eternal mountain.

That sounded like a recipe for unhappiness—knowing I would always want more, yet thinking I had done the biggest thing possible—until I had yet another realization—life is full of paradoxes and the trick of life is seeing every thing, every day, even every moment of life as a big adventure—being able to see the world with eyes of wonder. When I realized this, serendipity smiled upon me, as it often does and I discovered I had grown the ears to understand this quote:

If a man is called to be a street sweeper, he should sweep streets even as Michelangelo painted, or Beethoven played music, or Shakespeare wrote poetry. He should sweep streets so well that all the hosts of heaven and earth will pause to say, here lived a great street sweeper who did his job well.

~ Martin Luther King, Jr.

Would you do it again?

After my trip and re-discovering the meaning of life, I realized the obvious irony that I still have to live my life. I don't think I've experienced anything more than a handful of enlightening moments, but I am reminded of one of my favorite Zen sayings, "Before enlightenment chop wood carry water, after enlightenment chop wood carry water." (As a side note, I've come to believe everyone is standing on their own peak of enlightenment, with their own unique view of the universe. In other words, everyone has their own gift of genius, which some exercise more than others.)

Are you sick of riding your bike? I miss the freedom of cycling, but life is full of infinite adventures and joys waiting to be discovered, and not only can I choose my adventure, but I can create my adventure. So one adventure I dream of having is practicing seeing the "mundane" world with eyes of wonder. I want to plant some tomato seeds and nurse the miracle of fragrant plump, red, juicy tomatoes hanging on a vine like a concentrated drop of sunlight, and making spicy tomato sauce, that make my dinner guest's tongues tingle with pleasure and eyes water with joy.

During my trip, I reached the limits of my physical body many times; yet, I never came close to reaching the potential of my mind. I suspect that my mind's potential is unlimited, and that if I were skilled enough, if I could break out of my culturally-imposed box, if I could master being a human being—I could fly. People used to laugh at me when I told them I wanted to cycle around the world. What will they say now if I tell them I want to learn to fly with my mind and to do and create things that are unimaginable and impossible? Would they still laugh? And if they laughed, maybe I would simply say, "If you could do anything, what would you do? "

On the edge of Table Mountain, Cape Town, South Africa waving hello-goodbye.

Every ending is a new beginning.

~ Proverb

134

Thanks to everyone
who escorted my
journey one village
at a time.

Question IX:

Do you have any advice?

Some people are living their dreams, some don't care to try, and many seem too afraid to dream; nonetheless, the pattern of questions people ask eventually reaches critical mass with: How can I live my dream?

By now the ambitious reader will have absorbed everything I have to offer into who they are; so there is not much left to say. Besides, I'm not comfortable being a role model, because I often feel my greatest talents were having a lot of angst, ignorance and stubbornness to fuel my quest, and I may be good at preaching all this stuff, but I'm still practicing. That being said, if you must know—my answer is—there is no answer. The possibilities are endless in an ever-changing infinite world. And the best part about the world is you can create and add to it, so it's not something set in stone, that if you memorize all the facts, you can figure one perfect answer. So I encourage you to go out and see the world for yourself. **Why not start exploring your neighborhood?** Why not consider yourself ambassador of [Your Name] and go on a diplomatic mission and exchange some cultural values?

The following pages contain a few stepping stones, framing my discoveries in an ancient meditation technique said to be tens of thousands of years old, which might help you discover your passion, create your path, and take your first steps. In other words, align your thoughts, emotions and actions. At the least, you will discover with certainty a few things you won't want to do.

Jacques-Louis David, 1801.

Imagination rules the world.

~ Napoleon Bonaparte

The magical spell to making your dream a reality

This magical formula represents thousands of hours of trial and error, and research, and finding people that could actually demonstrate the technique—Oh!—and, don't forget, I had to ride my bicycle around the world to find it. So, this is my the boon of my adventure; what I like to think of as my gift to the world.

Step 1) Desire it! If you could do anything, what would you do? Take the first step in creating a new reality—dream big. How do you feel about that dream? Are you passionate about it? How can you fuel that fire? Are you afraid of it? Do you doubt it? Ask yourself how your fears and doubts are protecting you, and use them to your advantage!

Step 2) Plan it! Take that micro-reality of a dream and make it bigger by giving it more energy. What steps do you need to take on this journey to reach your destination? Declare your commitment to yourself and the world. The more people you inspire the merrier. The merrier for you and the merrier for them. Even if you decide to be a gourmet baker, someone has to grow the ingredients, and someone has to eat your bakery. Talk about it with your friends. Get valuable feedback as to how to make your dream come true. Watch the passion grow in other people.

Step 3) Do it! Strangely enough, a good idea and a cup of coffee will get you a cup of coffee. We live in a 3-dimensional world that requires honest effort. Even magic takes effort. So, get your community together and get going. They didn't build Rome in a day, but remember you're doing this because you said it would be so, and you thought it would be fun and exciting. Continue to fuel your passion, savor accomplishments every step of the way. Prove it to yourself. Take a small step of action now.

Sounds easy, right? Risk the exercise on the following pages and see if you can create a dream and turn it into a reality right now.

Cautions!

1) This dream is only part of the big-picture dream of your life. It's only what you think you want at this stage of your life. Allow it the room to evolve and change or maybe even evolve into something apparently completely different.

2) Do you have some hidden baggage in your subconscious? Do you **feel** like you can't do it or you don't deserve it? Emotions like these could be sabotaging all the good intentions and hard work in the world. Dig it up and throw it out.

3) Your desire is what keeps you pursuing your dream. The fact that you haven't achieved it doesn't mean that you won't, it only means that you haven't. Desire is only a sense of purpose about life. Don't take the imaginations of your dreams too literally—we all experience failures of imaginations.

4) Quitting and failure are two valid options. If you smash into the tree, it is only because you were trying to avoid the rock. And if you realize a more passionate goal in life, perhaps you avoid both. However, knowing when it's the appropriate time to change your mind is the artistic trick. Also, try purposely failing. Pick a dream too big. Try. Fail. Watch what happens.

5) Remember: if you don't feel the "pain" of your efforts, you won't know or feel you've accomplished anything. (Is drinking a glass of water an accomplishment? It was to me one day. Page 30.) Likewise, since you've never done it before, you don't know how to do it; therefore, it's not supposed to be easy.

6) Finally, if you begin dreaming and never take a step of action, you risk creating frustration, doubt, fear of failure and reenforcing all the other pitfalls of being human. Contrarily, do you think never dreaming equals never failing?

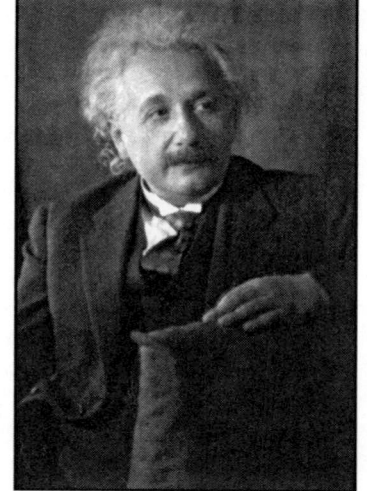

The most beautiful experience we can have is the mysterious. It is the fundamental emotion that stands at the cradle of true art and true science. Whoever does not know it and can no longer wonder, no longer marvel, is as good as dead, and his eyes are dimmed.

~ Albert Einstein

Step 1—The magic time capsule

As I mentioned, creating reality begins with a dream. So begin creating reality right now—start dreaming!

Write all your thoughts on a piece of paper and keep it safe for 10, 20, 30 maybe even 100 years. When you're ready, someday far in the future, read what you've written. You'll be surprised how much you've accomplished. It will seem like magic. I did it over 13 years ago and recently stumbled across my list. I accomplished things I had forgotten I wanted to accomplish. I even accomplished things I thought impractical and impossible. Who would have believed I'd climb Mount Everest? Not me.

1) Ignore the naysayers—just for a moment, you can always go back to doubting—and imagine anything is possible and dream big. The bottom line is that you only have one chance at life. So, if you could do anything, what would you do?

2) Why do you want a dream? Would you really attempt to make it real? Having a dream and not trying is harder than having a dream, trying and failing. What is the cost of not following your dream? What is the benefit of succeeding in your dream? Maybe you don't want a dream. That's okay, too. Are you willing to accept the costs and benefits of not having any goals?

3) Imagine everything you want and don't want. Do you really want it? Or do you think you need it? Is society (television, friends, family, et cetera) telling you that's what is important? Are you setting artificial limitations on yourself?

4) What if passion is the secret of life? What is your biggest passion? What would you do if you had no limitations of time, energy, space or money? What would you do if you weren't afraid? Keep dreaming until your passion is burning inside of you like a fire. Now is your chance to do anything.

5) What do feel you are missing in your life? Is there a matching dream? Are you afraid of something? How can you use your fears like a secret ingredient to spice your dream? Maybe you are already living your dream and you didn't know it? Can you simply change your attitude about your life?

6) Fish your mind's database for ideas: What dreams do you have including your friends and family? What kind of career do you want? How can you make the world a better place? What will the world say about your legacy? Do you care what the world says? Do you want to invent something? Discover something? Break a world record? Do you want to be a philanthropist, scholar, scientist, artist, laborer, or nothing at all? Do you want to do something "impossible" like explore new planets? Or fly? Or be omniscient? What do you want to do before you die? What is your top 10 list of places to go and things to do? Do you want to take an inner journey and explore the mysteries of the human mind?

7) Take a break. Let your imagination wander. Go to sleep and ask yourself to dream your dream tonight. Don't worry. You'll know it when you find it; and, when you find it, your dream might take you for a ride.

¿if you could
do anything,
what would
you do?

*Twenty years from now you will be more
disappointed by the things you didn't do
than by the ones you did do. So throw
off the bowlines, sail away from the safe
harbor. Catch the trade winds in your
sails. Explore. Dream. Discover.*

~ Mark Twain

Step 2—How do you eat an elephant?

You should have a whole list of dreams now. Some of those dreams didn't exist yesterday. Where did they come from? You've just pulled a rabbit out of a hat, haven't you? Ready to turn one of your dreams into reality? Get those emotions flowing again. Hint: give your dream more reality by writing your plan down on a piece of paper.

1) If you could plant a seed that would turn into a reality what would it be? Pick your smallest easiest impossible dream as a test. Or, go for the gold medal and pick the dream that makes your soul sing.

2) What are some steps to make that dream a reality? Do you need to make a list? Do you need to learn something? Acquire something? What is your time line? Break the one big goal into small and easy goals. How do you eat an elephant? One spoonful at a time.

3) What can you do? What do you need help with? Who would enjoy helping you or advising you? What obstacles do you need to remove?

4) Are you sure you're really willing to do it? If not, go back and get a different dream. If so, how can you find the courage to face the unknown knowing that it will probably be the most difficult thing you've ever done, yet also the most joyful?

5) What is the key ingredient missing? What do you need to change or accept about yourself or the world to begin your journey? Do you think it's too big and overwhelming? Does it seem too small and unimportant? Has the world presented a roadblock? Can you go around? Or, is the roadblock a stepping stone?

6) What inspiration can you find from the goals you have achieved in your past? Have you ever taken any similar steps in the past? Now that you have a dream and a rough plan, how are you a different person?

7) Imagine taking the steps one by one, how does it feel? Are you inspired? Are you afraid? What are your fears telling you? How do your fears protect and guide you? Maybe your limitations are the keys to your greatest potential for growth.

It is not the critic who counts; not the man who points out how the strong man stumbles, or where the doer of deeds could have done them better. The credit belongs to the man who is actually in the arena, whose face is marred by dust and sweat and blood, who strives valiantly; who errs and comes short again and again; because there is not effort without error and shortcomings; but who does actually strive to do the deed; who knows the great enthusiasm, the great devotion, who spends himself in a worthy cause, who at the best knows in the end the triumph of high achievement and who at the worst, if he fails, at least he fails while daring greatly. So that his place shall never be with those cold and timid souls who know neither victory nor defeat.

~ Theodore Roosevelt

Step 3—Reap a destiny

"Sow a thought, reap an act, sow an act, reap a habit, sow a habit, reap a character, sow a character, reap a destiny." ~ Anonymous.

This step is very important. Remember, if you've begun to dream and you don't take a step of action, you risk creating a nightmare of regret and frustration. So, time to start living your dream. Get out there and just do it. Have fun. Make mistakes. Get your hands dirty. Fall down. Get up. Try again. Change your mind. Quit. Fail. Get a new dream. You can't do it wrong, provided you're doing it. And once you achieve one "impossible" goal you will forever know that you can triumph over the doubt of yourself.

1) Consult your action list. What is the easiest smallest step of your easiest and smallest impossible dream?

2) If you took that step of action right now, would you be living your dream?

3) Do one thing on your list. Take one small step on your journey right now.

4) What did it feel like to take that small step? Are you a better person? A stronger person? A different person?

5) Did you succeed? Did you fail? Even if you failed, you many not have created your small goal, but you created learning something about yourself.

6) You did it. You just created a reality out of a small part of a big dream. Savor the sense of accomplishment. If you accomplished failure, feel that too. No one said this is easy, otherwise everyone would be living their dream. Like anything in life (even avoiding living your life) this exercise will take imagination, passion and effort. Acknowledge that you have one more tool in your toolbox.

7) Use the passion generated by the first action to fuel the next step of action. If you don't feel passionate create the passion! Imagine having achieved your big dream, how would it feel? How would you be different? Would your life seem meaningful and fulfilling? Who created that meaning? What opportunities would your dream create for your friends and family? Would your community benefit? Knowing anything is possible, what would you do next?

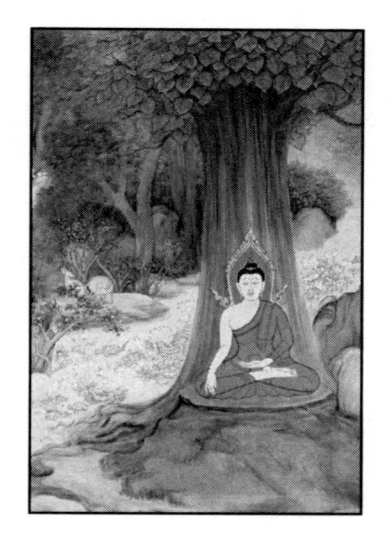

*You cannot travel the path until
you have become the path itself*

~ Buddha

Appendix—
The metric system

I have decided to use the metric system in my book, because it's the standard everywhere except the USA, Mynamar, and Liberia. In addition, I find the metric system to be very beautiful and simple. Like my bicycle trip, the length of the metric meter was originally defined by the circumference of the planet. Specifically, the distance from the equator to the pole was measured and assigned to be 10,000,000 meters, which is a rather arbitrary number except that ten happens to the number of fingers that we have, and one meter made a convenient unit, similar to the empirical yard. One liter was defined as the volume of a cube of water ten centimeters squared, which also defined the weight of one kilogram. Temperature was defined according to the freezing (0°) and boiling point (100°) of water and also based on units of ten. The metric system made it very easy to plan my days, estimating such things as the inclination of roads, distances to the summit, how far I could I ride, and how much food and water I would need.

Conversion Table
1 Kilometer (KM) = 0.62 miles
1 Meter (M) = 1.09 yards
1 Liter (L) = 0.26 gallons or 1.05 quarts (2.2 pounds)
1 Kilogram (KG) = 2.2 pounds

1 mile = 1.60 kilometers
1 yard = 0.91 meters
1 gallon or 4 quarts = 3.78 liters
1 pound = 0.45 kilograms

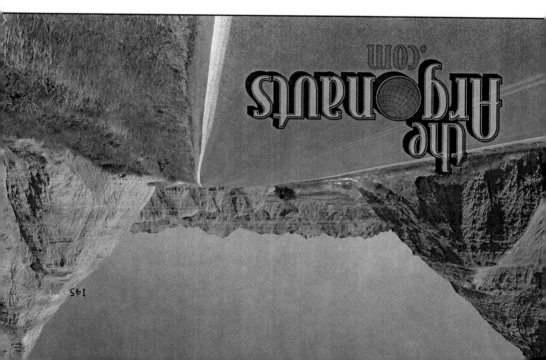

the Argonauts.com

Teacher's guide and more surprises

Visit the website for some great bonus material:

~ Exclusive **surprise bonus chapter** for people who bought the book:
http://www.theArgonauts.com/falling-uphill/bonus

~ **Reader's group guide** for your book club and a **teacher's guide**
with activities to inspire your students, such as quizzes, maps and trivia.

~ More photos and the short film:
"Quest for happiness—Around the world on a bicycle."

~ **Do you have another question?** Ask Scott.

~ Schedule Scott for speaking events and slideshows.

~ Order *Falling Uphill* signed by the author. (Bulk discounts available.)

~ Join the *Falling Uphill Fan Club* on Facebook and share your thoughts.

~ And much more of course....

Falling Uphill—The Audio Book as read by the author.
Travel the world from the comfort of your own home or
while driving to work or while exercising or anywhere....
Hours of entertainment. Available for immediate
download. **Visit http://www.theArgonauts.com**

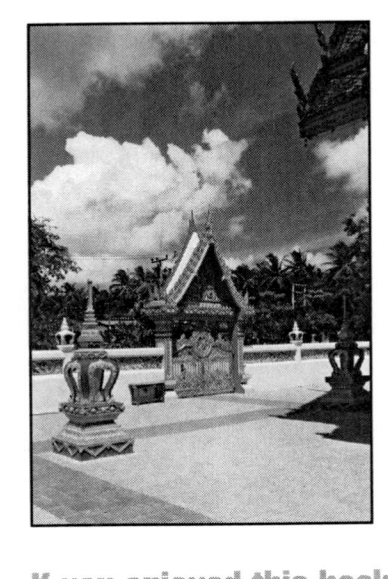

A karmic gas station.
Buddhist temple. Laos.

If you enjoyed this book,
please tell a friend.
Your help is appreciated.

LaVergne, TN USA
27 August 2010
194912LV00004B/6/P

ABOUT THE AUTHORS

LINDA CHAVEZ is a Fox News political analyst, a syndicated columnist, and the host of a syndicated talk-radio program. A former labor union official, she was President George W. Bush's original nominee for Secretary of Labor, though she withdrew her name from consideration. She is now president of the nonprofit, grassroots organization Stop Union Political Abuse. Chavez is the author of two other books, *An Unlikely Conservative* and *Out of the Barrio.*

DANIEL GRAY, a writer living in Washington, D.C., is a former director of communication for the National Right to Work Committee. He has done work for numerous political organizations and candidates.